SAVING STALIN'S IMPERIAL CITY

SAVING STALIN'S IMPERIAL CITY

Historic Preservation in Leningrad, 1930–1950

Steven Maddox

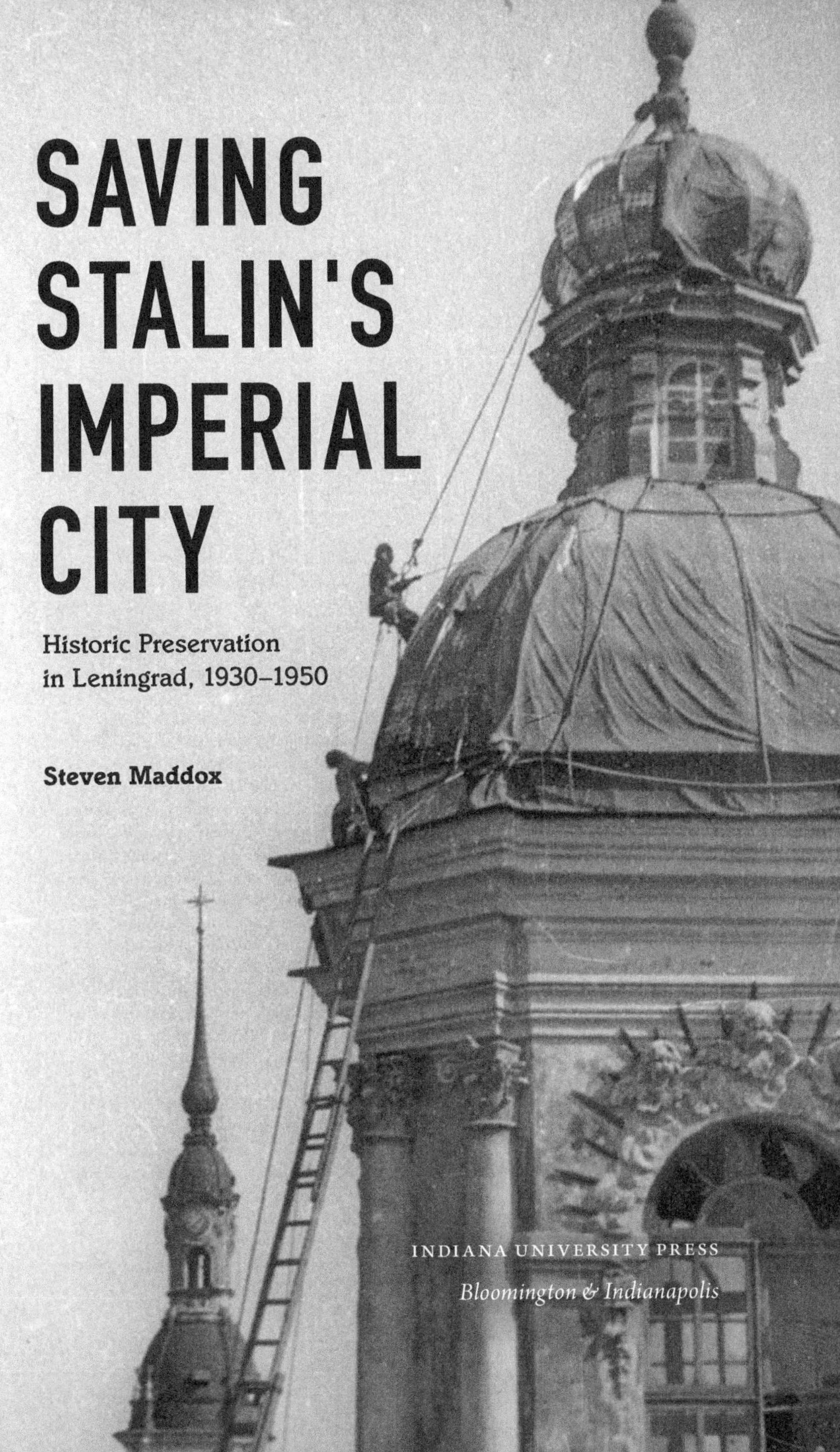

INDIANA UNIVERSITY PRESS
Bloomington & Indianapolis

This book is a publication of

INDIANA UNIVERSITY PRESS
Office of Scholarly Publishing
Herman B Wells Library 350
1320 East 10th Street
Bloomington, Indiana 47405 USA

iupress.indiana.edu

Telephone 800-842-6796
Fax 812-855-7931

∞ The paper used in this publication meets the minimum requirements of the American National Standard for Information Sciences–Permanence of Paper for Printed Library Materials, ANSI Z39.48–1992.

Manufactured in the United States of America

Library of Congress Cataloging-in-Publication Data

Maddox, Steven, [date]
Saving Stalin's imperial city : historic preservation in Leningrad, 1930-1950 / Steven Maddox.
pages cm
Includes bibliographical references and index.
ISBN 978-0-253-01484-9 (hardcover : alkaline paper) – ISBN 978-0-253-01489-4 (ebook) 1. Historic preservation – Russia (Federation) – Saint Petersburg – History – 20th century. 2. Historic buildings – Conservation and restoration – Russia (Federation) – Saint Petersburg – History – 20th century. 3. Monuments – Conservation and restoration – Russia (Federation) – Saint Petersburg – History – 20th century. 4. Architecture – Conservation and restoration – Russia (Federation) – Saint Petersburg – History – 20th century. 5. City planning – Russia (Federation) – Saint Petersburg – History – 20th century. 6. Saint Petersburg (Russia) – Buildings, structures, etc. 7. Saint Petersburg (Russia) – History – Siege, 1941-1944. 8. Memorials – Russia (Federation) – Saint Petersburg – History – 20th century. 9. Historic preservation – Government policy – Soviet Union – History. 10. Soviet Union – Cultural policy. I. Title.
DK573.M33 2015
363.6′909472109043 – dc23

2014017906

1 2 3 4 5 20 19 18 17 16 15

TO GILLIAN AND CLARKE

CONTENTS

ACKNOWLEDGMENTS

THIS BOOK COULD NOT HAVE BEEN WRITTEN WERE IT NOT FOR the continuous support I received from family, friends, and colleagues over the years. The project began at the University of Toronto. There I was fortunate to be among a wonderful cohort of graduate students. Many of them read parts of this book and provided valuable feedback. I would particularly like to thank Sarah Amato, Ariel Beaujot, Wilson Bell, Auri Berg, Max Bergholz, Heather DeHaan, Sveta Frunchak, Geoff Hamm, Janet Hyer, Tomaz Jardim, Alex Melnyk, Tracy McDonald, and Nathan Smith for their help and encouragement. I was also surrounded by an incredible group of mentors at Toronto, including Bob Johnson, Thomas Lahusen, Peter and Susan Solomon, Alison Smith, and Lynne Viola. Many thanks to Bob for our long conversations on history, fishing, and teaching. His encouragement and support have meant a lot over the years. Lynne Viola has been a model supervisor, colleague, and friend. I cannot thank her enough for the support and advice she generously offered me as a student and now as a professor. *Spasibo tebe,* Lynne!

Many others have left their imprint on this book. Peter Aterman, Richard Bidlack, Maya Haber, David Hoffmann, Andy Janco, Catriona Kelly, Lisa Kirschenbaum, Ben Loring, Brigid O'Keeffe, and Serhy Yekelchyk read individual chapters and provided excellent feedback along the way. David Brandenberger, Steve Norris, and Karl Qualls have always been available to read and comment on drafts (often with very short notice). Sean Guillory, Christoph Gumb, Jeff Hass, Jenny Kaminer, Nikita Lomagin, Matt Lenoe, Oscar Sanchez, and Andrew Sloin all discussed my arguments with me and offered insightful comments. I value not only their help with the book, but even more their friendship and good humor. I rarely get to see these people, so it is with great excitement and anticipation that I look forward to our annual get-togethers at the ASEEES! I am especially indebted to Ryan Gingeras and Mike Westren. They have been true friends since we met in graduate school and both have helped shape this book in more ways than they realize.

Friends and colleagues at Canisius College, my academic home since 2009, have been extraordinarily supportive as I revised the book for publication. Tom Banchich, Dave Costello, Dave Devereux, Julie Gibert, Rene de la Pedraja, Larry Jones, and Nancy Rosenbloom read and offered constructive criticism on chapters, while Matt Mitchell read the entire draft. Many thanks to them for their help. Thanks are also due to all other members of the History Department—Richard Bailey, Keith Burich, and Bruce Dierenfield—for their support over the years.

While doing research in Russia, I was fortunate to have support from a wonderful group of friends, most of whom I have known since my undergraduate trips in the 1990s. The Efimovs (Tania, Dima, and Sasha) have been like a family to me ever since I lived with them in Cheboksary for six weeks in 1997. It is hard to explain how much I learned from them, and to express how thankful I am for their friendship. Maya Efimova, likewise, did everything possible to make me feel at home in Moscow. Many thanks to her for putting a roof over my head whenever I came to town. Pavel and Viktoria Shpilevsky provided accommodations when necessary in St. Petersburg, while Sergei Antonov, Edik Kudriavtsev, Sasha Pirogov, and Vlad Smirnov have always offered good cheer and their most sincere friendship to this *kanadets*. I cannot thank them enough for all they have done for me over the years.

My research in Russia has been generously funded by grants from the Social Sciences and Humanities Research Council of Canada, the University of Toronto, and Canisius College. I would like to thank the dedicated staff at the Russian archives and libraries I worked in. Three people in particular were incredibly generous with their time, expertise, collegiality, and friendship. Iulia Iur'evna Bakhareva at the Archive of the Committee for State Control, Use, and Preservation of Monuments of History and Culture of St. Petersburg (KGIOP) took a special interest in my project when we first met in 2005, and has offered generous support and advice ever since. Vera Igorevna Popova at the former St. Petersburg Party Archive (TsGAIPD), too, never hesitated to help this Canadian jump the hurdles of Russian archive bureaucracy. At TsGAIPD Taisa Pavlovna Bondarevskaia insisted that I have lunch in her office every day, offered help whenever it seemed getting access to documents would be problematic, and proved to be a true friend to me and my wife during our year-long stay in Petersburg. Sadly, Taisa Pavlovna did not live to see the completed project. She will forever be in my thoughts.

I would like to extend my gratitude to my editors at Indiana University Press. The project began with Janet Rabinowitch and was then passed on to Bob Sloan when she retired. It has been a pleasure to work with both of them. Many thanks to Jenna Whittaker, June Silay, and Nancy Lightfoot for answering the several thousand questions I had, and to my copyeditor, Eric Levy, for his keen eye and constructive suggestions.

Parts of this book have been published before in modified form. Sections of chapter 2 appeared as "'These Monuments Must Be Protected!': Stalin's Turn to the Past and Historic Preservation during the Blockade of Leningrad," *Russian Review* 70, no. 4 (October 2011): 608–626. Parts of chapter 3 were published as "The Memory of the Blockade and Its Function in the Immediate Postwar Restoration of Leningrad," in Nikita Lomagin, ed., *Bitva za Leningrad: Diskussionnye problemy* (St. Petersburg: Evropeiskii Dom, 2009), 272–302. I am grateful to the *Russian Review* and Evropeiskii Dom for permitting me to republish them here.

Finally, I would like to thank those closest to me. My parents, Tom and Nell Maddox, have been a constant source of love and support. My sister Kelly-Anne helped me discover my passion for research and writing and urged me to continue to pursue my interests in Russian history, no matter how remote they seemed to a Quebec French literature specialist. My mother-in-law, Marion Clarke, likewise encouraged and supported my work. Above all, I would like to offer my sincerest gratitude to my wife, Gillian Clarke. She has been there through the highs and lows of this book project and never once doubted that it would see the light of day, even when I did. I dedicate this book to her and to our daughter, Clarke Maddox.

INTRODUCTION

ON THE NIGHT OF 27 JANUARY 1944, LENINGRADERS GATHERED along the granite-clad embankment of the Neva River to view the fireworks display in celebration of the end to the German siege of the city.[1] Aleksandr Boldyrev, a professor at Leningrad State University who survived the siege, described the scene in his diary:

> At exactly 8:00, 24 volleys from 324 guns deafeningly roared out. Multi-colored flares filled the sky, banishing the night. The city! You saw the reflections from the enemy's bombs exploding, you turned crimson in the bloody glow of enormous fires, the lights from German planes turned your nights into day . . . two and a half years, two and a half years. . . . Today the signs of victory and liberation illuminate you![2]

Boldyrev and the other survivors gathered along the Neva could finally breathe freely. The terror had passed, but everywhere they looked they saw destruction – tangible signs of Hitler's intention to annihilate the city, its population, and Russian history embodied in the cityscape.

For 872 days the *Wehrmacht* had surrounded Leningrad and subjected it to terror on an unimaginable scale. The impact of the siege was enormous: close to a million people died from starvation, bombings, and artillery shelling, the infrastructure suffered extensive damage, and hundreds of the city's famous historic and cultural monuments (buildings, statues, and landmarks under state protection) were destroyed or horribly disfigured. Yet the destruction would have been far more extensive were it not for the efforts of party officials and preservationists (artists, architects, and cultural specialists working at Leningrad's Administration for the Protection of Monuments) to protect the city's heritage sites throughout the war. When it became clear in the late summer of 1941 that the city would come under siege, several preservationists refused evacuation to the "safety" of the rear, choosing instead to endure tremendous suffering in order to save the city's monuments from destruction.[3] Likewise, when the siege was lifted and the danger to Leningrad had passed, preservationists and local authorities privileged historic monuments in plans for restoration, in spite of the incredible damage inflicted upon the city and chronic material shortages experienced throughout the Soviet Union. In doing so, they cast the restoration of historic monuments as a commemoration of the nearly nine-hundred-day siege, and proudly trumpeted the historical uniqueness of Leningrad's "unparalleled" wartime experience.

This book is a story of preservation, restoration, and commemoration in Leningrad. It is at once a history of the successes and failures in historic preservation during a time of cataclysmic upheavals and hardships, and of Leningraders' determination to preserve the memory of the siege. It stresses the counterintuitive nature of Stalinist policies, which allocated scarce resources to save historic monuments when the very existence of the Soviet state was threatened, and again after the war, when housing, hospitals, and schools needed to be rebuilt. Preservation proved to be extremely difficult, but necessary, as the occupying forces attacked and deliberately destroyed the country's historic monuments. When the war ended, preservationists made a concerted attempt to restore monuments in all areas that had been occupied by German forces. Leningrad was at the forefront of this restoration. Through "healing the wounds," Leningraders argued, they were writing the memory of war into the city's – and by extension, the state's – "great" historic narrative. Rather than leaving monuments and landmarks in ruins, local officials urged Leningraders to continue the "battle" on the restoration "front" to see their city and its history rise like a phoenix from the ashes. As in other Soviet cities undergoing restoration, this process was fueled by more traditional commemorations that glorified the city's wartime experience, encouraged civic pride, and mobilized residents to restore their hometown (*rodnoi gorod*).[4] During the war and immediate postwar period, therefore, the restoration of historic monuments and commemorations of the siege were intimately intertwined, served similar purposes, and were mutually reinforcing.

The events discussed here are part of the war and postwar reconstruction as experienced by the Soviet Union as a whole. This period deserves special attention, for the cataclysm of war became the central event in the lives of Soviet citizens.[5] Every family and individual in the Soviet Union was involved in, and traumatized by, the Great Patriotic War, as it is known in Russia. Over the course of four years, approximately twenty-seven million people were killed, twenty-five million were left homeless, and thirty-seven million were separated from their families and homes due to conscription, evacuation, and deportation.[6] When the war finally ended on 9 May 1945, Soviet citizens faced the gargantuan task of rebuilding their homes, industries, farms, villages, cities, and lives. Due to the degree of destruction, the postwar period was hardly one of peace and rest.[7] Civilians and returning soldiers moved on to the "labor front" and the Soviet leadership expected them to continue making sacrifices for the country's restoration. It is against the background of total war and harsh postwar conditions that this story of restoration and commemoration is set. And it is this context which brings into sharp relief the counterintuitive nature of Soviet policies as the leadership set out to save and restore historic monuments during a time of extraordinary cataclysm.

When Germany invaded the Soviet Union on 22 June 1941, it engaged in an unprecedented form of warfare – a "War of Extermination" – aimed at the destruction of the "Judeo-Bolshevik" system.[8] The Nazi leadership had devised intricate plans for the Soviet Union, including the "General Plan for the East" (*Generalplan ost*), which called for the creation of *Lebensraum*, or living space, for the German people and the annihilation of approximately thirty million people living there. This territory was to be thoroughly Germanized and turned into an agrarian utopia, where fertile lands could be "efficiently" tilled by the *Volk*. Monuments of Russian history and culture, therefore, had no place in the future German empire, and such reminders of a past civilization were to be erased from the topography of *Lebensraum*.

In preparing for Operation Barbarossa, Hitler made his intentions for Russian architecture, monuments, and landmarks clear. Although special commissions were established to "protect" objects that the Nazis deemed culturally valuable via confiscation and transportation to Germany, buildings and monuments symbolizing Russia's past and cultural heritage were treated with the utmost contempt and disrespect.[9] Before the war in the East began, for example, Hitler demanded the physical destruction of Moscow and Leningrad; as symbols of Russian and Soviet civilization, they were to be "razed to the ground."[10] From early in the war, German troops were encouraged to destroy monuments and landmarks. Field Marshal Walther von Reichenau, concerned about some soldiers' unease with Germany's genocidal policies, issued an order in October 1941 which called for unrestrained violence against the enemy population and "symbols" of the Bolshevik system. The order, which was subsequently praised by Hitler as exemplary and circulated to all units fighting in the Soviet Union, stated,

> During their retreat, the Soviets often set buildings on fire. The Army is interested in extinguishing them only to the extent to which accommodations must be preserved for the troops. Otherwise the disappearance of symbols of the former Bolshevik rule, including buildings, falls within the framework of the war of extermination. Neither historic nor artistic considerations are of any importance in the eastern territories.[11]

Reichenau's order thus called for the annihilation of the Soviet Union's national patrimony and heritage. Subsequently, German troops pillaged and razed historic monuments of all sorts – monasteries, museums, palaces, statues, homes of Russian cultural figures such as Lev Tolstoy and Ivan Turgenev, among other things – both during the occupation and upon retreat.[12]

The Germans' attack on monuments in the Soviet Union was not unprecedented.[13] Throughout history, buildings and monuments which connote identity, nationality, and community have been intentionally destroyed or damaged during wartime.[14] Opposing forces target historic monuments and landmarks as a means of wiping out the culture of the enemy and erasing the history and memory they embody.[15] Art historians Margaret Olin and Robert Nelson write that "because a monument can achieve a powerful symbolic agency, to damage it, much less to obliterate it, constitutes a personal and communal violation with serious consequences." They argue that "attacking a monument threatens a society's sense of itself and its past."[16] Once damage is done to a monument, the meaning of it, and the memories it represents, are altered. Studies of iconoclasm suggest that destruction meant to deface, deform, or obliterate objects treasured by cultures often results in the transformation of the object's meaning, as extra layers of memory are attached to it.[17] The deliberate destruction of culturally significant monuments and landmarks in the Soviet Union, therefore, modified these objects not only physically but symbolically; they became sites of memory which embodied the story of Russia's tsarist past and the genocidal intentions of the Nazi regime.[18]

The restoration of historic monuments in the postwar years added yet further layers of memory. According to sociologist Tony Bennett, not only destruction but also restoration of historic sites decisively alters their meaning. He argues that the past as embodied in heritage sites "is inescapably the product of the present which organizes it."[19] This is especially true in places such as Leningrad, where there existed an intense will to remember and commemorate the war in the restoration process. Whereas some argue that the restoration of monuments was a means of forgetting the hardships of war and moving on, the destruction of Leningrad's historic sites was constantly recalled in the immediate postwar years.[20] Restoration was accompanied by publicity and propaganda campaigns reminding people that Hitler's forces intentionally attacked monuments, resulting in immense destruction. The central and Leningrad press frequently published exposés on the attempted annihilation of monuments, lengthy publications emerged on the topic, and exhibitions devoted to wartime preservation and postwar restoration were held throughout the period.[21] "What were once unintentional monuments," writes historian Robert Bevan, "by their rebuilding can become new, intentional monuments to the events which caused their destruction."[22] Rather than erasing the memory of the war from the city's streets and facades, the restoration of historic monuments was celebrated as a victory over destruction and a fitting commemoration of Leningrad's wartime experience. Iconoclasm and restoration, therefore, made symbols of empire into sites of Soviet memory, legitimacy, and authority.

Why did the Soviet leadership seek to protect objects from a bygone age in Leningrad? At first glance, it seems to make little sense that the regime would devote resources to restoring monuments from the tsarist and imperial past during the war and postwar periods when there were so many other pressing needs. But when placed within the context of the development of Soviet patriotism, preservationist policies appear not only rational, but necessary.[23] Beginning in the early 1930s, as the threat of war in Europe loomed large, the Soviet leadership adopted a patriotic stance and called on Soviet citizens to love and protect their country. This was a radical departure from the proletarian internationalism that the leadership had promoted since the revolution. The move toward promoting patriotism was part of a larger series of changes and adaptations in Soviet policies under Joseph Stalin. Indeed, in the 1930s the party leadership renounced its mistrust of the family unit, prohibited abortions, promoted pro-natal policies, changed its approach to education and discipline, and turned toward bombastic Russian nationalism.

These changes in Soviet policies have been seen as a "Great Retreat" from socialism and a return to prerevolutionary norms and values. Originally formulated by Nicholas Timasheff in 1946, the Great Retreat thesis suggests that the Stalinist leadership realized that Communist ideology and practice were unpopular among the population and thus sought to gain popular support by returning to tsarist values and institutions.[24] In recent years, however, some historians have argued against the idea of a Great Retreat, stressing, quite correctly, that the Soviet leadership never abandoned its commitment to socialism and continued to work toward the development of Communism.[25] According to David Hoffmann, with socialism proclaimed to be achieved by 1934, the Soviet authorities could relax their revolutionary policies and use traditional institutions and culture to support and legitimize the state while remaining committed to the development of socialism in the Soviet Union.[26] Far from being evidence of a repudiation of socialism, the policies adopted in the 1930s were mobilizational strategies common to all modern states threatened with war in the interwar years. Indeed, given the fact that the Stalinist leadership continued to build socialism, albeit in a less radical fashion than during the years of the First Five-Year Plan, Timasheff's broad argument for a "retreat" seems problematic. Certain elements of the "retreat" were in fact already apparent in the years immediately following the 1917 revolution, and were thus only enhanced under Stalin. Perhaps it might make more sense to argue, as does Matthew Lenoe, that the Stalinist leadership was pragmatic about its mobilizational policies in the 1930s and adapted them to the conditions of the time.[27] This was certainly the case when it came to the evolving policies on Soviet patriotism, Russian history, and historic monuments.

A key element of the emerging Soviet patriotism was a growing reverence for great figures and events from the prerevolutionary period. The use of history to mobilize and prepare the population for war developed throughout the 1930s and became a central component of Soviet propaganda during the Second World War, when Stalin explicitly called on the population to be inspired by heroes from the tsarist era. The patriotic rehabilitation of Russian history invested monuments throughout the Soviet Union with newfound significance as embodiments of a glorious past. Whereas prior to the mid-1930s the state followed a contradictory policy toward historic monuments, in the years leading up to the war new laws and organizations emerged to preserve and ensure the inviolability of the Soviet Union's cultural heritage. Most studies of the Stalinist leadership's treatment of monuments from the past emphasize the iconoclastic nature of the regime.[28] To be sure, not all monuments were safe from destruction in the Soviet Union, even as the state began to venerate historic sites as windows onto a glorious past. Yet, as this study shows, the ideological move toward promoting Soviet patriotism led to policies which increasingly promoted heritage preservation, something that came into focus more clearly after the Germans invaded the Soviet Union and systematically sought to destroy monuments as a means of erasing evidence of Russian history and culture.

The country's preservationists were mobilized to protect cultural and historic monuments and landmarks. In fact, there was a high degree of cooperation between preservationists (both party and nonparty members) and the Soviet leadership in drafting and implementing legislation and measures to protect the country's national patrimony. Stalinist policy toward historic monuments was not dictated simply from Moscow, but was rather a negotiation between the state and heritage specialists, who lobbied for effective legislation and preservation practices. The state's cultivation of Russocentrism and glorification of Russian history meshed well with the desires of preservationists, who were particularly enthused by the Stalinist reappropriation of the past, which allowed them official sanction to save the monuments they so deeply loved.

The former imperial capital was particularly important as a symbol to be preserved. Leningrad's historic cityscape, which Russia's rulers consciously developed as an icon of imperial power and might, had long been the subject of praise, admiration, national pride, and international renown.[29] Its baroque and neoclassical architecture, grand boulevards, and historic sites commemorating heroic military victories in Russia's past exemplified the state power that the Stalinist leadership sought to project to its citizens and the outside world. The intentional destruction of the Second World War exposed the vulnerability of monuments and awakened the Soviet authorities to the need for greater protection. Given the state's growing reliance on Russian history for mobilizational purposes, the loss of monuments in Leningrad and elsewhere came to be seen as unacceptable.

The story told here is ultimately one of identity formation in the Soviet Union under Stalin. The constant threat of war during the 1930s and 1940s pushed the central authorities to impose upon the population an identity that was fiercely patriotic and loyal to the Soviet fatherland. For the Soviet leadership, war was always on the horizon. The very "building blocks" of the new state were formed in the Civil War when the Bolshevik regime was threatened by domestic enemies, as well as foreign interventionists determined to destroy the fledgling Communist system.[30] The threat of war was never far off during the 1920s, and it took on new proportions in 1927 when war with Britain seemed imminent, giving the Stalinist leadership the opportunity to scrap the New Economic Policy and launch the First Five-Year Plan.[31] Yet it was during the 1930s, when the threat and reality of war intensified, that the Stalinist leadership felt compelled to embrace a patriotic identity in order to mobilize the population to protect the socialist fatherland. Hitler's aggressive rhetoric and position toward the Soviet Union proved much more threatening and concerning than anything preceding it. Germany's subsequent attempts to annihilate the Soviet state and its people forced the propaganda apparatus to rely more and more on patriotic themes in mobilizing the defense of the country and stimulating defiance of the Nazis.

Compounding the foreign threat were internal developments which worried the Soviet leadership. Throughout the 1930s, repressive state policies did little to endear people to the system. The impact of collectivization on villages, the forced deportation of hundreds of thousands of supposed "kulaks" to remote regions of the country's interior, the various campaigns against socially marginal elements, and the terror of 1937–1938 left deep scars on the population.[32] The Stalinist authorities were thus confronted with a disgruntled population and feared that "anti-Soviet" elements could act as a fifth column in the event of war.[33] Historians Oleg Budnitskii and Galina Zelenina write that "on the eve of war there was a considerable number of people who dreamt about the death of Soviet power; to see this come to fruition, several of them were willing to cooperate with any external force capable of destroying this [Soviet] power."[34] Indeed, with the German invasion these fears proved, in part, to be valid, as thousands of peasants and urban residents openly welcomed – and many worked with – the Wehrmacht as liberators from Soviet terror.[35] On the day that the Germans invaded, for example, Lidiia Osipova, an anti-Communist poet living in a suburb of Leningrad, who worked for the press established by the Nazi occupation authorities, wrote the following in her diary:

> Is it possible that our liberation is drawing near? Whatever the Germans are like, they cannot be worse than ours. . . . Everyone senses that finally, what we have all waited so long for has arrived. . . . And there is no doubt that the Germans will win. Forgive me, Lord! I am not an enemy of my own people, my motherland. I am not a degenerate. But we need to face the truth: we all, all of Russia, passionately want the enemy, whoever it might be, to win. This cursed order has robbed us of everything, including our sense of patriotism.[36]

This disdain for, and opposition to, certain aspects of the Soviet state did not come to an end after the war. Even though victory provided a degree of legitimacy to Stalin and the Soviet system, many people remained recalcitrant in their opposition to Soviet policies. This was especially true in territories first annexed after the signing of the Nazi-Soviet Pact, and then reoccupied in the late stages of the war (Latvia,

Lithuania, Estonia, and Western Ukraine). Indeed, the incorporation of new territories swelled the western border regions of the country with a population that was genuinely opposed to Soviet power.[37] But there was dissatisfaction in the Soviet heartland as well. Many Soviet citizens grew increasingly disillusioned with the system which they had hoped would allow for a degree of liberalization after the war. To be sure, in the immediate postwar period there was an expectation that the people would be rewarded for their service to the motherland.[38] Veterans, especially, who made up approximately 10–15 percent of the population (some twenty to twenty-five million of them), felt a profound sense of entitlement at war's end, and their growing disappointment following demobilization from the Red Army led to resentment toward, and frustrations with, the Soviet regime.[39] War vets returned to the Soviet Union with stories of vastly superior living standards in Europe and questioned why their supposedly "superior" civilization was so far behind the capitalist West. As Mark Edele notes, those who were unwilling to keep this information to themselves were at risk of being arrested for "anti-Soviet agitation" in the late Stalin years.[40]

In the immediate postwar years, then, the Soviet leadership found itself in a precarious position. On one hand, the victory over Nazi Germany proved to be a triumphant moment for the Soviet people, and the significance of this victory would be used to trumpet the power of the state and people for years to come. On the other hand, however, large segments of the population were either disillusioned with the system, openly hostile to Soviet rule, or unwilling to conform to the behavior expected of them by the party leadership.[41] This was particularly troubling given that the authorities experienced a profound sense of insecurity and anxiety as a result of the tremendous wartime destruction and losses. As the Soviet Union furiously sought to overcome the disastrous effects of war, hostilities with the West developed, making it seem as if another, more violent nuclear war was imminent.[42] By mid-1947, the rift between the Soviet Union and its former allies had become unbridgeable, splitting the world into two hostile and opposing camps, to use Andrei Zhdanov's formulation. Disunity and opposition to Stalinist rule, real or imagined, fueled the insecurity and anxiety felt by the Soviet leadership as the Cold War emerged in the immediate postwar years.

Soviet domestic policies reflected these fears and sought to address them. In light of the potentially destabilizing forces at home, which could prove especially problematic in the event of a new war, the authorities sought to combat nonconformity and potential disloyalty by continuing to instill in the population a sense of devotion to the fatherland and an understanding of superiority over the West. While some would argue that bombastic displays of Soviet – which increasingly meant Russian – patriotism reached their peak during the aptly named Great Patriotic War, it would be more correct to see the continuation of (and even growth in) the state's attempts to instill in its population a sense of patriotic duty and loyalty in the late Stalinist era. "Soviet patriotism is a mighty force in the battle for Communism," wrote the author of a postwar tract on the topic. "And if the cultivation of Soviet patriotism was always one of the central tasks of the Communist Party's ideological work, then in present conditions the education of Soviet patriotism acquires exceptionally important significance. The cultivation of Soviet patriotism has now become one of the most urgent, most vitally essential problems of the communist education of the working people."[43]

To cultivate Soviet patriotism and a sense of devotion to the motherland in the early Cold War, the state relied in part on repression. Repressive campaigns were inaugurated in 1946 in the cultural sphere to punish those who showed too little appreciation for the Soviet system and those who supposedly "kowtowed to the West." As Juliane Fürst notes, the postwar repressive campaigns were fueled by the "regime's desire to bring order to the post-war ideological world, which had acquired a worrying amount of parallel discourse."[44] These campaigns were expressly designed to "eliminate servility before the West" and bolster Soviet patriotism.[45] Along with repression, the party leadership simultaneously developed a propaganda campaign which encouraged the Soviet people to appreciate their heritage and glorify their achievements. The propaganda apparatus promoted xenophobia, called on cultural producers to emphasize past Russian achievements in their works, and sought to root out any foreign influences in Soviet society. In postwar propaganda, literature, art, and official pronouncements, the Soviet people were presented as the heirs of powerful Russian martial traditions developed over centuries of defending the country against foreign foes, as well as successors to a long line of cultural and scientific geniuses who made significant contributions to world literature, art, and science. Postwar Soviet propaganda thus encouraged people to look to the "glorious" Russian past and the recent victory in the Great Patriotic War as proof of the superiority of Soviet civilization over the West.

The preservation of historic monuments and commemorations of the war were therefore vitally important to the cultivation of a patriotic Soviet identity and should be seen within this larger context of disunity, anxiety, and mobilization. Elizabeth Campbell Karlsgodt, a historian of French cultural policy during the Second World War, recently noted that "policy choices reflect the nation's desire to preserve vestiges from the past, as indicators of civilization and a superior culture. At the same time," she continues, "assertions of grandeur rooted in a glorious heritage from the past can betray anxieties about a nation's military, diplomatic, and economic strength in the present."[46] Monuments and landmarks of all sorts provided a connection to history and served as places of inspiration, where lessons about heritage and the Russian past could be taught and learned. These sites of (selective) memory, which had been transformed into sites of Soviet legitimacy by the war, therefore helped overcome the threat of "servility to the West" and served as a common heritage that could unite the Soviet people. Likewise, the myth of war, which emphasized unity in the battle against Nazism, was a rallying point of pride and distinction for all. These two lines of patriotic sentiment were especially pronounced and entwined in Leningrad, a city which literally embodied the "glory," "power," and "might" of the Russian and Soviet states from the time of Peter the Great through to the Second World War. Indeed, the heroism shown by Leningraders during the 872-day siege was a testament to the steadfastness, determination, and strength of the Soviet people in the war against fascism. Leningrad and its monuments were, therefore, powerful mobilizational symbols that the state could draw upon as the Soviet Union entered into the Cold War in the early postwar years.

The following chapters discuss the Stalinist use of the tsarist past and memory of the war for distinctly mobilizational purposes. In recent years, several studies of wartime and postwar preservation in Germany,

France, and England have emerged.[47] Yet the actions of the Soviet leadership and preservationists have received only superficial and anecdotal treatment at best.[48] *Saving Stalin's Imperial City* therefore helps fill this void. Chapter 1 sets the stage for the war and postwar period by analyzing the development of St. Petersburg/Leningrad from the eighteenth century. It traces the emergence of the city as a display of imperial power and discusses the development of a preservationist movement in the early 1900s, the members of which began to work with the Soviet regime after the October Revolution. These preservationists had an important impact on the party's approach to historic and artistic monuments. Although the state's policy toward its national patrimony was often contradictory during the 1920s and 1930s, by the time the Soviet Union was drawn into the Second World War, a clear policy of heritage preservation had been established.

Chapter 2 turns to the Second World War and focuses on the efforts of Leningrad's authorities and preservationists to protect the cityscape during the siege. Soviet architects were aware of the threat that modern warfare posed to historic monuments, but they had not expected that the Germans would deliberately target and destroy the country's national patrimony. At the beginning of the war, therefore, heritage specialists focused their work on prophylactic actions, such as securing the artistic detail on buildings, and burying or encasing statues to protect them from shells and bombs – preparations which drew on the work of preservationists in the West, especially France and England. When it became clear that the Germans were deliberately targeting monuments for annihilation, city authorities, on the advice of Leningrad's Administration for the Protection of Monuments, took extraordinary measures to protect monuments, including the use of Red Army soldiers to bury famous statues as the enemy neared the city in August 1941, as well as the refusal to evacuate heritage specialists from the city until all preservation tasks were completed.

Chapters 3 and 4 focus on the restoration of Leningrad's historic city center and the world-famous palace and park complexes in the city's suburbs. Chapter 3 argues that historic restoration was conceived of as a commemoration of Leningraders' experiences in the unprecedented siege of the city. Through restoration, argued Leningrad's preservationists, the "red thread of the blockade" would be inscribed in the city fabric. Restored landmarks, such as the Admiralty, therefore became symbols of Leningrad's – and the USSR's – victory over fascism. This chapter further situates Leningrad's restoration in its larger pan-European context and shows how the city's planners put the restoration of historic monuments at the top of their agenda, in spite of the tremendous shortages of resources. By 1950, preservationists, architects, and urban planners could proudly proclaim that the majority of historic monuments in the city center had been restored to their prewar state.

In the suburbs a very different story unfolded, which is detailed in chapter 4. Given the levels of destruction, Soviet authorities believed that the grand imperial palaces from the eighteenth century could not be restored and their ruins should be removed to make way for new structures. Horrified by this suggestion, Soviet heritage specialists capitalized on the state's changing meaning of Soviet patriotism and successfully argued that the palaces were needed as irreplaceable witnesses to the history and culture of Russia during its golden age and as a testament to the USSR's commitment to defending these accomplishments against Nazi barbarism. When restoration began, museum exhibitions that had a variety of themes related to Russian history were staged in palaces that were, for the most part, still in ruins. As I argue in this chapter, these palaces became ideological training grounds for the Soviet people as the exhibits held in them emphasized the connection between the Russian past, the most violent war in history, and the Soviet people's determination to overcome the destruction.

While local officials and preservationists worked to restore historic monuments in the postwar period, they also sought to create a space devoted solely to the official memory of the siege. Chapter 5 tells the story of the creation of the Museum of the Defense of Leningrad and the anniversary celebrations which were staged to commemorate the final lifting of the siege on 27 January 1944. These commemorative spaces and events need to be seen in the context of the Soviet leadership's efforts to preserve the memory of the Great Patriotic War as a foundational, and even sacred, event in Soviet history. Just as attempts were made to inscribe the memory of the blockade symbolically and literally into the existing city landscape, so too did Leningraders seek to memorialize their struggle against the "fascist enemy" in more traditional commemorative venues. Moreover, as this chapter shows, commemorations themselves became mobilizational tools: Leningrad's authorities used commemorative sites and events to inspire new residents of the city to participate in restoration efforts by establishing a connection between them and the glorious history found in cityscape.

The final chapter of the book places historic restoration and commemorations in the context of the emerging Cold War. In an era of renewed international tensions, the central authorities sought to restore the economy quickly and bolster Soviet patriotism, the focus of which was the people's experience in the war and one thousand years of Russian history. But as the Soviet leadership strove to create a population unified by a common history, it increasingly argued that commemorations of the siege "perverted the history of the war" by presenting Leningrad "in isolation" from the all-Union wartime experience. As a threat to the emerging myth of the war, Moscow ended commemorations of the siege in the wake of the Leningrad Affair, a vicious purge of party and soviet leaders beginning in 1949. The tremendously popular Museum of the Defense of Leningrad was shut down, and plans to build a monument to the blockade that would fit into the historic cityscape were shelved. At the same time, however, historic preservation continued, but it was stripped of its commemorative function. The intimate and entangled relationship that developed between restoration and siege commemorations, therefore, came to an end, at least officially.

ONE

OLD PETERSBURG, PRESERVATION MOVEMENTS, AND THE SOVIET STATE'S "TURN TO THE PAST"

AT THE TURN OF THE TWENTIETH CENTURY, EUROPEAN intellectuals were becoming increasingly interested in locating their nation's past in historic monuments. Across the continent, institutions, organizations, and interest groups formed to protect and preserve the "tangible links" to their nation's revered history.[1] In 1903, Alois Riegl, a prominent Austrian art historian, wrote an essay on what he called the "modern cult of monuments." He focused on the way people assign meaning and value to the built environment, and argued that there are essentially two types of monuments: deliberate and unintentional. Deliberate monuments are those sculptures, statues, buildings, and other forms of expression that are meant from the moment of their creation to mark an occasion or preserve the memory of a person or event. Unintentional monuments, on the other hand, are those which are attributed value as monuments, or defined as such by viewers, at a later date; their commemorative value is assigned only after they are created. While unintentional monuments are not built to commemorate, they nevertheless have historical value as witnesses to a bygone age, event, or individual. Such places are infused with meaning by later generations and become "stone documents" which tell a certain story.[2]

The city of St. Petersburg has hundreds of deliberate and unintentional monuments. From its very founding in 1703, the creation of Peter the Great was deliberately constructed as a symbol of imperial power and prestige. The city is often described as a victory over nature – a magnificent creation arising out of the marshy Neva River delta. In little more than a century, St. Petersburg developed into a metropolis of baroque and neoclassical ensembles, the impressive appearance of which testified to Russia's place in Europe, the country's imperial "glory," and its military might. For the intellectuals in the imperial capital caught up in Riegl's "cult of monuments," the rigidly planned city stood as a monument to Peter's transformation of Russia. From the city's inception, successive rulers erected numerous monuments in the city to commemorate military victories over the Swedes, the Turks, and the French. Every street corner, palace, and architectural ensemble told a story of triumphs on the battlefield, important cultural figures, and famous leaders. It was for this reason that preservationists struggled in the early 1900s to save the old center of the city from the ravages of modernization and industrialization. Throughout this period, preservation-minded intellectuals took it upon themselves to protect the historic monuments of St. Petersburg. In doing so, they began a tradition of preservationism that crossed the revolutionary divide and continued into the Soviet period.

When the 1917 revolutions occurred in Petrograd – the name given to the city in 1914 to make it sound less German – preservationists grasped the opportunity to play a greater role in the protection of the country's historic and artistic monuments. In many ways their goals coincided with key figures within the Bolshevik leadership, who saw the need for selectively saving monuments from the tsarist era for the creation of a socialist society. With the exception of the period of the First Five-Year Plan (1928–1932), when the interests of modernization trumped all else, the central authorities increasingly worked with preservationists to maintain, conserve, and popularize the physical remains of the country's prerevolutionary heritage. When the leadership sought a useable past with which to mobilize the population and create a sense of patriotism and community in the 1930s, it rehabilitated many of the great heroes and events from the thousand years of Russian history. As a result, the state began to advocate and push for the protection and preservation of historic, artistic, and cultural monuments, both deliberate and unintentional. More than ever, the Stalinist leadership cooperated with preservationists and used the country's monuments as witnesses to a bygone age – stone documents used to instill in people a connection to the "glorious" past. This turn to the past invested historic monuments with unprecedented significance. They were sites at which the state's glorification of the country's history was made tangible. Consequently, the Soviet government attempted to strengthen preservation activities throughout the country. This was especially true in Leningrad, where the long tradition of preservation and reverence for the cityscape, combined with the newfound respect for the country's past, had a major impact on the actions taken to protect the city's historic monuments during and after World War II.

CREATING A MONUMENTAL CITY

The Neva River delta was an unlikely site at which to begin the construction of a city, let alone the future capital of the Russian Empire. Located in the northwest corner of Russia, the area where the Neva flows into the Gulf of Finland is extreme in all senses of the word. Were it not for Peter the Great's desire to revolutionize Russia and create a "Window to the West," the city that was constructed on this inhospitable site would likely not exist.[3] Yet within a century, Peter's city became one of the most impressive architectural creations in Europe, the monumental buildings, statuary, and general aesthetics of which were symbols of Russia's growing power and place in the world.

The first stones of the future city were laid in May 1703, after Peter seized the land from the Swedes. Founded to defend the area, especially the entrance up the River Neva, the city started out as a military outpost on Hare Island, the present-day site of the Peter and Paul Fortress. One year later, on the opposite shore of the river, Peter began construction of the Admiralty wharves. The emperor forced thousands of serfs and workers to move to the new construction site in the early 1700s.[4] He also obliged members of the royal court, aristocrats, artisans, merchants, and skilled workers to take up residence on the Neva and begin building homes, stores, and workshops in European architectural styles. As the city expanded over the years, it continued to be the hub of the Russian military – serving as home to the country's major regiments and its naval base – but it also became the political and commercial capital of the empire.[5]

Following the victory over the Swedes in the Great Northern War at Poltava in 1709, Peter began moving the empire's administrative apparatus to St. Petersburg, and by 1712 the transfer was complete.[6] Due to its importance as a military base, port, administrative center, and imperial capital, Peter pushed for the city to grow more quickly.[7] To facilitate this, he devoted nearly 5 percent of the state budget to constructing government buildings on the banks of the Neva and Vasilievskii Island.[8]

In the wake of the victory at Poltava, and the subsequent transfer of the capital, the city began to develop along the lines of a coordinated plan.[9] From this point onward, the state would play a major role in the architectural and aesthetic shaping of the city. The emperor issued a series of decrees which strictly outlined the parameters of future planning and the duties of individuals in the city's construction.[10] He ordered, for example, that stone be used for important buildings instead of wood, that structures on the river's edge be built in a certain style, and that buildings be aesthetically pleasing.[11] Because Peter wanted the city to develop along a European model, he employed hundreds of architects from Western Europe to practice their profession on the blank slate of St. Petersburg.[12]

His official residence in the Summer Garden and other structures built during this period exemplified the shift away from traditional Russian architecture toward a more monumental style of construction. Many of the buildings in the capital, including the palace of Prince Menshikov located on the southern shore of Vasilievskii Island, were grandiose structures that served an imperial purpose. It was at Menshikov's palace, for example, that Peter would hold official court gatherings and greet visiting delegates from abroad. Drawing on architectural designs from Europe, the majority of the monumental buildings constructed under Peter, including the Kunstkamera (his "curiosity cabinet"), the Twelve Colleges (the seat of government), and the Alexander Nevskii Monastery, were built in the style of northern baroque. The choice was deliberate, as Peter was fully aware of the use of the baroque visual arts in Europe to express power and glorify society's rulers.[13] By the 1720s, the main quality of the city had taken form: St. Petersburg was a city of magnificent monuments on a grand scale.[14]

As the new capital of the Russian Empire and the "Window to the West," St. Petersburg was from the very beginning meant to be a prestigious city whose artistic and architectural appearance could rival those of any European capital. The element of prestige was key. Peter knew that visitors to his new capital, especially those from Europe, would spread the word about St. Petersburg's phenomenal growth and splendor upon their return to their homelands. The architecture of the city therefore served a political purpose: to express the power of the monarch, the wealth of the nation, and the strength of the military.[15] In constructing grandiose buildings, bridges, and sculptures, and providing a uniform layout of the city streets designed to awe and impress, Peter set a pattern for successive rulers to develop the city as a symbol of the majesty of the Romanov dynasty.[16] Historian Richard Wortman notes that "the sumptuous, highly ritualized presentations of the Russian monarchy produced at enormous cost of resources and time, indicate that Russian rulers and their advisers considered the symbolic sphere of ceremonies and imagery intrinsic to their exercise of power."[17] The external appearance of St. Petersburg, therefore, acted as a visual display of the power and glory of the Russian state under Peter the Great. Following the defeat of King Charles XII of Sweden in the Great Northern War, Peter turned Russia into a major European military and political power. The form that the city would take over the next two hundred years was a reflection of that new stature.[18]

Peter's successors, beginning with Empress Anna, continued to develop the city as a display of imperial prowess.[19] Russian rulers devoted nearly limitless funds to beautify and increase the imperial magnificence of the city.[20] Under Anna's rule, the city's central districts were purged of undesirable structures. This initiative was given added impetus by a series of fires in 1736 and 1737 that burned down the majority of wooden buildings between the Neva and the Moika (the central, or Admiralty, district).[21] Anna used this opportunity to enact a series of new laws meant to control the development of the city, decreeing that wooden buildings in the Admiralty district were to be removed and that new structures must be built using stone, making it prohibitively expensive for many tradesmen to build there. Anna also forbade members of the royal court to take up residence in the imperial palace, which spurred the building of a considerable number of palaces and mansions in the center. To reinforce control over the development of the city, in 1737 Anna created the Commission for the Orderly Development of St. Petersburg.[22] Throughout the eighteenth century, Russian rulers held firm to the need for control over urban development and continued to push slums to the outskirts in order to develop the grandeur of the city's center.[23]

Each successive Russian ruler followed the guidelines set by Peter in creating a cityscape that displayed the might of the state. When Elizabeth took the throne after Anna's death in 1740, she further developed the style of the capital by employing the Italian-born architect Bartolomeo Rastrelli, who created the Winter Palace, Smolnyi Cathedral, the Catherine Palace in Tsarskoe Selo, and many other baroque architectural landmarks. It was under Catherine the Great and her grandson Alexander I, however, that St. Petersburg reached the apotheosis of its imperial appearance. Almost immediately after her coronation in 1762, Catherine began to work at perfecting the symbolism of the capital, moving away from the baroque architectural extravagance of Elizabeth's reign.[24] She announced an architectural planning competition in 1763 to set new goals and bestow further grandeur and dignity on the city.[25] The new plans stressed the ensemble principle, in which continuous facades would line the streets, and granite embankments would clad the rivers and canals, making for an urban organic whole. Geographer James Bater notes that two basic principles for the planning of St. Petersburg were articulated during Catherine's reign: the construction of large squares and monumental buildings to increase the city's magnificence, and the development of "harmonious" and "continuous" facades along the city's main streets.[26]

The period between Catherine's reign and the first part of Nicholas I's marked the height of organized, rigid planning – a period during which the ruler became one of the most important arbiters of city aesthetics. Catherine established the Masonry Construction Commission, for example, to oversee all development in the capital.[27] Alexander I continued his grandmother's policies of control over urban development by creating a number of organizations and committees to supervise and scrutinize building in the city, and later throughout the empire. In 1816, Alexander established the Committee of Construction and Hydraulic Works to bring the capital to "aesthetic perfection." Like Peter the Great,

Alexander was determined that the seat of Russian government should be second to none and serve as a reflection of the Russian nation and its military might.[28]

In order to further transform the capital into a city exuding power and magnificence, Catherine, and to a greater extent Alexander, employed classical architecture. The neoclassical style expressed the grand goals of the Alexandrine period. Alexander wanted to shape the center of the city to reflect the "new seriousness of state power."[29] Both Catherine and Alexander filled the center of the city with monumental buildings in the neoclassical style, creating whole ensembles linked by large squares and parade grounds. The buildings and ensembles constructed during this period expressed state power on a monumental scale comparable to that of Imperial Rome.[30]

The pinnacle of neoclassical monumentalism in city planning came during the empire's rise to prominence in European affairs after Russia's victory in the Patriotic War against Napoleon in 1812. During the first third of the nineteenth century, urban planners shaped St. Petersburg into the harmonious and austere architectural ensemble for which it has received praise as one of the most beautiful cities in the world. Throughout this period one sees the construction of elegant neoclassical buildings by a number of architects, including Andrei Voronikhin (the Cathedral of the Kazan Mother of God, the Mining Institute), Thomas de Thomon (the Stock Exchange), Andrian Zakharov (the third and final reconstruction of the Admiralty), and Vasilii Stasov (the Barracks of the Pavlovskii Regiment). Yet more than any other architect, it was Carlo Rossi whose architectural designs, for such buildings as the Mikhailovskii Palace, the Senate and Synod, the building of the General Staff on Palace Square, and the Alexandrine Theater on Nevskii Prospekt, completed the neoclassical monumentalism of the capital. All of these buildings were painted in yellow, representing imperial gold, and lined with white columns, linking the city to the great traditions of ancient Rome and expressing the power and might of the Russian empire.[31]

By the early 1830s, the monumental style of building was coming to an end. Over the course of 130 years, Russia's rulers had sculpted a city out of the Neva River delta which matched, or surpassed, the most impressive and elegant cities in Europe, exactly as Peter had intended.

The river and canal embankments in the center of the city were now lined with buildings connecting the architectural ensembles. The massive parade grounds which dotted the city gave the impression of a powerful empire. The space between the building of the Senate and Synod and the Winter Palace, for example, was a series of squares designed for no other purpose than to display Russia's military might. What is more, several of these structures were built in commemoration of the victory over Napoleon, including the Kazan Cathedral and the building of the General Staff. The product of intense construction and aesthetic perfectionism, by the end of Alexander I's reign St. Petersburg's built environment reflected the consolidation of Russia's status as an imperial power and its military might.

It was during the reign of Nicholas I that the state relaxed control over what could be built and where. The rate of urban growth outpaced the capacity of officials to supervise and regulate construction. The onset of industrialization over the next several decades had severe consequences for a city that was rigidly planned as an expression of imperial "magnificence."[32] As the city's population grew to nearly half a million by the 1850s, and to over nine hundred thousand by the 1890s, the need for housing, administrative buildings, and office space stimulated construction on a much less monumental scale and put increasing pressure on the capital's celebrated cityscape.

Although grand palaces continued to be built in the city, there was a general turn away from the creation of neoclassical ensembles toward individual structures built in eclectic styles by an emerging middle class composed primarily of industrialists, merchants, and entrepreneurs.[33] Here, as in the other major cities of the Russian Empire, architects turned to pseudo-Gothic, neo-Renaissance, and a mixture of various styles with lavish facade detail, which many found to be vulgar, distasteful, and inappropriate for the capital of the empire. The second half of the nineteenth century also saw the beginnings of a revival in national architecture – quite in line with Nicholas's policy of Official Nationality and the admiration for Muscovy seen during the conservative and nationalistic reigns of Alexander III and Nicholas II – as Eastern-style cupolas and bell towers began to dot the Petersburg skyline.[34] The transition away from neoclassical architecture to a mix of styles led to criticism from artistic and cultural enthusiasts in the capital.[35] Many people viewed the St. Petersburg of the eighteenth and early nineteenth centuries – "Old Petersburg" – as an architectural masterpiece, whose harmonious and stern ensembles stood as a monument to Peter's transformation of Russia and the power of the empire. The development of industry, the influx of people into the city, and the resulting changes to the cityscape during the last fifty years of the nineteenth century threatened this monument and sparked a movement to preserve the city's artistic and historic heritage.

HISTORY, AESTHETICS, AND PRESERVATION

Toward the end of the nineteenth century, various groups began to protest the developmental trends in St. Petersburg and attempted to prevent further construction in the architectural styles of eclecticism and national revival, which they believed to be distorting the external appearance of the imperial capital.[36] Advocates for the preservation of the city's aesthetic appearance called for an end to indiscriminate construction in the city center and a return to the neoclassicism of Catherine's and Alexander's reigns. They also sought to prevent the destruction of monuments in the capital and throughout the empire. As elsewhere in Europe around the turn of the century, a growing number of people in Russia – and especially in St. Petersburg – became increasingly concerned with both the aesthetic value of historic monuments and the past they represented. And in the twilight years of the Russian Empire, these preservationists sought a more influential role in the decision-making process concerning the country's heritage.

The state had shown some interest in developing a system of monument preservation in Russia. Throughout the nineteenth century, officials began to question what exactly should be considered a monument and how a system of protection could be devised.[37] Beginning in 1826, the Ministry of Internal Affairs made several attempts to prevent the unauthorized alteration, renovation, and destruction of old buildings belonging to the state. The ministry required that governors, mayors, police, and church authorities strive to prevent the destruction of monuments whenever possible. These demands were repeated in a general mandate (*Obshchii nakaz*) issued by the ministry in 1837, and in subsequent edicts passed by the Senate and Synod in 1842 and 1848. To the dismay of many, destruction and mistreatment of monuments continued.[38] In 1898 the ministry and the Imperial Archeological Commission initiated a project to create a list of monuments throughout the country and draft legislation for their protection.[39] Although the idea was well-intentioned, the deliberations about the form of the legislation dragged on for years, hampered by the need to accommodate a number of conflicting interest groups. When a draft finally reached the Duma in 1912, prominent preservationists rejected it because they believed it would actually hinder the protection of the country's historic monuments.[40] The lack of decisive action by the state to provide legislation led preservationists to believe that the tsarist authorities were at best ambivalent about the preservation of monuments throughout the empire and in the capital itself.

In the absence of effective legislation to save the country's historic and artistic monuments, the initiative fell to civil society, which responded with a preservation movement centered in the capital. In the years leading up to 1917, one of the movement's major goals was the preservation of St. Petersburg itself, especially "Old Petersburg," a term which served as a "rallying cry for historic preservation."[41] Calls for improved treatment of monuments came from a group of influential artists and intellectuals, including Sergei Diaghilev, Alexander Benois, Dmitrii Filosofov, Igor Grabar', Giorgii Lukomskii, Petr Veiner, Nikolai Vrangel', Petr Stolpianskii, Vladimir Kurbatov, and others. The members of this "cult of Old Petersburg," as Katerina Clark describes it, were devoted to preserving the city's monumental architecture, and made their opinions known in a series of important journals devoted to art and antiquity, including *World of Art* (*Mir iskusstva*, 1899–1904), and *Bygone Years* (*Starye gody*, 1907–1917).[42]

These journals, and the people involved with them, played a decisive role in bringing the necessity for preservation to public attention, even if their idea of what needed to be preserved was selective and influenced by the artistic tastes of the period. As a platform for popularizing the need to preserve monuments, the journals offered discussions of all sorts of architecture and art, and encouraged people to preserve and protect what they considered to be the "treasures" of Russian history. One of the preservationists' goals was to increase the appreciation of St. Petersburg as a work of art that should not be spoiled through building in styles that conflicted with the "stern and harmonious" aesthetic of the city.[43] In an important article from 1902 in *World of Art,* Alexander Benois called for a reappraisal of the empire's capital and its cityscape. He noted that the city had been disfigured by urban development over the preceding fifty years, and that contemporaries heaped unfair scorn and insults on the city as a whole. He argued, however, that St. Petersburg was not deserving of the negative image it had received during that period and summoned readers to appreciate, preserve, and protect the beautiful city: "One wants artists to fall in love with Petersburg, and, having sanctified and promoted its beauty, save it from ruin, prevent barbarous distortions of it, protect its beauty from the encroachment of crude ignoramuses who treat it with such incredible disregard due largely to the lack of protesting voices, voices of defense, and voices of delight."[44] Benois and other preservationists believed it necessary to promote preservation because the government was doing precious little to help in this matter, and in certain cases was actually facilitating destruction. They hoped to rally support for their cause by stressing the possible destruction of St. Petersburg as an irreplaceable historic and artistic monument and witness to the nation's past.

Although the aesthetic appearance of the city was a key element in their thinking, preservationists realized, and emphasized to the public, that the monuments populating the city also embodied the history of St. Petersburg and imperial Russia. Deliberate monuments built throughout the city commemorated the country's heroes, victories in war, and the empire's might. Peter's Summer Palace, for example, was not only his residence, but also a monument to victory over the Swedes. The emperor had the facades of the modest palace decorated with allegorical depictions of the military triumph and Russian naval power.[45] The victory over Napoleon was particularly well represented in monuments such as the Alexander Column on Palace Square, the building of the General Staff designed in honor of the victory, the Narva Gates erected to greet the returning soldiers, and the statues of Mikhail Kutuzov and Michael Andreas Barclay de Tolly in front of the Kazan Cathedral (itself a monument to victory in 1812). In addition, numerous statues, obelisks, and other commemorative structures were placed throughout the city as a reminder for future generations of the empire's military prowess.

Unintentional monuments likewise served as reminders of the past. On the one hand, major buildings such as the Admiralty and the Peter and Paul Fortress were monuments to Peter's resolve to create a city on the banks of the Neva, just as the Winter Palace projected an image of imperial power and might. On the other hand, smaller, more modest buildings and structures too came to be understood as commemorative sites. Building number twelve on the Moika Canal, for example, was revered as the final residence of Russia's greatest poet, Alexander Pushkin. Preservationists viewed these monuments both as magnificent works of art and as windows onto the city's history. When the journal *Bygone Years* was first published in 1907, its editors claimed that it was "devoted to the memory of the past."[46] Indeed, contributors to the journal declared that the historic monuments of the city were places at which "the spirit of the age and the shadows of the past linger in the air."[47] The destruction or distortion of the monuments, therefore, signified a loss of not just an element in the cityscape, but a living witness to the country's history.

Nearly each issue of *Bygone Years* included articles devoted to monuments that were threatened with destruction in the capital and throughout the country. Articles on "vandalism" committed by businesses and governmental departments (mis)using and renovating buildings brought public attention to the destruction of historic monuments, and shamed individuals and institutions into addressing the problem and rethinking their actions. In a 1913 article entitled "Recurrent Acts of Vandalism by Governmental Departments," for example, the author discussed how a certain ministry damaged, "with a clear conscience," the building in which it was located because of the need for additional space. In a pointed criticism of the authorities, the author wrote, "If we should expect from anyone the most cultured attitude to one's property, as well as a small material concession for the sake of preserving works of art, then should we not expect it namely from the department controlling the property of the first proprietors in Russia – the tsarist family?"[48] Contributors to preservation journals, therefore, acted as watchdogs over Russia's historic monuments, as well as moral authorities when it came to relics of the past. Preservationists used such exposés of vandalism and destruction to urge the tsarist authorities – and the public – to play a larger role in the protection of the country's heritage.

The people involved with these journals (especially *Bygone Years*) set up organizations and commissions to focus on the matter of preservation. In 1907, the capital's preservationists established the Commission for the Study and Description of Old St. Petersburg, which was initially headed by Benois. The commission had no legal power to punish individuals and institutions for damaging the city's monuments through renovation or demolition, but like *Bygone Years,* it acted through media campaigns designed to influence public opinion and expose the vandalism caused by property owners, thereby shaming them into preserving the premises they occupied.[49] The commission then created the Museum of Old Petersburg in 1907, which would play an important role in preservationist activities. Although it received some small subsidies from the government, as did most privately run cultural institutions, the museum's main support came from individuals sympathetic to its cause.[50] Two years later, in 1909, contributors to the journal formed the Society for the Defense and Protection of Monuments of Art and Antiquity in Russia, whose goal was the "logical development of the ideas" promoted by the editors of *Bygone Years:* "'To impede destruction, support and assist in the protection of all monuments in Russia which have artistic or historic value, irrespective of the era in which they were created.'"[51] These initiatives were able to operate and become as influential as they did because wealthy individuals – who in many cases were members of the imperial family or held high positions in the tsarist bureaucracy – backed their goals ideologically and financially.[52]

Preservationists continued to voice their complaints and concerns about the lack of attention paid to the destruction of the past by the government and private individuals throughout the late imperial period – and they had good reason to do so. Many of the city's historic monuments were threatened with demolition, had lost their artistic detail and original form through renovations, or had been destroyed altogether in the interests of creating new structures. A historian involved in the preservation movement, G. K. Lukomskii, lamented the loss of not only "tens of buildings" during the first fifteen years of the twentieth century, but also the hundreds of small places (corners, building entrances, signs, gates, balconies, pavilions, doors, etc.) which gave character to Old Petersburg.[53] He expressed his frustration with the lack of progress in changing people's attitudes toward the city's history and built environment, and the authorities' unwillingness to provide for the protection of monuments, by stating, "So much has been written in journals and newspapers, so much has been said in meetings on this topic, but the opportunities for such acts of vandalism remain the same."[54] Like many other people at the time, Lukomskii was incensed by the lack of progress made in official circles to having historic monuments put under protection by the state.

Frustrated by the disregard shown to historic and artistic monuments, preservationists sought a larger role in protecting Russia's cultural heritage. Ironically, it was only with the February Revolution and the overthrow of the Russian monarchy that preservationists grasped the opportunity to carry out their goals of protecting monuments and landmarks in the city and throughout the country. The experience they accumulated in advocating for preservation during the first two decades of the twentieth century provided their cause with a momentum that took them across the revolutionary divide. Many of the country's prerevolutionary preservationists would, in fact, go on to work with the Provisional Government and subsequently the Bolshevik regime in creating laws and policies to protect the country's built heritage.

REVOLUTION AND PRESERVATION

When the revolution came in February 1917, preservationists began to fear for the fate of the palaces, mansions, statues, and valuable property that had been associated with the privileged classes. There was good reason for anxiety. During the French Revolution the "masses" attacked, burned, pulled down, and destroyed many of the monuments associated with the *Ancien Régime.*[55] The people's rage toward the old order had found expression in the destruction and defacing of objects which symbolized the monarchy and its supporters, and Petrograd's preservationists feared that Russia's monuments and landmarks might meet the same fate. But the French Revolution also brought into being the idea of the people's heritage – *patrimoine* – and led to the nationalization and protection of many culturally valuable objects.[56] A similar development occurred in Russia after February 1917. Just as in the French case, during and after the Russian revolutions there were attempts both to destroy the symbols of the tsarist regime *and* to protect them.

The February Revolution unleashed iconoclasm throughout the country, but the destruction was especially pronounced in the capital, which embodied the very essence of empire and autocracy. Historians Orlando Figes and Boris Kolonitskii argue that by destroying imperial symbols, people were attacking the old regime itself. Iconoclasm, they note, was a "central part of February."[57] The revolution witnessed attacks on tsarist symbols, such as the double-headed imperial eagle, destruction or veiling of imperial statues with red banners, and, as was the case with the Bastille, attacks on imperial prisons.[58] The situation could have been much worse with respect to the city's historic monuments. There was some looting of mansions and palaces, as well as acts of desecration, but overall the majority of people restrained themselves from indiscriminate destruction of cultural property (in the capital, at least). In April, Alexander Benois expressed his surprise and astonishment that more had not been destroyed. "Of all the miracles of this fantastic moment that we have lived through (and which is far from over)," he wrote, "what astounds me most is the almost complete absence of excesses of vandalism."[59]

The relative lack of damage to historic and artistic monuments was in part due to the actions taken by Petrograd's preservationists and several others in the city's cultural community – actions which found support in the new structures of power. Shortly after the abdication of the tsar, the capital's cultural activists met at Maxim Gorky's apartment to discuss the issues facing the country's built heritage. They decided to lobby the new government for the creation of a ministry of arts, which would give them a voice in the cultural development of the country.[60] The Gorky Commission, as it came to be called, set as one of its main goals the protection of national treasures. Over the course of the first two months following the revolution, the commission worked diligently to impress upon people the need to preserve the heritage they had inherited from the old regime, and to safeguard monuments of the past by creating a series of museums out of the imperial palaces and mansions.

Representatives of the commission reached out to the Provisional Government and the Petrograd Soviet and received official sanction from both.[61] In an appeal written by the Gorky Commission and made by the Petrograd Soviet, the Russian people were summoned to protect the "inheritance" left to them by the "former owners," for the paintings, statues, and buildings were, according to the appeal, "embodiments of your spiritual strengths and those of your forefathers." The appeal concluded by stressing the usefulness of monuments for building a new culture: "Citizens, do not touch a single brick, protect monuments, buildings, old things, documents – all of this is your history, your pride. Remember that this is the soil from which your new national art will grow."[62] The authorities clearly shared the commission's belief that the country's heritage was in danger, and stressed the need to preserve all of the cultural riches left in the hands of the people.

The Gorky Commission, however, was short-lived. Due to a number of problems between members, including ideological cleavages and accusations of dictatorship over the arts, the commission broke apart.[63] It was succeeded by a series of other commissions, which throughout the spring and summer of 1917 continued its work. Some of their main activities included protecting Petrograd's imperial suburban palaces from looting, providing an inventory and catalogue of the city's moveable artworks, and further advocating for the preservation of the country's historic monuments. From the very beginning of the revolution, therefore, activists had a much greater say in the politics of cultural protection than during the late imperial period, and they actively cultivated a working relationship with the organs of power.[64]

The October Revolution of that same year signified a radical departure in almost all respects from the policies employed by the tsarist bureaucracy, the Provisional Government, and the Petrograd Soviet. The Bolsheviks came to power vowing to create a new system and society on the ruins of the old. And while it might be expected that their attitudes toward imperial heritage would be decidedly negative, this was not the case. The October Revolution revealed a contradictory and uneasy relationship to the monuments of the past. On the one hand, certain influential avant-garde groups, such as the Russian Futurists and Proletkult, called for the complete destruction of the vestiges of the past in the name of creating a society that was entirely new.[65] On the other, many of the leading Bolsheviks held much less radical positions and called for using the past to build a new future.[66]

Public pronouncements made shortly after the revolution illustrate the Bolsheviks' initially contradictory policies. Within the first six months of October, the authorities called on people to save the country's cultural heritage *and* to tear it down. In the first instance, the commissar of enlightenment, Anatolii Lunacharskii, called on the citizens of Russia to "take care of the people's property." In his November 1917 appeal (which is reminiscent of the one made by the Petrograd Soviet earlier), he declared that the "laboring people" inherited not only "natural riches," but "vast cultural riches: buildings of stunning beauty, museums full of beautiful and rare objects, instructive and ennobling of the soul, libraries preserving enormous spiritual valuables, etc. All of this now truly belongs to the people." Calling for the preservation of "our common treasure," Lunacharskii emphasized the educational function of the "inheritance," stating that "even the most benighted, who have been held in ignorance by oppression, will become enlightened and understand what a source of joy, strength and wisdom artistic works can be."[67] The appeal did not encourage people to admire the history represented in their cultural inheritance. Rather, stress was placed on the aesthetic value of these treasures, as well as the lessons that could be learned about the creative genius of the Russian people.

Appeals of this sort were accompanied by actions designed to protect monuments. Immediately after the October Revolution, the Bolsheviks assigned soldiers to guard important historic sites and prevent destruction and looting in Petrograd, Moscow, and other cities.[68] The People's Commissariat of Enlightenment (Narkompros) also employed the commissions set up after the February Revolution in their work, encouraging them to continue their activities in cataloguing and preserving cultural artifacts.[69] Commissions in Petrograd, Moscow, and provincial towns worked with Narkompros to discourage looting and vandalism, prevent the inappropriate use of premises designated as cultural treasures, and carry out a host of other preservationist activities.[70] More importantly, in May of 1918, Narkompros established the Section for Museums and Preservation of Monuments of Art and Antiquity. Headed by the influential art historian Igor' Grabar', the Museum Section sought to account for, protect, and develop museums and museum exhibits out of the relics of the prerevolutionary period.[71]

Yet while the Bolsheviks created official organs to promote preservationists' goals and urged people to preserve the embodiments of the past, they also called for the selective demolition of monuments which symbolized the monarchy. Of the monuments erected in honor of the tsars and their servants, those which possessed historic or artistic interest were to be preserved; those that did not, according to a decree from April 1918, were to be removed from the streets, squares, and other public places and consigned to warehouses or "turned to some socially useful purpose." Several of the "more ugly idols," the authorities suggested, were to be removed by 1 May 1918 and replaced by new socialist monuments.[72]

Influential people within the Bolshevik leadership, therefore, were unwilling to entirely banish the tsarist heritage from socialist culture. Sheila Fitzpatrick, among others, has noted the problem of reducing the Bolshevik Party and Russian intelligentsia into "monolithic entities." She notes that a "variety of all values and opinions on cultural policy were represented within the Bolshevik Party." Most notable was the split between Old Bolsheviks, such as the moderate Anatolii Lunacharskii, whose views resembled those of the non-Bolshevik Russian intelligentsia, and the militant Communists, who favored forcible politicization of culture.[73] Vladimir Lenin himself was, in many ways, a traditional Russian intellectual who defended the interests of the intelligentsia against the radicals on the far left who set out to destroy the old culture.[74] Opposed to the indiscriminate destruction of monuments from the past, Lenin believed that a new socialist culture could not appear out of thin air, and it needed a base from which to grow.[75] Although some tsarist monuments and symbols became victims of revolutionary iconoclasm, many others continued to play a role in the cultural landscape of the socialist society. Thus, because Bolshevik calls for destruction were selective, famous monuments which dotted the Petrograd cityscape, such as the Bronze Horseman, were spared destruction during the first revolutionary years. Even certain statues symbolizing the most tyrannical and conservative periods of tsarist rule, including P. P. Trubetskoi's statue of

Alexander III on Znamenskaia Square (erected in 1909) and P. K. Klodt's impressive monument to Nicholas I on St. Isaac Square (1859), were not destroyed.[76]

Over the course of the 1920s, Bolshevik policies toward monuments continued to promote preservation and destruction, depending on the object in question, and the new authorities worked with prerevolutionary preservationists to save the country's heritage from destruction, looting, and vandalism.[77] Religious symbols and structures were particularly vulnerable. But as Catriona Kelly argues, very few churches were destroyed in Leningrad, and she notes that preservationists were influential in deciding what was to be preserved, destroyed, or reappropriated for other uses: "The tastes and perceptions of the officials in the monuments preservation service," she observes, "played a critical role in what survived and what did not."[78]

The majority of preservationists' work during this period involved the creation of museums out of the imperial palaces and mansions of the "former classes" and "disenfranchised."[79] In June 1918, for example, Narkompros turned the palaces of Tsarskoe Selo, one of the suburban residences of the tsars outside of Petrograd, into museums for the people. By 1920 the other imperial suburban residences at Peterhof, Gatchina, and Pavlovsk had also become museums, as had many of the grand private palaces in the city's center (Stroganov, Usupov, and Sheremetev palaces).[80] Residences of famous cultural figures were converted into museums during this period, as was the case with Lev Tolstoy's Moscow home and his former country estate, Iasnaia Poliana.[81] When the Civil War ended in 1921, a network of museums was fully operational throughout the country. Between 1918 and 1920, following a Soviet government decree calling for the registration of all monuments of art and antiquity, over 550 old mansions, nearly one thousand private art collections, and over two hundred separate pieces of art were accounted for by the Museum Section of Narkompros.[82] The Soviet authorities continued to create museums and use them for educating the populace throughout the period of the New Economic Policy.[83]

Much of the work to create museums and preserve monuments was carried out by voluntary organizations. The early years of Soviet rule – especially the relatively liberal period of the NEP – saw the promotion of local studies (*kraevedenie*) and voluntary organizations devoted to studying the regions of the country. In Petrograd, the Society for the Study, Popularization, and Artistic Protection of Old Petersburg and Its Surroundings (better known as the Society for Old Petersburg, which in 1925 became the Society for Old Petersburg–New Leningrad) was created to ensure the preservation of the city's monuments. The society was formed and directed by many of the same individuals who had called for preservation under the last tsar, and who had worked under the Provisional Government to save monuments from destruction.[84] The society's goal was to study the historic and artistic monuments of the former imperial capital, provide for their protection and preservation (especially in the context of new development under the Soviet state), and popularize cultural heritage to the people.[85] It organized excursions to historic and cultural sites, created museums–including an Alexander Pushkin museum in the poet's last place of residence on the Moika Canal–and arranged lectures and musical shows which exhibited the culture of Old Petersburg. All of the society's activities were designed to further the preservationists' cause and guard the center of the city (Old Petersburg) as if it were a "nature preserve."[86]

Throughout the early years of Soviet rule, therefore, the Bolsheviks did not wholly dismiss the country's heritage. As monuments to Karl Marx, Lenin, and other revolutionary heroes were being constructed, selected elements from the past were used for building a new culture. But as Richard Stites has noted, the authorities did not use monuments and museums to glorify history and create a connection with the tsarist past; that past was presented as a time of decadent, oppressive rulers who enslaved and exploited the people. Rather, in the 1920s the authorities "depoliticized" monuments of all sorts and "neutralized their former symbolic power."[87] In preserving monuments and creating museums, the Bolsheviks reinvested the symbols of the old order with new meanings. No longer were palaces and imperial treasures just symbols of oppression. They were now the people's property, earned during the upheavals of revolution. In fact, the very act of preserving such treasures as collective property buttressed the ideology of the regime, since they now served as concrete reminders not only of a past that had been overthrown, but also of a future in which all wealth was to be held in common, free of tyranny, oppression, and inequality.[88] Rather than creating a culture out of thin air based entirely on overthrowing the past, the October Revolution signified the beginnings of a new society which borrowed heavily from the old. And during this period, several cultural activists from the tsarist era played a decisive role in preserving the country's heritage, as their goals coincided with those in the Bolshevik leadership.

STALINISM AND HISTORIC MONUMENTS

The official policy toward monuments from the past underwent a series of dramatic changes beginning in the late 1920s when Stalin launched the First Five-Year Plan. The goal of the plan was to rapidly industrialize the Soviet Union, bring the peasantry firmly under Soviet control through the collectivization of agriculture, and prepare for an inevitable war. Ever since the October Revolution, Soviet leaders felt as if their state was under siege from the "hostile capitalist countries" surrounding it. Shortly after the Bolsheviks came to power, Russia experienced a devastating civil war, in which the Bolsheviks struggled to hold onto power against moderate socialist parties and forces of the old order, the Whites. At the same time, the Bolsheviks also had to contend with foreign interventionists, who sought to dislodge the Communists from power and bring Russia back into the war against Germany. When the Great War ended in November 1918, interventionists aimed to defeat the "Red Threat" and prevent it from spreading to the West.

With the end of the Civil War in early 1921 came a period of peace. However, the lessons of the war taught the Bolshevik leadership to view the Soviet Union as a besieged fortress. Although relations with foreign governments improved somewhat during the New Economic Policy (1921–1928), by 1927 the possibility of war once again became very real. A series of foreign policy debacles in China and Poland, as well as a British police raid on an Anglo-Soviet trade mission in London over allegations of espionage, led to a war scare. While Stalin likely did not believe that war was in fact imminent, many in the country did, leading to mass anxiety and calls for decisive action.[89]

The war scare that emerged was used by the Stalinist leadership as a pretext to abandon the New Economic Policy, modernize the country, and strengthen its defenses and fighting capability. In February 1931, Stalin delivered a speech at the First All-Union Conference of Leading Personnel of Socialist Industry, in which he justified the necessity for embarking on, and continuing with, fast-paced industrialization. Stalin proclaimed that in the past Russia had suffered a series of defeats at the hands of "Mongol khans," "Turkish beys," "Polish and Lithuanian gentry," "British and French capitalists," and "Japanese barons." "All beat her," Stalin argued, "because of her backwardness, because of her military backwardness, cultural backwardness, industrial backwardness, agricultural backwardness." Providing the rationale for the development of Soviet industry, he proclaimed that "we are fifty or a hundred years behind the advanced countries. We must make good this distance in ten years. Either we do it or we shall go under."[90]

Between 1928 and 1932 the country modernized at alarming speeds. Although the drive to modernity demanded the development of heavy industry, it also required the construction of new towns and the replanning of existing ones. Inevitably, the protection and preservation of monuments diminished in importance, and indeed, plans to modernize the country were often drawn up without any consideration of the effects they would have on its cultural heritage.[91] If preservationists were victorious in the cultural wars of the 1920s, during the First Five-Year Plan radicals gained the upper hand. Vandalism and iconoclasm were, in fact, widespread, as many physical reminders of the past, especially religious structures in both the countryside and cities, were destroyed for ideological and practical (urban-planning) reasons.[92] Moscow's historic cityscape was especially affected by the destruction of the Five-Year Plan.[93] Major landmarks, including the Cathedral of Christ the Redeemer, the wall of Kitaigorod, and the seventeenth-century Sukharev Tower, were demolished, in spite of protests from the preservation community.[94] Leningrad's appearance was likewise dramatically affected by this, as several of the city's church buildings were flattened or refashioned for other uses.[95] "The demonumentalization of the 1930s," notes Stites, "far surpassed that of the revolutionary period."[96]

Theoretically, the funding for Stalin's modernization was to come from agricultural products requisitioned from newly formed collective farms. Grain was to be sold on the foreign market, allowing the Soviet leadership to purchase materials needed for industrial construction. Grain, however, was not the only source of revenue – industrial growth was in part financed by the sale of many of the Soviet Union's artistic treasures. During the Five-Year Plan, major museums such as the State Hermitage in Leningrad lost thousands of works of art, which were then auctioned off in the West for foreign currency.[97]

In the rapid drive to industrialize and catch up with the West, preservationists' calls to protect monuments and cultural artifacts fell on deaf ears. In this atmosphere, outright condemnation of the state's disregard for cultural heritage could, and often did, result in repressive measures. Preservationists who sought to protect monuments in the face of industrialization were labeled "obstructionists," and some were viciously attacked as "bourgeois specialists."[98] In the late 1920s, for example, Vladimir Kuzmich Makarov was fired from his position of chief curator at the Gatchina Palace-Museum outside Leningrad for concealing museum valuables that the state had earmarked to sell abroad. He was later arrested and sent into administrative exile in Cherepovets.[99] In another case, one of the most influential preservationists in the country, Petr Dmitrievich Baranovskii, was officially reprimanded in 1931 for voicing his disapproval of the destruction of historic monuments in the capital. In 1933 he was arrested under article 58 of the criminal code (counterrevolutionary crimes) and in 1934 was sent to a prison camp in Siberia.[100]

With the end of the First Five-Year Plan, there was a gradual return to rational and sober planning, a general demilitarization of labor and life, and a move away from iconoclastic rhetoric and appeals. In comparison with the period between 1928 and 1932, the rest of the decade was one of consolidation. An industrial base had been established, as had the country's defense capability. But the threat of war had not waned. Throughout the 1930s, in fact, the possibility of a major conflict grew more and more likely. Indeed, if the Soviet leadership was concerned about the possibility of war before the Five-Year Plan, international events in the early 1930s heightened the leadership's sense of vulnerability. In 1931, the Imperial Japanese Army invaded Manchuria and established the puppet state of Manchukuo. Decidedly anti-Communist, the Japanese presence on the Soviet Union's eastern frontier provoked anxiety and heightened the possibility of conflict. Less than two years later, in January 1933, Hitler's National Socialist Party came to power in Germany, vowing to defeat the Soviet Union, enslave its population, and use its land for *Lebensraum,* or "living space" for the German *Volk.* In 1935, V. M. Molotov underlined the danger these two states posed:

> We must bear in mind that the direct danger of war against the U.S.S.R has increased. Certain influential circles in Japan have long been openly talking of a war on the Soviet Union. Nor should it be forgotten that there is now a ruling party in Europe which has frankly proclaimed its historical mission to be the seizure of territories in the Soviet Union. Not to perceive the approach of a new war is to close one's eyes to the principal danger.[101]

In response to the foreign threat in the 1930s, the Soviet leadership encouraged a move away from radicalism in all spheres of Soviet politics, culture, and society, and promoted a patriotic Soviet identity to mobilize the population for war.[102] From the revolution through the 1920s, the Bolsheviks adhered to Karl Marx's approach to patriotism, insisting that the "working class has no fatherland." In 1931, however, Stalin himself called on people to defend the independence of the socialist "fatherland" given that capitalism had been overthrown during the Five-Year Plan.[103] Other signals from above indicated that a shift was taking place in the way Soviet citizens were to view themselves and the world around them, including a 1934 editorial in *Pravda* which announced that people were to love the fatherland and be vigilant about defending it.[104] "Henceforth patriotism became the highest law of the land," writes David Brandenberger, "serving as a litmus test of loyalty to the party, state, society, and economic system. Defense of the motherland was now to be treated as a greater priority than the advancement of the worldwide socialist cause."[105] At approximately the same time, the authorities decreed that the teaching of history in schools was unsatisfactory and hereafter students were to be introduced to chronological narratives and important historical events and figures from the tsarist era. This new method of teaching was to replace the more abstract, sociological approach to history that had been promoted by the party throughout the 1920s, and was meant to instill in students a strong connection to their country and the Soviet people's shared history.[106]

Hand in hand with the teaching of history in schools came the rehabilitation of select individuals and events from the country's past. As the 1930s progressed, the embrace of Russian history gained momentum. The authorities actively sought out a "useable past" to unite the population, create a sense of community, and promote Soviet patriotism. By the mid-1930s, legendary tsars such as Alexander Nevskii, Ivan the Terrible, and Peter the Great, and cultural icons such as Alexander Pushkin and Lev Tolstoy, were lauded as exemplars of Russia's great past. The Stalinist leadership also began to valorize national heroes from the other Soviet republics in the mid- to late 1930s. Taras Shevchenko, Bohdan Khmelnytskii, and other individuals from the Ukrainian past, for example, were rehabilitated and celebrated beginning in 1938–1939.[107] Indeed, as Brandenberger argues, the terror of 1937–1938 wiped out Soviet heroes from the revolution and the Civil War, meaning that alternative figures from the country's past had to be used as positive models to promote a patriotic Soviet identity.[108]

With the turn to the past, the authorities began to pay even greater attention to the plight of historic monuments – invaluable stone documents – in which the state's new heroes found reflection. "Monumentalist art and architecture, formerly instruments of the old order," argues David Hoffmann, "now helped legitimate the new socialist order and symbolized its accomplishments. Patriotic appeals, elsewhere used to foment bourgeois nationalism, in the Soviet Union inspired defense of the socialist motherland."[109] Throughout the 1930s an attempt was made to create a viable system of monument protection. Due in part to a desire to prevent the reoccurrence of the First Five-Year Plan's destruction of the country's patrimony, the state sought to establish new legislation and institutions to deal specifically with the issue of preserving historic monuments. In 1932 the central authorities created the Interdepartmental Committee for the Protection of Monuments of the Revolution, Art, and Culture. The goal of the committee was to guarantee that earlier decrees about the protection and preservation of monuments were implemented. The committee was to compile a list of monuments to be placed under state protection; deal with questions regarding the use, renovation, and restoration of monuments; and handle budgetary issues.[110] These steps were meant to ensure that more attention would be paid to monuments than had been previously shown. Even though preservationists and the central authorities had on a number of occasions called for the safeguarding of relics from the past, many of the country's monuments were left unattended to or were not provided with the required protection. The creation of the committee was followed a year later by a law stipulating the need for increased vigilance in the protection of historic monuments. This law called for the end to the abuse, demolition, alteration, and negligent use of buildings with historical significance by local authorities throughout the country.[111]

As new laws were devised to protect the county's monuments, the state began to encourage cooperation between preservationists and bureaucratic agencies to preserve embodiments of the past. In February 1934, for example, a meeting was held between preservation activists and members of the Leningrad soviet's special inspection committee (*spetsinspektsiia*) working on city improvement and beautification, at which the need for working together to maintain the historic cityscape was discussed. In the months prior to the meeting, several architects and artists connected with the Society for Old Petersburg – New Leningrad published a declaration in *Krasnaia gazeta,* stating that they would work together to provide patronage over the city's monuments and landmarks. The Union of Architects saw this as a positive step, developed a set of instructions for such work, and drafted a resolution for the city soviet which would provide direction for this "institute of patrons."[112] By the time of the February meeting, more than 150 preservationists had volunteered to work as patrons and the group had held eight of their own meetings to discuss measures to preserve the city's monuments. The people involved in this "institute of patrons" devoted themselves to acting as a "helper" to "our organ of monument protection," which had few resources and was staffed by one person.[113] Given these limited resources and the growing concern over the condition and treatment of the city's monuments, the *spetsinspektsiia* urged preservationists to turn to the state for help. A representative from the *spetsinspektsiia,* Comrade Rammo, stated that they "understand perfectly well" the "enormous importance" of preserving monuments in Leningrad and that they would do whatever they could to help the patrons when necessary: "We beg of you to not shield us [from the work], but rather to pile [it] on us and make demands of us. We will not turn you down."[114] Rammo went on to state that at the present time only two or three people in the *spetsinspektsiia* were working on matters of monument protection, but should more work be needed "then you can be certain that the remaining comrades will also begin working in this direction."[115] Such cooperation between Leningrad's authorities and the preservation-minded public was indicative of the state's understanding that monuments could be used to teach Soviet citizens about heroes from the past and great events in the country's history, cultivate patriotism, and mobilize the population to protect the motherland.

As the Stalinist leadership celebrated prerevolutionary heroes from all areas of the Soviet Union and offered them as patriotic examples for citizens to model themselves on, it continued to push for increased security over historic monuments and cultural landmarks as the decade progressed. In the same year that the state staged impressive celebrations to commemorate the poet Alexander Pushkin on the hundredth anniversary of his death in 1837, it also transferred control over historic monuments to the newly created All-Union Committee for Artistic Affairs, and soon after created the Department for the Protection of Monuments under the purview of the Russian Administration of Artistic Affairs.[116] Step by step, the Soviet authorities worked with the country's preservationists to centralize and more efficiently coordinate the preservation system.

Although central organs had been created for the first time to work exclusively on the protection of the country's historic monuments, the problem of local compliance with decrees and the provision of consistent oversight had to be contended with. For this reason, local Departments for the Protection of Monuments were organized in regions and large centers throughout the Soviet Union, including Leningrad in 1938.[117] Efforts to create a viable preservation system continued into the early 1940s, with the creation of the Commission for the Preservation and Restoration of Architectural Monuments in July 1940.[118] Although not all objects from the past were protected (throughout the 1930s hundreds of religious buildings were destroyed), and some attempts to provide protection proved unproductive, one sees a general attempt in the 1930s and 1940s to improve the rules and practices governing the treatment of historic monuments.[119]

The Stalinist leadership's embrace of the past had particular resonance in the former imperial capital. This city, more than any other in the country, was intimately connected with the history of the Russian empire since the time of Peter the Great. Leningrad's cityscape was filled with monumental reminders of imperial glory, heroic leaders, and great cultural traditions. Its ensembles and neoclassical appearance emphasized the power and authority that the Stalinist state wanted to project. The city itself became a physical complement to the state's new patriotic focus. What is more, monument protection had been more successful here than elsewhere throughout the first twenty years of Soviet rule. With the state's rehabilitation of history in the mid-1930s, Leningrad's preservationists were provided with a governmental organ devoted solely to protecting, preserving, and restoring historic and artistic monuments in the city. Leningrad's long tradition of preservation activism, coupled with the all-Union turn to the past, therefore provided for a powerful system of monument protection on the eve of World War II.[120]

TWO

THESE MONUMENTS MUST BE PROTECTED!: LENINGRAD'S IMPERIAL CITYSCAPE AT WAR

ON 22 JUNE 1941, NAZI GERMANY INVADED THE SOVIET UNION with the largest invasion force ever assembled – more than three million German soldiers aided by another five hundred thousand troops from countries allied to the Third Reich. Although a pact of nonaggression had been signed between the two states in August 1939, Hitler had no intention of adhering to it. During the first two years of war, his ultimate goal remained the destruction of the "Judeo-Bolshevik" state in the east and the conquest of territory that would be used as *Lebensraum,* or living space, for the German people.[1] Stalin and the Soviet leadership had no doubt that Hitler's forces would eventually attack, but they (Stalin in particular) were unprepared for the assault when it came, in spite of evidence that clearly outlined German plans.[2] Stalin refused to believe that Hitler would invade before he had conquered England; indeed, the Soviet leader was certain that Hitler would not risk a two-front war, which would put Germany in the same disastrous situation it faced during the First World War. Yet Hitler's plans for the invasion of the Soviet Union developed as early as the summer of 1940, during the Battle of Britain. In late July, Hitler told his army commanders to consider an attack on the Soviet Union, and on 18 December, when ill-fated attempts to conquer Britain were put on indefinite hold, Hitler issued a directive calling for the destruction of the Soviet state – Operation Barbarossa.[3]

When Germany invaded, the Soviet leadership was caught unawares. No defense plans had been prepared and the first weeks (if not months) of the war were characterized by confusion, chaos, and calamity for the Soviet forces. The Wehrmacht easily overcame Soviet opposition and rolled eastward, encountering little organized resistance as it occupied and exploited territories, committing countless atrocities against Soviet civilians. Less than three months after the invasion, German forces laid siege to Leningrad. Hitler had not planned on capturing the city; rather, the former imperial capital – the cradle of the Russian Revolution – was to be annihilated. The chief of the German Army General Staff, Colonel-General Franz Halder, noted Hitler's demands in his diary:

> It is the Fuehrer's firm decision to level Moscow and Leningrad, and make them uninhabitable, so as to relieve us of the necessity of having to feed the populations through the winter. The cities will be razed by air force. Tanks must not be used for this purpose. "A national catastrophe which will deprive not only Bolshevism, but also Muscovite nationalism, of their centers."[4]

Accordingly, between September 1941 and January 1944, Leningraders experienced unrelenting horrors. Hardly a day went by when they were not subjected to enemy fire; over the course of the 872-day siege, the *Luftwaffe* dropped a total of 107,000 bombs on Leningrad, and the troops entrenched on the city's outskirts fired 150,000 shells at military and civilian targets.[5] The besieging forces destroyed Leningrad's food supply depots in the first weeks of September and sought to prevent the transportation of materials and provisions into the city. As a result of the siege, nearly one million people died of starvation and bombings.[6]

Notwithstanding these appalling losses, local authorities and preservationists made strenuous efforts to protect and preserve the city's historic sites throughout the war. In fact, on the advice of people working in the Department for the Protection of Monuments, Leningrad's party and soviet leaders prioritized the protection of historic sites and landmarks, diverted manpower and resources from defense needs to preservationists, allocated the highest bread rations to people working to preserve the imperial cityscape, and continuously risked human lives to save symbols of the "glorious past" from destruction. "Preserving architecture when architects' and preservationists' lives are at risk is very difficult," wrote the Leningrad preservationist L. A. Il'in during the siege, "but it is a task that demands fulfilling."[7] And while this task reflected a desire of Leningraders and their fellow countrymen to see the city's imperial relics saved from the ravages of war, it also had ideological underpinnings. To be sure, following the invasion, Soviet propaganda organs increasingly relied on the Russian past to inspire patriotism and instill in the population a connection to a glorious, mighty heritage.

The effort to preserve Leningrad's heritage during the Second World War was part of an all-Union drive to save the embodiments of the nation's past from destruction. Preservationists throughout the country welcomed the state's newfound appreciation of the tsarist era, and, in all areas threatened with occupation, did what they could to prevent the destruction of historic and cultural monuments. Several landmarks and buildings in Russia's ancient cities, for example, were provided with protection from enemy bombing raids, including the Dmitrii Cathedral in Vladimir and the Millennium Monument in Novgorod, which was covered in a protective housing.[8] In other places, such as Iasnaia Poliana – the former estate of Lev Tolstoy – preservationists struggled to save cultural valuables before the German forces occupied the area.[9] All told, thousands of museum valuables were loaded onto trains and sent off to the east from Moscow, Leningrad, Novgorod, Smolensk, Tula, Kiev, and other places.[10] Once historic towns and sites were occupied, preservationists could do little or nothing to protect the embodiments of the past. The city of Sevastopol, for example, was almost completely annihilated during the siege and subsequent occupation. At the end of the war only 3 percent of its buildings were intact, and many if not most of its historic landmarks and monuments were badly damaged or destroyed.[11]

The all-Union drive to save historic monuments was especially pronounced in the former imperial capital. The city's residents have traditionally shown a deep connection to its historic monuments and landmarks. Inspired by the mythologized cityscape, many writers and artists of the nineteenth and twentieth centuries made the city's wide avenues, grand palaces, rivers, canals, and golden spires dominating the skyline the focus of their creative talents.[12] The renowned artist Anna Ostroumova-Lebedeva, for example, expressed her connection to the city's monuments when her friends tried to convince her to evacuate the city after the blockade had begun: "To leave the city and perhaps never see it again! Not see its white nights! Its canals . . . , the Neva, the spire of the fortress, the tower of the Admiralty and the monument to Peter the Great! I simply cannot do it!"[13] Moreover, more than anywhere else in the country, a strong preservation movement had developed in Leningrad. Many of the preservationists active since the early 1900s continued to devote themselves to the protection of Russia's heritage. Several preservation-minded individuals held important positions in the municipal administration, including Lev Il'in, who not only had been deeply involved with the prerevolutionary preservation movement but was the president of the Old Petersburg – New Leningrad Society and unofficial chief architect of Leningrad between 1925 and 1938.[14] Nikolai Baranov, who became the city's chief architect in 1938, was also a constant advocate of maintaining the historic cityscape. These preservationists, and others like them, were especially enthused by the ideological changes in the 1930s. Many of them chose to remain in Leningrad during the siege and committed themselves to saving monuments of historic and cultural heritage. The rehabilitation of the past, therefore, provided an official framework in which Leningrad's preservationists could carry out their ambitions to protect the country's heritage, and they chose to do so at a tremendous risk to their lives. And as the propaganda apparatus relied more and more on Russian history to inspire Soviet patriotism, the need for preservation became increasingly necessary, especially as the enemy sought to wipe out the embodiments of Russian history and memory.

HISTORIC PRESERVATION AND CONSERVATION FOLLOWING THE GERMAN INVASION

When the German forces invaded the Soviet Union, life was immediately turned upside down as the country's leaders called on the civilian population to prepare for war. Although the immediate response to the invasion was shock and dismay, the majority of Soviet citizens rallied to the side of the leadership to defeat the "fascist invaders." In Leningrad, for example, some 212,000 people not subject to mobilization into the Red Army volunteered for service in the locally organized People's Militia, the *narodnoe opolchenie,* during the first week after the war began.[15] In Moscow, too, thousands volunteered for service at the outbreak of war. Although these people, as John Barber notes, were motivated by a belief in a quick and decisive victory, as well as "patriotic anger at German treachery," there was most certainly a degree of compulsion and pressure exerted on people to join the war effort.[16]

The patriotic response to defend the fatherland seen at the beginning of the war, however, soon gave way to criticism of the Soviet war effort. Indeed, as the country's defenses collapsed and the Germans captured more and more Soviet territory, the belief in the "invincibility" of the Red Army was called into question. Throughout the country the authorities reported episodes of panic, defeatism, hoarding, and many other "unheroic" forms of behavior. Certainly not all Soviet people exhibited these "anti-Soviet" tendencies, but the very existence of such attitudes and actions worried the Stalinist leadership. Even more troubling was the fact that many people were uninterested in helping the Bolshevik regime survive the German onslaught. Thousands were, in fact, all too happy that Germany waged war with the Soviet Union. Indeed, in the western regions of the country – particularly in Ukraine, which suffered disproportionally during collectivization in the early 1930s, but also in the Baltics, where the Red Army destroyed the national independence of Estonia, Latvia, and Lithuania and imposed Soviet control in 1940 – many Soviet citizens mistakenly believed that the Germans would save them from Communist despotism, offer them national autonomy or independence, and disband the hated collective farm system throughout the countryside.[17] Such hopes were based on what the people in these regions had experienced under German occupation during the First World War, when officers and troops treated the local populations with a degree of respect and humanity. Consequently, in several areas of the country people greeted German troops as liberators and presented them with offerings of bread and salt as they entered villages, and for a variety of reasons, thousands of Soviet civilians actively or passively collaborated with the occupiers during the war.[18]

The invasion, anti-Soviet attitudes, and the willingness of some people to work with the enemy prompted the propaganda organs to devise campaigns to mobilize the population and inspire victory.[19] From the very beginning of the war, the leadership framed the conflict as an attack on the Soviet "fatherland" and sought to motivate the population to defend the country from the fascists with appeals to patriotic sentiment. On the day of the invasion, for example, Viacheslav Molotov's radio announcement made an explicit link between the current war and the Patriotic War of 1812 against Napoleon:

> This is not the first time that our people have had to deal with an attack of an arrogant foe. At the time of Napoleon's invasion of Russia our people's reply was war for the fatherland, and Napoleon suffered defeat and met his doom. It will be the same with Hitler, who in his arrogance has proclaimed a new crusade against our country. The Red Army and our whole people will again wage victorious war for the fatherland, for our country, for honor, for liberty.[20]

The propaganda apparatus thus continued and expanded the 1930s' use of heroic events and figures from the past to rally the people around a common cause, and people were called upon to pick up the mantle of Russia's great leaders who fought valiantly against foreign foes. Academics were immediately enlisted to write histories of Russian heroes who defeated foreign invaders. In Leningrad, historians wrote articles comparing the current conflict to previous wars with Germany, some chronicling the long list of Russian victories over the Germans from the time of Alexander Nevskii onward.[21] Several months later, on the twenty-fourth anniversary of the October Revolution, Stalin called on the Soviet people to "draw inspiration from the valiant example of our great ancestors – Alexander Nevskii, Dmitrii Donskoi, Kuz'ma Minin, Dmitrii Pozharskii, Alexander Suvorov, Mikhail Kutuzov."[22]

Throughout the war, the Soviet leadership continued to use tsarist imagery to steel the population against the Germans, who were presented in propaganda as barbarians determined to destroy everything in their path that had been created by the Russian and Soviet people.[23] In Il'ia Ehrenburg's "The Justification of Hate," first published in *Pravda* on 26 May 1942, he presents the Germans as civilized barbarians who carry out their murderous destruction and theft in a "businesslike and efficient manner."[24] Ehrenburg writes,

> Forced to retreat the Hitlerites consign everything to the flames: to them the Russian noncombatant population is as much an enemy as the Red Army. To leave a Russian family without a roof over their heads is considered a military achievement by them. At home, in Germany, they are forced to toe the line, they will not so much as throw a match on the floor or dare to walk on the grass in a public square. In our country they have trampled underfoot entire regions,

> defiled entire cities, turned museums into latrines and converted schools into stables. This is done not only by clodhoppers from Pomerania or herdsmen from the Tyrol, it is being done by assistant professors, writers, "doctors of philosophy," and "learned counsels" reared by Hitler.[25]

Ehrenburg thus stresses one of the constant themes in Soviet propaganda concerning the Wehrmacht's campaign on Soviet territory – the absolute and seemingly senseless destruction carried out by one of the most "cultured" and "civilized" peoples in Europe.

Given the danger posed by the advancing "Huns," Soviet authorities and preservationists worried about the fate of sacred sites which embodied the country's history and could be used to illustrate the heroic past for mobilizational purposes. Indeed, while efforts were taken to strengthen the system of monument protection in the mid-1930s, preservationists raised concerns about the possibility of an attack on the Soviet Union. The destruction of monuments witnessed in the First World War and Spanish Civil War prompted Soviet preservationists to think about what could happen if the country was attacked.[26] In Leningrad, where civic pride was tied to the historic cityscape and cultural institutions, plans to ship "moveable" monuments from palaces and museums were in place since 1936.[27] But what were preservationists to do with historic artifacts that could not be evacuated? How would they protect buildings, statues, and other valuable features of the cityscape from military actions? Many of the methods ultimately implemented in Leningrad and elsewhere in the Soviet Union resulted from prewar planning and were modeled on wartime preservationist activities in Western Europe.

On the eve of the German invasion of the Soviet Union, a longtime Leningrad preservationist, Vladimir Makarov, wrote a lengthy report summarizing the effects of modern warfare on historic monuments in the West, and outlined the actions taken by preservationists to protect them. Makarov, who had been arrested and exiled from the city in the late 1920s for interfering in the sale of artistic and cultural artifacts from Gatchina Palace, was subsequently rehabilitated and returned to work at preservation after the turn to Soviet patriotism in the mid-1930s. His study of preservation in Europe showed that in several countries, preservationist organizations, museums, and governments worked together to protect especially valuable monuments after the onset of the Second

World War. In England and France, for example, stained glass was taken down from church windows and concealed after the hostilities began. Many sculptures and other forms of public art were removed from their pedestals and transported to safe places.[28] Makarov's report detailed these activities and provided information on the latest methods for concealing buildings, statues, and other landmarks.[29] This study signaled the need to develop methods of monument protection in the event of war on Soviet soil, and following the German invasion, it served as a preservationist's guide for the extensive work to be carried out in Leningrad.[30]

Over the course of the summer, Leningrad's municipal authorities, architectural organizations, and preservationists cooperated to protect historic monuments. The prewar discussions, planning, and study of Western European preservation methods proved invaluable in executing work on a scale never before seen. This work began almost immediately after the invasion. "It makes sense that the attention of Leningrad's party and soviet leaders focused on defense matters," wrote the city's chief architect, N. V. Baranov, in his memoirs. "But what is more important to note is that even during this difficult period, the care for artistic heritage was not put on the back burner."[31] On 23 June, for instance, the head of Leningrad's Department for the Protection of Monuments, Nikolai Belekhov, presented the city soviet with a plan for preserving the city's historic and cultural valuables.[32] As a result, the soviet issued orders on 25 June to protect Leningrad's statues and camouflage historic sites.[33] Two days later, the Union of Soviet Architects circulated a letter to all republic-, provincial-, and municipal-level branches with instructions to ensure the protection of the country's "outstanding monuments of architecture and the repositories of cultural valuables from destruction caused by bombings."[34]

Several iconic buildings in Leningrad had golden domes, spires, and cupolas which the Germans could easily target and use as orientation points. The city soviet instructed Belekhov's department to devise plans to camouflage the "golden heights" in order to take away the advantage they offered to the Germans while ensuring the protection of these landmarks and symbols of the city. A number of tall structures with no historic or artistic value in the city (such as factory smokestacks) were quickly disassembled, as they could be easily reconstructed after the war.

However, because buildings such as the Admiralty, the Peter and Paul Fortress, and St. Isaac's Cathedral (among others) were irreplaceable witnesses to a bygone age, preservationists and municipal authorities were determined to conceal them in ways which prevented damage and destruction.[35]

By 1 July, Belekhov's team of preservationists, drawing on the experiences in Western Europe, proposed to have the golden spires and domes either painted with a dark substance or covered with thick fabrics, thereby making them difficult for German pilots to detect during air raids.[36] Preservationists worked on St. Isaac's Cathedral on the southern bank of the Neva first, and in the second week of July had the four belfries and the massive dome of the gigantic cathedral painted with a nonreflective coating.[37] Yet it was only in the fall, after the Germans besieged the city and started daily bombing raids, that the necessary plans and preparations for camouflage work on the other historic monuments with golden spires and domes began.

Whereas camouflaging sites throughout Leningrad was both a strategic and a historically conscious action, the decision to conceal the city's statues and artistic decorations adorning landmarks was motivated solely by a desire to preserve historic symbols. Just days after the invasion, the city soviet, on Belekhov's advice, ordered that several famous statues from the previous two and a half centuries be protected from air strikes. The original order involved eleven statues from the imperial and Soviet periods to be worked on within two weeks.[38]

Small statues were to be taken down from their pedestals and buried in nearby gardens and parks, as was done with the marble statues in the Summer Garden, Rastrelli's statue of Peter I at the Mikhailovskii Castle, the statues of the Dioscuri twins at the Cavalry Guards' Barracks, and others. Larger statues, such as the Bronze Horseman, the statue of Nikolai I on St. Isaac's Square, and the monument to Lenin at Finland Station, were to be covered with sand and then encased in wooden structures.[39] Several monumental statues not listed in the original order were also protected. The bronze statue of Anna Ioannovna (empress of Russia from 1730 to 1740), which was too large to be evacuated with the rest of the exhibits from the Russian Museum, was buried in front of the Mikhailovskii Palace.[40] Similarly, the four equestrian statues adorning the Anichkov Bridge on Nevskii Prospekt were removed from their pedestals and buried in the nearby Garden of Rest. Igor' Krestovskii, the preservationist assigned the task of overseeing the protection of statues, noted that many people had gathered to watch the four horses and their tamers as they moved along the street. "The conveyance of the four magnificent equestrian groups presented a curious sight," he wrote. "They moved along Nevskii slowly, hoisted onto special wooden platforms, lying on rollers, towed by tractors. Many people gathered. Everyone accompanied the beloved sculptures to their prepared 'graves' with great curiosity."[41]

Both of these measures were influenced by the actions of preservationists in the West. In London, for example, several monuments, such as the statue of Henry Irving near the National Portrait Gallery, were protected *in situ*, while others, including the statue of Eros at Piccadilly Circus, were taken away for protection.[42] At this early stage of the war, Leningrad's statues were not directly threatened, but the study of the effects of war on monuments in the West served as a sober warning of the possibility of destruction, prompting the authorities and preservationists to take preventative measures.

The work to protect Leningrad's statues was exceptionally labor-intensive and involved a tremendous amount of resources, time, and manpower from several of the city's establishments. During the first weeks of the war, the city soviet assigned at least twelve separate organizations work to deliver sand, dig holes, construct wooden coverings, and perform other tasks to facilitate monument protection. The Department for the Protection of Monuments assigned to each statue a team of experts made up of an architect, a sculptor, and a construction specialist.[43]

A report compiled by the department upon completion of work on the Dioscuri speaks to the complex, laborious process of monument protection that was carried out over a two-week period. Those assigned to this statue group dug holes that were two meters deep and three and a half by two meters wide. At the bottom of each hole a thirty-centimeter layer of clay was strewn. The construction specialists built intricate conveyance mechanisms out of wooden poles, plywood, metal tubes, and sliding blocks to remove the statues from their pedestals and transport them to the holes. The figures were placed horizontally on beds of sandbags laid out on specially built wooden platforms, which were then manually lowered into the holes. Once they were in place, workers nailed wooden sides to the platforms and covered the statues with sand. Boards were then nailed to the top, creating boxes, which were covered in tarpaper to protect the statues from the elements. Members of the team finally filled the holes with layers of clay, sand, and topsoil.[44] This process was replicated in several places throughout the city, including the Summer Garden, where as many as eighty-three marble statues were buried over the course of the summer.[45] Preservationists employed a wide range of techniques and adapted them as individual circumstances demanded. All, however, required great effort and meticulous care.

District soviets assigned workers to carry out the more arduous tasks involved, but due to the extraordinary amount of work taking place to fortify the city, few people were readily available to protect monuments. At some places, schoolchildren were mobilized to pick up the slack and work on statues. The future author Oleg Shestinskii, for example, was sent along with his classmates to help cover the Bronze Horseman with sand before it was enclosed in a wooden shell.[46] Surprisingly, people assigned to protect the city's statues were excused from participation in defense preparations (digging antitank trenches and constructing barriers outside of the city), as well as from mobilization into the Red Army and *narodnoe opolchenie*.[47] Even soldiers already in the Red Army were used to protect monuments. Several of them, for example, were listed among the twenty people assigned work to protect the Dioscuri.[48] Because these statues symbolized the "strength and glory of the Russian state," Leningrad's authorities diverted precious resources to protect monuments during the first weeks of the war, when the enemy seemed unstoppable.[49]

In the meantime, the situation in the country continued to deteriorate. The Wehrmacht defeated the Red Army in battle after battle, forced the disorganized Soviet troops to retreat further eastward, and occupied vast stretches of the country's western territory. As the summer wore on, the sense that something ominous was about to occur was in the air. Removal of industrial machinery, workers, nonworking dependents, children, and others began in July and continued – in a disorganized fashion – until early September. The local authorities evacuated approximately 636,000 people out of the city's prewar population of 3.3 million before the start of the blockade.[50] Food rationing had been introduced less than a month into the war. The Leningrad academic Dmitrii Likhachev noted in his memoirs that even in July he felt that famine would soon strike the residents of Leningrad.[51] On 21 August, *Leningradskaia pravda* announced that the Germans were closing in and could try to besiege the city.[52] Within a few weeks the invading forces cut the last railway line out of Leningrad, and on 8 September laid siege to the city. The actions taken during the summer were exceptionally important in the preservation of monuments during the war, but more work had to be done as monuments themselves became targets of German weaponry.

HISTORIC PRESERVATION DURING THE BLOCKADE

Several months into the war it became clear that Hitler's policy toward the historic and cultural treasures in the Soviet Union was fundamentally different than in Western Europe. While German forces damaged and even destroyed monuments in the West, Hitler generally respected and admired the monuments of countries he considered to be part of the same "European cultural club." In the East, however, monuments were not only pillaged but systematically targeted and destroyed.[53] The infamous "Reichenau Order," for example, best illustrates the approach German troops were instructed to take toward heritage sites in the Soviet Union. This order explicitly called for the destruction of historic structures in the occupied Soviet territory as "symbols of the former Bolshevik rule," noting that "neither historic nor artistic considerations are of any importance in the eastern territories."[54] The order, which received praise from Hitler, was circulated to all army commanders to be implemented as policy.[55] "At the time we did not know about the barbarism of the fascists in relation to cultural valuables," wrote Baranov, "and for that reason did not assume that the magnificent monuments of architecture, without any military significance . . . could become targets of bombings."[56]

Realizing that the German forces were deliberately destroying the country's heritage sites, Soviet authorities created the All-Union Commission for the Registration and Protection of Monuments of Art to account for damage, provide leadership in preservation, and prepare monuments for restoration in liberated areas.[57] Discussions about the destruction of historic monuments emphasized the Germans' intentions to "degrade" the Soviet people, "tear away from them the memory of their great past," and destroy "historic buildings which preserve the memory of great events and great people."[58] The preservationists remaining in Leningrad therefore redoubled their efforts to protect monuments as they were forced to overcome a series of obstacles and adapt to the horrific conditions of the blockade.

When the Germans reached the outskirts of the city, they began a relentless bombing campaign. In the month of September alone, there were twenty-three major raids on the city and two hundred shellings. Some days more than two hundred German planes were involved in aerial attacks.[59] "Bombing raids started, and there was talk of nothing else," writes Likhachev. "Every day they began, always at the same time, but as the enemy was so close that there was no chance of giving warning of the approach of aircraft the air-raid sirens were only heard when bombs were already falling on the city."[60] The author Vera Inber, who worked as a radio broadcaster during the siege, echoed these sentiments when she wrote in her diary that "it dawned on me that there is nothing anyone can do to be safe . . . it's all a matter of chance. We can try to avoid standing near windows, but that's about all."[61] Bombing and shelling continued to be a daily occurrence in Leningrad throughout the fall of 1941, resulting in major damage to city infrastructure and the loss of thousands of lives.

The bombardment led many to fear that the city's historic landscape would be destroyed. The director of the Academy of Science archives, Georgi Knyazev, for example, wrote in his diary about the anxiety that the bombing provoked: "As I go out through the front door the first thing I do is to make sure the sphinxes are still whole, that St. Isaac's is whole, and the Admiralty spire, and the angel with a cross on top of the Alexander Column [are still whole]."[62] While these raids were taking place, Leningrad's authorities consulted with preservationists to ensure that further actions were taken to protect and preserve the historic cityscape. The need to continue camouflaging the golden heights was high on the agenda.

Over the course of the summer, Belekhov's team of preservationists made the necessary preparations to continue camouflage work. Several suggestions were made about how to accomplish this. Some argued that scaffolding should be built around the golden spires and cupolas, which would allow workers to cover or paint them with relative ease. This was problematic, however, because there was neither enough time nor enough people to erect them, and the wooden scaffolds themselves could catch fire during bombings and shelling.[63] Others suggested that the spires and cupolas be disassembled. "This opinion was rejected immediately," wrote Baranov, "for we simply were not able to destroy these outstanding architectural and artistic treasures with our own hands!"[64] After much discussion, the Department for the Protection of Monuments decided to employ experienced mountain climbers to camouflage the spires and domes, and during the first weeks of September a small team was organized and trained.[65] On 28 September, just one day after the worst bombing raid since the siege began, city authorities ordered Belekhov's department to conceal the spires of the Admiralty, the Peter and Paul Fortress, and the Mikhailovskii Castle.[66]

Starting with the Admiralty – the very symbol of Peter the Great's revolution – the team of mountain climbers worked throughout the fall as conditions in the city continued to worsen. Their work was complicated by the stormy, windy, wet, and cold weather characteristic of Leningrad in the autumn months, and bombing raids made their tasks extremely dangerous. One of the mountaineers, Mikhail Bobrov, noted the danger in his diary: "Aloiz and I stood on the bell tower below the spire [of the Mikhailovskii Castle] and were deafened by the whistling and explosions of bombs." Two small bombs even landed in the courtyard of the castle while they worked, destroying a significant portion of the monument's inner wall.[67] Despite the danger, decrease in food rations, and cold, by December they had camouflaged all three spires. For now this work ended, but by late 1942, ten more golden spires and domes were camouflaged in a similar manner.[68]

No matter how much was done to conceal and camouflage buildings, spires, and statues, preservationists realized that bombs and shells could easily, and quite randomly, destroy many of the city's most prized historic monuments. When they began to check the archives at the Department for the Protection of Monuments for documents that could facilitate future restoration projects, preservationists discovered that there were few plans, drawings, and measurements for several of Leningrad's historic structures and landmarks.[69] Although preservationists had measured and recorded the dimensions of the statues that they concealed in the months before the blockade, it was only after heavy bombing began in September and October that they realized the acute need to document the size, shape, and details of the majority of the city's heritage sites. On the advice of preservationists, municipal authorities issued an order in mid-October to begin compiling measurements and details of monuments of "great artistic and historic importance . . . in danger of destruction."[70]

The Leningrad branch of the Union of Soviet Architects appointed fifty-five of its members to work with Belekhov's department in early November. The department assigned each to a team working on one of the twenty-three historic monuments originally slated for study.[71] Over the course of the next few months, as many as two hundred architects produced detailed drawings of the artistic decorations of buildings, took measurements of all dimensions, and photographed as much detail as they could.[72] Much of their work focused on documenting the exterior designs and details of architectural monuments, meaning that preservationists often found themselves outside during air raids and shellings. The danger posed by this work is not to be underestimated: Igor' Krestovskii, for example, recalled an episode in which he and his colleagues were nearly killed by exploding shells as they worked to conceal the monument to Nicholas I on St. Isaac's Square. The preservationists managed to make it to a nearby bomb shelter when the shelling began, but when they emerged after the danger had passed, they found the mangled corpses of two young girls near the statue.[73] Those working to provide measurements for architectural monuments likewise experienced the constant threat posed by enemy weaponry.

Because of the importance of historic monuments and the danger of this work, Leningrad's authorities gave these architects "first-category" ration cards.[74] This placed them on the same footing as workers in heavy industry supplying armaments to the front, a decision that proved critical. Since the middle of the summer the food supply had steadily deteriorated, and in the middle of November it reached crisis proportions. On 19 November it was announced that those citizens holding first-category ration cards would receive 250 grams of bread per day, while everyone else would receive only half that.[75] By working in teams to provide documentation for historic monuments, therefore, many architects and preservationists were saved from the slow death by starvation that took the lives of so many others. "Measurement workers are given industrial workers' ration cards," wrote the architect Esfir' Levina in January 1942. "Now, when there is so little food, the Leningrad soviet does not forget about architecture."[76] The urgent need to document these irreplaceable monuments for future restoration meant that preservationists themselves had to be supported and well nourished.

Increased rations were contingent, however, on the fulfillment of work. When teams failed to compile the necessary documentation for whatever reason, they were denied the extra rations. Others were warned that the rations could be rescinded if measurements were not completed and submitted in a timely fashion. This, noted Belekhov, was done to "stimulate further work."[77] The Department for the Protection of Monuments also stepped in to prevent architects working in documentation teams from being evacuated. The leader of the team working on the Admiralty, for example, was not allowed to leave the city until all documentation was completed and the materials necessary for restoration projects were delivered to Belekhov's department.[78] Clearly the impulse to preserve the city's historic monuments – witnesses to Russia's "glorious" past – took precedence over the lives of people working to protect them. These measures resulted in a significant amount of work being accomplished. In the first year of the blockade, preservationists and architects provided more than fifty of Leningrad's historic monuments with detailed documentation.[79]

Starting in November, if not earlier, food supply problems became the major preoccupation of nearly every resident of Leningrad. When the Germans besieged the city in early September, Hitler ordered that Leningraders be starved into submission. The deliberate starvation of Leningraders should be seen within the larger context of Nazi annihilation policies and the radical social engineering established in Hitler's "General Plan for the East." The "Hunger Plan," formulated on the eve of Operation Barbarossa in May 1941, envisioned the deindustrialization of the Soviet Union and the establishment of an agrarian utopia for the German people. The Hunger Plan called for destruction of large Soviet cities and the starvation of some thirty million Soviet people in the winter of 1941–1942 in order to feed the German soldiers and civilians during and after the war.[80] By mid-December literally thousands of people were dying each day in Leningrad from starvation. In the first twenty-five days of December, 39,073 people died from hunger.[81] The situation was much worse during the first three months of 1942. In January, 96,751 people died; in February the number decreased slightly to 96,015; and in March it decreased further, to 81,507.[82] "My husband and I survived the famine in Leningrad between 1919 and 1921," wrote the artist Anna Ostroumova-Lebedeva. "But that famine had nothing in common with the present one. Back then some sort of food could always be found in the city."[83] The author and war correspondent for *Pravda,* Vsevolod Vishnevskii, wrote that "longtime residents of Leningrad say that the hungry years between 1918–1920 were 'child's play' in comparison with the siege of Leningrad."[84] Given the circumstances, most Leningraders could do little more than desperately seek out food and fuel for themselves and their families.

The catastrophic conditions in the fall of 1941 and the winter of 1942 had a significant effect on the amount of work that could be done to preserve historic monuments. In late November, for example, the city soviet called on architects, preservationists, and construction organizations to continue the work begun in the summer to protect the statues and monuments of Leningrad. The soviet ordered that nineteen additional monuments, including the statues of Catherine the Great on Ostrovskii Square, the sphinxes on the University Embankment, the Alexander Column on Palace Square, and the statues of Russia's greatest generals, A. V. Suvorov on the Field of Mars and M. I. Kutuzov in front of Kazan Cathedral, be concealed, buried, or protected with sand and wooden structures.[85]

However, the lack of food, the extremely high death rate, and the shortage of materials needed to carry out the work meant that preservationists were unable to provide the needed protection in 1941. The difficulties faced by preservationists during the siege meant that some of these statues were even left standing without any form of protection until the end of the war, in spite of complaints made by local officials. During his 1943 visit to the city, Alexander Werth interviewed the city's chief architect, Baranov, who told him that once the "starving winter" began they were "just too weak and too hungry" to finish concealing monuments.[86] Given the difficulties in the winter of 1942, city authorities opted to leave monuments to the famous imperial war heroes Suvorov, Kutuzov, and Barclay de Tolly in place to inspire patriotism in the city's residents and the troops visiting from the front.[87] As the Soviet press noted, "Monuments to the great leaders of the Russian army remain uncovered . . . calling for heroic deeds and commanding victory."[88]

During the worst winter of the blockade, preservationists could do little more than provide documentation, monitor the city's monuments, make detailed reports about their condition after bombings and artillery attacks, and attempt emergency repairs, such as covering holes in roofs and boarding up windows to prevent further harm. As early as September, the Executive Committee of the Leningrad soviet had called upon district authorities to keep account of the effects of bombing raids on the city's buildings, with the goal of devising means to repair the damage.[89] This work was particularly important during the winter as damage was compounded by climatic conditions. Shattered windows and gaping holes in the lofts and ceilings of historic structures allowed wind, rain, snow, and frost to enter these monuments and ruin much of their artistic and architectural details.[90] The everyday duties of preservationists, architects, and people working in buildings under state protection therefore were concentrated on emergency, rudimentary repairs, and on accounting for the damage to be attended to when relief ultimately came.[91]

CONSERVATION AND PLANS FOR RESTORATION

Conditions began to improve in the city toward the end of the winter. In late 1941 the authorities had opened the thirty-mile "Road of Life" across the ice of Lake Ladoga, allowing trucks to transport food, fuel, and other needed supplies into the city. On the way back across the treacherous ice road, trucks transported military supplies produced in the factories of the besieged city. More importantly, the Road of Life was used to evacuate people from Leningrad. Between January and April 1942, 554,186 people left the city over Lake Ladoga.[92] With fewer mouths to feed and more available supplies, local authorities were in a much better position to sustain those remaining in Leningrad, and the number of deaths each month from malnutrition and starvation began to decline.

As conditions improved, preservationists began conservation work to prevent further damage to historic monuments. At stake was not simply the loss of beautiful buildings and decorations, but major elements of Russian history and culture that were used to foster a connection to the motherland and inspire patriotism in the war against the Germans. Local authorities and preservationists understood that ruined buildings would do nothing to foster confidence in victory, but restored monuments and an intact cityscape could bolster the population's morale and inspire the resolve needed to withstand the enemy's siege.[93] Construction organizations, therefore, were assigned to buildings to carry out conservation work, including repairing roofs, restoring walls, boarding up windows, and securing artistic details. Restricted by the conditions in which they found themselves, many of the organizations were unable to accomplish all of the tasks assigned to them. They faced a litany of problems, including an insufficient supply of workers, a lack of adequate funding and materials, and continued bombings which caused more damage than organizations could keep up with.[94]

Over the course of the blockade, preservationists continuously bemoaned the problems encountered in conservation. After reviewing the work carried out on monuments in the summer of 1942, and finding that several tasks had not been completed or were executed poorly, Baranov complained to the city party committee and soviet. He outlined the problems faced by the construction organizations and urged that more be done to preserve the city's eighteenth- and nineteenth-century buildings: "By decisively carrying out conservation, we will prevent serious damage to buildings, avoid a great deal of major repairs, and most importantly, preserve for the country and for Leningrad these unique monuments of art and architecture." Baranov argued for the need to privilege historic monuments in the conservation and restoration work taking place throughout the city. He wrote, "It would be easier to consent to the loss of tens of residential buildings . . . than to the heavy destruction of these unique masterpieces of art, the restoration of which may not always be possible."[95]

Given the problems encountered, municipal and central authorities provided funding to conserve monuments and supported the preservationists' drive to maintain Leningrad's historic cityscape. In April, for example, the city soviet allocated 750,000 rubles for emergency restoration work on fourteen buildings, including the Winter Palace, Peter the Great's Cottage, and the Kunstkamera.[96] Later in the year, local authorities and preservationists petitioned the central government for help in conserving historic monuments, and received an additional 470,000 rubles.[97]

The funding helped preservationists overcome some of the problems. Numerous reports compiled by Belekhov's staff throughout the blockade attest to successes in preservation, whether elemental conservation or major repairs. By November 1942, for example, preservationists had completed a considerable amount of this work. Out of thirty-six buildings damaged to a "significant degree" during the first year of the blockade, twelve were partially repaired and six had damage completely eliminated. Out of eighty-eight which had less damage, thirty-eight were fully repaired and forty-one were restored to varying degrees.[98] Preservationists and construction workers, for example, carried out significant repairs at the Admiralty. During 1942, twenty thousand square meters of the monument's roof were repaired, one thousand windows were covered with plywood, and many of the buildings, statues, and bas-reliefs were secured in place, all at a cost of 139,462 rubles.[99]

While conservation work was taking place, Leningraders began making plans to restore historic monuments in anticipation of the end of the siege. As early as March 1942, preservationists and architectural organizations actively started planning for the city's "resurrection" (*vozrozhdenie*). "It had become clear to us," wrote Baranov, "that the time had come not only to defend the city, but to begin intensive preparation for its restoration."[100] Over the course of the year, the Union of Architects held several architectural competitions to plan for the restoration of historic buildings, including Gostinyi Dvor, the eighteenth-century shopping arcade on the city's main thoroughfare, Nevskii Prospekt.[101] Other buildings in the historic center that had been destroyed were also the subjects of architectural competitions. "Even during the starving winter, the most difficult weeks of the blockade," wrote the author Vera Ketlinskaia, "architects confronted the task of preserving the external appearance of besieged Leningrad for history, and prepared for restoration work."[102]

The most serious plans for Leningrad's restoration came as the Soviet Union's fortunes in the war began to change. In 1943, the Red Army defeated the Wehrmacht in a number of important battles, and the victory at Stalingrad in February is generally seen as the turning point in the war. But for Leningrad, relief had come earlier. On 18 January 1943, troops from the Leningrad and Volkhov fronts met at the Shlisselburg fortress to the east of the city and partially broke the German blockade. A railroad connection to Leningrad was finally reestablished. Admittedly, the situation remained precarious; over the next year, the Germans bombed and cut the railroad line 1,200 times, and bombing and shelling actually intensified.[103] Nonetheless, Leningrad remained out of reach of the German troops, whose position on the outskirts of the city was becoming more and more uncertain.

The break in the blockade had an important effect on plans to restore historic monuments, and it had a significant morale-boosting influence on the population, who linked restoration with inevitable Soviet victory. As early as 21 January, just three days after the blockade ring was pierced, the Leningrad soviet overturned a decree from early in the war that made it possible to mobilize people into work outside of their professions. The soviet, assigning considerable importance to the city's historic landscape, ordered all establishments in the city employing architects to transfer them to the Department for the Protection of Monuments or to the Architectural-Planning Administration to facilitate preservation and planning for restoration.[104]

Some of the most significant work in preparing for restoration, however, took place in the latter half of 1943. Toward the end of the summer, the Leningrad branch of the Union of Architects began offering courses on the city's architectural heritage and its historic importance to engineers and architects, as well as party and soviet officials. From August until the end of the year, the union set up several courses to raise the qualifications of the city's architects and other professionals in preparation for peacetime, when restoration of the city's monuments could begin in earnest. The leadership of the union believed that seminars on Leningrad's architectural culture were needed given the extraordinary amount of work facing the city.[105] "The greatest amount of the upcoming work involves the most valuable – in the architectural sense – central regions of the city," noted a report to the city party committee from the Union of Architects. "Party and soviet workers," it continued, "must familiarize themselves with the history of the creation of Leningrad and its magnificent architectural riches." The ultimate goal of the courses, therefore, was to facilitate restoration by "arming" party and soviet workers with the necessary knowledge of the city's history and its construction, its architectural richness and monuments, "without which competent leadership and execution of restoration work in . . . Leningrad is impossible."[106] These party and soviet officials were to guide restoration in their districts by emphasizing the importance of monuments as embodiments of the glorious past that would be lost forever if not restored.

But teaching officials, engineers, and others about the historical significance of Leningrad's cityscape was not enough to heal the wounds on historic monuments and bring them back to life – what was required were professional restorers. Unfortunately, at the end of 1943 Leningrad no longer had a pool of restorers, since the majority of its restoration specialists had succumbed to starvation, been killed by bombs, or been sent to the front, never to be heard from again.[107] As a result, the Leningrad branch of the Union of Architects proposed the creation of a college to train teenagers to become master restorers.[108]

In the early fall, the Leningrad party leadership summoned the head of the Union of Architects in Leningrad, Valentin Golli, and the preservationist Iosef Vaks to Smolnyi and assigned them the task of creating a curriculum and establishing the college.[109] The union began preparations for the selection of prospective students, most of whom would have to leave the "mainland" (the term used to describe the unoccupied areas of the Soviet Union outside the city) and come to besieged Leningrad. It held a competition among young Leningraders in evacuation to decide who had the necessary talent to work at artistic and historic restoration, and selected 178 people between the ages of fourteen and seventeen to begin their training.[110] Students arrived in late November 1943 and the college was scheduled to open on 1 January 1944.[111]

Notwithstanding the Red Army's successes throughout 1943, in the fall of that year Leningrad was experiencing some of the worst artillery and bombing attacks since the beginning of the siege. The willingness of Leningrad's authorities to transport young people from the relative safety of evacuation in the Urals to the besieged city reflects the degree to which Leningrad and the country as a whole viewed the city's historic monuments as important. Within days of the students' arrival, the danger of bringing them to the city became clear. On 3 December, a German shell exploded in the courtyard of the college, killing six of the students and injuring eleven others; another student succumbed to injuries later in the hospital.[112] In the wake of this tragedy, Nikolai Baranov, who played a major role in bringing the students to Leningrad instead of setting up a college somewhere in the East, questioned the wisdom of this decision: in his memoirs of the period he wrote, "Now when rereading that page in my diary, I question whether we did the right thing. And although the history of the college began so dramatically, none of us – neither adults nor adolescents – renounced our intentions. The duty to Leningrad convinced us of the righteousness of our actions."[113]

The preservation of Leningrad's historic and cultural monuments during the Second World War was part of a larger all-Union effort to save symbols of the country's glorious past from destruction. Soviet authorities and preservationists were well aware of the danger posed by war and they built on techniques used in Western European countries to ensure the safety of the country's historic sites. In Leningrad, these efforts reached a fever pitch at a time when hundreds, sometimes thousands, of people were dying each day from starvation and enemy bombardment. The fact that many preservationists found themselves inside the besieged city gave them the opportunity to enact protective measures that their counterparts in occupied territories could not.

Leningrad's preservationists were inspired by an intense feeling of civic pride and adoration for the former imperial capital's mythologized cityscape. This connection with the city compelled preservationists and authorities to implement measures designed to ensure the survival of the historic monuments – and the stories they have to tell – for generations to come. The "duty to Leningrad," therefore, motivated Leningrad's architects, sculptors, mountaineers, and workers to risk their lives and devote enormous energies to historic monuments as bombs fell on the city and food supplies dwindled to starvation rations.

Civic pride alone, however, was not enough to allow for preservation on the scale witnessed in Leningrad during the siege. Party and soviet authorities would have been unlikely to support such efforts and provide funding, materials, and laborers were it not for the state's newfound appreciation for a thousand years of Russian history. As the propaganda apparatus cultivated a patriotic Soviet identity while war loomed on the horizon, historic monuments became sacred sites at which the country's mythologized history could be both seen and touched. If the threat of war called for actions to protect historic monuments, the war itself telescoped the work of Soviet officials and preservationists throughout the country. Intentional destruction of the embodiments of Russian history and culture shocked the country's leadership and cultural community, signaling the need to heighten protection and conservation activities. Once the state turned to the past to foster a patriotic citizenry, its leaders and preservation advocates could not sit idly by as the enemy targeted the very venues and objects used to portray and instill a connection with the glorious past. The importance of Leningrad's historic monuments as embodiments of nearly two and a half centuries of tsarist and Soviet history necessitated their protection, especially during the horrors of the siege.

On 27 January 1944, Leningraders celebrated the lifting of the German siege of the city. For 872 days they had been gripped by terror. The inhuman deprivations that Leningraders suffered and the determination to survive they displayed would work to create a powerful mythology of the siege. With the city liberated from the blockade, Leningraders began the painstaking work to bring their hometown back into order. Just as during the blockade, Leningrad's authorities and urban planners privileged historic monuments and landmarks in the postwar period as the "battle" moved on to the restoration front.

THREE

PROJECTING SOVIET POWER: HISTORIC RESTORATION AS COMMEMORATION IN POSTWAR LENINGRAD

AFTER LIFTING THE SIEGE OF LENINGRAD, SOVIET FORCES continued to better the Wehrmacht in battle after battle. The Red Army recaptured Sevastopol and forced the Germans out of the Crimean Peninsula in May 1944, and by July, Stalin's troops had liberated Minsk from occupation and pushed Hitler's armies from Soviet territory. The areas of the country which had been occupied were utterly devastated. When the Wehrmacht retreated, it massacred civilian populations, drove thousands more westward as slave laborers, and burned whole villages to deprive partisans and Soviet forces of resources. As a result of occupation and war, 25 percent of the Soviet Union's physical assets had been destroyed, and 14 percent of its population was lost to death and displacement.[1] The housing shortages that were commonplace before the war became drastically more acute in the postwar period. In many places where battles had been fought, the majority of homes had been either fully destroyed or rendered uninhabitable.[2]

Leningrad too suffered. Unlike cities such as Stalingrad and Sevastopol, where intense fighting took place on city streets, Leningrad had not been razed to the ground. Yet when the siege was lifted on 27 January 1944, Leningraders were faced with the problem of restoring local industry and providing housing for people living in the city, those returning from evacuation, and the new migrants who took the place of those who had died during the war. As a result of the German bombing and shelling, 205 brick residential buildings and more than 1,900 wooden buildings were destroyed.[3] Leningrad's industry was not spared the war's destruction. The overall damage inflicted upon the city's economy amounted to thirty-eight billion rubles (in 1961 prices),[4] which included the destruction of 840 industrial buildings and damage to a further 3,090.[5] The city's residential fund also suffered drastically: more than 3,300,000 meters of living space were completely destroyed, and another 2,200,000 meters were significantly damaged.[6] Consequently, the Soviet regime was faced with the enormous problem of rebuilding its economy, housing and feeding its population, and returning some form of normalcy to everyday life. It was in the face of this immense damage, massive shortages in materials and labor, and an acute need to rebuild industry and housing that Leningraders set out to restore the city's historic monuments and prewar appearance.[7]

At the April 1944 plenum of the Leningrad party committee, first secretary Andrei Aleksandrovich Zhdanov addressed the audience about Leningrad's restoration. The plenum took place just over two months after Soviet forces had lifted the siege of Leningrad, and only a few weeks after the State Defense Committee decreed that the conditions for restoration of Leningrad's industry and the city economy had been attained.[8] Although the war had not yet ended, and fierce fighting continued until the capture of Berlin on 8 May 1945, Leningrad was not given the luxury of waiting for peacetime. "Now our task is not reconstruction [*rekonstruktsiia*]," proclaimed Zhdanov, "but restoration [*vosstanovlenie*] of the city, restoration of Leningrad in the appearance that it had."[9] City planners could have taken advantage of the massive amounts of destruction to build newer, more modern structures and improve the city's layout, but new construction was not the priority. Rather, planners opted for an approach to postwar restoration that differed from other war-torn cities in Europe and the USSR.

Leningrad's restoration was guided by important considerations and pressing political needs of the period. Worried about the massive destruction caused by the war and the effects this could have on public opinion, the Soviet leadership sought to restore the necessities of urban living while at the same time restoring historic monuments damaged or destroyed in the war. The use of the historic past to mobilize the population had not waned with the defeat of Nazi Germany, but rather had become a dominant feature of the Soviet ideological apparatus. Consequently, historic monuments continued to occupy an important place in the Soviet propaganda arsenal aimed at bolstering patriotism and inspiring confidence in the socialist system. Just as during the war, preservationists throughout the country, and especially in Leningrad, embraced the opportunity to carry out their mission of ensuring the protection of the country's heritage sites, and this desire dovetailed well with the Soviet leadership's need to maintain an image of power expressed in well-maintained cityscapes.

Local authorities expected that the city center and its historic monuments would be restored by the end of the first postwar Five-Year Plan in 1950. Party and soviet officials, architects, preservationists, and the press presented the restoration as a monument to the blockade and a tribute to Leningraders' heroism and determination to defeat the "fascist menace." Such a campaign represented state efforts to underline the official story of the war, which emphasized heroism, unity, and sacrifice while silencing any and all negative aspects of the Great Patriotic War. But it was also a manifestation of local desires to commemorate the "triumph" of the 872-day siege in the city's urban fabric. Indeed, Leningraders saw the phoenix rising from the ashes as a testament to their determination and victory over the Germans. "We defended you, Leningrad," went the slogan of the day. "We'll restore you!"[10] The restoration of Leningrad's historic monuments, then, was an important part of the state's projection of political power onto the cityscape, as well as a continuation of preservationist policies designed to provide for the long-term survival of monuments to "Russian glory."

HISTORIC MONUMENTS IN LENINGRAD'S POSTWAR RESTORATION PLAN

Toward the end of the war, preservation, conservation, and restoration works were launched in all liberated areas of the USSR.[11] Due to the importance of historic monuments in cultivating a patriotic Soviet identity, the government created the Main Administration for the Protection of Monuments (*Glavnoe upravlenie po okhrane pamiatnikov*, or GUOP) under the Committee for Architectural Affairs in 1944 as the central organization to head up all restoration efforts.[12] War, and the damage that it caused, heightened the significance of the country's heritage in the eyes of the authorities. Reflecting on the treatment of historic monuments during the war, Belekhov stated that the preservationist community's position was strengthened due to the damage, and that during the war the higher authorities began to pay more attention to preservationists and the needs of the country's monuments.[13] As soon as territories were liberated from German occupation, preservationists began the painstaking work of conserving and then restoring monuments which embodied the people's history and formed crucial elements of the country's visual identity. As in other places, Leningrad's planners stressed the importance of historic monuments in the city's layout, as well as the role they played in local and national identity.[14]

During the blockade, Leningrad's architectural authorities began to rethink the prewar plans to shift the administrative center of the city to the south. The 1938 plan had envisioned development of a new city center, the focal point of which would be the recently built House of Soviets on Moskovskii Prospekt. Yet the extensive amount of damage inflicted upon the city prompted local authorities in 1943 to discard this plan, focusing restoration on the historic center, which was to remain the social, administrative, and governmental heart of Leningrad.[15] Instead of constructing new buildings in areas that had yet to be fully developed, Leningrad's city planners argued for the need to first rebuild and improve the historic areas of the city which had suffered damage. That is not to say that new construction did not take place; rather, restoration of Leningrad's monuments and the historic structures linking them became one of the main subjects of attention.[16] During the second half of the nineteenth century, hundreds of highly decorative buildings were constructed along the city's main thoroughfares and streets in the center. Many of these new structures uniting the architectural ensembles were used as apartment buildings. Their restoration, therefore, would provide the city with badly needed living space.[17] Yet at the same time, this focus on the center expressed a desire to preserve the historic landscape as a window onto the past and expression of state power. There were, therefore, practical, political, and commemorative motives behind the plans to restore Leningrad's city center.

This approach to Leningrad contrasted sharply with that experienced by other war-torn urban areas. Local authorities and architects in several German, English, and French cities saw the destruction of their centers as an opportunity to create new, more modern buildings and structures, reduce traffic congestion, and improve urban life as a whole.[18] "Almost everywhere," writes Jeffry Diefendorf in reference to Western Europe, "town planners viewed the bombing as an unprecedented opportunity to introduce radically modernising changes in the urban fabric on a scale that had been almost impossible in existing, built-up cities."[19] Similar approaches were adopted in some Soviet cities that had suffered colossal damage as a result of wartime battles. The architects who worked out the 1943 plan for rebuilding Stalingrad, for example, saw the city for what it was – a blank slate upon which to develop "a new type of city."[20] But even in Soviet cities that had suffered major destruction, the need to modernize was tempered by the desire to maintain urban heritage and a connection to the past. Local planners in Sevastopol, for example, came into conflict with the architectural authorities in Moscow about the latter's desire to create a new "Soviet-style" Sevastopol at the expense of the city's history and traditions.[21] Leningrad's planners expressed similar desires, but conflicts between center and periphery did not develop in the former imperial capital, largely because damage there was not nearly as calamitous as in other cities, but perhaps more importantly because the state's focus on the Russian past meshed well with the program of Leningrad's preservationists. Indeed, both the central authorities and local planners sought to retain the city's powerful historic appearance and identity.[22] New development was subordinated to restoration, and construction which did occur was to draw upon the architectural traditions of imperial Petersburg.[23]

As a general principle, restoration efforts in Leningrad focused first and foremost on buildings and structures which contributed to the city's aesthetic and powerful historic appearance.[24] Contemporaries, in fact, noted that the restoration was concentrated on the city's historic center, while in other places off the beaten path, reconstruction was slow in coming.[25] Indeed, local leaders prioritized the restoration of all buildings located on the main streets, squares, and embankments of the center.[26] Into this grouping fell such structures and complexes as the Winter Palace, Smolnyi, the Admiralty, the Mariinskii Palace, the Engineers' Castle, and many other structures from the eighteenth and nineteenth centuries. Likewise, local authorities wanted to restore the city's monumental statues as quickly as possible. The inclusion of sculptures into the architectural composition of ensembles was one of Leningrad's important city planning traditions, as they formed "an inalienable link in the landscape of the city."[27] These monuments and ensembles all played a major role in the overall appearance of the city, and it was this "wholeness" (*tsel'nost'*), or integrity, that planners sought to restore in the period after the blockade.[28] Baranov summed up this desire as follows: "The fundamental architectural peculiarity of our city, which produces an exceptionally strong impression, is the ensemble principle of building. The streets, squares, and embankments of Leningrad do not present a mechanical collection of buildings, but rather an organic system, in which every building is an element of a single whole."[29] In the ensemble principle, every building plays a part in the composition of the city, like organs in a human body that all depend on each other. To lose a link in the chain, therefore, would mean damaging architectural-organic harmony, as well as losing an important piece of history. It was in this sense that the head of Leningrad's Department for the Protection of Monuments, Belekhov, said that "we are like doctors, we battle with illnesses found in our monuments with the goal of prolonging their long-lasting service."[30]

Although the famous buildings of the previous centuries were the jewels of the city – the vital organs of the city organism – the buildings and spaces linking these monuments were of no less importance in the architectural plans of the post-blockade period. The residential buildings, offices, and other structures connecting the palaces and monuments were essential elements in the cityscape.[31] Throughout the eighteenth and nineteenth centuries, St. Petersburg's city planners and architects had realized the need to minimize the empty spaces between important architectural ensembles, which they did by placing freestanding monumental buildings at key locations throughout the city. These linked the grandiose palaces and complexes, with the result that baroque and neoclassical buildings were joined together by eclectic, highly decorative structures in an organic whole.[32]

Throughout the postwar period, much of the planning and work of Leningrad's architects was oriented toward preserving and restoring not just individual buildings, but all elements of the organic whole. Because of the important role played by historic and artistic monuments in the city ensemble, the question of their restoration was unavoidable.[33] Officials frequently invoked the need to restore certain buildings because of the role they played in the city "organism." In calling for work to be started on the Admiralty and the former Stock Exchange – two buildings which were part of the city's core ensemble on both banks of the Neva – for example, Baranov argued that the need for restoration was due to the "exceptionally important role" that they played in Leningrad's external appearance.[34]

Although organic integrity was the goal, the architects of Leningrad's postwar restoration plan did not believe it necessary to restore absolutely everything that had been destroyed. Popular slogans urged that Leningrad should be made "more beautiful, and better" than it was before the war. According to Baranov, this meant that restoration should not simply be a "mechanical reproduction" of what existed before 1941.[35] There was no question about the restoration of monuments that were listed under state protection. But the city's preservationist and architectural authorities felt that certain structures they deemed to be out of sync with the surroundings, that had little or no artistic or historic value, or that were simply the result of poor planning and had been badly damaged, were to be replaced by more fitting constructions. Such damage allowed architects to improve buildings and whole areas in certain parts of the city. A building at the corner of Fontanka and the city's main thoroughfare, Nevskii Prospekt (which had only recently had its historic name changed back from 25th of October Prospekt), for example, was transformed from a structure considered to be of no special artistic value into one which better fit into the architectural style of the city's main street. Similarly, planners redesigned several other places in the historic center, including the area surrounding the Finland Station, the alley leading to the Engineers' Castle, and the square at Smolnyi.[36] All of these designs drew on the city's architectural traditions and used monuments and landmarks as their focal points.

In other cases, planners used the damage to visually and symbolically connect the Great Patriotic War to events in Russian history.[37] A building on the corner of Pestel' Street and Solanoi Lane, for example, was destroyed during the war and its ruins were subsequently removed. In its place architects created a small square featuring a monumental composition on the facade of an adjoining wall, which commemorated the Soviet defense of the Hankö Peninsula between June and December 1941. Located directly opposite the new square was the Church of St. Panteleimon the Healer, which was erected during the reign of Peter the Great to commemorate the Russian naval victory over the Swedes in the Battle of Gangut (Hankö) in 1714.[38] In constructing the memorial opposite a landmark which commemorated Peter the Great's naval achievements, planners sought to make the connection between the Soviet present and the era of imperial expansion, suggesting continuity in Russian military might and prowess.[39]

RESTORATION AS COMMEMORATION

When the restoration of Leningrad began, many felt the need to preserve the memory of the blockade and to have the 872 days reflected in the architecture of the city. To be sure, inscribing the events of the blockade into the city chronicle through restoration and new creations was often discussed in the immediate postwar period. At a 1945 meeting of the city's cultural-enlightenment workers, for example, participants reviewed the details of the plans to restore Leningrad and stressed the need to inform the restoration of the city with the memory of the blockade. Leningrad's deputy chief architect, A. I. Naumov, stated that "if Leningrad presents a stone page of our history, a stone book of our traditions, then obviously now, when preparing for the large-scale creative task of restoring the city, we do not have the right to depart from this tradition. . . . [W]e must add to this stone book by writing the events that we survived during the war years into it."[40] Naumov argued that, like the Patriotic War of 1812, which is commemorated in ensembles such as Palace Square, the Kazan Cathedral, and other prominent monuments, the Great Patriotic War and blockade of the city should and must be represented in the architectural work of the postwar period. "We must now, and not only in the future," he stated, "reflect the historic events of the period of the defense of Leningrad. This red thread must run through the measures that we take."[41] Like their colleagues in other Soviet cities, Leningrad's architectural authorities were determined to make the war an important part of the city's biography, and their activities were indicative of a general desire to commemorate the war throughout the Soviet Union in the postwar years.[42]

Whereas urban planners in some Western European cities strove to leave certain monuments or towns in ruins to commemorate their wartime experiences, Leningrad's authorities sought other strategies to memorialize the war.[43] Here, the party and soviet leadership presented the actions taken by the architectural and preservationist communities to overcome destruction as a fitting commemoration of the blockade.[44] But the idea of preserving ruins to commemorate the war was not wholly dismissed in Leningrad. In fact, some people suggested leaving selective, minor damage as a reminder of what the city suffered through. In planning the restoration of the Rostral Columns on the spit of Vasilievskii Island, for example, Baranov and others argued that a few indentations from shrapnel should be left unrepaired as a monument to the heroic days of the blockade.[45] At other places in the city, including the Anichkov Bridge, the Church of the Spilt Blood, and St. Isaac's Cathedral, small amounts of damage were left to commemorate the wartime events.[46]

The official attitude on leaving whole buildings in ruins, however, was the exact opposite. Most of the country's cultural community – with the exception of a very small minority – argued for the need to conserve, repair, and restore historic monuments wherever possible. The Soviet leadership, architectural authorities, and preservationists regarded ruins as unsightly representations of loss, which had limited educational value.[47] The authorities could have used the ruins of historic monuments to portray the attacks on Russian and Soviet culture, but they felt that restored monuments suggested a powerful, victorious people. Moreover, they understood that leaving monuments in ruins would mean losing a connection to the past. Instead, public lectures, images of destruction in the press, and books about "fascist vandalism" drew people's attention to the intentional destruction, as well as the Soviet leadership's determination to overcome the devastation and restore what had been lost.[48]

An article published in the daily newspaper *Vechernii Leningrad* (Evening Leningrad) articulated this sentiment, arguing that removing war damage was not an act of forgetting, or wiping the events from memory. Rather, restoration represented a monument to the war and blockade, for the experiences which the Soviet people lived through "cannot be embodied by destruction inflicted by the enemy. Only life can embody it, blooming in the place of destruction."[49] The author of the article emphasized the connection between restoration and commemoration by writing,

> I have met people who maintained that it is necessary to leave a few destroyed buildings in an inviolable appearance as monuments to the heroic years of the blockade of our city. I think the naiveté of this suggestion does not need commentary.... Through the centuries the blockade, the feats of the people who remained in the besieged city, and the valor of the builders returning the city's unique magnificence, will be inseparable.[50]

Such articles in the press clearly indicate that the party authorities wanted the population to understand the restoration in prescribed ways. Having successfully defended Leningrad for nearly nine hundred days, to not restore the essence of the city – its historic monuments and landmarks – would have meant conceding to the Germans.[51] As in other places that had been damaged in the war, the restoration of cities – historic monuments and landmarks included – worked to lift morale and provide proof of the power of the authorities, the state, and the Soviet people.[52]

Of particular importance in this respect was the Admiralty. Established during the reign of Peter the Great, the Admiralty represented Peter's modernizing vision and the naval might of the Russian Empire.[53] Over the years it had become one of the city's most prominent symbols. Yet during and after the war, it acquired extra layers of meaning. It was no longer simply a symbol of Petersburg, but had been transformed into a symbol of Soviet defiance and a monument to the blockade of the city.[54] Once again dominating the skyline of the city's center, the Admiralty spire proclaimed the passing, once and for all, of the "Hitlerite horde."[55] Such was its iconic power that it was commemorated on the medal "For the Defense of Leningrad."

The symbol of the Admiralty was used by preservationists to represent the heroism of Leningraders. In the immediate postwar years, GUOP called for measures to be taken to popularize historic monuments throughout the country. It commissioned books, films, and other media to heighten people's knowledge of history and cultivate respect for the country's built heritage. One film script reviewed by GUOP (and subsequently suggested for production) addressed the transformation of the Admiralty into a monument to the blockade. S. P. Varshavskii's script, *Glavnoe Admiralteistvo v Leningrade,* depicted the historic building as the central monument in Leningrad, one which embodied the city's history from the time of Peter the Great through to the postwar period. According to the script, the film would begin with an aerial panorama of the historic center of the city, focusing in on the Admiralty's spire. Surveying the surroundings, the script pauses on the adjacent Decembrist and Palace Squares, sites of Russia's first armed insurrection against autocracy and the storming of the Winter Palace in October 1917. Varshavskii, therefore, sought to emphasize the progressive, revolutionary nature of the city found in the historic cityscape. Attention then once again turns to the Admiralty, which is depicted with the Bronze Horseman in the foreground. The script stresses Peter's role in transforming Russia, the history of the Admiralty, the might of the Russian navy, and the part it played in protecting the country's maritime borders.

At this point in the script the film fades to black and turns to Leningrad under siege. It presents the blockaded city at night with lights searching the skies for enemy aircraft, followed by German weapons trained on the Admiralty and scenes of destruction. In this way, Varshavskii focused attention on Hitler's intention to annihilate the city and the very embodiments of Russian history and culture. It then moves on to fireworks exploding over the Admiralty, signifying the lifting of the siege on 27 January 1944, and images of restoration, as artists, sculptors, and builders arrive to "heal" the Admiralty's "wounds." Part of the Admiralty's restoration involved the uncovering of the spire: "The golden spire, camouflaged with cloth during the war, again began to sparkle above the hero-city, and the Admiralty's shining spire has become a symbol of courage, steadfastness, and heroism of the defenders of Leningrad in their battle for the Soviet motherland." In the final scene, the script indicates that the camera will pan to a medal that reads "For the Defense of Leningrad" and focuses in on the outline of the spire, thereby solidifying the link between Russian history and the Great Patriotic War.[56] The Admiralty, which embodied the history of the city and was revered as a monument to Peter's transformation of Russia, was transformed by the war; it now symbolized Russia's glorious past and the story of Leningraders' heroism during the blockade.

The same can be said of the Bronze Horseman, Falconet's iconic monument to Peter the Great. The uncovering of the statue in May 1945, for example, inspired an article published in *Leningradskaia pravda,* which illustrated a link between the city's historic landmarks, the victory in the blockade, and the transformative power of restoration. In the article, the author relates a conversation he had with an elderly Leningrader. The old man discussed the importance of the Bronze Horseman to Leningraders, as well as his desire to be present when it was finally uncovered. After walking past Decembrists' Square every day to see if work had begun, he found out that it would be uncovered at night. That May evening he prepared for the event, and went to bed early, but because of anxiety, he overslept. Cursing himself all the way to the square, he arrived to see Peter and the horse "standing in all their beauty." Although he explained how upset he was with himself for not getting there on time, he went on to say that "joy was stronger than shame as I walked around this horse, unable to take my eyes off of it." The old man finished his account by describing what young children from the neighboring courtyard had drawn on the monument immediately after it was uncovered: "I took a glance at Peter's chest and saw, [drawn] in chalk, childlike, large and clear, according to all the rules, a giant medal – 'For the Defense of Leningrad.'"[57]

The old man's story, however embellished by the editors of the press, shows the significance of the city's monuments to ordinary Leningraders, not just to the preservationist community and the authorities. It underlines the role played by art and architecture in inspiring and educating people about the city's history, heroes, and importance in the postwar period, just as it had during the blockade.[58] The story is also indicative of what the Soviet leadership wanted the people to think and feel about the Great Patriotic War. In describing how the medal "For the Defense of Leningrad" was displayed on Peter the Great's chest, the article emphasizes how the restoration of the monument was intimately linked to memories and commemorations of the blockade.[59] Like the Admiralty, the uncovered Bronze Horseman was transformed into a symbol of the Soviet people's defiance and refusal to surrender, and it taught a number of important political lessons to present and future generations: that the Soviet people had bravely withstood the Nazi onslaught; that the Soviet leadership was sincerely devoted to preserving culture and heritage; and that restoration was evidence of a powerful state quickly overcoming the destruction of war.

The rhetoric of restoration, likewise, frequently conjured memories of wartime heroism and encouraged Leningraders to repair the damage inflicted on the city. Using tropes that had been employed since the days of the Civil War, the local press referred to the restoration of the city as a "battle" in which people were summoned to participate. They were called upon to fight for the restoration of their "glorious city," just as they had fought during the war. Thus, on the first anniversary of the lifting of the siege, for example, an article commemorating the blockade commented, "The widely unfolding restoration works have opened a new page in the heroic battle of Leningraders. With love and pride Leningraders work at resurrecting their native city."[60] This battle, much like the "red thread" of the blockade, became a part of the city's heroic chronicle.[61] Images of a phoenix rising from the ashes, or of resurrection, were often invoked when connecting the struggles of restoration with wartime heroism. "Just as the warrior cleans the marks of a hot battle from his face," went one call to workers, "so the city-victor arises anew in the beauty and magnificence of its prospects and squares, buildings, and parks."[62] Bringing the powerful imperial appearance back to their beloved city, the Leningraders working at restoration, proclaimed local authorities, "piously preserve the memory of the great events of the Patriotic War."[63]

SUCCESSES AND FAILURES ON THE "RESTORATION FRONT"

Over the course of the first postwar years, Leningrad's architects, preservationists, and workers made significant progress in restoring the historic cityscape. By the late 1940s the vast majority of monuments had been "resurrected" (*vozrozhdeny*) or were in the process of being restored to their former appearance.[64] Central preservation authorities commended Leningraders for their efforts, noting that more work had been done there than anywhere else in the Soviet Union. In 1948, for example, the head of GUOP, Sh. E. Ratiia, after reviewing the work taking place in Leningrad, noted that "there is hardly a monument under state protection in the city that is either not restored, or not undergoing restoration." He went on to state that the restoration was "exceptional in both its range and quality."[65]

There were several factors accounting for the successes in historic restoration. A culture of preservation had been fostered among city planners, architects, and artists over the years, which led to a commitment to preserve select structures created in the first two and a half centuries of the city's history. As the state rehabilitated the past in the mid-1930s, organizations devoted to preservation and restoration were formed and continued their work in the postwar period. Leningrad's Department for the Protection of Monuments, established in 1938, was transformed into the State Inspectorate for the Protection of Monuments (*Gosudarstvennaia inspektsiia po okhrane pamiatnikov,* or GIOP) shortly after the siege was lifted in 1944. Its responsibilities consequently increased, as did its authority and influence. Prewar artistic workshops, likewise, continued to carry out restoration during the postwar period. Created just before the war, the Museum of City Sculpture also worked at restoring the city's monumental statues and sculptures. When the war ended, Leningrad's monuments benefited from the creation of other institutions which dealt specifically with their restoration. Two architectural-artistic trade colleges were opened, the students of which were to play important roles in the city's restoration. While attending the colleges, students gained practical experience working with seasoned preservationists and master restorers on the facades and interiors of the city's historic monuments and landmarks.[66]

Another institution working on the restoration "front" was the Leningrad Architectural Restoration Workshops (*Leningradskie arkhitekturno-restavratsionnye masterskie,* or LARM). One of several specialized restoration workshops established in Soviet cities with large numbers of damaged monuments in 1945,[67] LARM carried out many of the most important restoration projects in Leningrad and its suburbs, conducted research needed for accurate restoration, and compiled lists of projects for restoration.[68] LARM quickly grew into a large association of restorers performing work at several sites. In the first year and a half of its existence, its staff more than doubled from 163 people to 347.[69] During this period it was responsible for the restoration of more than fifty of the city's architectural monuments, including the Russian Museum, the Stroganov and Sheremetev Palaces, and the Leningrad Philharmonic.[70]

By the early postwar period, then, Leningrad was becoming more and more equipped and able to restore its historic monuments and landmarks. Yet it was the state's reliance on Russian history for mobilizational purposes which was the decisive factor in preservationist activities. The creation of new institutions devoted to conservation and restoration in the chaotic and resource-starved postwar years demonstrates the high level of cooperation between the local leaders and preservationists, as well as the commitment of the Stalinist state to preserve historic sites and use them as propaganda tools. Soviet leaders understood the need to use symbols to display state power and might to the population, and as the people continued to suffer from the effects of war, the Stalinist leadership sought to project state authority and legitimacy onto the urban fabric.

Any steps to return Leningrad's city center to its prewar appearance involved work that would reverse the prophylactic measures taken throughout the blockade. Especially important in this respect was the restoration of the city's decorative statues and symbols.[71] When the threat of destruction had been lifted, the city soviet ordered the statues put back in place and the spires and cupolas uncovered. In the spring of 1945, Leningrad's mountaineers – some of the very same people who risked their lives to camouflage the spires and cupolas in 1941 – removed the covering from the Admiralty, the Engineers' Castle, the Predtechenskaia Church, and the St. Nicholas Cathedral.[72] Meanwhile, work began on the restoration of the city's monumental sculptures and statues. In April 1945, instructions were sent to various organizations, stipulating a timeline for monuments to be uncovered and/or returned to their rightful places.[73] Given that summer was close at hand and Leningraders would soon be enjoying the city's beauty and charm in their leisure time, the authorities planned to have all statues back in their places by mid-June.[74]

Table 3.1. Appendix to Decision N.143-14-b of the Leningrad Soviet Executive Committee from 9 April 1945 – "On removing defensive covering from the city's monuments"

	Name	Address	Organization doing work	Date of completion
A.	Dismantling protective covering			
1	Monument to Nicholas I	Isaac's Square	October district soviet	01/05/1945
2	Monument to Peter I	Decembrist Square	October district soviet	01/06/1945
3	Improvement of the public garden	Decembrist Square	October district soviet	01/06/1945
4	Monument to Lenin	Finland Station	Kravnogvardeiskii district soviet	01/05/1945
5	Egyptian sphinxes	University Embankment 17. (Academy of Arts)	Vasilioostrovskii district soviet	01/05/1945
6	Monument to Kruzenstern	Lieutenant Shmidt Embankment (near Morskoi Korpus)	Vasilioostrovskii district soviet	01/05/1945
B.	Returning statues to their place			
7	Anichkov sculptural group	Anichkov Bridge	Stal'konstruktsiia	15/06/1945
8	Monument to Peter I (Rastrelli)	Engineers' Castle	Stal'konstruktsiia	15/06/1945
9	Dioscurs	Manège on Profsoiuz Boulevard	Monument Sculpture	01/06/1945
10	Manchurian Lions	Neva Embankment near Peter I's cottage	Monument Sculpture	15/05/1945
11	Sculptures of the Summer Garden	Summer Garden	Dzerzhinskii district soviet	15/06/1945
C.	Unmasking of spires and cupolas			
12	Admiralty spire	Admiralty proezd	GIOP	01/05/1945
13	Cupola of St. Nicholas Cathedral	Kommunar Square	GIOP	01/06/1945
14	Cupola and spire of Predtechenskaia Church	Ligovskaia Street at Obvodnyi Canal	GIOP	01/07/1945
15	Spire of the Engineers' Castle	2 Sadovaia Street	GIOP	15/06/1945
16	Spire and cupola of the Peter and Paul Fortress	Peter and Paul Fortress	GIOP	01/05/1945
17	Cupola of St. Isaac's Cathedral	Isaac Square	GIOP	01/07/1945

Source: GMGS, f. Otdel pamiatnikov i memorial'nykh dosok, d. 48, ch. 1 (unpaginated).

This was not an easy task, as it involved the coordination of several construction organizations and government branches at the local level. Removing statues from the ground and uncovering much larger statues like the Bronze Horseman required many workers and long hours. Returning statues to their rightful places was especially arduous and time consuming in the Summer Garden, where preservationists had organized the burial of marble statues and pedestals in more than a hundred places.[75] On 6 May 1945, for example, eighty-five soldiers from Leningrad's military divisions worked at removing statues from the ground. After laboring from nine-thirty in the morning until two o'clock in the afternoon, several statues and pedestals had been successfully exhumed, but much more work remained.[76] In some places machinery was needed to hoist the heavy statues from the ground once they were uncovered. In her description of the restoration of Rastrelli's monument to Peter I in front of the Engineers' Castle, for example, the artist Anna Ostroumova-Lebedeva noted an intricate system of wires, pulleys, and lifting devices used to raise Peter from his temporary grave back onto his pedestal.[77] Not only did work on the city's statues draw labor and machinery away from other jobs, but construction materials, which were in drastically short supply, had to be used to complete the work. Fortuitously, however, uncovering statues sometimes allowed for a recycling of construction materials. After the protective covering of the monument to Nicholas I on Isaac Square was dismantled, for example, that material was itself used as required by the October district soviet for restoration.[78]

People waited with enthusiasm for the removal of the protective covering from the city's monuments, for these were concrete, positive signs of Leningrad's "resurrection" after the blockade. Throughout the war, Leningraders lamented the removal of statues from the cityscape. During the blockade, the architect E. Levina commented on the removal of the famous equestrian group (created in the mid-1800s by the sculptor Petr Klodt) from the Anichkov Bridge, stating that "we walk along Nevskii and dream of the day when Klodt's horses will clamber up onto their pedestals on the Anichkov bridge."[79] These statues were one of the very symbols of the city, and for most people it was difficult to imagine Leningrad without them.[80] When the statues were returned to their rightful place on 2 June 1945,[81] those in attendance felt jubilation: "It was," wrote one commentator, "a moment of true exaltation for Leningraders."[82] In her diary, Ostroumova-Lebedeva expressed similar sentiments about the return of the monument to Peter I to its pedestal near the Engineers' Castle, stating that she "was very happy to have been there at one of the most joyful episodes in the restoration of our dear city."[83] Although work at some other monumental statues was delayed or passed on to other organizations, all projects to restore statues to their rightful places were fulfilled by the end of the first postwar construction season.[84]

The work to resurrect the city's statues and unveil its golden spires and cupolas was, in many ways, an easier task than the restoration of palaces, mansions, and other architectural symbols of the city. Here the city needed to prioritize, and one deciding factor was a building's significance in Russian and Soviet history. The Senate and Winter Palace, for example, conjured up images of imperial power and might, while Smolnyi and the Tauride Palace evoked the celebrated days of 1917; to have left them in disrepair would have been tantamount to a denial of their importance in history. Similarly, monuments such as the Admiralty and the Peter and Paul Fortress were symbols of the Petrine epoch and the storied founding of the city, and other famous monuments told the story of the Russian Empire during the eighteenth and nineteenth centuries. Hitler's attempt to erase this history by obliterating the city's monuments demanded that they be restored. "They would have liked to destroy our history," wrote the author Konstantin Fedin in 1944, "to erase the deeds and the glory of our fathers from the memory of our people."[85] It was thus both their importance to the country's historic narrative and the symbolic role these monuments played in the struggle against the Germans that led local leaders and preservationists to prioritize them in the restoration process.

Other, more practical considerations also played a role in decisions about restoration, including the amount of destruction suffered by individual buildings. In plans for restoring Leningrad, for example, Baranov suggested starting with buildings that suffered the least.[86] His chief motivation was to increase the amount of useable living space, but this policy was applied to historic monuments and landmarks as well: with materials and workers in short supply, small-scale works were often the easiest and least expensive to complete. At the Summer Palace of Peter I in the Summer Garden, for example, restoration began immediately after the war because it was one of the few "well preserved" monuments.[87]

What the building was used for and who was using it also frequently affected the pace and success of restoration. Premises which housed the more important government offices were among those at the top of this list. Smolnyi, the Tauride Palace, and the Mariinskii Palace, for example, were all buildings used by the city party committee and the Leningrad soviet, which meant that they occupied an important place in restoration plans.[88] No less important were the imperial palaces which housed museums of all-Union significance: the State Hermitage (Winter Palace) and the State Russian Museum (Mikhailovskii Palace). During the blockade, the most valuable collections from these two museums were evacuated, and preservationists constantly monitored them and employed conservation efforts to lessen the damage to the buildings themselves. Immediately after the blockade was lifted, architects and preservationists began restoration work on the facades and interiors of both museums. So important were these museums that in November 1945 the city soviet established a special commission, whose members included Baranov and Belekhov, to oversee the restoration of these monument complexes.[89]

Because these palaces housed two of the country's most important museums, they were well funded by the Ministry for Artistic Affairs, the Leningrad soviet, and GIOP. Due to the funds provided by Soviet authorities, the Russian Museum opened its doors to visitors on 9 May 1946 to commemorate the first anniversary of Victory Day.[90] This event was hailed in the press as a great "feat" (*podvig*) of restoration, which symbolized the Soviet people's ability to overcome adversity. The Hermitage likewise opened soon after the war ended, but because of the significant degree of damage to the museum, not all of the exhibits and rooms were accessible to visitors. Restoration work continued, however, and in April 1947 the city soviet evaluated the progress, noting that five million rubles had been spent on restoration in 1946, and another 1.28 million in the first quarter of 1947. Considering it necessary to complete the restoration of the building by the thirtieth anniversary of the October Revolution, the Leningrad soviet sent a petition to the central government for funding.[91] The government approved the request and allocated an additional six million rubles from its reserve fund to the Committee for Artistic Affairs to carry out the work.[92] As a result of the funding, major work was done in the complex of the State Hermitage, and by 1948, the facades and 152 exhibition halls had been returned to their prewar state.[93]

Although the interiors of the Hermitage and Russian Museum were priorities, Leningrad's authorities sought first and foremost to restore the facades of buildings in the historic core – the external appearance of state power and magnificence.[94] This was especially important as the number of tourists to the city grew with each postwar year. Almost all of the buildings in the city, especially in the center, bore the traces of war. A demobilized soldier described what he saw after returning from the front: "We drove over the wounded bridges of Leningrad streets, past ruins, along buildings where glass rarely shone among embrasures, covered by plywood on facades that were badly scratched by shrapnel."[95] The local authorities understood that such images did little to inspire confidence in the state, and therefore sought to quickly heal the wounds of war, if only on the exteriors. Facade work, therefore, commenced immediately after the siege was lifted. The local press promoted restoration by stressing that it was "shameful" to see destruction on the facades of monuments and sculptures adorning the city.[96]

Considerable steps were taken during the first postwar years to return many of the facades to their prewar state. From the very beginning of the restoration period in 1944, architects and preservationists lauded the impressive repairs at places like the Kirov Theater and the Theater of Musical Comedy, as well as on the facades of residential buildings lining the main streets.[97] In 1945 there were over 140 restoration projects completed on the facades of imperial monuments.[98] As time went by, the city's construction organizations accomplished more and more restoration work. In August 1946, for example, facade restoration was taking place at three hundred buildings on the streets of Leningrad, including Nevskii, Suvorovskii, and Mezhdunarodnyi Prospekts.[99] A few months later, the scaffolding was taken down from the Mariinskii Palace, the new home of the city soviet's executive committee. Freshly restored, the facade of the palace bore the symbol for the Order of Lenin, awarded to Leningrad for courage, discipline, and heroism during the blockade.[100]

The state of Leningrad's historic monuments continued to improve throughout the period as the economy began to stabilize and grow. However, progress was uneven and sometimes not quick enough for the authorities' liking. Up until 1947, at least, the Leningrad authorities complained that work to bring the architectural whole back to its prewar state was unsatisfactory and moving too slowly. In 1946, for example, plans for architectural monuments housing state ministries and other governmental institutions fell far short of what the city soviet had planned, as only 41 percent of the work slated for that year was accomplished.[101]

Local authorities blamed several construction organizations and building occupants for the slow progress, claiming that they continued to drag out the process of repairs and painting, leaving several buildings either partially completed or not worked on at all. By July 1947, members of the executive committee of the city soviet were rather concerned. Out of the sixty-six buildings under state protection where facade work was intended to be completed in that year, work had not started at thirty-five, including the Pushkin Theater on Ostrovskaia Square and the Philharmonic.[102] "The most important tasks in the restoration of Leningrad's most prominent ensembles and its main streets," declared one city soviet decision, "are under threat of not being met [*sryv*]."[103] This angered the authorities and prompted them to take measures to ensure that facades were restored.

One of the ways they did so was by pressuring construction organizations and institutions that occupied historic buildings. In July 1946, for example, the city soviet convened a meeting to discuss the restoration of facades.[104] In blunt terms, it threatened individuals and organizations responsible for restoration with punishment if work was not completed as scheduled. Baranov warned that if progress on facades was not taken more seriously, certain buildings (he cited the Stock Exchange on the pit of Vasilievskii Island as an example) could be passed on to different organizations.[105] In this he was joined by V. P. Galkin, vice chairman of the city soviet, who sternly warned those in attendance that "we demand the fulfillment of the executive committee's decision. Subjective and objective reasons will not be accepted by the executive committee, nor will it sort out who is guilty. We will not allow you to push blame onto contractors [*ne prinimaem ssylki na podriadchikov*]."[106] Organizations were told that no work was to begin on the interiors of buildings until facades were restored, and that the buildings could not be fully utilized until this was completed: "I warn you now," said Galkin, "that without painting the facades, we will not allow buildings to be occupied. I ask that you take this into account."[107]

Several organizations explained that there were too few workers on hand to complete the assigned tasks. Some had enough workers but no materials. Others argued that they had yet to receive funding sufficient to carry out the work, or stated that the contractors assigned to the monuments were overworked. Their protests, however, fell on deaf ears. Increasingly concerned about the state of the city's external appearance as an expression of state power, the authorities were unwilling to listen to what they understood as excuses. Work as planned and ordered was to be completed in a timely fashion.

By the construction season of 1947, Leningrad's party and soviet leaders had become incensed by the poor results of certain organizations and construction trusts in carrying out the executive committee's decisions about facades. At a meeting in July, the chairman of the Leningrad soviet, P. G. Lazutin, chastised individuals for underfulfilling plans, warning them that there would be consequences to pay.[108] The year 1947 was especially important to the authorities because in November, the country was to celebrate the thirtieth anniversary of the October Revolution. "The facades must be done," argued Lazutin, "because we want the city to look better by the thirtieth anniversary of October, because we gave our word to the country that we would make Leningrad better, more beautiful."[109] Institutions occupying buildings of historic value were to focus all their resources on facade restoration.

The authorities were unwilling to listen to explanations. They wanted work done and they wanted it done immediately. Making clear the position of the city soviet, Lazutin stated, "If you do not fulfill the decisions, then we will treat you differently. Do not forget that this is the Leningrad soviet – not a rural soviet, not the Pskov nor the Novgorod soviet, but Leningrad's, where the revolution was made. . . . We will fight for the decisions of the Leningrad soviet."[110] Officials and institutions deemed to have not fulfilled their restoration tasks were scapegoated and shamed in the press. As early as 1945, for example, the Leningrad media reported on poor work in the restoration of facades on historic buildings housing state institutions. Individuals responsible were named, as were their failings, and they were compared to others who were successfully carrying out work as planned.[111]

The sense of urgency regarding the restoration of statues, museums, and facades of historic buildings was indicative of the state's desire to use Leningrad's built heritage for propaganda purposes. This was especially important given the city's status as the second-largest urban center in the country, former capital of the Russian Empire, and "cradle of the revolution." Hundreds of thousands of people came to Leningrad each year to visit its historic sites and museums and walk along its canals and rivers. Throughout the postwar years, the Soviet leadership promoted tourism within the Soviet Union to draw attention to the people's long and "glorious" history, their achievements, and their "magnificent" culture. In the late Stalin years, the leadership used tourism as a means of cultivating and reinforcing a Soviet patriotic identity. According to Anne Gorsuch, postwar Soviet tourism was meant to create a devoted citizenry who saw the advantages of the socialist system over its capitalist counterpart. "Patriotic tourism," she writes, "engaged the tourist in rituals of public self-admiration in which the Soviet Union's prestige was perpetually reaffirmed."[112] In Leningrad, the local excursion bureau consistently stated that its main goal was to provide for the "education of workers in the spirit of Soviet patriotism through examples of the glorious revolutionary traditions of the past and the heroic present of Leningrad – the Hero City."[113] The bureau organized tours and visits to historic sites which focused on the founding and development of Petersburg, famous military and cultural figures associated with the imperial capital, the socialist development of Leningrad, and the city's experience in the Great Patriotic War.[114] Thus, when restoration projects proceeded slowly or had not begun at all, the ability of Soviet institutions, such as the Leningrad Excursion Bureau, to utilize the cityscape to promote Soviet patriotism was severely compromised. As a result, local leaders demanded the successful completion of restoration projects in a timely manner.

The problem was that even two years after the war, chaos reigned in the planning system. Literally thousands of restoration projects (industrial, residential, and architectural) were taking place in the city, all of which required labor and materials. These problems were compounded by other difficulties, including improper preparation for large-scale restoration projects and insufficient organization of labor.[115] Yet throughout the Soviet Union in the first postwar years there was a drastic shortage of labor and materials needed to repair the colossal amount of damage inflicted by the Germans. Leningrad's troubles were simply indicative of the situation in the country as a whole. Thus, organizations complaining about these problems were not deceiving the authorities – they were merely stating the truth. These issues were faced by organizations at most, if not all, restoration projects during the postwar period.

Over time, especially after 1947, pressure eased somewhat due to a gradual return of qualified workers from the Red Army, an increase in the number of trained restorers, and a constant improvement in the supply of materials.[116] Nevertheless, by the late 1940s, certain buildings – even some which played key roles in the city's ensembles and historical narrative – had witnessed very little, if any, restoration work carried out since the end of the war.

At places where little if anything was done, the institution occupying the premises was frequently deemed the main reason for inaction. This was a problem that had plagued historic monuments and landmarks since the revolution. The laws on historic preservation from the 1930s, for instance, were in part aimed at local authorities and building occupants who were inadequately caring for the monuments. Reports from the postwar period quite frequently cite unreliable occupants as the main problem hindering restoration activities throughout the Soviet Union.[117] Whereas the Hermitage Museum occupying the Winter Palace was reliable and well-funded, for example, this was not the case at some other architectural monuments. Several organizations and institutions did not have the necessary means and were thus unable to carry out all the restoration work on the premises they occupied.[118] At the palace housing the Herzen Pedagogical Institute on the Moika Embankment, for example, very little restoration had taken place between 1944 and 1949. Although the institute received funding specifically for restoration of the building, reports compiled by GIOP indicate that much of the money was used for other purposes. According to the reports, the building had deteriorated so badly that the upper floors of the palace could no longer be used.[119] The situation at one of Leningrad's major historic symbols, the Peter and Paul Fortress, was apparently not much better: "This is a black spot on the background of Leningrad's monuments," stated Belekhov at a meeting to discuss the work of GIOP in 1949. "In the past few years we have been trying to carry out even elemental improvements [*blagoustroistvo*], but nevertheless, the occupants of this monument complex refuse in every way possible to improve its condition."[120]

The Engineers' Castle is perhaps the best example of a major city monument where major damage and postwar shortages in combination with an unreliable occupant prevented significant repairs well into the 1950s. Built in the late 1790s by Catherine the Great's son Paul, and used for only a few months before the emperor was assassinated in his chambers, the castle was converted by the tsarist government into an engineering college in the 1820s. Since 1917, a military engineering college used it, although a military hospital occupied it during the war. The castle played a crucial role in the historic ensemble surrounding the Field of Mars, yet German bombing and shelling had left it severely damaged: one of its walls on the courtyard side had been completely destroyed, thereby exposing much of the interior to the elements.

Once the war was over, Leningrad's authorities and architects planned to have the castle fully restored. An article in *Leningradskaia pravda* in April 1945 stated rather optimistically that the castle would be restored to its former appearance by the fall of that year.[121] Throughout the postwar period, however, the college, the contracting organization, and the military administration did hardly anything to improve it, despite repeated appeals and warnings from GIOP and the city soviet.[122] Not surprisingly, the castle's condition continued to worsen. In February 1948, a commission made up of architects and restorers noted that "in spite of the significant destruction inflicted on the Mikhailovskii [Engineers'] Castle during the Great Patriotic War, restoration work has still not unfolded in the amount needed to provide for even minimal preservation of the monument's architecture, the technical condition of which worsens with every year."[123] The commission went on to note that the state of the building's exterior mirrored its interior, as decorative details of the facades and interiors were being destroyed by weather and improper use.

The major problem at the castle was a common one in the first years after the war: materials and restoration workers were in short supply. But when a neglectful occupant was added into the mix, the situation became catastrophic. Before the war, the building had been used properly, but after the blockade, the military engineering college was either unable or unwilling (or perhaps both) to spend the necessary time and resources on restoration. The central preservation authorities – GUOP – proclaimed that the Ministry of the Armed Forces, which was ultimately responsible for the castle, was the "worst transgressor in the use of funding allocated for restoration on building-monuments" throughout the USSR.[124] Leningrad's authorities, however, were unable to find a new institution which would treat the monument with respect. One observer, a certain Almazov, wrote a letter to the press about the castle. The letter was never published, but because it raised concerns, it was forwarded to GIOP. In his letter, Almazov commented on the problems of the organization occupying the premises, and went on to discuss the difficulty of finding a new institution which would properly care for the monument. "The organization currently using the castle," wrote Almazov, "has been trying for three years to dump the premises off on another and receive a better building, but the trouble is that as soon as the castle is looked over and the means to repair it estimated, nobody agrees [to accept the building]."[125] Given the amount of damage done to it during the war, it is not surprising that other organizations were unwilling to make it their home. GIOP suggested that the castle be given to the Public Library, but because the library did not have a contracting/construction organization, the search continued. By 1949 a successful replacement had not been found.[126] Due to its unreliable occupant, as well as the problems and shortages of the postwar period, the castle remained in a dilapidated state until restoration work began in earnest in 1952.[127]

Shortcomings of this kind made unrestored monuments extremely conspicuous among the successful restoration projects in the postwar years. The poor quality which sometimes characterized work – especially in the immediate postwar period – and the lack of activity at certain places aroused the anger not only of the authorities but also of ordinary Leningraders, who were anxious to see their city returned to its prewar state. Some of these concerned citizens, like Almazov, wrote to the press and the authorities to express their dissatisfaction about the state of the city's treasures and to demand that more work be done to return the city to its former glory.

According to published and unpublished letters, many Leningraders felt that the slow pace of restoration was unfitting of a city of such historic importance that had just withstood the German onslaught for almost nine hundred days. One letter printed in *Vechernii Leningrad* in early 1946, for example, stated that the lack of restoration work taking place on certain historic monuments was "disappointing." The author, an architect named S. Korulov, discussed the Kushlevskaia Dacha, built in the eighteenth century on the Sverdlov Embankment, and the Sampsionievskii Cathedral, a monument to the Petrine era, as two examples of historic monuments where work had yet to begin. Korulov expressed his hopes that the monuments would be restored in the coming construction season.[128] The head of Leningrad's Administration for Artistic Affairs, B. I. Zagurskii, was forwarded another letter from a concerned citizen writing to the press about the shameful state of the monument to the Victims of the Revolution on the Field of Mars. After reading the letter, Zagurskii petitioned the executive committee of the city soviet to allocate 350,000 rubles for its restoration. "The condition of this granite grave monument," noted Zagurskii, "has provoked the righteous indignation of the residents of Leningrad, who have even written directly to I. V. Stalin about this matter."[129]

In other letters, the authors invoked the Stalinist language of denunciation as they called on the authorities to take extraordinary measures to ensure the restoration of historic monuments. In one unpublished letter, a demobilized soldier commented on the poor quality of work carried out on the Winter Palace. The author exclaimed that the poor work was the result of "vandalism" (*varvarstvo*) and "wrecking" (*vreditel'stvo*). Ending his letter, he demanded answers to four questions:

> 1. Who is the main scoundrel who carried out the work on the Winter Palace (his surname).
> 2. Is he still walking on our Leningrad soil, or is he sitting in prison. If he is not in prison, then why not?
> 3. Who approved such criminally deficient work on the palace?
> 4. Does the Leningrad soviet know about this crying shame [*vopiiushchem bezobrazii*]?[130]

Such denunciatory language was also seen in an angry letter sent to the Central Committee's Department of Propaganda and Agitation from the director of Leningrad's Museum of the History of Religion, V. Bonch-Burevich. In his letter, the director expressed his concern about the "awful condition" of the building which housed the museum (the Kazan Cathedral on Nevskii Prospekt). The director noted that the building "suffered terribly" during the blockade and that the Soviet of Ministers had instructed the Academy of Sciences to provide the necessary materials to a contracting organization for restoration work. In spite of this, nothing had in fact been done and the condition of the building continued to worsen. The contracting organization, Lenakademstroi, according to the director, "is an absolutely worthless organization, and in my opinion, clearly an organization of wreckers." According to the director, the inactivity of the contracting organization was particularly galling due to the central importance of the building in Russia's historic narrative, for not only was this the Museum of the History of Religion, but more significantly, it was a monument to Russia's Patriotic War against Napoleon. Bonch-Burevich wrote,

> In the building . . . rests the remains of the General Field Marshal Kutuzov. . . . Every day no less than a thousand people come to the grave and they all intensely grumble that Soviet power can maintain the building – where the sacred remains of one of the greatest patriots of our fatherland are kept – in such a condition. Red Army soldiers, sailors, workers, students, and laborers all come here and it is simply shameful that we must let them into the building, which is in such awful condition. I consider this absolutely politically unacceptable.[131]

These letters reflect the concerns of individual Leningraders and Soviet leaders. By the late 1940s, most of the damage to the city's monuments had been restored, especially that inflicted on major imperial palaces. But while the authorities demanded the restoration of the city's historic sites and landmarks, the combination of postwar shortages and inaction on the part of organizations occupying the buildings left some monuments in a dilapidated state. As was often the case in the Soviet Union, plans deviated from reality. Arousing the exasperation of local leaders and ordinary Leningraders, these "black spots" on the background of Leningrad's restoration represented failures in the new battle. Like the authorities, letter-writers saw in the restored city a monument to the events lived through during the blockade. In ruins and unfinished work, however, they saw shame and vandalism, which was, as Bonch-Burevich noted, "politically unacceptable."

During Leningrad's first postwar years, history, memory, and commemoration were the driving forces behind the restoration of the city's monuments. Leningrad was vitally important in the state's attempts to mobilize the population around a shared heritage. Consequently, its monuments could not be left in ruins or removed from the cityscape, for that would mean losing important witnesses to the country's past. To that end, hundreds of millions of rubles were spent on "resurrecting" monuments from ruins throughout the period between 1944 and 1950.[132] Leningrad's authorities cast the restoration of the city as a memorial to the 872-day siege. Having defended Leningrad and shown their determination to care for its cultural and historic heritage, it was only fitting that Leningraders should work just as hard to "resurrect" the city. "The memory of the heroic and heavy days, survived by Leningrad," wrote the director of the Museum of the Defense of Leningrad in 1945, "inspires the warriors and laborers to new feats in work, to new strengths in the restoration of their hometown."[133] Through restoration of historic monuments in the city's center, Leningraders were rescuing the country's "glorious history" and writing the narrative of the blockade into the city's urban fabric. Restoration was a symbolic victory for the authorities and for ordinary Leningraders – it represented a "new page" in the "battle" of the heroic city.

The rhetoric surrounding restoration was indicative of the ambitions and desires of those who lived through the siege and wanted to see their experience commemorated in the cityscape. But it also reflected the political messages that the state sought to project in the postwar period. Soviet authorities used official pronouncements, stories in the press, and achievements in historic restoration to foster Soviet patriotism by highlighting the great historic traditions of the Russian people, the creative genius of their forefathers, and the heroic sacrifices made during the blockade and the Great Patriotic War. Working with the city's preservationists during a time of incredible scarcity, the Stalinist leadership devoted enormous resources to the restoration of historic monuments in order to project the power of the Soviet state and people onto the cityscape emerging like a phoenix from the ravages of war.

1. Removal of the equestrian statue group from the Anichkov Bridge. 1941.
Source: KGIOP, N. 89190.

2. Monument to Lenin concealed in protective covering in front of Smolnyi. 1941.
Source: KGIOP, N. 83134.

3. Monument to Peter the Great (the Bronze Horseman) concealed in protective covering on Decembrists' Square. 1943. *Source: KGIOP, N. 13510.*

4. Mountaineer concealing the cupola of the Nikol'skii Cathedral in July 1942.
Source: KGIOP, N. 10738.

5. Bomb damage from a direct hit at the Engineers' (Mikhailovskii) Castle on 9 April 1942. *Source: KGIOP, N. 11809.*

6. Marble statue in the Summer Garden returned to its pedestal. 1945.
Source: KGIOP, N. 15869.

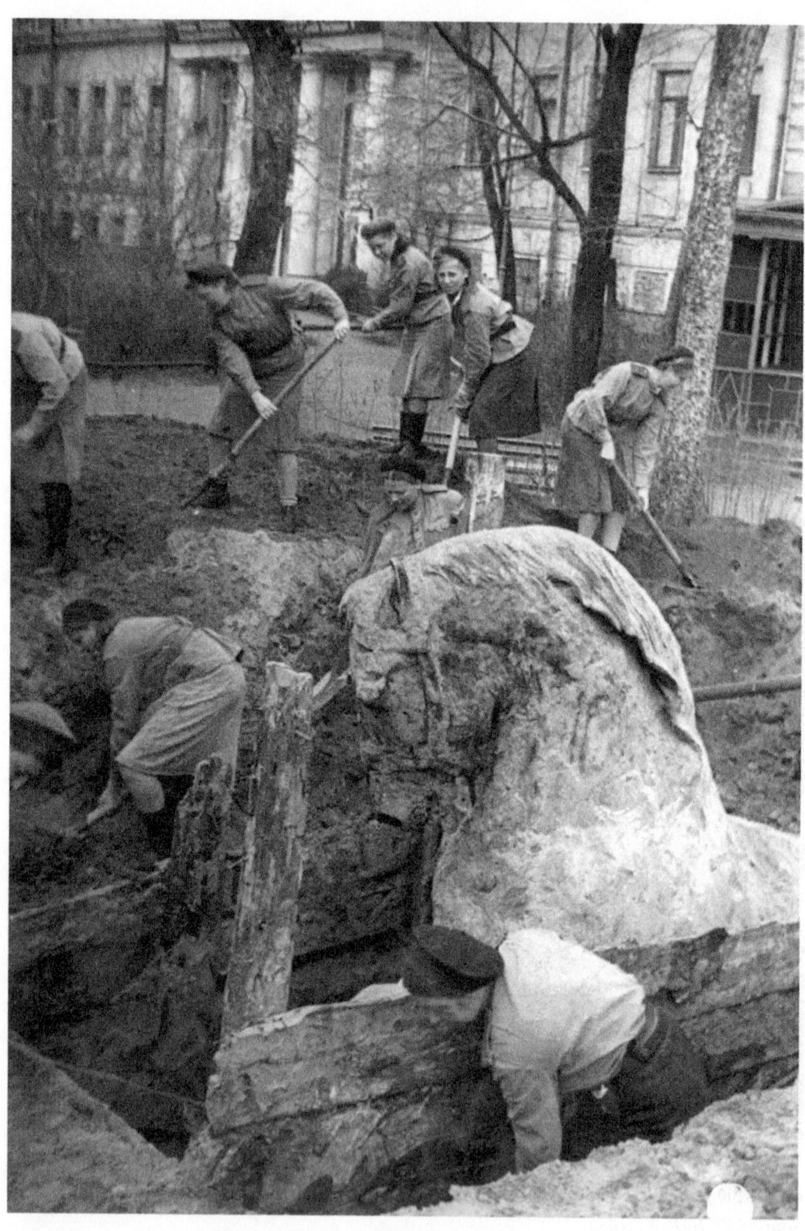

7. Removal of the equestrian statues from their burial sites in the garden of the Pioneers' (Anichkov) Palace before being returned to their places on the Anichkov Bridge. 1945. *Source: KGIOP, N. 16143.*

8. Monument to Peter the Great being hoisted back onto its pedestal in front of the Engineers' Castle. *Source: KGIOP, N. 15956.*

9. Workers removing the sand protecting the base of the Bronze Horseman. 1944.
Source: KGIOP, N. 31527.

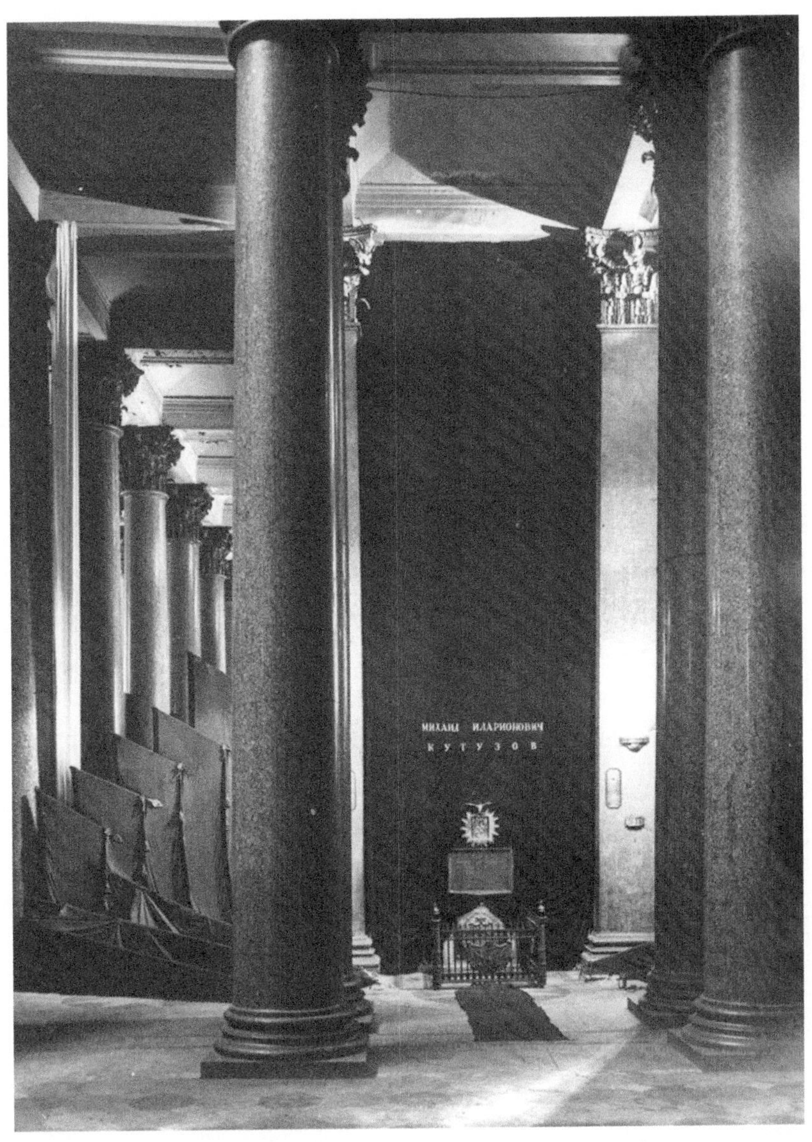

10. Mikhail Kutuzov's grave in the Kazan Cathedral. 1942.
Source: KGIOP, A-432, N. 14048.

11. D. M. Shpraizer's poster "Death to the Fascist Vandals for Defiling Our National Treasures." June 1942. *Source: KGIOP, XX/G-10 (3392).*

12. Ruins of the Peterhof Palace and the fountain cascade leading to the Gulf of Finland. 1944. *Source: Courtesy of KGIOP.*

13. German graveyard in front of the Alexander Palace in Pushkin. 1944. *Source: KGIOP, A-427, N.12599.*

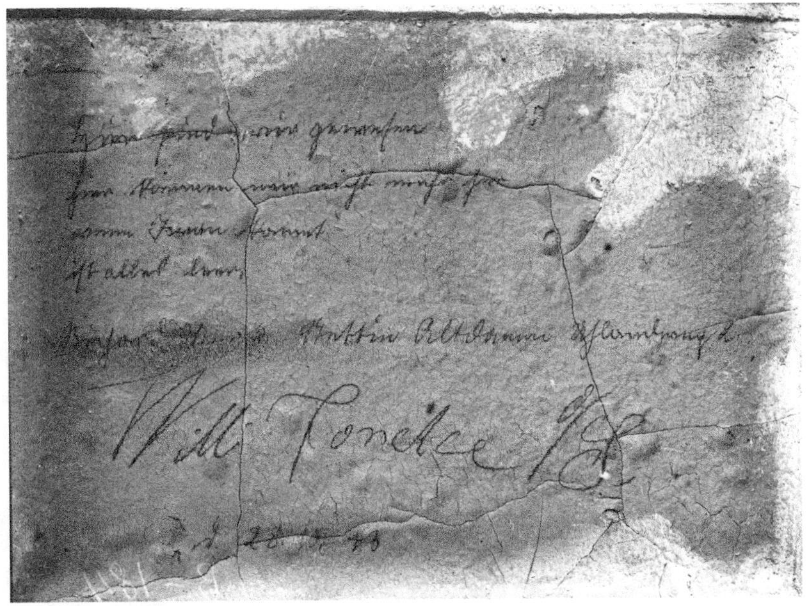

14. Message written on the wall of the Gatchina Palace: "We were here, but we will not return. When Ivan comes, there will be nothing left." *Source: Courtesy of GMZ "Gatchina."*

15. Catherine's Palace in Pushkin in ruins with an image of Stalin at the courtyard entrance. 1948. *Source: KGIOP, N. 21617/3.*

16. Fireworks over the monument to Suvorov at the Field of Mars marking the end of the blockade on 27 January 1944. *Source: KGIOP, N. 12703.*

17. Nikolai Nikolaevich Belekhov. *Source: Courtesy of KGIOP.*

FOUR

"WHEN IVAN COMES, THERE WILL BE NOTHING LEFT": REBUILDING AND REIMAGINING THE HISTORIC MONUMENTS IN LENINGRAD'S SUBURBS

THE RESTORATION OF THE IMPERIAL PALACES AND PARKS surrounding the city was a key element in Leningrad's postwar restoration. The Germans had taken Gatchina, Pavlovsk, Peterhof, and Pushkin at the end of August 1941. During the occupation they systematically pillaged, defiled, and partially destroyed the historic monuments in these suburbs. When they were forced to retreat from their positions, they burned and blew up much of what remained of the eighteenth-century landmarks. After the Soviet forces captured the suburbs in mid-January 1944, what they found could be summed up in what Richard Wurf, a rank-and-file German soldier, wrote on the wall of the Gatchina Palace: "We were here, but we will not return. When Ivan comes, there will be nothing left."[1]

Despite – and arguably because of – the vast scale of destruction (the Germans having carried out this promise), the country's preservationist community was determined to restore the suburban palaces to their prewar state. Immediately after the suburbs were liberated, preservationists and architectural authorities from Leningrad and Moscow held meetings and conferences to discuss restoration, as well as what the palaces would be used for. At the time, however, the colossal damage inflicted upon the palaces led some officials to believe that restoration was impossible. In the ensuing fight to have the suburban palace-park complexes restored, preservationists were able to draw upon official state ideology and argue that these historic sites were irreplaceable symbols of Russian power and imperial might. The preservationists' desire for almost complete restoration conflicted with the central authorities' early plans of only partial restoration, leading to a compromise calling for the restoration of the suburban palaces to varying degrees.

Over the course of the postwar period, preservationists and officials made a commitment to restoring the imperial monuments in Leningrad's suburbs. But that commitment was in certain respects inadequate. Although advocates of preservation made loud noises about the immediate need to restore palaces to their prewar grandeur, these buildings did not house hospitals, government organs, colleges, or other essential services as did many of the historic monuments in the city itself. In addition, postwar shortages limited the amount of work that could be done. Nevertheless, a series of conservation and restoration activities began which laid the basis for nearly complete restoration in the coming decades. The fact that the suburban palaces and parks were worked on at all, given the disastrous economic situation facing the country, highlights the importance attached to imperial monuments by the Stalinist leadership, as well as the tenacity of the country's preservationists, who were determined to raise them from the ruins.

In the early postwar years the suburban palaces and parks came to symbolize more than just imperial power, although this continued to be a key narrative in the cultural events held in restored rooms and halls. The discussions and reports about the palaces and parks, the exhibits they hosted, and the physical destruction itself all worked to add new layers of meaning to these monuments. They came to symbolize the destruction of war, but particularly the attack on Russian history and culture perpetrated by the Germans. As restoration proceeded, efforts were made to impress upon visitors the narratives of imperial glory and the Great Patriotic War. During restoration, therefore, the suburban palace-park complexes became unique venues for inculcating Soviet patriotism and promoting the postwar ideological program.[2]

SUBURBAN PALACES AND OCCUPATION

Before the Germans attacked the Soviet Union and occupied the region around Leningrad, the city's residents were drawn to the suburban palaces and parks to enjoy holidays and days off work. The world-famous sites had been used almost exclusively by royalty until 1917. Russia's emperors and empresses had constructed the palaces and parks of Gatchina, Lomonosov, Pavlovsk, Peterhof, and Pushkin in the eighteenth century as retreats for the imperial family and court.[3] Like the historic sites in the city center, the imperial palaces on the outskirts spoke to the image of wealth and power that Russia's rulers – like other European monarchs of the eighteenth and nineteenth centuries – wished to portray.

The small towns surrounding the imperial residences were popular destinations for the upper and middle classes throughout the imperial period.[4] As in Britain and other industrializing nations during the nineteenth and early twentieth centuries, suburbs were places in which the upper classes could spend time away from the overcrowded, unhealthy urban environment. As time went by, more and more people began to make use of these greener, fresher environments for rest and relaxation.[5] In St. Petersburg, the suburbs became the most popular and fashionable places of rest for the city's residents.[6]

After the October Revolution, the Bolsheviks brought the palaces and parks under the control of the Commissariat of Enlightenment as the "people's property." The commissariat then turned them into museums and places of rest and entertainment. The parks, with their ponds, fountains, forest paths, and pavilions, provided a relaxing atmosphere with clean air, which proved to be a welcome retreat from the congested and dirty industrial areas of the city. Visitors could rent rowboats, play tennis, ski in the winter, and take part in any number of cultural entertainments and sports.[7] In addition, these opulent specimens of art, architecture, and landscape design offered a window onto the country's history and cultural heritage. The founder of Leningrad's Puppet Theater, Lyubov Shaporina, for example, recorded her impressions of a visit to Peterhof in her diary in September 1936, emphasizing how the surroundings created a connection with the past. "It is so beautiful here," she remarked. "A fairy tale frozen in time, la belle au bois dormant [the Sleeping Beauty]. Here things don't seem to belong, it's a vision of the past. . . . And the sea! It may be just a puddle, but still it's the sea, and of course the spirit of Peter lives on in these parts."[8]

Up to the outbreak of the war, Leningraders visited the suburban palace-park complexes to rest and encounter the past. Thousands of people streamed to the suburbs to enjoy their days off away from the hustle and bustle of the city. More than 100,000 people per year visited the Pavlovsk Palace-Museum in the period leading up to the war,[9] and as many as 150,000 visited Peterhof, the suburb famous for its fountains based on the design at Versailles, on summer weekends.[10] Almost all Leningraders, including high-level officials, used the suburban palace-park as a retreat throughout the 1930s. The city's chief architect, Nikolai Baranov, for example, often visited the suburbs with his family to relax. They made the trip to Peterhof on the day that the Germans invaded, and Baranov noted how the park was packed with well-dressed people admiring the fountains and the seaside vista.[11] This would be one of the last days that the suburban palaces and parks were open to visitors for over three years.

Four days after the war was announced, the city's authorities and museum workers began to implement plans to save the treasures of Leningrad's suburbs from destruction.[12] Leningrad's party and soviet leadership ordered all palace-museums to close their doors to the public and instructed directors to begin measures to conserve the buildings, exhibits, sculptures, and fountains.[13] Just as in the city itself during the first days of the war, museum workers and others labored frantically to protect the historic and artistic monuments. "These were days of unbelievable haste," wrote the director of the Pavlovsk Palace, Anna Zelenova, in her reminiscences of the period.[14] Their sense of urgency was warranted, as it did not take long for the Germans to make their way east to Leningrad. Before the suburbs were occupied, the enemy had begun firing on Soviet positions in and around the towns near the city.[15] In these conditions, the staff of the suburban palaces and parks had to move quickly in order to protect the monuments from destruction.

A key component of the plans to save the city's artistic and cultural heritage was evacuation. Valuables from areas threatened with destruction, including Leningrad's suburbs, were sent to the East almost immediately after Germany declared war.[16] Although hundreds of the most valuable treasures were evacuated, many museum pieces remained in the palaces, including some of the larger exhibits, furniture, and statues in the parks. With the threat of German occupation looming, museum workers did whatever possible to hide the suburbs' treasures. Ia. I. Shurygin, one of the museum workers at the Peterhof Palace (and its postwar director), noted that it was impossible to evacuate the statues. In all of the suburbs, as in the center of the city, several statues were taken down from their pedestals and buried in the grounds of the parks to protect them from the "tornado of war."[17] In other cases, museum workers used their intimate knowledge of the palaces to their advantage. In Peterhof, for instance, some of the bronze statues decorating the main fountain ensemble, the Great Cascade, were removed from their positions and hidden in a gallery under the palace;[18] in Pavlovsk, many of the exhibits were similarly stored in a secure underground cellar which was sealed with bricks made to look old and dirty in order to camouflage the hiding place.[19]

Yet these measures were improvised, because the plans that Leningrad's museum workers had drawn up in the mid-1930s to protect the suburbs did not take into account the possibility of occupation.[20] Soviet authorities had assured the people that the Red Army was invincible, and that if war should break out, it would take place on foreign soil.[21] Consequently, the museum workers themselves did not expect that the suburbs would fall into German hands and that the palaces and parks would be left unprotected – even the director of the Pavlovsk Palace was still working on the removal of valuables when the Germans entered the park.[22] By early September, the military situation had forced all museum workers to leave the palaces and move what they could for storage to St. Isaac's Cathedral in the center of Leningrad.[23] Days later, when the enemy occupied the suburbs, there was nothing that could be done to protect the monuments, for even the Red Army was forced to take up a position closer to the city itself.

News of the occupation of the suburbs was not taken well in the city. When the artist Anna Ostroumova-Lebedeva, for example, heard from an acquaintance on 15 September that the Germans had occupied the town of Pushkin, she was deeply troubled, writing in her diary only, "What a disgrace! What anguish!"[24] From the moment the suburbs were occupied until the time they were liberated in January 1944, Leningrad's cultural community worried about the fate of the famous palaces and parks. During the two-and-a-half-year occupation of the suburbs, very scant information about the state of the palaces and parks reached the city,[25] and rumors began to circulate that the Germans had completely wiped them off the face of the earth. "Detskoe Selo [Pushkin] no longer exists," wrote Ostroumova-Lebedeva on 20 September 1941. "It burned and the train station was blown up."[26] Although she later learned that the situation *at that point* was not as bad as she had heard, such fears were gradually confirmed as the war progressed. In March 1942, art historian Anna Petrovna Chubova wrote to friends on the "mainland" (a term Leningraders used for the Soviet Union beyond the German ring around the city), noting that she was "unable to write calmly about the destruction of our poor palaces."[27] The palaces and parks of the suburbs were sites of strong sentimental value to many Leningraders, and the idea that the invading forces had destroyed them was difficult to bear.

News from soldiers on the Leningrad front was particularly disheartening. The future author and blockade chronicler Daniil Granin, who was stationed in Pushkin before the occupation, had the opportunity to observe the palaces from a vantage point between the suburb and the city. "Through binoculars," he wrote, "one could see how the palace had turned black and was going to ruins.... One day a fire started in the palace. We watched as the black column of smoke rose into the frosty air."[28] Two years later, on the other side of the city, the British war correspondent Alexander Werth spoke with a Red Army captain while peering out over a lookout post. Gesturing in the direction of Peterhof, the captain told him about the condition of the monuments in that suburb, noting that "the palace is burned; the park destroyed, the fountains either sent as scrap to Germany, or mixed up with the earth. I was there not long ago. It's a horrible sight."[29] Soon the country as a whole was to learn of the palace's fate, as the press published a photo of it – confiscated from a German prisoner in 1943 – in ruins.[30]

These stories of devastation in the suburbs were supplemented by accounts in the press of German destruction of cultural-historic monuments in all the occupied areas. Once the Red Army liberated regions from occupation, specialists from the Academy of Architecture published reports of the senseless damage inflicted on the country's built heritage.[31] Accounts of the destruction of New Jerusalem in Istra, Lev Tolstoy's estate at Iasnaia Poliana, the historic monuments in Kalinin, and many other sites made Leningraders expect the worst about the fate of the suburban palaces and parks.[32] With the liberation of the area surrounding Leningrad in mid- to late January 1944, these fears were confirmed: of the grand imperial playgrounds, there was almost nothing left.

ASSESSING THE DESTRUCTION

When the Red Army recaptured the suburbs from the Germans, the extent of the destruction of the palaces and parks became known. While the level of damage suffered by individual monuments in the suburbs differed, in every case the destruction was significant, if not total. Once Soviet sappers had the opportunity to de-mine the palaces, as well as the parks surrounding them, groups of specialists traveled to the suburbs to review the damage and provide the necessary details to the appropriate government departments and the public. "Traces of war and death," as Baranov noted, were everywhere in the once lively suburbs.[33] One could walk for hours, observed the director of the Peterhof palace-park complex, and find only "despondent, lifeless places marked with destruction and theft."[34] "We knew that the Hitlerites plundered and maimed a great deal," wrote Anna Zelenova, director of the Pavlovsk Palace, "but what we had occasion to see after the banishment of the fascist invaders from Petrodvorets, Gatchina, Pushkin, and Pavlovsk, exceeded our worst expectations."[35] The destruction became the subject of numerous accounts in the press, all of which presented the damage as a deliberate act of barbarism meant to erase Russian culture, memory, and identity.

Of all the destruction reviewed in the weeks following the liberation of the suburbs, that suffered by the grand palaces provided the clearest example of attacks against Russian heritage. The Germans had ransacked the palaces and parks and stolen whatever valuables they could. They had shipped furniture, paintings, statues, and all other valuable moveable property back to Germany.[36] In perhaps the most famous example of this kind of theft, the Amber Room in the Catherine Palace in Pushkin was stripped bare.[37] Although the room has recently been reconstructed, the fate of the stolen amber walls is still the subject of considerable debate and research.[38]

The Alexander Palace in Pushkin suffered the least amount of damage out of the five major suburban palaces that were occupied. The neighboring Catherine Palace, however, was ravaged. When specialists arrived in Pushkin to review its condition, they found a ghost of the former tsarist residence. Shells, bullets, and fire had severely damaged the facades.[39] The artistic valuables of the interiors, such as the parquet floors, which the occupiers had not stolen and taken back to Germany, had been used as fuel for warmth.[40] Due to a fire that the Germans set in the first days of the occupation, much of the palace's decoration was destroyed, and the building itself stood without a roof over a large part of it for more than two years. "All that was preserved by the great roof of the palace disappeared," wrote the author Konstantin Fedin, "as did the roof itself."[41] Indeed, the damage to the palace made it very difficult for people to see its former magnificence. The city's chief architect likened the shell of the palace to a "skeleton," as did Fedin, who noted that the semicircular wings of the palace reminded him of "the curved arms of a skeleton, still hugging the parade courtyard."[42] What had once been an architectural "fairy tale" was reduced to a "mournful, devastated cemetery of architecture, painting, and sculpture covered in snow."[43] But the Catherine Palace escaped the full extent of the damage planned for it. When the Germans were forced to retreat, they placed eleven high-explosive bombs of up to three tons in the basement with the aim of annihilating this symbol of Russian culture and history. Soviet troops found and disarmed them before they could explode.[44]

Much the same was encountered in the other suburbs occupied by the Germans. In Pavlovsk, the occupying forces set fire to the palace just as the town was liberated, resulting in an inferno which lasted for five days. As a result of the occupation and fire, the palace was left without a roof, many of its interiors were destroyed, and the frescoes and details decorating the monument since the beginning of the nineteenth century were badly damaged.[45] In a similar act of iconoclasm, the Germans set fire to the palace in Gatchina before being driven out by the Red Army. According to reports, they doused the interiors with gasoline and set the palace ablaze as they left.[46] When the first group of museum workers came to review the palace on 1 February, from far off it appeared as if it remained in decent shape. When they approached it, however, they realized that the destruction was near total.[47] Not long after the fire, the palace was visited by Fedin, who described the damage. Standing on one of the palace's towers, looking over its layout, he observed how "inside the walls, where all the valuable contents of the historic palace were, my eye could find nothing except chaotic mounds of metal rubbish, bent steel rails, and stone fragments."[48]

Of all the monuments of Russian imperial power in the suburbs of Leningrad, the worst damage was inflicted upon the Great Palace of Peterhof. Standing atop a cascade of fountains, looking out over the Lower Park and the Gulf of Finland, this palace was the preeminent symbol of Petrine Russia. When the Germans captured Peterhof, shelling caused the Great Palace to catch on fire. Museum workers who had not managed to leave the suburb witnessed the catastrophe and were forced at gunpoint to watch as it burned. They pleaded with the Germans to let them extinguish the fire, explaining the historical significance of the palace, but "they would not allow it," said one of the workers. "We cried."[49] Not only did the Germans let the palace burn, but they also blew up its central section and part of the cascade of fountains in front of it – both to desecrate this embodiment of Russian culture and to fortify their position against Soviet tanks.[50] A report in the central press about Peterhof after its liberation noted that "the Peterhof Palace is destroyed, burned. This sight is so cruel, so terrible, that at first it seems unreal. Only deformed cells of walls with gaping windows look onto the seaside."[51] The parks, pavilions, and smaller palaces of the suburbs fared no better.

Discussions of destruction in the suburbs of Leningrad emphasized the historic importance of these places, as well as their role in narrating the country's past. Particularly important in this respect was the notion that historic monuments could tell the history of modern Russia.[52] A newspaper article written on the day that Leningrad was liberated proclaimed that the suburbs "were always connected to the history of the motherland by the Russian people. . . . There were many monuments of antiquity here, through which one could visually follow the history of the state for more than two hundred years."[53] The report of the Extraordinary State Commission for the Establishment and Investigation of the Crimes of the German-Fascist Invaders and their Accomplices echoed this notion that monuments were stone texts of the country's past. Before detailing the damage done to the suburbs, the report outlined the history of the palaces and parks, noting that they embodied the history of modern Russia. Peterhof, for example, is a symbol of Peter's maritime reorientation of the country and the defeat of the Swedes in the Great Northern War. The monuments in Pushkin, likewise, "are tightly connected to several important events in the history of Russia," including the victory over the Turks in 1770.[54] The presentation of destruction, therefore, was almost always prefaced by a discussion of the historical significance of the monument in question.

The palaces may not have represented the most positive aspects of Russia's past, but they nevertheless served as windows through which the past could be seen and experienced. The Gatchina Palace, for example, was one of the favorite residences of the Romanovs during the "most gloomy period" of the dynasty, the nineteenth century. "No other emperor's palace contained so much autocratic essence of the Russian monarchy," wrote Fedin, "and for that reason, the Gatchina castle was an irreplaceable material monument of our history."[55] The fact that the palaces played such an important role in the country's culture and heritage made their destruction particularly alarming. As a Red Army captain observed while discussing the loss of the country's heritage with a British journalist, "You cannot imagine with what reverence our young people tiptoed along the parquet floors of the [Great Peterhof] palace.... There was no reverence for the wicked old Tsars in this tiptoeing. But there was reverence for this great piece of our national heritage. It belonged to us, to our culture, don't you see, and now, now there's nothing but rubble; and it's the same everywhere."[56] The author Nikolai Tikhonov also commented on the attack on Russian history in Peterhof by writing, "That living piece of our history is dead, it has been killed."[57]

It was clear that the damage in the suburbs of Leningrad had not resulted from unavoidable military actions, but had been deliberately inflicted by the Germans over the entire course of the occupation. Vandalism, destruction, and theft were "intrinsic elements" of German operations, all of which had the goal of erasing the culture of the enemy.[58] The authorities quickly circulated accounts of this deliberate damage to the Soviet people, and used the exposés to publicly prosecute the Germans for their crimes against Russian heritage, mobilize hatred for the enemy, and demonstrate a higher level of culture (or love for culture) in the Soviet Union.[59] This use of cultural destruction for the purposes of propaganda, writes historian Nicola Lambourne, was a practice used by all belligerents during the Second World War, employed by states to both manipulate feelings and mobilize the population: "Each side encouraged hatred of the enemy by characterizing the other as barbarians, not destroying architecture thoughtlessly and accidentally, but rather intentionally and systematically."[60]

By presenting the Germans' actions in the suburbs as deliberate acts employed to erase Russian history and culture, the Soviet authorities invested the palaces and parks with a deeper significance.[61] The monuments were no longer just symbols of the imperial past; rather, they were now wartime targets that stood as examples of German barbarity. The understanding of historic monuments changed throughout Europe during the Second World War, argues Lambourne. They came to mean something different, "whether it was an exaggerated or jingoistic version of their earlier significance or a new revised version, taking account of bomb damage."[62] Historian Adrian Bantjes contends that iconoclasm and deliberate destruction rarely achieve their purpose of relegating an image to oblivion. "Far from annihilating the icon," he writes, "[iconoclasm] actually can have a 'positive' impact, transforming instead of obliterating the object and its meaning(s)."[63] The meaning of the suburbs had indeed been altered to reflect the suffering and destruction of the war. No longer could people visit, talk about, or think of the palaces and parks without recalling the cruel acts that the Germans committed against them.

Given the important position that the palaces occupied in the Russian and Soviet historical imagination, reports of their destruction called forth a corresponding level of hatred for the Germans.[64] "We will avenge you, Peterhof!" and "The Stones of Peterhof Call for Revenge," cried newspaper articles, promising that the loss of the magnificent examples of Russian architecture would not go unpunished.[65] Implicit in these calls for vengeance was a desire to resurrect that which had been destroyed during the war.[66] The author of one article, for example, proclaimed, "We will restore all that the German barbarians destroyed, and the new Peterhof will shine with the light of victory, in which our past will merge with our great future."[67] Many other articles and reports in the press stressed the future restoration of the suburban palace-park complexes. "In spite of the enormous mutilations . . . ," stated one report, "they will be restored."[68]

WHAT TO DO WITH THE RUINS?

Although the press optimistically called for the restoration of the suburban palaces, the level of destruction and the conditions faced by the country as a whole made it seem that restoration would be difficult, if not impossible. Some people felt that it would be best to leave the ruins as a monument to the events experienced by the country during the Great Patriotic War. The Soviet writer and war correspondent Il'ia Ehrenburg, for example, wrote that "the external appearance of the palace in Pushkin can perhaps be preserved, but the palace in Peterhof is incurable [*neizlechim*]; it would be best to leave it as magnificent ruins, like the ruins of the Acropolis, reminding future generations of architectural genius and the barbarity of the fascists."[69] The war correspondent Harrison Salisbury agreed and noted that most of the surviving Leningrad intelligentsia felt the same way.[70] There is also evidence to suggest that when some members of the local and central authorities viewed the palaces immediately after they were liberated, they felt that the palaces could not be restored.[71]

Although there were some voices that did not call for restoration, the country's preservationists did.[72] Many believed that if they did not work at restoring the suburban palaces and parks, they "would be unworthy sons of the motherland and our beautiful city!"[73] The preservationist V. K. Makarov, for example, in his "Appeal about the Restoration of Leningrad's Suburbs" addressed to the artistic workers of the city, wrote, "Future generations will not forgive us if we – people who have known, seen, and felt the cultural heritage of the Great Motherland that is now in danger – do not take all measures to restore the artistic monuments of Peterhof, Pushkin, Pavlovsk, and Gatchina."[74]

This task, however, would not be easy, for there were a number of problems facing the planners and authorities in the first months after the war. Even if it was possible, how much should be restored? What would the palaces be used for? Where should the process begin? These questions and others plagued the authorities and preservationists alike. What would eventually become of the suburbs resulted from the debates and discussions of this period, as well as the persistence and tenacity of preservationists, who could not bear to accept the loss of such important historic and cultural monuments.

The fate of the suburbs was a question that concerned many people. The most insistent voice for restoration came from the preservationist community in Leningrad, especially from the staff of the suburban palace-museums, the city's architects and artists, and GIOP. Belekhov insisted immediately after the suburbs were liberated that restoration was possible, and began petitioning the authorities in Moscow and Leningrad to provide for the conservation of the palaces before restoration could begin.[75] In addition, a series of meetings was held to decide what exactly should be done with the "skeletons" in the towns surrounding Leningrad. On 18 February, one such meeting was held in the Leningrad House of Architects, the main speaker at which was Belekhov. At the meeting the "infamy" of the Germans was stressed as speakers called for the mobilization of the public for restoration.[76] F. F. Oleinik, a young preservationist fighting on the Leningrad front, attended the meeting and voiced his opinion about the need to restore. He argued that leaving the palaces in ruins as "monuments to fascism" was unacceptable. "Beauty was created here," exclaimed Oleinik, "and the loss of this beauty makes all humanity feel poorer. We must reconstruct it. Our beautiful palaces are wounded, they are waiting for us."[77] Another participant in this meeting, M. Tikhomirova (the chief curator of the Peterhof Palace-Museum), noted that all in attendance felt this way and expressed their desire and enthusiasm to see the palaces and parks restored. The level of damage, however, made it clear that priorities must be set and compromises made. Restoration would not be complete, but rather would have to be carried out "to various degrees."[78] Those attending the meeting agreed that a special commission of preservation experts should be convened to assess the damage and discuss the possibility of restoration.[79]

On 21 and 22 March, GIOP convened another meeting of preservationists and museum workers to discuss the commission's findings and set goals for the restoration of the palaces. Discussions focused on the theme of Russian culture and its loss. Professor A. P. Udalenkov, an important figure in Leningrad's restoration, made the point that cultures need landmarks from which to grow, and that the suburban palaces were just such landmarks. Due to their significance to Russian culture, he argued, they must be restored: "We cannot say that these two centuries [the eighteenth and nineteenth] do not interest us and that we can pass them by. I suggest that we are obliged to preserve, to the best of our abilities, all that remains, to strain all of our energy, our minds, in order to search out genuine documentation for the restoration of all that was lost."[80] These restored palaces, noted many in attendance, should be used as museum premises which would reflect the history of imperial Russia. Peterhof's palace, for example, would be the home of an exhibition about the Petrine period. The Pavlovsk Palace, participants suggested, could be a museum reflecting the end of the eighteenth and beginning of the nineteenth centuries (the periods of Paul, Alexander I, and Nicholas I). The Catherine Palace in Pushkin, they argued, must be used as a museum of Russian art of the post-Petrine era. In Gatchina, the palace should become a museum of "Russian glory."[81] Even though the Germans had attempted to erase the history embodied in these monuments, Leningrad's cultural activists were determined to rescue the history of the nation from oblivion and present it to Soviet citizens in restored historic sites. The central parts of the palaces, therefore, should be restored to their original historic appearance and used for these purposes.[82]

The participants of the conference also emphasized restoring the palaces and parks as places of rest and recreation. After years of war and deprivation, citizens wanted an easier life.[83] The authorities, for their part, were interested in cultivating a healthy, cultured citizenry.[84] In Leningrad this struck a special chord, given the disastrous effects of the war and the blockade on the health and morale of the population.[85] The municipal authorities were intent on providing the people of the city the opportunity to enjoy their free time and recuperate in healthy surroundings.[86] With this in mind, the majority of conference participants agreed that those parts of the palaces and parks which were too badly damaged to repair immediately, or had never before been used as museum premises, were to be employed for such "contemporary needs." Much of the space on the first floor of the Peterhof and Catherine Palaces, for example, was to serve the needs of the people visiting the parks and museums on the upper floors.[87] The director of the Pavlovsk Palace, Anna Zelenova, proposed that its wings could be used as houses of rest. She also suggested that certain areas of the park be used for sport, including tennis courts which could be constructed on the "grave of Fritzes."[88] Not everyone agreed with this proposal, however. S. N. Balaeva, the chief curator at Gatchina, argued that the parks should not be used for sport because, as she stated, one could "freely play in other places. We must care not only for the present, but also the future. . . . We must not forget that we are preserving monuments of an epoch."[89] In spite of such protests, as the plans for restoration of the suburbs developed over the next year, a great deal of emphasis was placed on the use of the suburban parks and palaces as places of culture and rest for the people of Leningrad.

The arguments for restoring the palaces did not simply stem from the desire of cultural enthusiasts to see Leningrad's landscape and history restored, although this certainly played a key role. Preservationists felt that restoration was in fact possible. Even though destruction had been thorough, specialists argued that enough fragments and documentation remained to allow for accurate restorative work, and not just clumsy replicas of that which had been destroyed.[90] In Pavlovsk, for example, all the halls could "easily be restored" because, in spite of the fire that lasted a number of days, much of the molded adornment remained on the walls. A great deal was damaged, but according to reports, "the appearance of the rooms was not lost."[91]

Other than the decorations that remained, plans, drawings, blueprints, measurements, and photos existed that would facilitate the restoration process.[92] The collection of these materials had begun even before the suburbs were liberated. In August 1942, for example, the Committee for the Registration and Preservation of Monuments of Art had instructed the Leningrad Administration for Artistic Affairs to begin collecting materials that had been removed from the suburbs for future work on the palaces. This work continued throughout the war and facilitated conservation and restoration in the suburbs after they were liberated.[93] In April 1944, the Leningrad authorities circulated orders for all museum property and decoration in the suburbs to be collected to aid the process of conservation and restoration.[94] Furthermore, the evacuation of museum property and valuables during the war proved to be indispensable. Because so much had been kept out of harm's way, the possibilities for historically accurate restoration were greatly increased.

The idea of restoring the palaces to their original appearance for use as museum premises was supported by a special commission of experts sent from Moscow to review the ruins in May 1944. The commission was composed of representatives from the Committee for Architectural Affairs and the Committee for Artistic Affairs. "After attentively reviewing the damage," stated the chairman of the Committee for Architectural Affairs, Arkady Mordvinov, "we came to the conclusion that we can restore these magnificent works of architecture of our motherland in all their former brilliance and greatness."[95] Needless to say, this conclusion of Moscow-based experts gave added impetus to the movement for complete restoration of the suburban parks and palaces. By the summer of 1944, for example, more than thirty thousand rubles had been donated unsolicitedly to the cause of restoring the suburban monuments.[96]

Restoration, however, soon came up against a powerful opponent. At the April 1944 Leningrad party plenum, party leader A. A. Zhdanov discussed the State Defense Committee's designs for the suburbs of Leningrad. Rather than expressing enthusiasm for the restoration of historic monuments as museums, he announced that the suburbs would merely be used as places of rest. He noted that the suburbs and their monuments had "fallen into the death zone, and had experienced the greatest destruction and barbarity of the enemy." In calling for the restoration of suburbs as places of rest, he singled out Peterhof and Pavlovsk because their parks were preserved better than others.[97] Nothing was mentioned about the restoration of the palaces.

It became clear in the middle of June that in his capacity as the Leningrad party first secretary, Zhdanov would not support draft resolutions to the central government from the city soviet calling for the restoration of suburban palace-museums. Rather, he reaffirmed the State Defense Committee's decision to restore the parks in the suburbs without restoration of the palaces. It seems likely that Zhdanov was unwilling to put himself on the line by contradicting the orders set down by the State Defense Committee. It is also quite possible that the image of the palaces in ruins made him believe that they could never be restored, in spite of the commission's recommendation.[98]

The idea that the palaces might never be restored sent many members of the Soviet Union's cultural community into a state of panic. Immediately, Belekhov dispatched several letters to "allies" in Moscow to try to get Zhdanov's decision overturned. For the advocates of restoration, the idea of simply providing places of rest without cultural establishments was problematic. In making their case for the restoration of the palaces, they argued that places of rest needed museums and exhibitions to entertain and provide "recreational learning" [*poznavatel'nyi otdykh*] to the laborers of Leningrad.[99] The restored palaces and pavilions, and the exhibits to be held in them, would perform that function.

The proponents of restoration emphasized the fact that a commission of experts had proclaimed that the suburbs could indeed be restored to their former appearance. Zhdanov's callous attitude toward Leningrad's monuments of history was "especially offensive" given that it was "technically absolutely possible" to resurrect the beloved palaces.[100] Invoking precedents for restoration of palaces on a large scale, Belekhov pointed to the fact that some of the suburban palaces had burned and been restored in the past. He went on to discuss examples from the West, where historic monuments had been restored at various points throughout history. If these palaces in imperial Russia and in Western countries could be restored, went the argument, certainly monuments of history in the Soviet Union could be raised from the ashes.[101]

The advocates of restoration pleaded for preservationists in Moscow to organize public opinion among the leaders of "society" to support their cause. Several prominent people, including the author Alexei Tolstoi, members of the Moscow Theater of Arts, a number of academics, and Metropolitan Nikolai, had already "promised their participation in the battle for the restoration of the suburbs."[102] Belekhov asked the preservationists in Moscow to press the chairmen of the Committees for Architectural Affairs (Mordvinov) and Artistic Affairs (Khrapchenko) to present the Soviet government with projects for restoring the suburbs. "The fate of one of the most magnificent pages in the history of the culture of our country," wrote Belekhov to A. I. Shchusev (a member of the commission which recommended the restoration of the palaces), "depends on how comrades Mordvinov and Khrapchenko will respond."[103]

Although the details of exactly how the projects for restoration finally were approved are unclear, what is certain is that Khrapchenko and Mordvinov advocated for the restoration of both the suburban palaces and the parks. They headed up the commission of experts which concluded that restoration was possible and desirable, and they continued to call for measures to be taken to protect, preserve, and restore what remained after the liberation.[104] Discussions also continued to take place in the Leningrad soviet about the need to restore. One of the leading figures in the palaces' restoration, A. M. Kuchumov, noted that several meetings about the suburbs were held at Baranov's office in May and June. Those in attendance supported the Moscow commission's decision to restore the palaces, as well as the outcome of the March conference, which called for historic museums to be located in them.[105] Even Stalin himself appears to have become involved. Belekhov forwarded information to him demonstrating the feasibility of restoration and asked for assistance.[106] Makarov recorded in his diary that at the end of May 1944, the prominent cultural activist I. E. Grabar' had approached him to take a leading role in restoration. According to Makarov, Grabar' had a copy of a decree from Stalin stating that the palaces were to be restored and that funding would be allotted. "In the past few days," he wrote, "one senses a great breakthrough in the relationship to the suburban palaces."[107] In the end, the persistence of Leningrad's preservationists in having the State Defense Committee's decision overturned met with success.

What eventually evolved out of these discussions and disputes was a mixture of historic restoration and cultural work aimed at providing the laborers of Leningrad with places of rest. Control over the palaces and parks themselves, for example, was transferred from the Leningrad Administration for Artistic Affairs to the newly created Department of Cultural-Enlightenment Work of the Leningrad city soviet.[108] The restoration of the suburban palaces and parks was "one of the main, and most difficult, goals" of the department's Five-Year Plan.[109] The Leningrad authorities called for partial restoration of the Catherine and Alexander Palaces in Pushkin, the Pavlovsk Palace, and several of the smaller palaces and pavilions in all suburbs by 1950. The Great Palace in Peterhof was to have its exterior restored to complement the fountain and park ensemble.[110] The Gatchina Palace, however, was not slated for restoration during this period because of the level of destruction and the lack of authentic detail remaining to facilitate the process. "The restoration of the suburbs and their cultural-historic valuables," announced the press, "is a testimony to the exceptional care of the Soviet government for monuments of culture, as well as for the rest and relaxation of laborers."[111] It was also a testament to the determination of preservationists and the influence they had in ensuring that these historic monuments be restored, in spite of opposing voices.

RESTORATION

Once given the opportunity to begin restoration, the country's preservationists approached the task with the Bolshevik mindset of storming a fortress. The planners in the Department of Cultural-Enlightenment Work and at GIOP believed that the palaces could be raised from the ruins in just a few years. Leningrad's restoration practice in the period immediately after the war was oriented, like many Soviet projects, toward the complete restoration of destroyed monuments.[112] The process in the suburbs, however, would prove to be frustrating, chaotic, poorly supplied, underfunded, and ever-changing. Several "advances" were made in the "battle for restoration" during the period under discussion, but much more work remained to be done in the years following the first postwar Five-Year Plan.

The first stage of restoration involved conserving what was left of the monuments as quickly as possible to prevent further damage from the elements. While the disputes, disagreements, and discussions continued about what to do with the palaces and parks, efforts to clear the rubble, perform landscaping, collect valuable decorative fragments, and preserve the ruins had begun. Ia. I. Shurygin, the director of the Peterhof palace, noted that museum workers, recognizing how much money would be needed for restoration, believed that it was "necessary to take care of all that managed to be preserved during the war and resurrect it after victory."[113] In April 1944, the city soviet circulated orders to immediately begin conserving the palaces and bring the surrounding areas, including the parks, into "elementary order." Museum workers were ordered to estimate the amount of construction work needed and submit plans to the Leningrad city soviet no later than June of that year.[114] Conservation was slated to continue until the end of 1945. According to the postwar plan, by that time all artistic detail was to be protected by constructing roofs over the palaces and sealing off window openings and doorframes, and the parks were to be opened to the public.[115]

With the onset of spring in 1944, many of the city's workers were sent to the suburban parks to help preserve what remained of them. The authorities had no illusions about restoring the parks by the summer of 1944, but they were intent on having them in order and open to the public in the spring of 1945. During the summer of 1944, for example, Leningrad authorities assigned one hundred people to the Administration of Palaces and Parks in Pushkin to clear rubble and fallen trees from alleys and open spaces, repair and clear the park's paths, and fill trenches and craters.[116] Similar measures were taken in other parks. Much of the work was done during *voskresniki* – weekend days during which workers were recruited to labor at restoration projects during their time off. Recruited workers were assigned specific days for this additional work. People arrived in the suburbs from all districts of the city on their designated days to bring the parks into order and perform other tasks. "Several times we went to the parks of Pushkin, Pavlovsk, and Petrodvorets [which were] mutilated by the fascists on *voskresniki,*" recalled a former worker at the Kirov factory.[117] During one *voskresnik* in Peterhof on 16 July 1944, for example, 1,368 people took part and managed to perform a great deal of work over the course of the day.[118] In May 1945, the Leningrad soviet obliged the city's *Komsomol* (Communist Youth League) to organize mass *voskresniki* to prepare the Pushkin parks for their opening in June. The soviet also dispatched a thousand soldiers to the parks for seven days to ensure that the work was accomplished.[119] These *voskresniki* proved to be an exceptionally important source of labor during a period when few people were available to work full-time in the suburbs. Without the use of these workers, the conservation and restoration would have been much more difficult and prolonged, if not impossible.[120]

Museum directors were often left to their own devices to carry out the necessary work on both the palaces and parks, and of necessity were forced to be resourceful. Because Pavlovsk was not technically one of Leningrad's districts, for example, it was assigned fewer workers for *voskresniki* than were other suburbs. To overcome this disadvantage, Zelenova, the director of the palace, made agreements with several organizations whereby, in return for preservation work, the organizations received all the deadwood that they cleared from the parks to use for fuel.[121] The director of the Peterhof Palace made a similar agreement with a military college located nearby.[122] He also found other means to accomplish his goals when the regular channels proved insufficient. A few days before the opening in 1945, for example, city authorities reviewed the state of the park and declared that much more work needed to be done before it could be opened to the public. Short of labor, Shurygin turned to a prisoner-of-war camp located not far from the palace for assistance. During the evening and night of 20 June 1945, two hundred German prisoners labored to bring the park into order.[123]

Initiatives like these, as well as the mobilization of the city's population on their days off, allowed for much work to be done at a very low cost. In addition, the authorities were able to draw on a large pool of workers because much of the work was unskilled. As a result, more and more work was successfully completed every year in the suburban parks, and the prospect of seeing them restored to their prewar appearance by 1950 became a real possibility.[124]

The suburbs' historic monuments, however, proved to be much more troublesome. From the very beginning, restoration was plagued with problems. Indeed, most of Leningrad's construction agencies were occupied with rebuilding and restoration projects in the city center, and the city as a whole suffered from a shortage of skilled labor.[125] As a result, under pressure from preservationists, local officials reached out to state institutions to facilitate the conservation and restoration process. In June 1944, for example, the chairman of the city soviet, P. S. Popkov, wrote the commander of the Leningrad front, Marshal L. A. Govorov, to request that the Military-Construction Administration help in building roofs over the palaces in order to protect what remained.[126] Govorov, according to Baranov, had earlier promised to provide any help necessary in the restoration of Leningrad's historic monuments.[127] An agreement was made about the measures to be taken to preserve the palaces, but more than a month later, the work had not begun because of the lack of an available labor force.[128]

With the fall quickly approaching, the preservationists turned to the People's Commissariat for Internal Affairs (NKVD) for assistance. Emphasizing the importance of the palaces to "our national pride," and the need to "preserve the artistic treasures for the culture of the peoples of the Soviet Union," Belekhov petitioned the head of the country's security apparatus, L. P. Beria, for one thousand German POWs to work at conservation. This, according to Belekhov, "is our last hope to carry out the emergency work needed for preserving the palace-museums during the fall and winter."[129] Much to the disappointment of the Leningrad authorities, this request was denied because the NKVD could not spare the security staff needed to guard the prisoners.[130]

Not all requests, however, were turned down. In late 1944 and the beginning of 1945, the Leningrad city soviet and party committee petitioned the State Administration for Aviation Construction of the NKVD to take on the responsibility for preserving the Pavlovsk Palace from further destruction. An agreement was reached which stipulated that the organization was to restore the roof over the palace and carry out other more specialized construction activities.[131] German POWs were also used in Pavlovsk, despite Beria's original refusal. Until at least May 1947, 180 prisoners carried out conservation and restoration work at the palace.[132] The palaces of Pushkin and Peterhof were also provided with construction organizations to facilitate their preservation.[133] "Armed" with skilled workers, it seemed as if the "battle" to bring history back to life could begin.

Conservation and restoration, however, were mired in other problems. Even when Leningrad's authorities provided workers and construction agencies, they were unable to work because they had nothing to work with. The massive restoration projects taking place in the city and throughout the country meant that resources for construction were very slim. The construction organizations in Pushkin and Peterhof, for example, complained that they were not allocated the necessary materials to do the conservation work assigned to them. "The Sixth Trust could provide an additional 50–60 people for the restoration of the roofs on the Catherine and Alexander palaces," noted its head engineer, "but because of the absence of round and sawed lumber, nothing can be done."[134]

The problem with materials was acute for the first years after the liberation of the suburbs. At each location the lack of metal, wood, and other materials necessary for conservation and restoration prevented meaningful work from being accomplished. At a meeting of the directors of the suburban palace-museums in May 1945, the problem with material supply was reviewed. The director of the Pavlovsk Palace, Zelenova, noted that the NKVD organization working there did not even have enough material to construct scaffolding. "Three hundred workers are here in Pavlovsk," she exclaimed, "highly qualified, forged, real roof workers, real carpenters, plasterers, bricklayers, and stove-setters. Three hundred people sit without work and nobody will allow me to hold them any longer." Zelenova was forced to give the workers menial tasks to keep them occupied so that they would not be taken away and included in work at other places in the city.[135] To make matters worse, a representative from the Central Committee for Cultural-Enlightenment Establishments in Moscow made it clear that, at least for the near future, Leningrad could not count on a supply of materials. Because of this lack of materials, the palaces in Pushkin, Pavlovsk, and Peterhof had three construction organizations working at 35 percent of their capacity.[136] The supply of construction materials gradually increased as the industries producing them were restored, but the problem continued to hinder restoration throughout the period.[137]

Nevertheless, just as in the city center, the situation in the suburbs continued to improve as postwar life slowly began to return to normalcy;[138] and with the announcement of the Five-Year Plan in 1946, the prospects for the monuments and parks began to look much better, at least for the foreseeable future. The plan allotted twenty-seven million rubles for restoration. This amount was clearly insufficient for complete restoration, but it would allow for the beginnings of conservation and restoration in the immediate postwar period.[139] After the first couple of years of mixed results, it now seemed as if restoration was possible. Although problems continued to hamper the efforts, and the goal of complete restoration by 1950 was soon dropped, a significant amount of restoration work was completed.

In the face of massive shortages and problems, those tasks which were performed successfully were symbolically important. As each year went by, the directors of the suburban museum complexes could claim more and more "advances on the restoration front." Particularly important in this respect was the restoration of the fountain system in Peterhof. Planners argued that the fountains of the upper and lower gardens would decide the fate of the entire palace-park complex, and therefore devoted tremendous resources to their restoration.[140] With the fountains in working order, there was a better chance of having the facades of the Great Palace restored because without them, it was argued, the palace-park ensemble would not be complete.[141] Although the process of restoring the entire hydraulic system took the best part of the postwar Five-Year Plan, the Great Cascade and the fountains lining the alley leading to the Gulf of Finland were restored by the end of the summer of 1947.

Progress was made in the other suburbs as well. In Pushkin, the famous Cameron Gallery of the Catherine Palace was restored in 1948 by LARM, and was again used as an exhibition hall. Other rooms of the Catherine Palace had also been brought back into order and were used for exhibits as well. In fact, by 1950 a total of twenty-six halls in the palace were used for exhibits.[142] In Pavlovsk, the restorers had made significant advances in the three years since the end of the war. They had repaired much of the structural elements of the monument, and had begun to work on the decorations in its halls.[143] The press noted that "among those who are raising the riches of Leningrad's suburbs from ruins, the restorers of Pavlovsk are in first place."[144] As a result of significant progress in restoration, the city soviet awarded the suburbs extra funding that was taken from other city projects, including housing, to help out the process. In September 1947, for example, 3.4 million rubles was allocated in varying amounts to the suburbs, followed a year later by an additional 1.5 million rubles. The funds were taken from other places in the city, including a construction project of a residential building on Moscow Highway (*Moskovskoe shosse*).[145]

By the middle of 1948, however, the prospects again began to look much bleaker. Funding was the main problem. Although the Leningrad authorities were active in petitioning Moscow to increase funds, there was simply no way to come up with the vast amount of money needed to get all the work done during the first postwar Five-Year Plan. Indeed, by 1948 the funding allocated for the restoration of the suburban palaces and parks had been exhausted.[146] At a meeting to discuss the restoration of the palaces and parks in Pushkin, for example, a district party representative commented that the museum workers "have huge appetites, they want to restore the old museum, they see it in their dreams, but they do not have the wherewithal to achieve it [*a vozmozhnosti u nikh drugie*]."[147]

The municipal and central authorities attempted to alleviate the funding problems throughout the period. Because the funds for the plan had run out in 1948, the Central Committee for Cultural-Enlightenment Establishments in Moscow stepped in to provide support. In the interests of seeing work continue, it allocated funding from the first year of the next Five-Year Plan to the Catherine and Pavlovsk Palaces.[148] Orders to carry out certain projects also came from Stalin and Molotov. In 1948 the Leningrad party committee and soviet petitioned the central government to pass a decree ordering the restoration of the Great Palace in Peterhof as an architectural-historic monument.[149] Moscow agreed wholeheartedly with the requests and decreed that the facades as well as several of the palace's rooms and halls and its parade staircase be restored to their former appearance by 1950.[150]

Although official sanction for the restoration of the Great Palace suggested a moment of victory, that victory proved illusory as funding shortages continued into the 1950s. Only 1 million rubles was allocated for work on *all* of the suburbs in 1949, when officials estimated that 6.3 million was needed to do the assigned work on the Great Palace in that year alone.[151] In spite of all efforts to have the palaces restored by the end of the first postwar Five-Year Plan, by 1950 workers had not even begun to restore the Great Palace in Peterhof, and the Catherine Palace in Pushkin stood without a roof over much of the building.[152] Out of all the palaces that were severely damaged during the war, only Pavlovsk's could claim to have completed conservation and moved on to full-scale restoration on the interiors.

EXHIBITING THE IMPERIAL PAST, WARTIME DESTRUCTION, AND POSTWAR RESTORATION

During this period of mixed results in restoration, the commitment to providing cultured places of rest and "recreational learning" never waned. The authorities invited the public to visit the suburbs, marvel at the work being done to breathe life back into the parks and monuments, and enjoy their days off in a healthy, relaxing environment. In addition, the Department for Cultural-Enlightenment Work used the ruined monuments undergoing restoration to promote narratives which sought to bolster Soviet patriotism and instill Soviet values, including respect for cultural heritage, pride in Soviet victory, and a belief in the state's ability to restore the country.

Throughout the postwar period several cultural events were held by the authorities to introduce Soviet citizens to the history embodied in the suburban monuments. As soon as parks opened in June 1945, excursions and exhibits began with the aim of narrating the history of the suburbs and presenting an ideal version of Russia's past and present. The cultural activities summoned up memories of great leaders (Peter I, Catherine II, Alexander I) as well as famous cultural figures, such as Alexander Pushkin, who was closely connected to the historic monuments in the town bearing his name.[153] Many events focused on the military victories of the imperial state throughout the eighteenth and nineteenth centuries.[154] Excursions to Peterhof, for example, presented the complex as a monument to the victory over the Swedes in the Great Northern War. In Pushkin an exhibit was devoted to the victory over the Turks at Chesme under Catherine the Great. In Gatchina exhibits devoted to the history of Russian arms reflected the might of the Russian military under the leadership of Alexander I.

The aim of all of the exhibits and excursions on the history of the suburbs was to teach visitors about their past and stimulate pride in their heritage. The instructions for guides leading excursions through the exhibit "Chesme Victory" in Pushkin, for example, highlighted the connection between past and present. The three main goals for guides were as follows:

> 1. Using works of art, show to the fullest possible extent one of the glorious victories of our fleet – the Chesme Battle.
> 2. Point out the sublime models of heroism and courage of the Russian sailors who secured this exceptional victory and added one of the brightest pages into the chronicle of our glory for the whole world to see.
> 3. Point out the connection between the heroic traditions of the former Russian fleet and the traditions of Soviet sailors, having emphasized that Soviet sailors piously preserve these traditions, are brought up on the fighting experience of our fleet's past, and are entering new pages into the book of Russian glory.[155]

In stressing the link between the "glory" of the past and the present, guides sought to strengthen the people's awareness of a long lineage of warriors fighting valiantly for their country. The exhibit took advantage of the monuments in Catherine's Park, many of which spoke to the "glory of Russian arms," including the Chesme Column, erected in 1778 to mark the "brilliant victory" over the Turks in Catherine's first Turkish War.[156]

During their visits, people were invited to relive history as they walked from monument to monument, or exhibit to exhibit. One of the most interesting aspects of these events is that they called upon visitors to experience the country's past through the lens of war and destruction. In narrating the history of the suburbs, guides and museum workers used the ruins of monuments to underline the significance of the war and its impact on the Soviet Union. According to the director of the Peterhof Palace and parks, destruction became a major focus of all excursions in the postwar years, and one that was quite popular. To emphasize exactly what had been lost, guides led visitors through the parks, presented destroyed monuments, discussed their historical significance, and displayed images depicting the palaces before the Germans arrived.[157] Similarly, exhibits in all of the suburbs on the history of the palaces included large sections devoted specifically to the destruction.[158] Often the exhibits were held in the partially destroyed eighteenth-century buildings, thereby making the message all the more explicit. An exhibit in the restored sections of the Catherine Palace devoted to its history, for example, included "several items demonstrating the barbarity of the German vandals, who destroyed the magnificent cultural valuables of the Russian people, in particular the Catherine and Alexander palaces."[159] An important theme in the Chesme Victory exhibit, likewise, centered on "the attack on the treasures of the people's soul," which according to the excursion "was an important part of the fascist ideologues' strategy and tactics."[160] Any visit to the suburban palaces and parks, therefore, put the vandalism and iconoclasm of the Germans on display for all to see, while emphasizing the official story of the war against the Soviet people. The narrative of war, then, became a key element in the history of the palaces and parks, an element that was to be remembered and recalled in the postwar years.

The restoration of historic monuments in the suburbs was also the subject of exhibits which celebrated the will to overcome the devastation of the war. A Leningrad academic, P. V. Preis, stressed the need to "imprint the vandalism of fascism" in the restoration of the suburbs. He suggested creating two models of equal size for each of the monuments being restored – one to depict the monument before the destruction, and the other to show it during the restoration.[161] This idea was implemented in a number of exhibits organized in the suburbs so that people could see the destruction caused by the Germans and be impressed by the plans to resurrect these historic sites. Not long after the restoration began in Pavlovsk, for example, an exhibit entitled "Pavlovsk after the German Occupation and the Battle for Its Restoration" was opened on-site.[162] The exhibit entitled "The Restoration of the Palace-Park Complex of Peterhof" displayed several hundred objects, including models of restored fountains and pictures depicting the palaces and parks in ruins.[163] Such exhibits, like the one in the Catherine Palace, it was noted, "present indisputable interest because they convincingly show the results of the creative work of the Soviet people at the restoration of this most valuable monument of Russian culture."[164] The exhibits and excursions glorified the restoration activities and presented them as a victory over the intentional destruction caused by the German "barbarians." They portrayed a victorious Soviet people rescuing their history from oblivion through painstaking, dedicated work. In doing so, they added an extra layer of narrative about the war and blockade into the story of these monuments of Russian culture and heritage. No longer simply relics of Russian history, the suburban palaces became Soviet monuments.

With the end of the postwar Five-Year Plan the dreams of Leningrad's museum workers, cultural activists, architects, and others had only partially come true. Their goal was to ensure that the suburban monuments of the eighteenth century, which embodied the power of imperial Russia, would be restored to the greatest extent possible. They were unwilling to accept the loss of such valuable historic and cultural monuments and fought to have them included in plans for Leningrad's restoration. Their efforts to make certain that restoration was indeed possible proved invaluable, for without their lobbying at the highest state and party levels, the imperial palaces from the eighteenth and nineteenth centuries would likely not have been "resurrected" in the postwar years. The major problem in the restoration of the suburban palace-park complexes, therefore, was not the will to restore. Rather, the economy of the immediate postwar period limited the amount of work that could be done on projects that were not of vital importance. On top of this, the level of damage was so catastrophic that any plans for restoration were bound to face obstacles and difficulties. Although several important projects had been successfully realized, the limited funding available for historic restoration in the suburbs, as well as the continuing problems with materials, proved to be a major hindrance in the first postwar years.

The problems which hampered the restoration of the suburban palaces and parks did not discourage their use as discursive instruments for condemning the devastation caused by the Germans, stressing the importance of national history, and displaying the will to bring history back to life. These monuments, therefore, came to symbolize more than just the imperial past. The discussions in the press about iconoclasm and destruction, as well as the cultural events held in and around partially destroyed palaces, pavilions, and parks, all worked to impress upon people what exactly was lost, how it was lost, and what measures were underway to retrieve it. Even while these monuments were being restored, the state made great efforts to ensure that the memory of the war and blockade would not be erased. During the postwar period, that memory became a central part of the country's historic narrative, and was harnessed by the authorities to promote Soviet patriotism and civic pride.

The activities in the suburbs also had broader implications for understanding the Soviet Union in the postwar period. The narrative focus in the suburban parks and palaces was on the destruction of heritage and history, but it also worked to reinforce the cataclysmic events faced by the Soviet people throughout the country. The destruction here emphasized the magnitude of the "treacherous attack" (*verolomnoe napadenie*) on a people determined to keep the peace, and the common struggle to drive the Germans out of the country. Likewise, the restoration work was representative of a country getting back on its feet and overcoming the destruction of war, in spite of the postwar difficulties. Throughout the country, people were working furiously to restore their communities and homes. The restoration of the palaces and parks, then, was a representation of the people's will to see the country resurrected from the ruins of war. The achievements in the restoration of the suburban palaces and parks thus suggested a powerful Soviet people overcoming seemingly insurmountable obstacles.

FIVE

BECOMING "LENINGRADERS": OFFICIAL COMMEMORATIONS OF THE BLOCKADE

IN THE IMMEDIATE POSTWAR YEARS, SOVIET AUTHORITIES AND citizens sought to preserve the memory of the war and create an image of a self-sacrificing people who heroically withstood the treacherous attack of the "fascist barbarians." Even before the war ended, the press began to valorize the Soviet people and their accomplishments. The leadership commissioned histories of the Great Patriotic War and ordered the collection of materials and documents to chronicle wartime events. Artists submitted proposals for war memorials to competitions organized by the Union of Architects, and central planners sought to reconstruct some of the country's destroyed cities as museum spaces dedicated to the war.[1] In short, throughout the Soviet Union there was a genuine popular desire to celebrate and selectively remember the most devastating conflict in the country's history, which fed into the creation of a state-sponsored myth of the Great Patriotic War.[2]

Leningraders, too, sought to memorialize the war, and plans for commemoration began well before the siege was lifted.[3] The city's party and soviet leadership spearheaded efforts to preserve and shape the memory of the blockade through official publications, commemorative sites, and annual celebrations marking the anniversary of the lifting of the siege on 27 January 1944. Official commemorations and personal recollections of the blockade complemented each other, notes Lisa Kirschenbaum. The official story drew on personal trauma to establish the "emotional authenticity" of the event, while individuals used the state's narrative to "invest their wartime experiences with historic significance."[4] Providing a sanitized view of the blockade, official commemorations of the city's wartime experience emphasized the heroic suffering and steadfast determination of the population: they mythologized Leningrad and the "Leningrader," transforming them into "heroic symbols" whose sacrifices and actions were meant to be emulated.[5]

While commemorations of the blockade were designed to ensure that the "Leningrad epic" would occupy a central place in the overall story of the Great Patriotic War, they were also employed by the state to overcome the destruction of war. Because the restoration of the city – its industry, housing, infrastructure, and historic landscape – was deemed the most pressing issue facing Leningraders once the blockade was lifted, local party authorities used commemorations to instill in the city's residents a sense of patriotism and civic pride and to encourage the population to sacrifice and work relentlessly at restoration.[6] Official commemorations such as the Museum of the Defense of Leningrad and anniversary celebrations of the lifting of the siege, then, were mobilizational tools *par excellence.* Intent on keeping alive the enthusiasm and patriotism for Leningrad that was shown during the blockade, while at the same time inculcating these traits in the fast-growing population (most of whom had not experienced the blockade or were not native Leningraders), commemorations were meant to shape people's perceptions and understandings of the war on the Leningrad front and provide positive examples for the city's restoration. By offering the Leningrad identity to newcomers, and stressing the importance of the hometown (*rodnoi gorod*), Leningrad's authorities sought to create a sense of attachment to the city that would make people sacrifice more to restore it.[7] The commemorations told a story of heroism, provided sites of mourning and celebration, and offered residents of the city a place in the community of heroes – the *blokadniki* – through emulation.

THE AUDIENCE FOR BLOCKADE COMMEMORATIONS

When the siege was lifted on 27 January 1944, Leningrad's population had undergone a dramatic change since the outbreak of the war. Nearly a million people had died during the 872 days, and close to a million more had been evacuated to the East. The majority of evacuees had left before the blockade began in September 1941, while others escaped during the winter via the so-called "Road of Life" over the frozen Lake Ladoga, and still more left in the spring of 1942. Although there may have been people who took advantage of the evacuations to "save their skins," the majority of people were given no choice. Thousands of workers, for example, were evacuated with their disassembled factories to work in the rear. Even if they were given a choice, the decision to stay or go was often very difficult, for many did not want to abandon their city, friends, and homes. Once the blockade and war ended, many of them were not allowed to leave their places of evacuation, which caused enormous discontent.[8]

Nevertheless, between 1944 and 1946 Leningrad's population had grown by at least 1.3 million as a result of in-migration, the demobilization of soldiers, and the return of evacuees.[9] Much of this growth came from Leningrad Province, which was devastated by the Wehrmacht as it retreated in 1944. Due to the destruction, peasants, unskilled laborers, and others looking for work, housing, and a better life in the aftermath of the war flooded into the city.[10] Blair Ruble has argued that the highly skilled workforce, which the Leningrad authorities had been so proud of, "had been swamped by yet another wave of migrants from the countryside."[11] As a result, the commemorations that occurred in Leningrad once the siege was lifted had to take into account the fact that the number of people who had lived in the city during the war was quickly becoming a minority, as was the number of "native-born" Leningraders. Local authorities felt the need to work with migrants and educate them about the city's history and the blockade to prepare them for life in the city.

Restoration required a reliable, dedicated workforce. Party leaders urged Leningraders to continue the "heroic work" they had performed throughout the blockade. According to the official rendition of Leningraders' heroism, nothing could break their steadfastness and courage. At the Leningrad party plenum in April 1944, party boss Andrei Zhdanov proclaimed that the residents of the city would not shy away from the tasks that lay ahead, for they were driven by an intense patriotism. "Leningraders displayed a miracle of heroism, as they took care to preserve their city from the enemy," noted Zhdanov. "This care for the city," he continued,

> has become a way of life. For a Leningrader visiting another city, it would be strange to see that only yardmen keep courtyards clean, for we have become accustomed during these years to clean our building premises ourselves. The mass participation of Leningraders in defensive measures, in anti-aircraft defense measures, [and in] protecting every inch of ground has become a way of life. . . . Such concern that the city not fall into the enemy's hands [and] that it remain ours, the loving care for our city, the lofty patriotism of Leningraders for their city, for their Motherland must all be carried over into the period of restoration. Moreover, it must not just be carried over, but it must be transformed . . . [and] the zeal for saving the city from the enemy must become zeal for restoration.[12]

Invoking the myth of the heroic Leningrader, he argued that they would be successful, because they "do not abhor any type of labor, including dirty work [*chernovaia rabota*]," and they showed this to be true during the blockade.[13]

Zhdanov suggested that a strong sense of patriotism and duty toward the city and country would guide Leningraders in their work. Such sentiments were echoed by his replacement as first secretary of the Leningrad party organization, Alexei Kuznetsov, who in a January 1946 speech extolled the unique qualities of Leningraders and called on the people to become patriots of their city. "I already promised you that I would be a faithful patriot of our city . . . ," proclaimed Kuznetsov. "They say that we Leningraders are great patriots of our city. God forbid that you say something bad about Leningrad in the presence of a Leningrader: he'll be terribly offended." As Leningrad patriots, Kuznetsov argued, they were duty bound to put all of their energies into restoring the city that they so deeply "love and cherish."[14]

Zhdanov, Kuznetsov, and others in the Leningrad party organization believed that those who lived through the blockade would continue to work as hard at restoration as they did at defense. However, they were not sure that migrants and returning evacuees would be as willing to make sacrifices and struggle for the restoration of the city.[15] Zhdanov made it clear that the patriotism and care for the city shown by Leningraders during the blockade must be taught to the people arriving after the war: "We must inculcate in migrants, and our own people, that no type of work is disgraceful if it serves to provide us with success in our affairs."[16] Much like the efforts to instill Soviet values and shape the identities of migrants who came to Soviet cities in the 1930s, the Leningrad authorities wanted new arrivals to work, in the words of the Orientalist A. N. Boldyrev, "in the Leningrad style, the blockade style."[17]

According to reports compiled by workers in the Leningrad party's Department of Agitation and Propaganda, there was indeed a perceived gap between the *blokadniki* and recent arrivals' desire to work at restoration. These reports perpetuated the idea that Leningraders who survived the blockade were more heroic and more self-sacrificing for their city, and information in them had an important impact on the policies and programs implemented by local officials in the postwar period.[18] According to the reports, party activists in a number of the city's districts felt that, in certain cases, those who did not experience the war in Leningrad were less willing to carry out the tasks assigned to them. One activist reported that although several of the returnees and migrants settled into restoration work well, "in their level of consciousness, and organization, new workers differ sharply from those who worked in Leningrad during the period of the blockade."[19] As these reports show, many believed that those arriving in Leningrad were lazy, tried to obtain easy jobs, had a high rate of absenteeism, and undertook assigned tasks "without making much effort."[20] Party workers attributed these "unhealthy moods" among migrants and reevacuees to the fact that they "judge and react to circumstances as they did before the war [*po dovoennomu*]." In stark contrast to the mythologized Leningrader, who lived and worked in the worst possible circumstances during the blockade, some of the newcomers, it was said, "do not feel the war [*malo chuvstvuiut voinu*]."[21] In light of this, district party committees gave orders to the secretaries of party organizations to carry out political work with those people returning to Leningrad from evacuation, and those coming for the first time.[22]

The perceived differences between those arriving in the city and the *blokadniki* led to tensions and hostilities. According to party mood reports, survivors of the blockade often voiced complaints that returnees and migrants did not want to work at the restoration of the city. One activist's report from May 1944 cast doubt on the newcomers' intentions, stating that "they arrived just to land in Leningrad, not to work." "We need to have conversations with them," the report continued, for "our workers do not like such people."[23] A worker from a factory in the Vasilievskii Island district voiced her complaints to a party activist about people coming to Leningrad after the blockade:

> Many people have returned to Leningrad from evacuation, but very few of them came to work. They do not work at establishments, at construction sites, or at the procurement of timber, rather, our teenagers do this work, to the detriment of their studies. All of those people who arrive set themselves up in kiosks or trade at the market. But invalids of the [Great] Patriotic War should be working in kiosks. How did this situation come about?[24]

Party activists' reports suggest that these complaints were widespread. For many people who lived in Leningrad during the blockade, the restoration of the city was a sacred duty which local officials presented as a commemoration of Leningraders' heroism and suffering. Not surprisingly, many considered inaction on the part of newcomers and returnees to be a sign of disrespect. Such complaints and accusations were even more pointed and emotional because there was a widespread sentiment that evacuees had turned their backs on Leningrad and left to find shelter in the East when the situation became difficult.[25] The "cowards," some argued, were the first to leave the city, and now when good workers were in demand those same people who had left Leningrad in its time of need "return before everyone else."[26] One worker expressed her desire, and that of her neighbors, to restore their building, but stated, "We do not want our labor to be used by the cowards and idlers who ran away from Leningrad, thinking only of how to save themselves."[27] "In general," went another report, "at the establishments of the [Volodarskii] district, there is a malevolent attitude felt toward those people who, in the difficult days, left Leningrad, and now are returning or are asking factories and plants to summon them."[28] At one factory, for example, activists noted that some workers were disturbed by the demands made by evacuees to be returned to the city. Feelings of resentment and betrayal were evident in some of their comments, including one which stated, "When it was difficult here nobody wrote, but now they are all asking to be returned. They shouldn't be allowed back."[29]

Returning evacuees also leveled accusations against those who remained in the city, which disturbed not only the average citizen but the authorities as well. The art scholar Nikolai Punin, who had been in evacuation himself, recalled the following representative conversation between people who remained and those who were evacuated: "'So, you sat it out in the rear?' – They respond: 'And you were waiting for the Germans?'"[30] Boldyrev noted in his diary a conversation at a gathering during the summer of 1944, in which a certain professor stated that the people who remained in Leningrad were "defeatists, who saved their personal property," or did not succeed in leaving because of "weakness or blunders."[31] Others proclaimed that those who had remained in the city did so not only because they wanted to stay with the Germans,[32] but also so that they would have the opportunity to loot the apartments of those who were evacuated: "We thought that you suffered," stated a returnee, but "you stayed for easy profit – you looted everything."[33] A report compiled by party activists in the Moscow district cited comments made by people returning from evacuation, which downplayed the severity of the blockade. The activist noted that "among certain people returning to the city from the rear, there are statements that they suffered greater hardships than Leningraders, that the period of the blockade was short, but they all [the evacuees] lived for two years in conditions of deprivation."[34] Such attitudes and sentiments – however inflated and manipulated by Soviet organs of surveillance – were antithetical to the story of heroism, determination, and personal sacrifice of all Leningraders during the blockade. They were explicit challenges to the official narrative of Leningrad's wartime suffering.

The tensions between *blokadniki,* evacuees, and migrants clearly posed a problem for local leaders who sought to shape public memory of the war and blockade in order to mobilize people to restore the city. As a solution to some of the tensions and supposed lack of desire on the part of returnees and migrants to work at restoration, Leningrad officials sought to instill a sense of civic identity and pride, and teach people to act as "Leningraders" would.[35] Municipal authorities employed commemorations for this purpose. There can be no denying the power of commemorative sites and events in forming identities, mobilizing populations, and instilling values and norms in citizens. Acts of remembering are crucial to any group's identity, as presentations and representations of a group's past play a powerful role in shaping its members' conception of who they are based on common experiences. Without the "assistance of mechanical reminders, souvenirs and memory sites," writes the historian John Gillis, we are often unable to fulfill the "enormous obligation to remember" our past.[36] Such memory sites and commemorations are always political and serve an agenda.[37] They embrace certain aspects of the past which glorify a nation, group, or individual. In more cases than not, commemorations are selective, and encourage forgetting as much as remembering in their attempts to shape memories, identities, and actions. In this process, the state is often the "major producer and choreographer of commemoration."[38] Through commemorations, the state's agents articulate a vision or an interpretation of an event and invite the viewer to participate in the commemorative activity. In the case of the Soviet Union, and Leningrad in particular, the memory of the war was widely employed to serve the regime, but "these acts of remembrance," notes the historian Catherine Merridale, "were not fake."[39] The goals of the state in official commemorations often corresponded to the desires of the population.

Leningrad's officials and party activists recognized the utility of commemorations in cultivating an acceptable memory of the war and mobilizing the population for restoration. At certain factories, propaganda work with newcomers and returnees involved special gatherings and conversations about how people had lived during the blockade, as well as discussions about the tasks standing before them in the period of restoration.[40] The large number of people coming to Leningrad, and the reports compiled by party workers, made it particularly "urgent" that all activists strive to socialize newcomers in "the spirit of Leningrad traditions."[41] The Department of Agitation and Propaganda of the Kirov district, for example, attempted to accomplish this by "educating laborers about the main qualities of Leningraders, preserving and developing the methods of work from the period of the blockade."[42] After noting the poor work of many returnees and migrants, as well as the tensions that were evident between workers, one activist stated that "we want to take the newcomers to the exhibition 'The Heroic Defense of Leningrad' – then they will certainly relate differently to the assigned work."[43] Through exposure to the monuments and memories of the blockade, therefore, it was believed that Leningraders and migrants alike would become Leningrad patriots and be inspired to work harder at restoring the city to its prewar state.

THE MUSEUM OF THE DEFENSE OF LENINGRAD

In the period following the blockade, the Museum of the Defense of Leningrad was the most important monument to the events experienced by the city and its residents during the war. Bringing together personal documents, photographs, military equipment, and other reminders of the war, it chronicled the events of the nearly nine hundred days and told the official version of the blockade story. Its materials, noted an article in the Leningrad press, "clearly reflect the unprecedented-in-history epic of the 900-day fight of the besieged city against the enemy."[44] The museum invited its visitors to take part in the ritualized performance of experiencing the blockade through the exhibits on display, and acted as a mobilizational tool which sought to inculcate both a love for the city and a desire to restore it.[45]

As an official commemoration of the siege, the museum offered citizens a sanitized representation of the blockade at which survivors could relive the heroism and tragedy of their experience. Like other commemorative sites in the Soviet Union and elsewhere, the museum silenced aspects of the war which reflected negatively on Leningraders or the party leadership. So while a narrative of suffering, deprivation, and starvation as a result of Hitler's plans to annihilate the city was clearly presented, the darker side of the blockade was either toned down or completely erased from the official memory of the war. Morally problematic activities such as theft, corruption, and black-market transactions, which were common in Leningrad during the war, were absent from the museum's layout, as were references to murder and cannibalism, which some people resorted to in order to survive.[46] Thus, the party apparatus sought to shape the public's understanding of Leningrad's wartime experience by stressing the heroic and feeding into the growing myth of the Great Patriotic War.

The museum became a monument that captured the imagination of Leningraders and all those who came to the city, but its origins were humble. It began as an exhibition, "The Heroic Defense of Leningrad," which in turn developed out of a smaller one entitled "The Great Patriotic War of the Soviet People against German Fascism." Leningrad's authorities opened this exhibition, which occupied one hall in the Leningrad House of the Red Army, in the fall of 1941. This exhibition was not unlike others taking place throughout the Soviet Union during the war, which the Stalinist propaganda apparatus used to mobilize support for the battle against Nazi Germany.[47] It was made up of trophy armaments taken from fallen German soldiers, as well as artwork depicting battles and events on the Leningrad front. The exhibition had three sections: "The Crushing Defeat of the Predecessors of Fascism – the Livonian and Teutonic Knights"; "The Great Patriotic War of the Soviet People against German Fascism"; and "Fascism Is Hunger, Fascism Is War."[48] Drawing on historic precedents to cultivate hatred of fascism, promote patriotism, and galvanize public opinion against the invaders who threatened to destroy their city, the exhibit enjoyed some initial popularity. Yet after the break in the blockade in January 1943, interest grew exponentially, and by the fall of that year, 94,500 visitors had come to view it.[49] Even before the blockade had come to an end, Leningraders were interested in seeing themselves and their experiences historicized in a museum setting. Official attempts to commemorate the war and blockade, therefore, were consistent with the desire on the part of the city's residents to have their epic memorialized.

As the blockade wore on, the tide of the war began to turn, and the popularity of the exhibition grew, Leningrad's leaders initiated plans to open a new exhibition that would commemorate the heroism of the city's defenders. Under the initiative of Leningrad's second party secretary A. A. Kuznetsov and Marshal L. A. Govorov, on 4 December 1943 the city party committee and the military soviet of the Leningrad front decided to organize the exhibition into one based on the "Heroic Defense of Leningrad."[50] "This was an excellent and opportune idea," noted a contemporary, for "everything was still fresh in memory, and a great quantity of... impressive exhibits were preserved."[51] Work immediately began on the construction of the exhibition in the buildings of the former Museum of Socialist Agriculture on Solianoi Pereulok. To organize it, the local party leadership established a commission drawn from the city's Department of Agitation and Propaganda, the Union of Soviet Artists, and the Administration for Artistic Affairs.[52] The commission then formed a team of experienced specialists from various museums and research institutes throughout the city, including the Institute for the History of the Party.[53] "Enemy shells were still exploding over the city, when preparations for the exhibition 'The Heroic Defense of Leningrad' began in Solianoi Gorodok," stated a contemporary about the creation of the exhibition.[54] In typical socialist realist fashion, faith in victory was so great that the largest halls in the exhibition told of the defeat of the Germans outside Leningrad before the event happened.

Organizing the exhibition, which was being constructed at a time of intensified German shelling, required a significant amount of work. Laborers first had to restore the buildings in which it would be held, as well as collect the materials to be put on display. N. D. Khudiakova, a member of the organizing team who worked at the exhibition and museum throughout the postwar period, described the process of collecting and systematizing materials, noting that "the entire city took part."[55] Local party committees and soviets, industrial establishments, social organizations, research institutes, military detachments, and other groups all played a role in restoring the building and donating materials. Even individual *blokadniki* contributed to the creation of the exhibition. When the news about the exhibition spread throughout the city, "residents themselves came to us," bringing photos, documents, and family and military relics.[56] Leningraders brought their personal effects to the exhibition, wrote Khudiakova in a diary entry from 17 January 1944, because "they were interested in the portrayal of their own work, their lives and their battle in the besieged city."[57] Local artists also played an important part, as many pieces of art produced during the blockade, especially those reflecting life in the city, the destruction of the historic cityscape, and battles at the front found a place in the exhibition's layout.[58] Given the good fortune experienced in collecting materials, and the energetic work put into the organization by all involved, the organizers created the exhibition in a very short period and presented it to city officials in its first variant at the end of February 1944.[59]

By the end of April, the exhibition was ready to be opened to the public. Since December 1943, when the decision was made to create the exhibition, organizers had collected 7,382 separate exhibits and documents. Of these, 5,839 would find a place in the exhibition, which was spread out in twenty-six separate halls and took up nine thousand square meters of floor space.[60] The massive exhibition opened its doors on 30 April to an invited group of one thousand people, which included high-ranking officers from the Leningrad front and prominent officials.[61] This festive event began with a review of the exhibits, followed by a meeting dedicated to the exhibition's opening. In the days that followed, the exhibition's guides organized excursions for people invited from local establishments, and on 7 May the exhibition was opened to the public.[62]

Even before the exhibition was completed, Leningrad officials, realizing the importance of the exhibits to the memory of the city's ordeal and the blockade's place in the city narrative, petitioned to have it turned into a museum of republic stature, as opposed to regional stature.[63] Turning it into a museum would facilitate research and popularization work, provide for senior research positions, and encourage the creation of a permanent staff.[64] After several petitions to Moscow, the central government granted the request, and on 5 October 1945 it decreed that the exhibition be turned into a museum of second-category republic stature.[65] Following this, the exhibition closed its doors to allow for reconstruction of the layout, which was completed by the second anniversary of the lifting of the blockade on 27 January 1946.

When the Museum of the Defense of Leningrad opened, its organizers had added eleven new halls and significantly increased its size and scope.[66] It was conceived of as a "political-educational and research establishment," which would study, popularize, and present the history of the "unprecedented" battle of Leningraders on the front as well as in the city. The blockade, according to the museum's narrative, became the culmination of the city's historic development. Just as the war was presented as a formative moment in Soviet history, the blockade was depicted as the defining moment in the history of Petersburg/Leningrad.[67] Victory in the blockade was attributed to the revolutionary and military traditions of the city, and the museum aimed to pass these traditions on through Bolshevik propaganda.[68] "Walk through the halls of the museum," stated an article in the Leningrad press, "and you will see how the glorious traditions of the Petrograd workers multiplied and grew in strength, how our beautiful city grew and matured."[69] The museum therefore offered its viewers the opportunity to revisit the blockade and to embrace the city's history and identity as their own.

The museum painted a truly heroic picture of the defense of Leningrad under siege, with exhibits displaying a history of the war as experienced by the city. Both the exhibition and museum discussed the blockade as bookended by the city's "glorious" history and the new battle to be fought on the restoration front. The introductory hall, for example, emphasized Leningrad's "fighting revolutionary traditions," its status as an "impenetrable fortress," and its close connection with the "military glory of the Russian people." It developed a story of Leningrad's exceptionalism by presenting it as a city of monuments, of great cultural figures, of scientific and artistic achievements, and one of the country's most important industrial centers.[70] It also emphasized the work which lay ahead in the restoration of the city. Pictures of the suburban palaces before and after the Germans destroyed them, for instance, provided a poignant illustration of both the city's history and the tasks faced by all Leningraders in the immediate future.[71] One of the museum's guides discussed the use of such photographs in its layout: "We say that Leningrad is one of the most beautiful cities in the world, famous for its suburbs. Using the photographs for support, we say that we have presented the suburbs, and when we come to the victory hall, we show the suburbs after the Fascist barbarians had been there, and people leave with a definite impression."[72] Museum workers created a narrative to show that in the wake of the war, the city of Lenin was "in the avant-garde of socialist construction in the USSR [and was] successfully healing the wounds inflicted by the war."[73] The museum's educational value, therefore, had a much wider scope than just the war as experienced by Leningrad. Indeed, as an educational tool, it attempted to inculcate the history of the city in people, encouraging them to make sacrifices and restore their "hometown" (*rodnoi gorod*).

The museum mythologized Leningraders as a steadfast and courageous people who made sacrifices for the good of the front, the city, and the country. The museological narrative made it clear that in the face of the German attempts to storm Leningrad, the city's residents had held their positions. Through the period of the "hungry blockade" (to which three halls were devoted), Leningraders continued to produce armaments for the front and the country as a whole, and due to their heroic efforts, people in the city and at the front were able to decisively defeat the Germans in the month of January 1944.[74] It goes without saying that there was no criticism of the party leadership for failing to adequately supply the city with food, nor were the consequences of starvation discussed to any significant degree. As in all sections of the museum, Leningraders' heroism and the guiding role of the party were stressed to the visitors. The museum, like other official commemorations, argues Lisa Kirschenbaum, "celebrated individual acts of heroism and invited Leningraders to recognize themselves as actors in the Leningrad 'epic.'"[75] Such commemorations also invited newcomers, as well as Leningraders who had been in evacuation, to emulate the *blokadniki* and their sacrifice for the restoration of the city.

Leningrad's authorities had created what they called a "museum of a new type, the layout of which is based on genuinely scientific elaboration and possesses great interests and impressionability [*obladaet bol'shim interesom i vpechatliaemost'iu*]."[76] Vaunting the museum's uniqueness and importance, its organizers proclaimed it to be "the only historical museum in the world whose visitors are both contemporaries and participants of the events eternalized in it."[77] For both organizers and visitors – especially those who had lived through the war in Leningrad – the exhibits in the museum provoked strong emotions. The documents, photos, maps, military equipment, and artwork all had the effect of resurrecting in people's memory the great days of defense.[78] Nikolai Tikhonov, the future head of the Union of Writers, wrote in the museum's guestbook that "with a feeling of gratitude I walked through the halls . . . and the not so distant past stood before me in its magnificent essence."[79] These impressions were echoed by Vera Inber, who recalled a visit to the exhibition with her husband: "I.D. and I talked very little – a nod of the head, a gesture, a word, and we understood each other. Nearly three years of our lives passed before us."[80] One of the museum's great strengths, according to its first director, L. L. Rakov, was the illustration not only of the "external" side of the events on the front and in the city, but also of "the feelings and thoughts which possessed the defenders of the great city of Lenin."[81] The exhibition and museum "completely illuminates the heroic days of Leningrad," wrote a group of students in the visitors' book. "This inspires us to restore our beloved hometown [*rodnoi gorod*]. And we will do this."[82]

The museum had tremendous political-propaganda significance for laborers in the city and soldiers at the front. But even more importantly, Leningrad's officials believed that the exhibition and museum played an influential role in instilling "the greatest of Leningrad's traditions among youth and newcomers to Leningrad."[83] After walking through the museum's halls, for example, a group of children (*rebiata*) wrote their impressions in the visitors' book: "At the exhibition it was as if we were reliving the years of the blockade of our beloved city. The exhibition reminded us of Leningrad's battle with the fascist monsters, who tormented the city during the two-year [*sic*] blockade. Those children who were in evacuation learned about . . . Leningrad in the days of its difficult life."[84] Realizing the potential of the museum as an educational tool, Leningrad's authorities sought to expand its size and funding. Indeed, further expansion of the museum was listed as one of the goals in Leningrad's postwar Five-Year Plan.[85] The Department of Cultural-Enlightenment Work of the city soviet funded the museum very well. Out of all the establishments under its purview – including individual suburban palaces, parks throughout the city, and other museums and libraries – the Museum of the Defense of Leningrad consistently received a large share of the overall budget.[86]

Using the funding provided, organizers added new halls and materials to develop the story of the blockade, including exhibits on the restoration of the city in the postwar Five-Year Plan, partisan activity behind German lines, and the local anti-aircraft defense, among other subjects.[87] Expansion was not confined to the walls of the already enormous system of buildings in which the exhibits were displayed. The museum used the territory surrounding its buildings as an exhibition space to display the military technology and artillery employed by both sides in the battles for the city.[88] Expanding beyond the museum, the Department for Cultural-Enlightenment Work planned to open an affiliated exhibition in the Kirov Central Park of Culture and Rest,[89] as well as create mobile and temporary exhibits that could be taken to locations throughout the city and Leningrad province.[90]

The expansion and development of new displays, halls, and exhibits was facilitated by the collection of new materials, documents, and artifacts from the city and areas in Leningrad province – a process that continued throughout the period under discussion. Museum workers made extensive field trips to areas where battles had taken place in search of materials to put on display.[91] Personal documents belonging to a soldier from an infantry regiment were found, for example, on Siniavinskie Heights and were presented to the museum.[92] "The museum is carrying out large-scale works in the collection of new documents, exhibits, and memoirs," announced the Leningrad press. "Materials on the people's militia, the destruction of cultural monuments, and the work of Leningrad radio during the blockade are being collected. The city's workers provide great help in this matter to the museum."[93] The museum encouraged donations through announcements over the radio and ads placed in factory newspapers, and the city's residents responded on a mass scale. In the first three months of 1949 alone, for example, Leningraders donated around one thousand new documents, photos, and other artifacts reflecting various aspects of the blockade.[94] The museum continued to receive many valuable exhibits from citizens and organizations throughout the city during the postwar period. A large collection of materials on the People's Militia (*narodnoe opolchenie*) was donated, which included approximately three hundred valuable diaries of participants in the defense of Leningrad.[95] The mountain climbers who concealed the city's spires, cupolas, and industrial sites donated a photo album as an exhibit to display their service in the defense of the city and its historic landscape.[96] Leningraders' interest in seeing themselves and their actions memorialized in the museum, therefore, had not waned in the five years since it was opened. Their participation in the expansion of the museum suggests the extent to which the party's commemorative goals resonated with the city's residents.

Museum workers cooperated with research establishments and individuals wishing to study the history of Leningrad's defense by offering them access to their holdings and providing archival services.[97] Researchers employed at the museum also used the archival holdings to write histories of various facets of the defense of Leningrad, life in the city, and other themes pertaining to the blockade. One of the museum staff's main goals was to publish works that would shed light on heroic aspects of the siege and glorify the actions of individual Leningraders. "Work on writing articles, brochures, [and] monographs is tightly connected with the work in collecting new exhibits," stated museum director V. P. Kovalev at a meeting to discuss its work. "This work is especially important," he continued, "since with every day the number of materials of the wartime become fewer, and the number of participants in the heroic epic thin out."[98] Throughout the early postwar period, the museum published a large number of leaflets, articles, and papers. The topics and themes of these works varied from purely military matters to issues such as "The Destruction of Artistic and Architectural Monuments by Fascist Barbarians," "The Work of Leningrad's Doctors during the Blockade," and "The Women of Leningrad in the Defense of the City," among others.[99] These publications, like the museum itself, were meant to illuminate a number of perspectives of the blockade narrative.

Workers from the museum actively sought to propagandize and popularize its message throughout Leningrad, interest people in the history of the city and the blockade, and draw people into the museum itself. They used a widespread program of advertising for this purpose, including radio announcements, leaflets, posters, and advertising space on streetcars. Museum workers distributed these advertisements in factories, institutes, movie theaters, and elsewhere.[100] In the first half of 1948, for example, activists dispersed more than sixty thousand posters, leaflets, and other advertisements throughout the city.[101] The local press also publicized the museum to keep the public informed of any changes in its status, exhibits, and events taking place there. Indeed, Leningrad's newspapers published at least seventy-one articles about the exhibition and museum between 1944 and 1948.[102]

The museum also maintained close contact with the organizations in the city. Museum workers organized lectures and talks for the public both on and off the premises, and on orders from party authorities, researchers, and workers delivered free talks at factories, organizations, military divisions, schools, and other establishments with the goal of inspiring workers through stories of Leningraders' heroism during the

Table 5.1. Comparative Data for 1948 on Attendance at the Museum of the Defense of Leningrad from City Districts Organized by the Department of Agitation and Propaganda

District	Number of organizations and establishments visiting the museum	Number of excursions	Number of people
Oktiabrskii	140	185	7,400
Frunzenskii	83	124	4,960
Dzerzhinskii	102	120	4,800
Kuibyshevskii	90	112	4,480
Petrogradskii	73	108	4,320
Nevskii	59	107	4,280
Vyborgskii	69	92	3,680
Moskovskii	75	88	3,520
Kirovskii	63	83	3,400
Vasileoostrvoskii	55	82	3,280
Kalininskii	54	75	3,000
Leninskii	59	69	2,760
Zhdanovskii	61	66	2,640
Smol'ninskii	50	65	2,600
Sverdlovskii	38	59	2,360
Totals	1,071	1,437	57,480

Source: TsGAIPD SPb, f. 25, op. 18, d. 92, l. 13.

blockade.[103] Each year the number of talks given outside the museum increased. From 1946 to 1949 alone, the museum organized 670 talks and lectures at various places throughout the city.[104]

The city party committee played an influential role in promoting attendance at the museum, and thereby a more widespread dissemination of the blockade narrative. City officials understood that the blockade's message of sacrifice for the city could best be inculcated in migrants, and Leningraders themselves, through attendance at the museum. In light of this, party activists organized group excursions from most, if not all, of the city's places of work. Official party publications, such as *Bloknot agitatora* and the Leningrad press, summoned activists to make wide use of the exhibition and museum, noting that it offered the "richest" of materials for both "working on oneself in preparing for talks" and "mass agitational work among the laborers of Leningrad."[105] Such calls were well received by activists throughout the city, who saw an opportunity to expose people who had not lived through the war in Leningrad to the realities of the city's experience. At times when it was felt that museum attendance had declined in certain districts, both the museum and the Department of Agitation and Propaganda pushed for more work to be carried out by activists in those districts. The parties involved noticed a higher number of people attending the museum from areas in which activist work on the blockade was carried out daily.[106] Indeed, activists played an important role in organizing excursions to the museum from the city's factories, plants, and institutes. According to party activists' reports, these excursions made "great impressions" on people and provided a "new flood of strength" among workers.[107]

Throughout the early postwar period – until mid-1949 – the Museum of the Defense of Leningrad was the second-most-popular museum in the city, behind only the State Hermitage. By May 1949, five years after it opened, 1,565,300 people had visited the exhibition and the museum, a truly astounding number given that the museum had been closed for certain periods of time to allow for the reconstruction of halls and exhibits.[108] Although the attendance record was impressive, it must be noted that it involved a certain element of coercion; organized excursions were often mandatory, meaning that people could receive reprimands at their places of work if they did not attend the museum with their coworkers. The party leadership wanted to see museum attendance increase to ensure that the state-sponsored memory of the blockade – which promoted a narrative of Leningrad exceptionalism and silenced issues that ran counter to the heroic myth of the war – would become a central part of people's lives in the postwar period. The museum thus evolved into a place of pilgrimage, learning, and propaganda that could be visited year round.

YEARLY COMMEMORATION RITUALS AROUND 27 JANUARY

Each year residents of Leningrad celebrated the complete lifting of the blockade on 27 January. Hundreds of events took place throughout the city to mark the "unforgettable date" and provide a forum at which the scripted memory of the blockade could be remembered, celebrated, and taught to the people living in Leningrad. Karen Petrone has argued that the state used Soviet celebrations of the 1930s to create ideal Soviet citizens. The celebrations themselves, according to her, were templates used to form and inculcate this identity.[109] A similar process took place in Leningrad in the postwar period, one which attempted to mold the city's residents into ideal Leningraders based on the mythologized image of the heroic and selfless *blokadniki*. The celebrations mixed memories of loss together with images of heroic steadfastness, all of which served as reminders (and examples to follow) of sacrifice and victories on the military and labor fronts. Like the events commemorating Victory Day, those marking the liberation of Leningrad involved all residents and were carefully scripted by the local party and soviet leadership.[110]

The memory of the blockade became the focus of the entire city in the days before the anniversary. Although major celebrations and commemorative events took place on 27 January, municipal authorities began preparations weeks in advance, providing an educational lead-up to the date. Throughout the city, party activists and Leningrad's defenders worked to spread the word and stress the importance of the blockade in the history of the city and the unfolding restoration. Preparations often began as early as 10 January, with meetings involving the directors of houses of culture, activists, and cultural-enlightenment workers.[111] The party leadership provided activists with instructions on how to carry out propaganda work surrounding the blockade anniversary. In 1947, for example, the authorities asked the director of the Museum of the Defense of Leningrad to deliver a lecture on the liberation of Leningrad to the leading workers of cultural-enlightenment establishments of the city, which would allow them to organize events at their places of work and provide a succinct official version of the blockade story.[112] Articles in the party publication *Bloknot agitatora,* aimed at party activists, also provided materials to be used in discussions about the blockade, its implications, and the tasks facing all Leningraders.[113]

Events which reached the general population began soon after the preparatory meetings. In the Vasilievskii Island district, for example, commemorative events connected with the 1947 anniversary were scheduled to begin on 12 January and last until 30 January.[114] Cultural-enlightenment workers organized lectures, discussions, and readings on the blockade at red corners, libraries, dormitories, and factories in all districts of the city leading up to 27 January.[115] They also set up exhibits about the defense of the city and screened films reflecting the life and battles of Leningraders. During the days before the anniversary date, city and district officials organized group tours to the Museum of the Defense of Leningrad as well as meetings with participants in the defense, and led excursions to battle sites outside the city.[116] The city party committee recruited hundreds of generals and military officers each year to give talks, lectures, and presentations about the blockade.[117]

All of these events provided city officials with an opportunity to reach as many people as possible, spread the story and memory of the blockade, and stress the importance of using the examples of Leningraders to work harder in the restoration of the city. "The anniversary of the enemy's blockade of Leningrad," stated a party report about the events in the Dzerzhinskii district, "was carried out under the banner of mobilizing the laborers for the restoration of the district, and a desire to completely resurrect the former glory of the beloved city, to make it more beautiful than it was before the war."[118] Given the importance of restoration, hundreds of events took place to mark the anniversary. The number of events could vary from year to year, but there is evidence to suggest that the anniversary of the blockade was one of the most widely celebrated red calendar dates each year. According to a Leningrad party report, in 1945 the anniversary of the lifting of the blockade had more events devoted to it (196) than all others listed, including the anniversary of Lenin's death (123) and Red Army Day (122).[119]

The anniversary celebrations provided the opportunity for people who experienced the blockade to come together and carry out rituals of mourning and commemoration. Thousands of *blokadniki* visited the Museum of the Defense of Leningrad and symbolically relived the experiences of the war.[120] Others made pilgrimages to battle sites, places where soldiers were buried, and the mass graves of Leningraders who had died in the city from starvation, cold, and enemy fire. District party committees organized workers into delegations and made trips to these sites. Party and soviet officials held funeral meetings at gravesites followed by the ceremonial laying of wreaths to the sounds of funeral melodies.[121] Even at these sites of memory and mourning, local authorities used the memory of the blockade to promote the restoration of the city. At a gravesite meeting of more than two thousand people in the Volodarskii district on 27 January 1947, for example, the party and soviet officials leading the meeting called on those gathered to "honor the memory of the heroes of the defense of the hometown through new successes on the labor front, to restore Leningrad and make it more beautiful and better."[122] In Leningrad, mourning and memory were harnessed, shaped, and used for productive and socially useful work.[123]

Yet the anniversary of the lifting of the blockade was not only a time of mourning, but also a period of celebration, marking one of the most joyous occasions in the lives of those who lived in Leningrad through the blockade. As such, officials aimed to entertain the population in ways that were both educational and festive. To mark the anniversary each year, Leningrad's authorities held celebrations throughout the city at houses of culture, involving, for the most part, "the best people" of each district – the most active party, soviet, Komsomol, military, and union leaders.[124] Soviet celebrations most often took the form of mass meetings, followed by entertainment and refreshments.[125] The anniversary celebrations followed this form in Leningrad. To mark these celebrations, the first and second secretaries of the respective district, as well as participants in the defense, gave speeches devoted to the memory of the blockade and the tasks facing the city in the period of restoration.[126]

The main official celebration, however, was held at the recently restored Kirov Theater, which had been badly damaged during the blockade but had recently been restored as a site of historic and cultural importance. Each year the city's "most important" representatives – including the very top brass of the Leningrad governmental and party organizations, all of whom were bearers of the medal "For the Defense of Leningrad" – packed the theater to commemorate the blockade, celebrate victory, and discuss the challenges facing the city in the present and the future. These meetings were followed by large concerts featuring some of the Soviet Union's most accomplished artists.[127]

The "festive gathering" at the theater in 1945 was especially important. As the first anniversary celebration, it provided a precedent and a model for those in the years to come. At this meeting, the chairman of the Supreme Soviet, M. I. Kalinin, presented Leningrad with the Order of Lenin – the Soviet Union's highest honor – for the "outstanding services of the laborers of Leningrad to the Motherland, for courage and heroism, discipline and steadfastness shown in the fight with German invaders in the difficult conditions of the blockade."[128] In his speech to Leningrad's "best people," Kalinin stressed the importance of the lifting of the blockade to Leningraders and the entire country. Like the Museum of the Defense of Leningrad, Kalinin emphasized the revolutionary qualities of the city and its people, and noted that it was these qualities which had allowed Leningraders to defend themselves and defeat the Germans. In the postwar period, these qualities, he argued, would allow for the quick restoration of the city.[129] The chairman of the Leningrad city soviet, P. S. Popkov, made similar connections with the city's past, blockade, and restoration by stating that Leningrad had "preserved and multiplied the glorious traditions of revolutionary Petrograd." Echoing Kalinin's remarks, Popkov argued that it was the "centuries-old history of our magnificent city [which] prepared it to fulfill the great role [during the blockade]." Those Leningrad qualities which were so evident during the blockade, he stressed, were to be used in the "conscious labor of restoring the city's industry, economy, and culture."[130] This became the dominant message proclaimed in the press and at all subsequent celebrations of the lifting of the blockade.[131]

Finally, yearly anniversary celebrations were meant to reflect the joy felt by Leningraders when it was announced that the Germans had been driven from the walls of the city. Whereas celebrations and concerts at the Kirov Theater and other venues involved mainly party and soviet officials, festivals [*narodnoe gulian'e*] were held at various locations in the city for the public in general. Designed to be inclusive, these gatherings invited everyone to share in the memories of liberation, celebrate the feats of Leningraders, and take part in the festivities. In every district of the city, main squares and parks became the venues for games, dances, speeches, and general merrymaking. These events were accompanied by the music of brass orchestras, accordions, and singing, which went until midnight. Campfires were lit at a number of the venues to fend off the cold.[132]

The highlight of the anniversary celebrations was the symbolic reenactment of the salute which signified the end of the blockade. Each year fireworks were set off in the evening over the Neva in the center of the city near the Field of Mars, the spit of Vasilievskii Island, Revolution Square, the Peter and Paul Fortress, and the Bronze Horseman.[133] A party report on the events from 1945 noted that "on the evening of 27 January, great anticipation prevailed: hundreds of thousands of workers watched the explosion [*sozhzhenie*] of celebratory fireworks."[134] Describing the salute that took place on 27 January 1949, the Leningrad press wrote,

> By 8 o'clock yesterday, thousands of people were drawn to the banks of the Neva. Here, five years ago, the powerful volleys from 324 cannons proclaimed to the world the brilliant victory of the soldiers from the Leningrad front, who completely liberated the city from the enemy blockade. And yesterday the thunder of 20 volleys and the fireworks illuminated the Leningrad sky, resurrecting in memory that unforgettable day.[135]

Like the all-city festivals which brought *blokadniki* together with evacuees and newcomers, the fireworks, and the joyous moment they symbolized, offered an opportunity both to reflect on the horrors, triumphs, and heroism of the 872 days, and to reinforce the meaning of the blockade. These anniversary celebrations as a whole, then, provided a powerful supplement to the commemorative services offered by the museum. By concentrating hundreds of events in the weeks leading up to the anniversary, the actual date of the lifting of the siege was invested with unprecedented significance for the city and its residents.

In a poem written in January 1943, a young Leningrad woman mused about the significance of the blockade, the need to commemorate it, and the will to restore the city. For her, and certainly many others, the blockade was a formative experience. The "falling walls," "hunger," and the sounds "which seemed to destroy the stars in the sky," were things that could never be forgotten. But those who "ran away" from the city's tortures, wrote the woman, "will never understand what the Leningrad blockade means."[136] Indeed, for someone who did not experience the blockade – its horrors, heroism, and victory – the very meaning of the 872 days could be something distant, impersonal, and unfathomable. Official commemorations of the blockade sought to address these issues. They were employed by the city's authorities to provide sites of mourning and memory for those who lived through the blockade. They were also used to create a sense of civic identity for all of the city's residents, but especially those who did not experience the siege. For all groups, whether they lived through the war in Leningrad or not, official commemorations – such as the Museum of the Defense of Leningrad and the anniversary celebrations – were used to cultivate a memory of the blockade (one which erased negative aspects of Leningraders' wartime experience), and mobilize people for the city's restoration.

Through commemorations, Leningrad's authorities were able to reach a large audience. Hundreds of thousands of people were exposed to lectures on the siege, the historical significance of the city, and the tasks facing them in Leningrad's postwar restoration. Official commemorations offered a ritualistic reenactment of the heroic and self-sacrificing story of the blockade; they created and perpetuated a story of Leningrad's – and Leningraders' – uniqueness. By actively engaging with the city's population and fostering a mythologized memory of the blockade, Leningrad's authorities provided a model to follow, which encouraged people to become "heroic Leningraders" through their labor in the restoration of the "glorious city."

SIX

COLD WAR COMPLICATIONS: SOVIET PATRIOTISM, HISTORIC RESTORATION, AND THE END OF BLOCKADE COMMEMORATIONS

THE POSTWAR RESTORATION OF HISTORIC MONUMENTS AND commemorations of the blockade took place against the background of growing international tensions and corresponding domestic anxieties. Whereas the Soviet Union had been an ally of the United States and Britain during the war, that relationship – fraught with tensions from the beginning – came to an end very soon after the defeat of Nazi Germany, and the former allies found themselves on opposing sides of the emerging Cold War. This new conflict was most immediately felt in the foreign policy of the Soviet Union, but it also had a tremendous impact on internal Soviet politics and everyday life.[1] The developing confrontation with the West, in fact, manifested itself in the ideological dictates of the postwar Stalin regime.[2] With the Cold War in full swing by 1947, Moscow was intent on imposing ideological conformity on the Soviet population, hoping to ensure loyalty and unity in the new battle with the West.

A key component of postwar Stalinist ideology was a renewed emphasis on Soviet patriotism, which dominated all aspects of internal affairs by the spring of 1947.[3] Like the patriotism fostered since the mid-1930s, the postwar patriotic line promoted love for the motherland and its past (which was increasingly identified as Russia and Russia's past). It was also guided by the emerging myth of the Great Patriotic War, which lauded the heroic Soviet people, the Soviet state, and above all, Stalin for saving humanity from fascism. These two pillars of Soviet patriotism and postwar ideology had an important impact on the commemorations in Leningrad and the restoration of the city's imperial monuments and landmarks.

The postwar emphasis on the Russian past in creating a unified, patriotic community of people led Soviet authorities to strengthen their commitment to preserving the embodiments of the country's history. The destruction of war made it painfully obvious that monuments, and the history they embodied, could easily be destroyed or lost. In a series of new laws, the Soviet government outlined the need for improving preservation and restoration activities, as well as rules to be followed with respect to the use of historic monuments in all areas of the Soviet Union. From late 1948 onward, those organizations and people who had fought to preserve the country's monuments received further encouragement in their work. Although they continued to face problems, the Stalinist state confirmed its commitment to restoring the country's heritage and improving the condition of historic and cultural sites.

The ideological demands of the period, however, had an adverse effect on commemorations of Leningrad's experience in the war. As the conflict with the West intensified, and the threat of a new, more devastating war loomed, the central authorities became more and more intolerant of local particularistic narratives that did not focus on the all-Union heroism of the Soviet people. When Leningrad's leaders came under attack in 1949, those people and institutions in the city most closely associated with promoting the memory of the blockade became caught up in the "Leningrad Affair," Stalin's most vicious postwar purge. Representatives from Moscow scrutinized the Leningrad party organization in the wake of the purge and found that Leningrad's commemorative narrative "perverted" the history of the Great Patriotic War. The particularistic myth of the blockade, and the local patriotism it promoted, was used as evidence of Leningrad's "disloyalty" and fueled the purge of the city's party and government organizations.

Early 1949, therefore, marked a radical departure from the previous years, when commemorations and restoration of the city's historic monuments were inextricably linked and intertwined. Restoration would continue, and, indeed, would achieve more and more positive results in bringing the country's history back to life. But it would continue without – at least officially – being portrayed as a commemoration of the blockade. The year 1949 represents a parting of the ways, a time when Leningrad's particularistic memory of the war was quashed while the embodiments of the past that served Soviet patriotism continued to be restored. The connection between commemoration and restoration in Leningrad became a victim of the postwar Stalinist ideological clampdown.

TIGHTENING THE IDEOLOGICAL REINS

The Soviet Union emerged victorious from the Second World War, but that victory was in many respects Pyrrhic. True, Soviet frontiers were expanded to the West, and much of Eastern Europe had come under the influence of Moscow, but that did not negate the fact that the Soviet Union faced major economic, demographic, and social problems as a result of the war, which created feelings of insecurity and anxiety among the top leadership. Consequently, at the end of the war Stalin sought continued cooperation with the United States and Britain to overcome the destruction.[4]

Growing tensions between the Soviet Union and the West, however, put an end to cooperation soon after the war.[5] Actions taken by both sides created an atmosphere of deep mistrust and hostility: the Truman administration cut off Lend-Lease immediately when the war ended, and several months later, in August 1945, dropped two atomic bombs on Japan; Stalin continued to exert pressure and influence on the internal workings of Eastern European states despite his promises not to, which by 1946 led Churchill to proclaim that an Iron Curtain had descended across Europe, separating East from West; and the announcement of the Truman Doctrine and Marshall Plan in 1947 prompted Andrei Zhdanov to declare to representatives from Eastern European Communist parties that the world had been split into two hostile and opposing camps.[6] Between 1945 and 1947, therefore, the gulf between the former allies became unbridgeable. As relations between the two camps worsened and rhetoric grew more hostile, the Soviet Union again, as in the 1920s and 1930s, found itself isolated and "besieged."

In response to the growing threat from abroad, which only exacerbated Soviet insecurities about its economy and its defense capabilities, the Stalinist leadership sought to stamp out Western leanings and cultivate a sense of devotion to the socialist motherland and its achievements by reverting to strict ideological orthodoxy. Indeed, there were several problems that concerned the leadership in the postwar years. The devotion and reliability of party cadres was one of these issues. During the war, millions of civilians and soldiers had joined the Communist Party without having gone through the usual screening and training.[7] The leadership worried about new members' level of "partymindedness" and ideological commitment to the cause.[8] The circumstances of the war had also compelled the party leadership to offer certain liberties – intellectual and religious – to the population, which meant that ideological control was not always strictly observed.[9] While many hoped for such policies to continue into the postwar years, their desire for liberalization was dashed as the Stalinist leadership strove to restore the system as it existed in the prewar years.[10]

The central authorities were further concerned about popular loyalty after the war. Most disturbing to Stalin was the fact that certain areas of the country had been completely out of Moscow's reach for extended periods, and as a result, the reliability of people in those regions was a source of grave concern. This fear was exacerbated by the fact that in certain parts of the western borderlands – including Western Ukraine and the Baltic republics – nationalist insurgencies carried on well into the postwar years.[11] Those returning from slave labor and prisoner-of-war camps in Germany were, likewise, treated with a great deal of suspicion regarding their wartime activities and political allegiances.[12] Indeed, between 1943 and 1953, the Stalinist security apparatus arrested approximately 320,000 people on suspicion of collaborating with the enemy during the war.[13] Even Leningrad, which had not been occupied, had shown a high degree of autonomy and independence in the decision-making process during the siege, and this ultimately led to tensions between Stalin and the Leningrad leadership.[14]

During the immediate postwar period, then, Moscow was intent on regaining control over the population and reasserting authority over center-periphery relations.[15] This called for action in a number of areas. In April 1946, Andrei Zhdanov was entrusted with increasing vigilance among new party members, the intelligentsia, and the population as a whole to ensure ideological conformity.[16] In a speech to workers at the Central Committee's Department of Agitation and Propaganda on 18

April 1946, Zhdanov emphasized "serious insufficiencies" in the realm of ideology, noting the need to "significantly strengthen" party leadership in ideological matters.[17] What resulted from this was an ideological campaign – the *Zhdanovshchina* – that was scripted and closely monitored by Stalin, and was aimed at eliminating a perceived "pro-Western orientation" among the intelligentsia and increasing the level of Soviet patriotism among the population.

From late 1946, the Soviet leadership demanded that all cultural and scientific matters be put at the service of ideology and used to bolster Soviet patriotism.[18] The arts and sciences were to conform to the new ideological demands. Those who did not live up to the state's new line were severely criticized, scapegoated, and repressed. The ideological crackdown targeted works that the party judged to be politically irrelevant or of no use in creating a loyal citizenry. Leningrad writers Anna Akhmatova and Mikhail Zoshchenko, for example, were attacked for the "anti-Soviet" and "individualistic" themes in their work, in a speech written by Stalin and delivered by Zhdanov. At the beginning of the *Zhdanovshchina,* two Leningrad-based journals (*Zvezda* and *Leningrad*) were attacked for their political "mistakes." The editors of both were accused of printing the works of Akhmatova and Zoshchenko, and for being "apolitical," a serious crime when journals were to be a medium of "education for Soviet people."[19] Some scientists also came under attack for their connections with, and "kowtowing" to, the West, as happened with professors Nina Klіueva and Grigorii Roskin, whose famous case marked the inauguration of "courts of honor." These courts were intended to eliminate "servility to the West" and "reeducate the *workers of state institutions* in the spirit of Soviet patriotism and devotion to the Soviet state's interests" (emphasis original).[20] The Stalinist leadership used nearly all propaganda avenues and channels to steel the population against the Soviet Union's ideological enemies.

Soviet patriotism became the ultimate vehicle for crafting a loyal population.[21] In propagandizing Soviet patriotism, the Department of Propaganda and Agitation of the Central Committee (Agitprop) instructed its activists to focus on the achievements of the Soviet system and its superiority over the West. The emerging all-Union myth of war became one of the key elements demonstrating supposed Soviet supremacy and uniting the people, and consequently Agitprop ordered that special attention be paid to the war in propaganda:

> In all political work it is necessary to persistently emphasize that there is no other people who could have made such great services to humanity, as the Soviet people has. It needs to be shown that the Soviet people, who opened a new epoch in the history of humanity – the epoch of socialist society, which saved world civilization from the fascist barbarians – is the leading, creative people.[22]

The myth of war fostered cohesion and unity among the population. "The supraclass, cross-ethnic aspect of the myth," notes Amir Weiner, "provided the polity with a previously absent integrating theme and folded into the body politic large groups that previously had been excluded."[23] Focusing on the superiority of the Soviet system, the myth of war offered a feeling of belonging, and a sense of pride in the socialist motherland and its achievements. More than anything else, the myth of the war helped forge a patriotic Soviet identity.[24]

The glory of Russia's past was the other crucial element in the construction of postwar Soviet patriotism. Soviet citizens were expected to learn about the history of selected events and heroes throughout the thousand years of the Russian state's existence. Like the myth of war, the Russian past was to act as a unifier and anchor for Soviet identity. "In presenting the magnificence of our socialist motherland, of the heroic Soviet people," Agitprop instructed, "it is necessary to explain that our people is right to be proud of its great historic past."[25] Party activists were to discuss the accomplishments of the Russian people in the period before the revolution, as well as Russia's military victories over the Mongol-Tatar Yoke and Napoleon, and Agitprop instructed that, in doing so, they should emphasize the contribution of these events to the development of European civilization. Special attention was also to be paid to Russia's contribution to world culture, music, literature, and science.[26] The non-Russian peoples of the other Soviet republics were, likewise, instructed to respect their national pasts and feel pride in national accomplishments, yet always in the context of Russia's great past: republican history had to complement and not undermine Russia's.[27]

The impetus for this came from international politics. The need to rebuild the country and to be on guard in the Cold War demanded a unified population with a common past, common goals, and common identity. Soviet patriotism was to be the bond that would unite the country's diverse population, as well as a source of inspiration to defend the country against its enemies. A postwar publication on Soviet patriotism, for example, highlighted the lessons learned from the Second World War and the people's patriotic determination to defend the motherland should another war ensue. "The Patriotic War was the most severe test of the strength and endurance of Soviet patriotism," declared the book's author, N. I. Matiushkin. "The results of the war," he continued,

> are a stern warning to the instigators of a new world war, to all enemies of peace. These results show that the Soviet people are in a position to honorably stand up for themselves with weapon in hand, in a position to crush and reduce to ashes any enemy encroaching on the freedom and independence of the socialist state. The toiling people, the creative people, is also a warrior people and a fighting people. The Soviet people have grasped and continued the heroic traditions of their forefathers, and have placed these traditions at the service of the interests of the Soviet motherland and all of progressive humanity.[28]

As this passage suggests, Soviet patriotism was guided by two distinct themes: one concentrating on the Soviet experience in the Great Patriotic War and the people's ultimate victory, and the other on the country's past and heroic traditions. "It would be precise to think of Soviet ideology during these years as characterized by a double axis," argues David Brandenberger. "On the one hand, the Soviet myth of war became the quintessential legitimation of Soviet power. On the other hand, a thousand years of prerevolutionary history continued to serve – as it had since 1937 – as another source of authority and legitimacy."[29] Soviet patriotism was based on the accomplishments of the tsarist period and the myth of war, both of which were used by the Stalinist authorities to foster a common culture and identity during the postwar years.[30]

COMMITTING TO THE PAST

Throughout the postwar period, as we have seen in previous chapters, the central and local authorities were concerned with restoring the embodiments of the country's past. Historian Serhy Yekelchyk, for example, has noted that in postwar Ukraine the new emphasis on history and heritage caused officials to distance themselves from the prewar Ukrainian leadership, which had destroyed many of the republic's most famous religious monuments for ideological and urban planning purposes.[31] These monuments provided a tangible connection to the people's heritage. Given that the country's past became one of the main components of postwar ideology, this connection to heritage was not only desired, but necessary. Historic, artistic, and architectural monuments were sites in which the past, and the professed ideology, were reified.

During the war preservationists pushed for the creation of new legislation to protect the country's historic monuments.[32] As soon as the country was liberated from the German forces, architectural and preservationist organizations – especially the recently formed Committee for Architectural Affairs at the Council of Ministers (USSR) and the Main Administration for the Protection of Monuments of Architecture under its purview – began to lobby for laws designed to protect the country's heritage. The destruction of historic monuments during the war heightened people's awareness of the vulnerability of monuments as unique artifacts through which the narrative of the motherland was told. With this in mind, in December 1944 the participants at an all-Union conference of architects discussed the need for the government to exercise control over the country's historic monuments and ensure their "proper maintenance and protection."[33] New legislation, argued conference participants, must provide for leadership, control, and help in the preservation of monuments "from above." Responsibility for, and the actual organization of, monument preservation needed to be placed with local organs of authority and the administration for architectural affairs in the given location.[34] Leningrad's Administration for Architectural Affairs was held up as a positive example in this regard.[35]

During the first postwar years a number of problems became evident in the efforts to preserve and restore Leningrad's monuments. Given that the situation in Leningrad was considered to be the best in the country, one can only imagine the difficulties faced elsewhere.[36] The failure of building occupants to carry out the work assigned to them in leases, inadequate funding, and a lack of control over certain monuments were some of the main issues to be dealt with in drawing up legislation.[37] Efforts to draft new laws for the protection of monuments were, in fact, a means of providing a system of organization that would allow for the long-term stability of the country's heritage. Due to the lack of appropriate legislation, a solution was needed.[38] Creating new laws to protect the country's historic, cultural, and artistic monuments, in light of the circumstances, would benefit the state as it increasingly relied upon the Russian past to promote a patriotic identity among the population.

From mid-1947 onward, the efforts of preservationists, architects, and the artistic community to get legislation passed came to fruition. In late 1946, the Administration for the Protection of Monuments of Architecture submitted a draft resolution to the Soviet government calling for legislation to ensure the protection of the country's architectural heritage.[39] The Soviet of Ministers of the Russian Republic passed the law "On the Protection of Architectural Monuments" on 22 May 1947. This law proclaimed the works of ancient Russian architecture "to be the inviolable historical-artistic legacy of the national culture and the property of the republic."[40] Echoing the ideological turn toward the Russian past, the law laid out a system of rules concerning the protection, use, and upkeep of architectural monuments. It stipulated that the Administration for Architectural Affairs in each locality, as well as local government organs, were to take responsibility for the preservation and proper use of monuments and landmarks. It specified that occupants were to sign agreements with the local administration, and that if they failed to uphold the terms of the agreement they could be evicted. Local governments (city and regional soviet executive committees, for example) were placed in charge of restoration, repairs, and related work on monuments. The funding for this was to come from local budgets and from the money provided by occupants of buildings and monuments. Finally, the law ordered that instructions about the use of monuments be compiled and confirmed in June of that year, and that a list of monuments under state protection be presented by December.[41]

This legislation was the first significant attempt to centralize the management of architectural monuments in the Russian republic since the 1930s. It clearly outlined the responsibilities of various parties, and made infractions of these obligations punishable by law.[42] Although the legislation stipulated that infractions could lead to institutions and organizations' being evicted, there were obvious problems with this. Depending on exactly who the occupant was, the matter could become quite complicated. In March 1948, for example, the president of the Committee for Architectural Affairs of the USSR wrote party hierarch Kliment Voroshilov to ask for his help in transferring the management of the Constantine Palace outside Leningrad from the Ministry of Armed Forces to the Ministry of Higher Education. Basing the request on the 1947 law, the president argued that the Ministry of Armed Forces had done nothing to restore the palace since the end of the war and was therefore subject to eviction.[43] The ministry, however, refused to move. The fact that a petition had to be sent to the vice president of the Soviet government suggests that, at least in some cases, enforcement was problematic. In the meantime, the Committee for Architectural Affairs worked out and submitted a draft of a new law to the Soviet of Ministers of the USSR that would be all-encompassing, focusing on the entire Union, not just the Russian republic.[44]

Unlike the 1947 legislation, which addressed the preservation of architectural monuments in Russia, the all-Union decree of 14 October 1948 took into account all monuments of culture (broadly defined, monuments of culture included architectural, artistic, and archeological monuments of historical significance) throughout the country. The legislation itself was a response to the "serious insufficiencies" plaguing the country's monuments. The decree opened by describing the current state of heritage protection in the Soviet Union. "Control over the preservation of historical and archeological monuments does not exist," it stated. "Leadership over the protection and restoration of monuments of architecture and art by the Committee for Architectural Affairs and the Committee for Artistic Affairs of the Soviet government is being carried out unsatisfactorily." It further asserted that institutions occupying heritage buildings were not providing for their preservation, nor were the local soviet executive committees showing the "appropriate care" for monuments of culture.[45] In presenting the problems in the system, the Soviet leadership was taking a stand, proclaiming that the current situation was unacceptable and stating its position on the country's heritage.

The new legislation was far-reaching in its ambition to provide for preservation. It laid the responsibility for the protection and supervision of the monuments on the governments of the various republics and on the local soviet executive committees. It called for the registration of all monuments in the Soviet Union, ordered that scientific-restoration workshops be opened in areas with a high concentration of monuments, and directed that a scientific-methodological council be created under the purview of the Academy of Sciences. A further eight pages of instructions and stipulations were appended, emphasizing the need to preserve the country's heritage.[46] The outcome of the new legislation was, therefore, a bifurcated system of preservation which saw the oversight of monuments shared by local and central government organs.[47]

Preservationists were enthusiastic about the law of 1948. At last there was a detailed all-Union document meant to provide for the protection of the country's heritage.[48] The architectural and preservation authorities in Moscow were interested in disseminating the law as quickly and widely as possible and bringing specialists together to discuss its implications. Soon after the announcement of the legislation, the Main Administration for the Protection of Monuments of Architecture arranged plans to distribute copies of it to architects and planners throughout the country.[49] The law was made widely known to the public with the hope that the problems encountered in preserving monuments of culture and history would soon be overcome. The Committee for Architectural Affairs also received permission from the party's Central Committee to bring specialists from all regions of the Soviet Union to Moscow in the second quarter of 1949 to discuss the principal questions concerning the law.[50]

The importance of these new laws is difficult to overstate. At the very least, they gave preservationists legal grounds to demand that restoration, repairs, and conservation be carried out by building occupants in a timely fashion. Local and central government organs used the law frequently in their correspondence with ministries, organizations, and institutions using buildings under state protection. The Committee for Architectural Affairs, for example, cited the law when writing to the Leningrad city soviet in early 1949, requesting that the executive committee spend nearly thirty-one million rubles on fifty-two monuments housing organizations under its purview.[51] The head of GIOP, Belekhov, also invoked the new law when demanding that restoration be carried out on monuments in the suburb of Pushkin. Noting the lack of work, Belekhov wrote,

> Seeing in this a direct violation of the Soviet government's decree from 14.10.1948 (N.3898) . . . as well as the instructions published by the Committee for Architectural Affairs . . . for the execution of the law, the Inspectorate categorically insists that immediate steps be taken to conserve this monument in the current year, in order to prevent further destructive actions during the fall and winter.[52]

The 1948 decree was a document that could also be cited by local governing bodies when petitioning Moscow for funding to provide for restoration, or used for confirming the use of monuments.[53] The new laws, then, provided a basis for grievances to be made about the state of the country's monuments, as well as demands that actions be taken to protect them from further harm.

Perhaps more importantly, the new laws – and especially the 1948 legislation – underlined the party's position on relics of the past. The country's monuments were physical manifestations of the tsarist and imperial historical narrative that was central to Soviet patriotic identity. Increasingly during the postwar period the party manifested, as Yekelchyk notes, "a desire for total ideological control over historic sites," and the laws served this desire.[54] The official endorsement of the restoration of architectural, artistic, historic, and cultural monuments was, then, a natural outgrowth of the promotion of Soviet patriotism, and preservationists welcomed the ideological turn because it bolstered their endeavor to restore embodiments of the past and save history for future generations. What is more, the laws are a testament to the power of preservationists to lobby for the protection of monuments at a time when resources were scarce and the difficulties facing the country as a whole were immense.

IDEOLOGY AND COMMEMORATIONS OF THE BLOCKADE

While the postwar ideological line promoted the restoration of the country's architectural, artistic, and historic monuments, it slowly silenced blockade commemorations. The authorities utilized the country's monumental heritage to create common roots and a common past for the population to rally around. Commemorations of the blockade did the opposite. Instead of presenting a united Soviet population defeating the

Germans in a battle for the Soviet Union, commemorations in the former imperial capital perpetuated a myth of the blockade that emphasized the unique fate of Leningrad, the "heroic feats" achieved by the city's residents on the front and in their everyday surroundings, and the "labor heroism" of those who continued to work in the city's factories and industries. This myth offered Leningraders an identity that was rooted in, yet also transcended, the experience and narrative offered by the Soviet state.[55] It allowed Leningraders to share in the victory of the Soviet Union and feel united as one people, but it also advanced a particularistic story of the blockade that belonged to Leningrad alone.

The myth of the blockade was articulated in a number of ways and by a multitude of actors. The Museum of the Defense of Leningrad and the celebrations of the anniversary of the lifting of the blockade worked to promote civic identity as a tool for mobilizing the city's long-term residents and newcomers to restore Leningrad. These became the cornerstones of the blockade myth and provided for its articulation. Other vehicles of mythmaking, of course, included the numerous works of literature written by people who survived the blockade, including Ol'ga Berggol'ts, Nikolai Tikhonov, and Vera Inber.[56] Yet perhaps the most consistent and vocal articulators of the blockade myth were the party and soviet authorities who had experienced the siege firsthand. It was people like Aleksei Kuznetsov, the Leningrad party boss, and Petr Popkov, the chairman of the city soviet (and party boss after Kuznetsov's promotion and move to Moscow in March 1946), who pushed for the creation of the museum, scripted the anniversary celebrations, and sponsored the publication of works which glorified Leningrad's wartime experience.[57] "The entire initiative behind publishing document collections on the history of the defense of Leningrad," observes Russian historian Andrei Dzeniskevich, "came from the city's party leadership. These people actively sought to immortalize the feat of Leningraders, and they acted without waiting for orders and permission from above."[58]

Although Leningraders articulated the city's epic through the museum and anniversary celebrations, many felt the need to further memorialize the heroism of the blockade in stone. Local authorities envisioned erecting a massive monumental ensemble to the defenders of the city immediately after the blockade was lifted.[59] The party's city committee established a commission headed by Alexei Kuznetsov to develop plans for a monument to the defenders of Leningrad in November 1944.[60] The commission sought advice from a wide variety of party and soviet workers, architects, artists, and sculptors, as well as other representatives of Leningrad's intelligentsia, about the possible name for the monument, its location in the city, and the form the monument should take.[61] In a report produced by the commission, the author (who was most likely Nikolai Baranov), emphasized the importance of drawing on Leningrad's city-planning tradition of utilizing architecture and sculpture to depict the "military feats of the heroic Russian people."[62] The report went on to argue that the war with Germany, and especially the heroic defense of Leningrad – "one of the most brilliant pages of the epic" – must be reflected in the city's appearance.[63]

The commission decided that the monument should be built on Moskovskii Prospekt near the House of Soviets, where it would become the center of an area devoted entirely to the blockade.[64] Nikolai Baranov discussed the construction of this monument in a paper delivered at a meeting of the city soviet's executive committee in December 1945. He argued that although a series of monuments was planned for areas outside the city, a large monument must be constructed in Leningrad itself. The planning for the monument entitled "To the Heroic Defenders of Leningrad" was to begin in 1946. Due to the centrality of the blockade in the city's narrative and its importance to Leningrad's identity, this monumental structure, Baranov emphasized, must surpass the monument to the victory in the war of 1812 (the Alexander Column on Palace Square): "The events that we experienced have much greater significance, and therefore, we do not have the right to make a lesser monument, but rather it must be more impressive; we must not erect just one monument, but create an architectural ensemble, in which the monument will be the main element." The commission's decision to erect the monument near the House of Soviets made sense, argued Baranov, because "the entire ensemble of the square would be nothing other than a monument, which would immortalize the events that Leningrad lived through."[65] After a series of petitions and requests to build the monument were sent to the Central Committee in Moscow, permission was granted and construction was slated to begin during the first postwar Five-Year Plan. Indeed, the official plan for the reconstruction and development of Leningrad in the new Five-Year Plan stipulated that construction of this monumental ensemble, along with monuments at mass graves, would commence.[66]

This idea resonated with many of the people living in Leningrad after the blockade. A worker at the Kirov factory, for example, expressed his desire to see the epic commemorated in the age-old fashion. "I would erect a huge monument on the most crucial and nearest border of the defense of the city," he wrote in his memoirs, "which would reflect the unprecedented heroism of Leningraders. A monument, in memory of those heroes who died in defense of Leningrad, and those heroic Leningraders who died of hunger."[67] Similar thoughts were echoed by a young woman in a poem about the destruction of the city and the experience of the siege. "We'll gather together the Rastrelli granite / Destroyed at the hands of defilers / And we'll erect a monument and let the centuries preserve / The proud story of Leningraders' glory."[68] Bringing together images of the city's historic architecture and expressing the need to eternalize the Leningrad epic in stone, these memoirs and diary entries show how important the blockade was to Leningraders' understanding of their own identities and the history of the city.[69] Average Leningraders, like the city's authorities, were producers, carriers, and articulators of the myth.

Throughout the first postwar years, then, Leningraders were determined to tell and glorify their story. Although a new monumental ensemble was meant to supplement the existing commemorations and to immortalize the history of the blockade in stone, the ideological stringency accompanying the Cold War prevented its construction and led to imposed amnesia about the Leningraders' struggles.[70] At precisely the same time that the government was expressing its commitment to preserving the country's great heritage, the narrative of Leningrad's wartime experience began to change. The first alterations took place in early 1948. The official story of the blockade began to focus more on the struggle of the entire country with the Germans in the Great Patriotic War, and the victory at the gates of Leningrad was increasingly attributed to Stalin. The press coverage surrounding the anniversary celebrations also began to emphasize Stalin's role in saving Leningrad. The emphasis on the city's unique experience was shifted to Stalin's greatness and the help given to the besieged city from the entire country.[71] No longer, for example, was the idea of creating the "Road of Life" across Lake Ladoga attributed to Zhdanov and the Leningrad party; instead, Stalin was now hailed as the initiator of this and all other actions which alleviated the plight of Leningraders in the city and at the front.

This change in the narrative of the blockade was also reflected in the plans for the Museum of the Defense of Leningrad. The museum's administration, for instance, instructed its staff to begin reworking several of the exhibits in order to portray the experience of war on all fronts, not just in Leningrad. In his report for 1948, the director of the museum, V. P. Kovalev, noted the new ideological line:

> The battle of Leningraders and warriors at the front outside Leningrad with the German-Fascist invaders must not be portrayed in isolation [*otvorvanno*] from the general battle of the Soviet people with the Hitlerite monsters, and for this reason, the museum must develop exhibits which clearly characterize the most important victories attained by the soldiers of the Red Army on the fronts of the Great Patriotic War.[72]

Just as the victory in the war was proclaimed to be secured by Stalin, the credit for the heroic defense of Leningrad increasingly shifted away from those who articulated the particularistic myth.[73] At this point the party leadership still hailed the blockade and the struggles on the Leningrad front as one of the greatest events in the war. But over the course of 1948 and 1949, the significance of the blockade diminished, as officials treated it less as an event in and of itself and more as an episode in the all-Union war. The ways in which Leningraders had presented the city's wartime experience impinged on the official promotion of Soviet patriotism through its challenge to the myth of the Great Patriotic War as a collective accomplishment.

The decisive change came in January 1949, in the wake of the fifth anniversary of the end of the siege. Less than a month after the anniversary celebrations, the Politburo accused two of Leningrad's wartime leaders – A. A. Kuznetsov and P. S. Popkov – of a host of crimes, including squandering state funds on a wholesale trade fair in Leningrad that was not approved by the Soviet government, and promoting themselves as "special defenders of Leningrad's interests."[74] A few days later, Georgii Malenkov traveled to Leningrad with an entourage of nearly two hundred officials to speak at a united city and regional party plenum.[75] At the plenum he stated the accusations of the Politburo, proclaimed that the Leningrad leadership was attempting to distance itself from the Central Committee of the party, and argued that their actions had "set them down an anti-party path."[76] Not only were Kuznetsov and Popkov suddenly turned into anti-party enemies, but the "plague" quickly spread to other members of the Leningrad leadership, including the two other top officials in the city's administration, Ia. F. Kapustin and P. G. Lazutin.[77] On 1 October 1950, a military board of the Supreme Court of the USSR sentenced them and two other highly placed officials with connections to Leningrad (N. A. Voznesenskii, a Politburo member and vice chairman of the Soviet of Ministers of the USSR, and M. I. Rodionov, a member of the Orgburo and chairman of the Soviet of Ministers of the Russian Republic), to death. Several others were given long-term prison sentences.[78] Over the course of the next few years, many of the people who had been in positions of authority in Leningrad during the blockade, as well as their families, were swallowed up in a bloody political purge known as the Leningrad Affair.[79] On 15 August 1952 alone, for example, the police arrested fifty people who worked as district party committee and soviet executive committee members during the blockade, and handed them long prison sentences.[80]

Historians have tended to see the purge as a result of a battle for power that developed in the early postwar years between two factions in the top party leadership. When the war ended, Zhdanov was recalled to Moscow to oversee ideological matters and gradually rose to become Stalin's most trusted underling. Shortly after taking his position in Moscow, Zhdanov arranged to have Kuznetsov promoted to secretary of the party's Central Committee in the spring of 1946. The promotion of Zhdanov and Kuznetsov came at the expense of Malenkov and Lavrentii Beriia. With Zhdanov in control of Agitprop, Kuznetsov took over Malenkov's former position supervising party cadres and Beria's leadership of the state security apparatus. The Leningraders then promoted former associates, mainly from Leningrad, into influential positions in Moscow and throughout the USSR. Malenkov and Beria's waning power motivated them to collaborate in a struggle against Zhdanov and the Leningraders. According to the conventional interpretation, when

Zhdanov died in August 1948, Malenkov and Beria seized the opportunity to defeat their opponents (left defenseless with the death of their patron in the Politburo), and regain Stalin's favor by raising his suspicions about the Leningraders.[81]

Recently historians have nuanced the factional fighting argument. While acknowledging the importance of tensions between the groups, some have argued that the Leningrad leadership was purged for violating the principles of governmental and party discipline.[82] Others see the purge as an attempt to "uproot" a patronage network in the party elite,[83] or to destroy a "Leningrad cabal" that Stalin no longer had faith in.[84] And yet another interpretation suggests that the root of the purge lay in attempts to promote Russian autonomy within the USSR by creating a Russian Communist Party centered in Leningrad.[85] Certainly no single reason can be pinpointed to explain this final Stalinist purge, and it is clear that the Leningrad Affair developed out of a combination of factors. But given the ideological rigidity provoked by the Cold War, the promotion of local identity and the particularistic myth of Leningrad's wartime experience must be seen as contributing factors in the attack on Leningrad's leadership and the memory of the blockade.[86] Malenkov and Beria certainly used the particularistic myth of the blockade as evidence of disloyalty in their efforts to have Stalin attack Leningrad. And – more importantly – the story of the blockade and Leningraders' heroism became an additional victim of the purge.

Amir Weiner has argued that in the postwar period, promoting narratives of war and wartime suffering that did not fit into or that challenged the official myth of war could and did lead to the "collective exclusion" of certain groups of people.[87] The Jewish Anti-Fascist Committee, for example, became the object of persecution, in part because it attempted to document the suffering of the Jewish people during the war and expressed "Jewish particularism."[88] Between 1941 and 1945, the Soviet leadership used the committee to mobilize support from Jews outside the Soviet Union in the battle against fascism. In the postwar period, the party leadership believed that the committee's continuing activities, including the publication of *The Black Book*, which told of Jewish suffering at the hands of the Nazis, presented the history of the Jews in the Great Patriotic War and early postwar period "in isolation" from the rest of the Soviet people.[89] When the war ended, the committee was no longer needed to mobilize support against the Germans. Similarly, by 1949 the memory of the blockade, in Moscow's opinion, had outlived its usefulness as a mobilizing force to "resurrect" the second-most important city in the country. Now that the economy had been restored to its prewar levels and the central government felt itself to be on more solid ground than in the immediate postwar period, Moscow was no longer willing to tolerate the powerful myth of the northern capital's wartime experience when the international situation demanded unity at home.

Leningrad and the memory of the blockade thus came under attack following Malenkov's visit. The central leadership was intent on bringing the memory of the war in Leningrad back under the state's ideological program and subjecting the city's leadership to strict control from above. Those Leningrad leaders purged over the course of the Leningrad Affair were replaced by Stalin's people sent from Moscow.[90] In the months that followed the February meeting, Agitprop dispatched several commissions to scrutinize the work of the Leningrad party organization and document their findings for the Central Committee. The results of the reviews, given the postwar insistence on Soviet patriotism, were not surprising. Reports sent to Agitprop noted that Leningrad party organizations focused too much on the city itself, to the detriment of the country as a whole. A review of the House of the Party Activists (*Dom partaktiv*), for example, noted that the material prepared by the Leningrad party organization for the *Short Course of the History of the Party* "is one-sided and impresses on the readers an incorrect presentation about the special, supposedly decisive role of Leningrad and the Leningrad party organization in the life of the country." The report went on to state that the city's party organization presented the Great Patriotic War, as experienced in Leningrad, in a one-sided fashion, leaving out battles on other fronts.[91] Another report noted that agitation work and the city's cultural-enlightenment establishments were not living up to the tasks set by the central leadership. Party journals, including *Bloknot agitatora,* as well as Leningrad's radio stations, were accused of devoting very little attention to the Union as a whole.[92] Leningrad's propaganda organs, the report noted, needed to expand their focus to include all-Union matters. The Leningrad Affair therefore opened the party organization up to increased scrutiny and provided a pretext for the Central Committee to find faults and lay blame. The reviews showed the Stalinist leadership that local authorities had created a cult of Leningrad based on the city's unique history and the myth of the blockade.

Soon after the purge began in Leningrad, the changes in the blockade narrative that were witnessed in 1948 were greatly intensified. Indeed, over the course of 1949 and the years leading up to Stalin's death, all mention of Leningrad's wartime experience ceased. Books focusing on the blockade that were published during and after the war were pulled from the shelves of bookstores and libraries throughout the country.[93] Between 1949 and Khrushchev's de-Stalinization of the mid 1950s very little, if anything, was published about the "heroic nine-hundred-day struggle." At the same time, discussion of the blockade was drastically curtailed in the press. Although an article or two appeared each subsequent year on the anniversary of the lifting of the siege, the coverage in Leningrad shrank significantly. In the first five years following the city's liberation, Leningrad newspapers devoted three to four pages to the blockade every 27 January. In 1950 only one article appeared on page 2 of *Leningradskaia pravda,* and any mention of the anniversary completely disappeared from the central newspapers.[94] From this time onward, much more attention was given to the other major battles during the war (e.g., Stalingrad), and the victory at the gates of Leningrad was presented as the result of the work of the entire Soviet people, and especially Stalin. Not only did reports of the anniversary vanish from the press, but popular celebrations also came to an end.[95] Moscow, in fact, silenced all forms of local celebrations that broke away from the ideological line by presenting Leningrad as a special victim of the Great Patriotic War. By attacking the institutions which propagated the uniqueness of Leningrad's wartime experience, the Stalinist leadership intended to place more emphasis on the all-Union myth of war in an effort to promote Soviet patriotism.

The most vital blow to the Leningraders' memory of the blockade struck the Museum of the Defense of Leningrad. Soon after the Leningrad Affair began, the museum was closed "temporarily" to reorganize parts of the layout. At first there was nothing strange in this: the museum had been closed temporarily to renovate and update exhibits in the past.

This time, however, the museum never reopened. Since 1948 the museum had come under increasing pressure to present the defense and blockade of Leningrad in a way that emphasized the connection with the rest of the country and the assistance provided to Leningrad by the Soviet people. Like other institutions in Leningrad following the purge, the museum was closely scrutinized by representatives of the central party leadership and found to be seriously lacking in several respects. Malenkov, for example, reviewed the museum's guidebook (published in 1948) during his stay in the city and "screamed" that the museum was full of anti-Soviet exhibits, that it had "perverted Stalin's role in the defense of Leningrad, that only the suffering of Leningraders is emphasized in the museum, and that the role of the Central Committee of the party in the defense of Leningrad is not presented, etc., etc."[96] In effect, Malenkov accused the museum of creating a special myth of Leningrad's fate during the blockade.[97] Following this, Agitprop sent commissions to Leningrad to review and assess the museum, as well as provide guidelines for restructuring the exhibits and museological narrative.[98]

The museum became a lightning rod for the memory of the blockade as a whole, as well as for those who articulated that memory. The changes seen in the museum's narrative reflected the overall change in the limits of presenting exceptional events that could offer a sense of identity other than that proposed by the central leadership. A meeting of the museum's party organization in October 1949 echoed Malenkov's comments by noting that the museum's greatest fault was that it "perverted the historic events of the Great Patriotic War of the Soviet Union and in its content carried an anti-party character." Its layout, the gathering continued, "conducted an anti-party line of artificial separation of the battle of Leningraders from the general battle of the entire Soviet people, setting Leningrad off from the rest of the Soviet country."[99] Those very same Leningrad party and soviet leaders who were purged during the Leningrad Affair were now accused of using the museum for their own purposes – to split Leningrad off from the Central Committee, to acclaim their "sham contributions" in the defense of Leningrad at the expense of Stalin's role, and to minimize the role of the entire country in saving the city.[100] The tasks of the museum's party organization in late 1949, then, were many. Two of the most important were to concentrate on the ideological content in the new layout, and to uncover all the evidence of the former leaders' "enemy activities" and "tear them out by the roots."[101]

Over the next few years, museum staff – those who had not been removed from their positions and imprisoned for perverting the history of the war – worked furiously at correcting the "mistakes" and "anti-Soviet" elements that had poisoned the layout of the institution.[102] Much of their work focused on providing a narrative of the blockade that presented it as a component of the Great Patriotic War instead of a unique event of significance in and of itself. Workers were sent to regions and cities as far away as Odessa to search for materials showing that Leningrad was supported continuously by the entire country throughout the siege, and that Stalin had personally saved the city and its residents. At the museum's request, the central party committees of Kazakhstan, Tadzhikistan, Uzbekistan, Georgia, and other regions sent materials to show the help offered to Leningrad.[103] By 1951, the newly proposed layout of the museum bore very little resemblance to the museum as it existed until the summer of 1949. In order to fulfill the ideological demands of Moscow, the layout, in the words of its new director, L. A. Dubinin (appointed by the Central Committee), "is undergoing a fundamental change."[104]

Try as the museum staff might, there was very little that could be done to present Leningrad's wartime experience as anything but exceptional. No matter how the layout of the museum was changed, no matter how many images of Stalin were added to its walls, the museum could not but "bear witness" to the experience and heroism of Leningraders during the siege.[105] After closing in August 1949, the museum, contrary to the hopes of its employees and the people of Leningrad, never reopened.[106] On 18 February 1953, after more than three years of work to turn the museum into something it was never meant to be, the Leningrad city soviet ordered that it be liquidated and its exhibits distributed to other museums throughout the city.[107]

It is tempting to see the attack on the blockade narrative as simply a consequence of the local party leadership's fall from grace: that is, once they were unmasked as enemies, everything associated with them or that bore their imprint had to be destroyed as well. This was certainly a factor contributing to the closure of the museum and to the silence imposed on the story of the blockade. But it would be shortsighted not to see the attack on Leningrad's party leadership emerging from the local patriotism and particularistic myth of the war that they promoted. As was the case with other sites, events, institutions, and, indeed, people who promoted the memory of the blockade, the museum, in offering a particularistic history of the Great Patriotic War, had become ideologically dangerous and had to be silenced.

As the Cold War developed, the Stalinist leadership sought more than ever to create a loyal and unified population by inculcating a sense of Soviet patriotism in its citizens. The new ideological stance as expressed by Soviet patriotism stood on two pillars: a connection with the country's heritage, and the myth of the Great Patriotic War. In the words of David Brandenberger, "If Lenin's formula in the early 1920s had been 'communism equals Soviet power plus electrification,' by the late 1940s, Stalin's corollary apparently held that 'Soviet power equals the history of the Russian people plus the myth of war.'"[108]

To promote awareness of the thousand years of Russian history, the Stalinist leadership enacted laws to protect the embodiments of the country's past. By late 1948, historic and cultural monuments throughout the USSR were guaranteed protection in a series of new laws which sought to save them from destruction and abuse. The new legislation was part of an ideological commitment to heritage. The country's monuments were a means of unifying the population through the presentation of a common, heroic past, and the restoration of cultural monuments was thus not only desirable, but politically useful.

Commemorations of the blockade, however, were deemed to have the opposite effect. Instead of being accessible to all, the myth of the blockade offered a particularistic history of the war in Leningrad and on the Leningrad front. Throughout 1948, the central leadership in Moscow attempted to downplay the siege as a unique event which took place in isolation from the war on other fronts. When the Leningrad Affair began in February 1949, the city's wartime narrative and those who articulated it were exposed to scrutiny from Moscow. Their story was found to be heresy, and as a result, the city's leadership and institutions of memory came under attack. By the late 1940s, memories that challenged the all-

Union myth of the war as a pillar of Soviet patriotism were quashed to assure adherence to the postwar ideological line.

In 1949 the processes of restoration and commemoration in Leningrad, which had been intimately connected throughout the immediate postwar period, diverged. The restoration of Leningrad's imperial monuments continued, but during Stalin's final years it was not hailed as a commemoration of the events which Leningraders lived through. Nor was the memory of the blockade used to fuel restoration. This parting of ways between restoration and commemoration can best be understood in the context of the increasing ideological stringency of the postwar period.

CONCLUSION

ON 7 NOVEMBER 1938, SOVIET AUTHORITIES RELEASED SERGEI Eisenstein's film *Alexander Nevskii* to coincide with the twenty-first anniversary of the October Revolution.[1] The film tells the story of Nevskii, a thirteenth-century Russian prince, who was summoned by the people of Novgorod to protect Russian soil from the invading Teutonic knights. Prince Alexander, who had previously defeated the Swedes on the River Neva, earning himself the moniker "Nevskii," accepted the task and called on the people to join him in his patriotic endeavor. Eisenstein's film portrays the Russian people rising in unison to defend their lands from the invaders, who are seen burning cities and slaughtering women and children with a callous determination. After a series of skirmishes, the decisive battle takes place on Lake Chud', where Alexander's tactics overwhelm the Teutonic forces, who fall through the ice and drown. Afterward, the victorious people of Rus' celebrate their victory in the liberated city of Pskov, where they are witness to the triumphant prince's message: "Go and tell everyone in foreign lands that Rus' lives! Let them come to us as guests without fear. But whosoever comes to us with the sword shall perish by the sword! Such is the law of the Russian land, and such shall it always be!"[2]

The patriotic message in Eisenstein's film was clear: the people of the Soviet Union were to draw inspiration from their Russian ancestors who fought valiantly to protect their lands from foreign foes. The use of this particular historical event was not coincidental; the film was produced at a time when Nazi Germany threatened the stability of Europe and the very existence of the Soviet state. Hitler's annihilationist policies toward the Soviet Union and its people were not lost on Stalin. *Alexander Nevskii,* then, served as a warning of Hitler's intentions (and the film was incredibly prescient in its depiction of German atrocities), but it also aimed to inspire confidence in Soviet strength and superiority over the German foe in the thirteenth *and* twentieth centuries. Through the film, the Soviet leadership demanded unity and sacrifice to defend the country, while warning its citizens of the consequences of betraying the fatherland.[3] Eisenstein's film is but one example of the Stalinist state's use, beginning in the 1930s, of the Russian past to mobilize the population for war. Subsequently, during the Second World War, the Soviet propaganda apparatus relied to an even greater extent on the historic events and personages to drum up patriotic sentiment. Although prewar claims of invincibility proved problematic during the first years of the war, when the German forces seemed unstoppable, by 1945 Alexander Nevskii's words rang true – Nazi Germany did, in fact, perish by the Soviet sword.

In the wake of victory, Nevskii's patriotic message continued to resonate, as new enemies surfaced to threaten the socialist state with the onset of the Cold War. Emerging victorious out of the Second World War, the people took great pride in their accomplishments, and Soviet patriotism had received a major boost. From the moment of invasion on 22 June 1941, the central authorities limited discussion of pain and suffering, and sought to silence references to collaboration, defeatism, and other negative aspects of the war. Instead, the authorities developed a myth of the war which embellished the heroism and unity of the people, and underlined the willingness of Soviet people to sacrifice for the good of the fatherland. In the postwar years, the propaganda apparatus deployed this myth in tandem with examples from the "glorious" Russian past to further inspire patriotic devotion to the fatherland and express supremacy over capitalist enemies in the West. The Soviet people were instructed to turn inward and look to the great Russian traditions and accomplishments for inspiration. However, as tensions between the Soviet Union and its former allies developed, and the threat of another war loomed large, the absolute destruction of the war mitigated against Stalinist claims of superiority and might.

In areas of the country where the war was fought, the Wehrmacht had razed entire regions to the ground. As a result, the central authorities sought to restore the country's economy, housing, industry, and infrastructure in the immediate postwar years. In doing so, the Stalinist leadership strove to project an image of power and strength to its population and the outside world. Soviet planners envisioned grandiose urban projects to depict the prestige of the state. Attempts were made to reconstruct destroyed cities as monuments to the Great Patriotic War at the expense of local urban planning traditions and heritage. Soviet architects, urban planners, and preservationists debated plans for reconstruction and restoration, but ultimately sought to both commemorate the victory over the Germans and preserve the country's built heritage.[4] Cities and towns that were restored to reflect the war and the Russian past, therefore, could help lend legitimacy to the leadership's claims of Soviet supremacy as the Cold War developed.

In Leningrad the desire to maintain the historic cityscape and preserve the memory of the blockade led to a series of preservationist and commemorative policies and initiatives. At a time when construction materials and labor power were in drastically short supply – when schools, hospitals, and other essential services needed to be restored and reconstructed – Leningrad's planners worked furiously to resurrect the venerated imperial cityscape. The local party organization called upon the architectural and artistic community to return the "former glory" to the imperial monuments populating the city's center and suburbs, and they expended tremendous resources to accomplish these goals. The authorities used restored monuments to present an image of a well-ordered and mighty state. The monuments also served as educational spaces to complement the Stalinist rehabilitation of Russian history. Soviet citizens could visit monuments and landmarks to learn about events in the "glorious" past, and they could partake in walking tours of the city and encounter the history embodied in the many deliberate and unintentional monuments which were built in the 250 years since Peter the Great founded the city.

The success of restoration in Leningrad was very much the product of the convergence of the state's embrace of the Russian past with the deep-rooted tradition of historic preservation in the city. Well before the Stalinist propaganda apparatus turned to figures from Russian history to inspire patriotism, intellectuals in the former imperial capital fought to save select artistic, cultural, and historic monuments from all forms of abuse and neglect. When given the opportunity to work with the state to oversee the protection of monuments and landmarks, these preservationists eagerly offered their services and lobbied for the adoption of new laws, policies, and practices to ensure the inviolability of the country's patrimony.

One of Leningrad's urban-planning traditions involved commemorating military victories in architecture and sculpture. In the postwar years, municipal authorities and preservationists actively worked to imprint the memory of the war onto Leningrad's historic cityscape. Local officials cast the very process of restoration as a commemoration of victory over the Germans: by overcoming the destruction of war, Leningraders, officials argued, were writing the history of the blockade into the city's "stone chronicle." As preservationists restored historic monuments by "healing the wounds" inflicted upon them during the war, they enthusiastically worked to document and publicize the German army's attempts to annihilate artifacts of Russian heritage and culture on the territory that was slated to become *Lebensraum*. In the postwar years, then, imperial monuments gained new layers of meaning and were transformed into Soviet monuments.

Leningraders also demanded that the city's wartime experience find expression in more traditional commemorative venues and sites. The city's architectural authorities projected the construction of a series of stand-alone monuments and monumental complexes to commemorate the blockade. Such monuments were to complement those erected during the previous two centuries in commemoration of Russian military victories over the Swedes in the Great Northern War, Napoleon in 1812, and the Turks at various occasions. At the same time, party officials established commemorative venues and events to preserve the selective memory of the city's wartime experiences. The Museum of the Defense of Leningrad and yearly anniversary celebrations of the lifting of the blockade, for instance, were a reflection of both the all-Union impetus to remember the war and Leningraders' striving to eternalize and glorify their unprecedented struggle during the 872 days.

While these commemorations contributed to the Soviet myth of the war by emphasizing the heroic and the tragic, they also presented a powerful alternative myth – the myth of the blockade – which espoused a particularistic "Leningrad" version of the Second World War. The Stalinist leadership allowed and even encouraged blockade commemorations in Leningrad during and immediately after the war, but by the end of the postwar Five-Year Plan it viewed the Leningrad patriotism emerging from them as problematic. With the country's economy officially restored by 1948, the leadership no longer needed to rely upon the memory of the blockade to mobilize the city's population for restoration. And as tensions in the Cold War came to a boiling point, the authorities sought to present a united front to the world and its own population. The powerful myth of the blockade, which supposedly focused too much on Leningrad's own wartime experience at the expense of the all-Union narrative, complicated and competed with the central myth of the war. Given the state's use of the myth to cultivate Soviet patriotism, the central leadership argued that the particularistic narrative offered by Leningraders "perverted" the history of the war. When the Leningrad Affair began in February 1949, those people and institutions who articulated the myth of the blockade most forcefully came under attack and the memory of the blockade was erased from public consciousness.

In spite of Stalin's attempts to quash the memory of the blockade as a competing myth in the last years of his reign, the powerful narrative of the city's wartime experiences could not remain suppressed. With the cultural Thaw of the 1950s, the myth of the blockade once again became a central feature in the city's memory and landscape. During the de-Stalinization launched by Nikita Khrushchev, the new leadership rehabilitated the Leningraders purged and executed between 1949 and 1953, announcing in December 1954 that Beria had concocted the Leningrad Affair at the behest of Stalin.[5] The rehabilitation of Leningraders, in combination with the somewhat sporadic freedoms offered by the Thaw, had a profound effect on the reemergence of the blockade as a central event in the lives of Leningraders. Khrushchev decided to allow the Soviet public to produce war stories that did not attribute victory solely to Stalin, a decision that was upheld by his successors.[6] Shortly after the "Secret Speech" in 1956, Leningraders once again began to openly commemorate the blockade. Participants in the battles outside Leningrad, intellectuals who lived in the city, and others began to publish books, memoirs, and semifictional accounts about their experiences during the war.[7] Over the next several decades the story of the blockade became an important part of the burgeoning war cult, which began under Khrushchev and flourished during the Brezhnev regime.

The freedoms of the post-Stalin period and the war cult permitted the articulation of the blockade narrative in numerous forms. Leningraders continued the process of writing their story into the cityscape. They expressed their wartime experiences in stone throughout the city in ways that were not permissible during Stalin's last years. In 1956 construction began on the memorial complex at the Piskarevskoe Cemetery, one of the mass graves where hundreds of thousands of Leningraders were unceremoniously buried during the siege. The memorial was unveiled on 9 May 1960, sixteen years after the siege was lifted in January 1944. On the centerpiece of the memorial one finds the inscription "Nothing is forgotten, no one is forgotten." As a monument to the victims of the blockade, this somber yet powerful complex speaks to the pain and suffering experienced by Leningraders during the war. It also emphasizes the tremendous will to remember and commemorate the event that more than anything else defined the identity of the city and its residents in the postwar years. The Piskarevskoe memorial was only one of a series of monuments constructed in and around Leningrad between the 1960s and the 1980s to commemorate the siege. During this period, the Leningrad leadership placed hundreds of memorial plaques on buildings in the city to memorialize events that took place during the war. Some of these plaques identified damage done by bombs and shells, many marked places where people died from bombardment, and others were reproductions of signs which warned citizens that "this side of the street is more dangerous during artillery raids."[8] On 9 May 1975, the massive monument to the Heroic Defenders of Leningrad – located at the southern edge of the city on Victory Square at the end of Moskovskii Prospekt – was opened to the public.[9]

The blockade also became the subject of new museum exhibits. On 27 January 1964, to mark the twentieth anniversary of the lifting of the blockade, local authorities opened a permanent exhibition consisting of thirteen halls in the State Museum of the History of Leningrad devoted to the war in the city and at the front.[10] Several years later, a grassroots movement successfully petitioned to have the Museum of the Defense of Leningrad recreated. In 1989, at the height of glasnost, the famous museum reopened in the same building in which it was formerly located. Although the organizers of the movement to reopen the museum requested all thirty-seven halls occupied by the old museum on Solianoi Pereulok, the resurrected museum was allocated only one hall.[11] The memory of the blockade, therefore, did not disappear. Rather, over the course of the post-Stalin period it grew stronger and more resilient. It became part of a growing cult of war that was much more open to personal tragedy and suffering than Stalin's myth had ever been.

The rehabilitation of Leningrad's wartime narrative in the post-Stalin years allowed for a reconnection of blockade memory with the historic cityscape. With the revival of the blockade story, museum workers, preservationists, and historians published monographs and personal accounts about the battle to protect the city's monuments during the war and restore them in the postwar period.[12] This process continues to the present day, as more and more diaries, memoirs, and document collections recount the efforts of Leningraders to save the city's historic monuments and the history embodied in them.[13] The cityscape figures prominently in the wartime narratives produced by the state and individuals who lived through the blockade. One might not find many physical traces of the war on the buildings, statues, and streets of the city, but each monument has a story to tell about the war, and those stories are eagerly told by museum workers and preservationists, and memorialized by plaques and exhibits. The restored cityscape stands as a commemoration of Leningraders' determination to protect the city, to overcome the destruction of war, and to preserve its imperial heritage. Writing in 1978, Joseph Brodsky argued that the memory of the war could never be expunged from the cityscape: "Today, thirty-three years later, however repainted and stuccoed, the ceilings and façades of this unconquered city still seem to preserve the stain-like imprints of the inhabitants' last gasps and last gazes. Or," he continued, "perhaps it's just bad paint and bad stucco."[14]

NOTES

INTRODUCTION

1. I use the terms "siege" and "blockade" interchangeably throughout the book.

2. A. N. Boldyrev, *Osadnaia Zapis' (Blokadnyi dnevnik)*, ed. V. S. Garbuzova and I. M. Streblin-Kamenskii (St. Petersburg: Evropeiskii Dom, 1998), 320.

3. A Leningrad architect-preservationist, E. Levina, was one of those who refused evacuation in order to protect the city's historic monuments. In her diary she scorned architects leaving the city in February 1942 for not devoting themselves wholly to saving historic Leningrad: "I'm not going to the Union [of Architects] so that I won't see them. I know that this isn't right, that evacuation will save many lives, and that the city needs only those able to stand on their feet. I know they will work in evacuation and after the war come back, but some sort of demon makes me avoid those who are leaving so I won't say something rude to them." E. Levina, "Pis'ma k drugu," in *Leningradtsy v dni blokady: Sbornik*, ed. E. Korol'chuk and A. Volkova (Leningrad: Leningradskoe gazetno-zhurnal'noe i knizhnoe izdatel'stvo, 1947), 202–203. On the evacuation of Soviet citizens to the rear during the Second World War, see Rebecca Manley, *To Tashkent Station: Evacuation and Survival in the Soviet Union at War* (Ithaca, NY: Cornell University Press, 2009).

4. Karl Qualls, *From Ruins to Reconstruction: Urban Identity in Sevastopol after World War II* (Ithaca, NY: Cornell University Press, 2009), 124–156.

5. For an overview of the war on Soviet territory, see Richard Overy, *Russia's War: A History of the Soviet War Effort: 1941–1945* (New York: Penguin, 1997).

6. Anna Krylova, "'Healers of Wounded Souls': The Crisis of Private Life in Soviet Literature, 1944–1946," *Journal of Modern History* 73, no. 2 (June 2001): 309. For more on the death toll during the Second World War, see P. B. Evdokimov, ed., *Liudskie poteri SSSR v Velikoi Otechestvennoi voine: Sbornik statei* (St. Petersburg: Russko-Baltiiskii informatsionnyi tsentr BLITS, 1995).

7. See Elena Zubkova, *Russia after the War: Hopes, Illusions, and Disappointments, 1945–1957*, trans. Hugh Ragsdale (Armonk, NY: M. E. Sharpe, 1998).

8. For recent English discussions of the nature of war in the Soviet Union, see Stephen G. Fritz, *Ostkrieg: Hitler's War of Extermination in the East* (Lexington: University Press of Kentucky, 2011),

Hannes Heer and Klaus Naumann, eds., *War of Extermination: The German Military in World War II, 1941–1944* (New York: Berghahn Books, 2000), and Geoffrey P. Megargee, *War of Annihilation: Combat and Genocide on the Eastern Front, 1941* (New York: Rowman and Littlefield, 2006).

9. See the introduction to M. A. Boitsov and T. A. Vasil'eva, eds., *Kartoteka "Z" operativnogo shtaba "Reikhsliaiter Rozenberg": Tsennosti kul'tury na okkupirovannykh territoriiakh Rossii, Ukrainy i Belorussii, 1941–1942* (Moscow: Izdatel'stvo Moskovskogo Universiteta, 1998).

10. Alex J. Kay, *Exploitation, Resettlement, Mass Murder: Political and Economic Planning for German Occupation Policy in the Soviet Union, 1940–1941* (New York: Berghahn Books, 2006), 185.

11. The so-called "Von Reichenau Order" (*Verhalten der Truppe im Ostraum*) was issued on 10 October 1941. http://www.ns-archiv.de/krieg/untermenschen/reichenau-befehl.php (last accessed on 29 October 2013).

12. A German officer arrested for war crimes in the Soviet Union stated that when his company was retreating in early 1944, the troops were given orders to destroy all buildings with economic and cultural significance. USHMM (United States Holocaust Memorial Museum Archive), RG-06.025, Reel 1, Pskov Trial, case number H-19094, Tom 1, l. 25. Karl Qualls notes further that Wehrmacht maps of Sevastopol indicate that historic monuments were in fact deliberately targeted for annihilation. See Qualls, *From Ruins to Reconstruction*, 16.

13. See Michael Meng's discussion, for instance, of Nazi Germany's wartime destruction of Jewish monuments and landmarks as part of Hitler's genocidal project, in Meng, *Shattered Spaces: Encountering Jewish Ruins in Postwar Germany and Poland* (Cambridge, MA: Harvard University Press, 2011), 60–68.

14. For a discussion of historic monuments as wartime targets, see Nicola Lambourne, *War Damage in Western Europe: The Destruction of Historic Monuments during the Second World War* (Edinburgh: Edinburgh University Press, 2001). On the destruction of cultural monuments during the First World War in Europe, see Alan Kramer, *Dynamic of Destruction: Culture and Mass Killing in the First World War* (New York: Oxford University Press, 2007).

15. For an excellent discussion of the effects of war on historic monuments, see Robert Bevan, *The Destruction of Memory: Architecture at War* (London: Reaktion Books, 2006).

16. Robert S. Nelson and Margaret Olin, introduction to *Monuments of Memory, Made and Unmade* (Chicago: University of Chicago Press, 2003), 3–4.

17. Adrian A. Bantjes, for example, argues that "iconoclastic attacks are seldom successful in achieving their purpose, which is not just the physical elimination of the image but its relegation to a state of oblivion. Recent research . . . suggests that iconoclasm, far from annihilating the icon, actually can have a 'positive' impact, transforming instead of obliterating the object and its meaning(s)." See Bantjes, "Making Sense of Iconoclasm: Popular Responses to the Destruction of Religious Images in Revolutionary Mexico," in *Iconoclasm: Contested Objects, Contested Terms*, ed. Stacy Boldrick and Richard Clay (Burlington, VT: Ashgate, 2007), 171.

18. On the transformation of meaning through destruction, see Sarah Farmer's discussion of the preservation of ruined villages to commemorate a German

massacre committed against French villagers in 1944, in Farmer, *Martyred Village: Commemorating the 1944 Massacre at Oradour-sur-Glane* (Los Angeles: University of California Press, 1999), chap. 3 in particular.

19. Tony Bennett, *The Birth of the Museum: History, Theory, Politics* (New York: Routledge, 1995), 129.

20. Lisa Kirschenbaum, for example, sees the restoration as a means of effacing the memory of the war. See Kirschenbaum, *The Legacy of the Siege of Leningrad, 1941–1945: Myths, Memories, and Monuments* (New York: Cambridge University Press, 2006), chap. 4.

21. For more on these exhibits, see "V soiuze arkhitektorov (khronika 1942–1945 gg.)," *Arkhitektura Leningrada,* no. 1 (1945): 28–31, and "Leningrad zimoi 1941–42 gg. Risunki arkhitektorov," *Arkhitektura SSSR,* no. 2 (1943): 16–18.

22. Bevan, *The Destruction of Memory,* 176.

23. See David Brandenberger's discussion of the development of Soviet patriotism in the 1930s, in Brandenberger, *Propaganda State in Crisis: Soviet Ideology, Indoctrination, and Terror under Stalin, 1927–1941* (New Haven, CT: Yale University Press, 2011), 98–119. See also his authoritative work on the Stalinist rehabilitation and use of the Russian national past, *National Bolshevism: Stalinist Mass Culture and the Formation of Modern Russian National Identity, 1931–1956* (Cambridge, MA: Harvard University Press, 2002).

24. Nicholas Timasheff, *The Great Retreat* (New York: E. P. Dutton, 1946). See also Matthew Lenoe, "In Defense of Timasheff's *Great Retreat,*" *Kritika: Explorations in Russian and Eurasian History* 5, no. 4 (Fall 2004): 721–730.

25. This line of scholarship was first developed by Stephen Kotkin in *Magnetic Mountain: Stalinism as a Civilization* (Los Angeles: University of California Press, 1995).

26. David L. Hoffmann, *Stalinist Values: The Cultural Norms of Soviet Modernity, 1917–1941* (Ithaca, NY: Cornell University Press, 2003), 7.

27. Matthew E. Lenoe, *Closer to the Masses: Stalinist Culture, Social Revolution, and Soviet Newspapers* (Cambridge, MA: Harvard University Press, 2004), 247–248.

28. Timothy Colton, *Moscow: Governing the Socialist Metropolis* (Cambridge, MA: Belknap Press of Harvard University Press, 1998); Emily D. Johnson, *How St. Petersburg Learned to Study Itself: The Russian Idea of Kraevedenie* (University Park, PA: Penn State University Press, 2006); Richard Stites, *Revolutionary Dreams: Utopian Vision and Experimental Life in the Russian Revolution* (New York: Oxford University Press, 1989).

29. See, for example, the articles in Helena Goscilo and Stephen M. Norris, eds., *Preserving Petersburg: History, Memory, Nostalgia* (Bloomington: Indiana University Press, 2008).

30. Peter Holquist, *Making War, Forging Revolution: Russia's Continuum of Crisis, 1914–1921* (Cambridge, MA: Harvard University Press, 2002), 3, 144, 286.

31. Lynne Viola et al., eds., *The Tragedy of the Soviet Countryside,* vol. 1, *The War against the Peasantry, 1927–1930,* trans. Steven Shabad (New Haven, CT: Yale University Press, 2005), 16–17.

32. On the impact of collectivization, see in particular Sheila Fitzpatrick, *Stalin's Peasants: Resistance and Survival in the Russian Village after Collectivization* (New York: Oxford University Press, 1996); Lynne Viola, *Peasant Rebels under Stalin:*

Collectivization and the Culture of Peasant Resistance (New York: Oxford University Press, 1999); Lynne Viola, *The Unknown Gulag: The Lost World of Stalin's Special Settlements* (New York: Oxford University Press, 2009); and Viola et al., eds., *The War against the Peasantry.* On repressive campaigns throughout the 1930s, see Paul Hagenloh, *Stalin's Police: Public Order and Mass Repression in the* USSR, *1926–1941* (Baltimore: Johns Hopkins University Press, 2009) and David Scherer, *Policing Stalin's Socialism: Repression and Social Order in the Soviet Union, 1924–1953* (New Haven, CT: Yale University Press, 2009).

33. See Oleg Khlevniuk, "The Objectives of the Great Terror," in *Soviet History, 1937–1938: Essays in Honour of R.W. Davies,* ed. Julian Cooper, Maureen Perrie, and E. A. Rees (London: Palgrave Macmillan, 1995), 158–176.

34. O. V. Budnitskii and G. S. Zelenina, "Ideinyi kollaboratsionizm v gody Velikoi Otechestvennoi voiny," in *"Svershilos' Prishli nemtsy!" Ideinyi kollaboratsionizm v SSSR v period Velikoi Otechestvennoi voiny,* ed. O. V. Budnitskii and G. S. Zelenina (Moscow: Rosspen, 2012), 7.

35. For recent work on collaboration, see Martin Dean, *Collaboration in the Holocaust: Crimes of the Local Police in Belorussia and Ukraine, 1941–44* (New York: St. Martin's, 2000); Igor' Ermolov, *Tri goda bez Stalina: Okkupatsiia; Sovetskie grazhdane mezhdu natsistami i bol'shivakami* (Moscow: Tsentrpoligraff, 2010); Boris Kovalev, *Natsistskaia okkupatsiia i kollaboratsionizm v Rossii, 1941–1944* (Moscow: Tranzitkniga, 2004); Per Rudling, "The Khatyn Massacre in Belorussia: A Historical Controversy Revisited," *Holocaust and Genocide Studies* 26, no. 1 (Spring 2012): 29–58; M. I. Semiriaga, *Kollaboratsionizm: Priroda, tipologiia i proiavleniia v gody Vtoroi mirovoi voiny* (Moscow: Rosspen, 2000); Rolf-Dieter Mueller, *The Unknown Eastern Front: The Wehrmacht and Hitler's Foreign Soldiers,* trans. David Burnett (New York: I. B. Tauris, 2012).

36. Lidiia Osipova, *"Dnevnik kollaborantki,"* in Budnitskii and Zelenina, *"Svershilos' Prishli nemtsy!,"* 65. Osipova's real name was Olimpiada Georgievna Poliakova. Both she and her husband, Nikolai Nikolaevich Poliakov, wrote for collaborationist newspapers during the German occupation of Soviet territory.

37. Alexander Statiev, *The Soviet Counterinsurgency in the Western Borderlands* (New York: Cambridge University Press, 2010). See also N. I. Vladimirtsev et al., eds., *Pribaltiiskii natsionalism v dokumentakh* NKVD, *MVD i MGB SSSR* (Moscow: Ob"edinennaia redaktsiia MVD Rossii, 2011).

38. The Soviet intelligentsia, in particular, felt that the system would undergo liberalization after the war. See Zubkova, *Russia after the War,* 88.

39. Mark Edele, *Soviet Veterans of the Second World War: A Popular Movement in an Authoritarian Society, 1941–1991* (Oxford: Oxford University Press, 2008), 53. On veteran discontent, see also Zubkova, *Russia after the War,* 23–30.

40. Edele, *Soviet Veterans,* 10. See also his "More than Just Stalinists: The Political Sentiments of Victors, 1945–1953," in *Late Stalinist Russia: Society between Reconstruction and Reinvention,* ed. Juliane Fürst (London: Routledge, 2006), 167–191.

41. See, for example, Juliane Fürst's work on the attitudes and behavior of youth in late Stalinism, *Stalin's Last Generation: Soviet Post-War Youth and the Emergence of Mature Socialism* (New York: Oxford University Press, 2010).

42. For more on the development of the Cold War under Stalin, see Vladislav M.

Zubok, *A Failed Empire: The Soviet Union in the Cold War from Stalin to Gorbachev* (Chapel Hill: University of North Carolina Press, 2007).

43. N. I. Matiushkin, *Sovetskii patriotizm – moguchaia dvizhushchaia sila sotsialisticheskogo obshchestva* (Moscow: Gosudarstvennoe Izdatel'stvo Politicheskoi Literatury, 1952), 386.

44. Juliane Fürst, "Introduction – Late Stalinist Society: History, Policies and People," in Fürst, *Late Stalinist Russia*, 9.

45. For a discussion of Stalin's role in the unfolding ideological campaigns of the postwar years which developed in tandem with the Cold War, see Yoram Gorlizki and Oleg Khlevniuk, *Cold Peace: Stalin and the Soviet Ruling Circle, 1945–1953* (New York: Oxford University Press, 2004), 31–38.

46. Elizabeth Campbell Karlsgodt, *Defending National Treasures: French Art and Heritage under Vichy* (Stanford, CA: Stanford University Press, 2011), 6.

47. See, for example, Lambourne, *War Damage in Western Europe;* Rudy Koshar, *Germany's Transient Pasts: Preservation and National Memory in the Twentieth Century* (Chapel Hill: University of North Carolina Press, 1998), Kirilly Freeman, *Bronzes to Bullets: Vichy and the Destruction of French Public Statuary, 1941–1944* (Stanford, CA: Stanford University Press, 2009); Elizabeth Karlsgodt, *Defending National Treasures.*

48. Lynn H. Nicholas, *The Rape of Europa: The Fate of Europe's Treasures in the Third Reich and the Second World War* (New York: Knopf, 1994), 185–202.

1. OLD PETERSBURG, PRESERVATION MOVEMENTS, AND THE SOVIET STATE'S "TURN TO THE PAST"

1. Rudy Koshar, for example, notes that between the 1890s and the outbreak of World War I, historic preservation "became a significant public activity" in the German Empire. Koshar, *Germany's Transient Pasts*, 17.

2. Alois Riegl, "The Modern Cult of Monuments: Its Essence and Its Development," trans. Karen Bruckner and Karen Williams, in *Historical and Philosophical Issues in the Conservation of Cultural Heritage*, ed. Nicholas Stanley Price, M. Kirby Talley Jr., and Alessandra Melucco Vaccaro (Los Angeles: Getty Conservation Institute, 1996), 69–83. A translation of Riegl's article can also be found as "The Modern Cult of Monuments: Its Character and Origins," *Oppositions* 25 (1982): 21–50.

3. For a discussion of the Petrine Revolution, see James Cracraft, *The Revolution of Peter the Great* (Cambridge, MA: Harvard University Press, 2003)

4. James Cracraft, *The Petrine Revolution in Russian Architecture* (Chicago: University of Chicago Press, 1988), 176–178.

5. As early as 1704, Peter began to refer to the construction site as the capital of Russia, and it is possible that he was already planning to move the throne to St. Petersburg. S. P. Luppov, *Istoriia stroitel'stva Peterburga v pervoi chetverti XVIII veka* (Leningrad: Izdatel'stvo Akademii Nauk SSSR, 1957), 17.

6. Iu. A. Egorov, *The Architectural Planning of St. Petersburg*, trans. Eric Dluhosch (Athens: Ohio University Press, 1969), 8.

7. During this time the city continued to grow at a dramatic pace. In 1710, for example, it was home to a permanent population of approximately eight thousand people, and thousands more seasonal migrants. James H. Bater, *St. Petersburg: Industrialization and Change* (London: Edward Arnold, 1976), 20.

8. W. Bruce Lincoln, *Sunlight at Midnight: St. Petersburg and the Rise of Modern Russia* (New York: Basic Books, 2002), 25.

9. William Craft Brumfield, *A History of Russian Architecture* (New York: Cambridge University Press, 1993), 204; Luppov, *Istoriia stroitel'stva Peterburga,* 15. Before the capital moved to St. Petersburg, construction in the city had been largely unregulated. Peter was, of course, devoted to creating a European city that would be the antithesis of backward, chaotic Moscow, but military matters proved to be more important for the time being. The merchants, nobles, and artisans whom Peter had forced to take up residence in the city built structures in ways they saw fit and in areas they desired.

10. Bater, *St. Petersburg: Industrialization and Change,* 20.

11. James Hassell, "The Planning of St. Petersburg," *The Historian* 36, no. 2 (February 1974): 250.

12. Cracraft, *The Petrine Revolution,* 155–156.

13. Cracraft, *The Revolution of Peter the Great,* 89. Peter was so intent on having his new city appear monumental that he had many of the wooden structures, including the Cathedral of Peter and Paul in the fortress, painted to resemble stone and brick. See Brumfield, *A History of Russian Architecture,* 205.

14. Lincoln, *Sunlight at Midnight,* 31.

15. Egorov, *The Architectural Planning of St. Petersburg,* 11.

16. Blair A. Ruble, *Leningrad: Shaping a Soviet City* (Los Angeles: University of California Press, 1990), 24.

17. Richard Wortman, *Scenarios of Power: Myth and Ceremony in Russian Monarchy,* vol. 1, *From Peter the Great to the Death of Nicholas I* (Princeton, NJ: Princeton University Press, 1995), 3.

18. James Cracraft and Daniel Rowland, for example, note that Russian rulers "used architecture not merely to project an image of state power, but to define and legitimize that power." See James Cracraft and Daniel Rowland, "Introduction," in *Architectures of Russian Identity: 1500 to the Present,* ed. Cracraft and Rowland (Ithaca, NY: Cornell University Press, 2003), 2.

19. Bater, *St. Petersburg: Industrialization and Change,* 27.

20. Zoe Bakeeff Peterson, "The Architectural Heritage of Leningrad," *American Slavic and East European Review* 4, nos. 3/4 (December 1945): 34.

21. Egorov, *The Architectural Planning of St. Petersburg,* 30.

22. Bater, *St. Petersburg: Industrialization and Change,* 28.

23. Lincoln, *Sunlight at Midnight,* 91. Lincoln notes that in comparison with other capital cities such as London, Paris, and Vienna, St. Petersburg had few backstreets and alleys because of the tendency to relegate slums to areas outside of the center.

24. Brumfield, *A History of Russian Architecture,* 261.

25. Egorov, *The Architectural Planning of St. Petersburg,* 43.

26. Bater, *St. Petersburg: Industrialization and Change,* 35. The desire to create continuous facades throughout the city, however, proved logistically impossible. As an alternative, the city planning authorities under Catherine and later Alexander focused on placing freestanding monumental buildings at various points throughout the developing city. "These grand-scale edifices," notes Julie Buckler, "visually unified the spaces of the city along the perspectives of avenues and embankments, and lessened the impact of the 'gray areas' in between them." Julie

Buckler, *Mapping St. Petersburg: Imperial Text and Cityshape* (Princeton, NJ: Princeton University Press, 2005), 1–3.

27. This commission was dissolved after Catherine's death in 1796. Brumfield, *A History of Russian Architecture,* 348.

28. Hassell, "The Planning of St. Petersburg," 249–254.

29. Wortman, *Scenarios of Power,* 210.

30. Lincoln, *Sunlight at Midnight,* 82.

31. In reference to Rossi, Bruce Lincoln writes, "No other builder ever linked modern Russia and Ancient Rome more closely, for Rossi saw in the heritage of Rome a means for expressing the full grandeur of Russia's destiny. And in doing so, he transformed St. Petersburg into an imperial metropolis that had no rival in the modern world." See Lincoln, *Sunlight at Midnight,* 112.

32. Bater, *St. Petersburg: Industrialization and Change,* 39–40.

33. Buckler, *Mapping St. Petersburg,* 29.

34. Buckler, *Mapping St. Petersburg,* 44; Brumfield notes that the Russian revival style was comparatively muted in St. Petersburg, where other eclectic styles dominated. See Brumfield, *A History of Russian Architecture,* 419; On the conservatism of Nicholas I's regime, see Nicholas Riasanovsky, *Nicholas I and Official Nationality in Russia, 1825–1855* (Berkeley: University of California Press, 1961).

35. In chapter 1 of Julie Buckler's *Mapping St Petersburg,* she discusses the reactions to the new style of architecture that began to dominate the Petersburg landscape during the period of capitalist development, especially after the Great Reforms. She quite rightly notes that what was thought of as distasteful during the mid-nineteenth and early twentieth centuries is now very much appreciated as a characteristic feature of the city's architectural layout.

36. Ruble, *Leningrad,* 40.

37. Iu. N. Zhukov, *Stanovlenie i deiatel'nost sovetskikh organov okhrany pamiatnikov istorii i kul'tury, 1917–1920* (Moscow: Nauka, 1989), 19–23. Francoise Choay notes that the impetus to study historic monuments and preserve them is a phenomenon which began in the nineteenth century. See Choay, *The Invention of the Historic Monument,* trans. Lauren M. O'Connell (New York: Cambridge University Press, 2001).

38. Zhukov, *Stanovlenie i deiatel'nost,* 23.

39. Zhukov, *Stanovlenie i deiatel'nost,* 26–27.

40. Johnson, *How St. Petersburg Learned to Study Itself,* 67.

41. Johnson, *How St. Petersburg Learned to Study Itself,* 43. The term was first popularized by Mikhail Pyliaev in his nineteenth-century book *Staryi Peterburg* (St. Petersburg: Izdatel'stvo A. S. Suvorina, 1887).

42. Katerina Clark, *Petersburg: Crucible of Cultural Revolution* (Cambridge, MA: Harvard University Press, 1995), 59. *Bygone Years,* according to some sources, was the most popular journal in Europe at the time. The number of subscribers between 1907 and 1914 grew from one thousand to five thousand, and that number continued to grow during World War I. See Johnson, *How St. Petersburg Learned to Study Itself,* 65.

43. Johnson notes that preservationists involved in the journals believed that before the middle of the nineteenth century, when eclecticism spoiled the city's classical appearance, St. Petersburg was a successful work of art. Johnson, *How St. Petersburg Learned to Study Itself,* 48.

44. Alexander Benois, "Zhivopisnyi Peterburg," *Mir iskusstva* 1 (1902): 5.

45. Brumfield, *A History of Russian Architecture,* 216, 276.

46. V. Vereshchagin, "Starye gody," *Starye gody,* January 1907, 1.

47. A. Rostislavov, "Zhertva 'sobytii,'" *Starye gody,* January 1907, 21–23.

48. P. V., "Ocherednye vandalizmy vedomstv," *Starye gody,* January 1913, 49.

49. Johnson, *How St. Petersburg Learned to Study Itself,* 68.

50. Johnson, *How St. Petersburg Learned to Study Itself,* 69–70.

51. Quoted in Zhukov, *Stanovlenie i deiatel'nost,* 36. See also Khristina Tur'inskaia, *Muzeinoe delo v Rossii v 1907–1936 gody* (Moscow: Institut etnografii i antropologii im. N. N. Miklukho-Maklaia Rossiiskaia Akademiia Nauk, 2001), 47–48.

52. Zhukov, *Stanovlenie i deiatel'nost,* 36; Clark notes that the movement for Old Petersburg depended largely on the patronage of the imperial family and upper nobility. See Clark, *Petersburg,* 64.

53. G. K. Lukomskii, *Staryi Peterburg: Progulki po starinnym kvartalam stolitsy* (St. Petersburg: Kolo, 2002), 6. This book was originally published in 1917 by the publishing company Svobodnoe iskusstvo.

54. Lukomskii, *Staryi Peterburg,* 30.

55. See, for example, Richard Clay, "Bouchardon's Statue of Louis XV: Iconoclasm and the Transformation of Signs," in *Iconoclasm: Contested Objects, Contested Terms,* ed. Stacy Boldrick and Richard Clay (Burlington, VT: Ashgate, 2007), 93–122. See also Dario Gamboni, *The Destruction of Art: Iconoclasm and Vandalism since the French Revolution* (London: Reaktion Books, 1997), 31–40.

56. See Stanley J. Idzerda for more on the tensions between iconoclasm and preservation during the French Revolution. "Iconoclasm during the French Revolution," *American Historical Review* 60, no. 1 (October 1954): 13–26.

57. Orlando Figes and Boris Kolonitskii, *Interpreting the Russian Revolution: The Language and Symbols of 1917* (New Haven, CT: Yale University Press, 1999), 48.

58. Figes and Kolonitskii, *Interpreting the Russian Revolution,* 48–57; Richard Stites makes the comparison between the attack on the Bastille as a symbol of the old regime in France and attacks on certain buildings in Russia. See Stites, "Iconoclastic Currents in the Russian Revolution: Destroying and Preserving the Past," in *Bolshevik Culture: Experiment and Order in the Russian Revolution,* ed. Peter Kenez and Richard Stites (Bloomington: Indiana University Press, 1985), 6.

59. Alexander Benois, "Chudesa i blagorazumie," in *Aleksandr Benua razmyshliaet,* ed. I. S. Zil'bershtein and A. N. Savinov (Moscow: Sovetskii Khudozhnik, 1968), 55.

60. Clark, *Petersburg,* 65.

61. Johnson, *How St. Petersburg Learned to Study Itself,* 74; Alexander Benois provides a step-by-step discussion of the commission's formation, as well as its initial meetings with the Petrograd authorities. See Alexander Benois, *Moi dnevnik: 1916–1917–1918,* ed. N. I. Aleksandrova and T. V. Esina (Moscow: Russkii Put', 2003), 136–160.

62. "Vozvanie Soveta rabochikh i soldatskikh deputatov," in *Okhrana pamiatnikov istorii i kul'tury: Dekrety, postanovleniia, rasporiazheniia Pravitel'stva SSSR i Pravitel'stva RSFSR, 1917–1968,* ed. G. G. Anisimov (Moscow: Sovetskaia Rossiia, 1973), 14. Benois discusses one of the first meetings of the Gorky Commission at which a text of the "Appeal to the Masses" was composed. See Benois, *Moi dnevnik,* 153.

63. Richard Stites discusses the problems that existed between people who advocated for the preservation of historic monuments, such as Benois, Gorky, and Nikolai Rerikh, and those who believed that "overprotection" would inhibit innovative art, including Maiakovskii, Meyerhold, and Nikolai Punin. See Stites, *Revolutionary Dreams*, 76.

64. It is clear that the preservationists wanted to attain some form of power and control over the fate of monuments. According to Johnson, preservationists in Petrograd welcomed the position offered to them by the February Revolution, for they no longer felt as if they were outside the system. See Johnson, *How St. Petersburg Learned to Study Itself*, 74. Clark goes further than Johnson in discussing the preservationists' motivations. For her, preservationists had a utopian streak and their calls for neoclassical revival represent a desire for "power and control": "The movement to revive Empire style in St. Petersburg can be read as an instructive chapter in the story of intellectuals 'reach for power' at about this time. The Preservationists sought greater control over the ways the arts were administered by the state." See Clark, *Petersburg*, 64.

65. For a discussion of Proletkult, see Lynn Mally, *Culture of the Future: The Proletkult Movement in Revolutionary Russia* (Los Angeles: University of California Press, 1990).

66. Katerina Clark and Evgeny Dobrenko with Andrei Artizov and Oleg Naumov, eds., *Soviet Culture and Power: A History in Documents, 1917–1953*, trans. Marion Schwartz (New Haven, CT: Yale University Press, 2007), 4.

67. "Obrashchenie Narkoma Prosveshcheniia A.V. Lunacharskogo k grazhdanam Rossii 'Beregite narodnoe dostoianie,' 3(16) noiabria 1917," in A. P. Nenarokov, ed., *Kul'turnoe stroitel'stvo v SSSR, 1917–1927: Razborka edinoi gosudarstvennoi politiki v oblasti kul'tury; Dokumenty i materialy* (Moscow: Nauka, 1989), 20–22.

68. Such sites included the imperial palaces in Petrograd's suburbs and Moscow's Kremlin, among others. Stites, *Revolutionary Dreams*, 76.

69. G. A. Boguslavskii, "Kul'turnoe nasledie i khudozhestvennyi mir Petrograda v 1918–1920 godakh," in *Peterburgskoe chteniia, 97: Materialy entsiklopedicheskoi biblioteki "Sankt-Peterburg-2003*, ed. T. A. Slavina et. al. (St. Petersburg: Russko-Baltiiskii informatsionnyi tsentr BLITs, 1997), 201–202; Johnson, *How St. Petersburg Learned to Study Itself*, 79–81.

70. Stites, *Revolutionary Dreams*, 76–77.

71. For a detailed discussion of the Museum Section's creation, see Zhukov, *Stanovlenie i deiatel'nost*, 91–109.

72. "Dekret o pamiatnikakh respubliki: 12 aprelia 1918," in Anisimov, *Okhrana pamiatnikov istorii i kul'tury*, 15–16. The decree stipulated that specialists in Moscow and Petrograd would decide on what should be demolished.

73. Sheila Fitzpatrick, *The Cultural Front: Power and Culture in Revolutionary Russia* (Ithaca, NY: Cornell University Press, 1992), 3.

74. Kendall Bailes, *Technology and Society under Lenin and Stalin: Origins of the Soviet Technological Intelligentsia, 1917–1941* (Princeton, NJ: Princeton University Press, 1978), 47.

75. Stites, "Iconoclastic Currents in the Russian Revolution," 17.

76. A. N. Chistikov and N. B. Lebina argue that the lack of funding during the Civil War slowed the destruction of certain monuments in Petrograd. See Chistikov and Lebina, *Obyvatel' i reformy:*

Kartiny povsednevnoi zhizni gorozhan (St. Petersburg: Dmitrii Bulanin, 2003), 20.

77. Johnson, *How St. Petersburg Learned to Study Itself,* 81.

78. Catriona Kelly, "Socialist Churches: Heritage Preservation and 'Cultic Buildings' in Leningrad, 1924–1940," *Slavic Review* 71, no. 4 (Winter 2012): 811.

79. Johnson, *How St. Petersburg Learned to Study Itself,* 79.

80. Boguslavskii, "Kul'turnoe nasledie i khudozhestvennyi mir Petrograda," 202.

81. See the decrees about nationalizing Tolstoy's residences in April 1920 (Moscow home) and June 1921 (*Iasnaia Poliana*). "O natsionalizatsii doma L'va Tolstogo v Moskve," in Anisimov, *Okhrana pamiatnikov istorii i kul'tury,* 26; "O natsionalizatsii usad'by Iasnaia Poliana," ibid., 28–30.

82. See "Dekret Soveta Narodnykh Komissarov o registratsii, prieme na uchet i okhranenii pamiatnikov iskusstva i stariny, nakhodiashchikhsia vo vladenii chastnykh lits, obshchestv i ucherezhdenii ot 10.10.1918," in Anisimov, *Okhrana pamiatnikov istorii i kul'tury,* 22–24. For the decree and instructions for carrying it out, see N. M. Serapina, ed., *Ermitazh, kotoryi my poteriali: Dokumenty 1920–1930 godov* (St. Petersburg: Izdatel'stvo Zhurnal Neva, 2002), 18–22; see also Stites, *Revolutionary Dreams,* 77.

83. E. D. Kul'chinskaia, "Ot museefikatsii k unichtozheniiu naslediia. 1920-e gody," in *Pamiatniki arkhitektury v Sovetskom Soiuze: Ocherki istorii arkhitekturnoi restavratsii,* ed. A. S. Shchenkov (Moscow: Pamiatniki istoricheskoi mysli, 2004), 22.

84. See *Obshchestvo Staryi Peterburg, 1921–1923* (Petrograd, 1923), 10–11.

85. P. M. Blinov, "Obshchestvo 'Staryi Peterburg – Novyi Leningrad,'" *Pamiatniki Otechestva: Al'minakh Vserossiiskogo obshchestva okhrany pamiatnikov istorii i kultury,* no. 2 (1987): 46.

86. *Obshchestvo Staryi Peterburg,* 9.

87. Stites, *Revolutionary Dreams,* 78.

88. Carol Duncan asserts that this was the case in the creation of the Louvre after the French Revolution. See Duncan, "Art Museums and the Ritual of Citizenship," in *Exhibiting Cultures: The Poetics and Politics of Museum Display,* ed. Ivan Karp and Stephen Lavine (Washington, DC: Smithsonian Institution Press, 1991), 93.

89. Viola et al., eds., *The Tragedy of the Soviet Countryside,* 16. For recent research on the War Scare, its use as a political tool, and the popular perception of it, see Olga Velikanova, *Popular Perceptions of Soviet Politics in the 1920s: Disenchantment of the Dreamers* (New York: Palgrave Macmillan, 2013).

90. Joseph Stalin, *Works,* vol. 13 (July 1930–January 1934) (Moscow: Foreign Languages Publishing House, 1954), 40–41.

91. Kul'chinaskaia, "Ot museefikatsii k unichtozheniiu naslediia," 24; Johnson, *How St. Petersburg Learned to Study Itself,* 81.

92. Stites, *Revolutionary Dreams,* 227.

93. Moscow lost many historic and religious monuments during the first years of the 1930s. See E. D. Kul'chinskaia, "Teatralizatsiia i mifologizatsiia kul'tury: Unichtozhenie i pereomyslenie naslediia. Konets 1920-kh–1930-e gody," in Shchenkov, *Pamiatniki arkhitektury,* 35–38.

94. Colton, *Moscow,* 260–268.

95. Chistikov and Lebina, *Obyvatel' i reformy,* 15. For a listing of the churches and other buildings destroyed in Leningrad during this period, see V. V. Antonov and A. V. Kobak, eds., *Utrachennye pamiatniki arkhitektury*

Peterburga-Leningrada: Katalog vystavki (Leningrad: Khudozhnik RSFSR, 1988).

96. Stites, *Revolutionary Dreams*, 227.

97. See M. B. Piotrovskii, ed., *Gosudarstvennyi Ermitazh: Muzeinye rasprodazhi 1928–1929 godov; Arkhivnye dokumenty* (St. Petersburg: State Hermitage, 2006); Serapina, ed., *Ermitazh, kotoryi my poteriali;* Anne Odom and Wendy Salmond, eds., *Treasures into Tractors: The Selling of Russia's Cultural Heritage, 1918–1938* (Seattle: University of Washington Press, 2009); and Sean McMeekin, *History's Greatest Heist: The Looting of Russia by the Bolsheviks* (New Haven, CT: Yale University Press, 2008).

98. Many of the local studies organizations that developed during the NEP were disbanded and the Academy of Sciences, which administered the Central Bureau of *Kraevedenie*, was purged. See Johnson, *How St. Petersburg Learned to Study Itself*, 87, 172–176. For more on purges of the Academy of Sciences, see A. S. Shchenkov, "Kratkaia kharteristika obshchekul'turnoi situatsii," in Shchenkov, *Pamiatniki arkhitektury*, 11–12. For attacks on old specialists during the Five-Year Plan and cultural revolution, see Bailes, *Technology and Society*, chaps. 3–6.

99. N. S. Tret'iakov, ed., "'My . . . dolzhny schitat' sebia mobilizovannymi dlia bor'by i pobedy . . .' Iz dnevnikov khranitelei prigorodnykh dvortsov-muzeev Leningrada: 1941–1945 gg.," *Otechestvennye arkhivy*, no. 1 (2007): 82–97; A. N. Farafonova, "'Ia v Gatchinu ne vernus', no nikogda ne perestany interesovat'sia eiu . . .' Vladimir Kuzmich Makarov," http://gatchinapalace.ru/special/publications/nevernus.php (accessed 5 July 2013).

100. Colton, *Moscow*, 267.

101. V. M. Molotov, *The International Situation and the Soviet Union* (New York: International Publishers, 1935), 7.

102. For an analysis of the Soviet embrace of patriotism, see Brandenberger, *Propaganda State in Crisis*, especially 98–119. See also his *National Bolshevism.*

103. Serhy Yekelchyk, *Stalin's Empire of Memory: Russian-Ukrainian Relations in the Soviet Historical Imagination* (Toronto: University of Toronto Press, 2004), 14.

104. "Za rodinu," *Pravda*, 9 June 1934.

105. Brandenberger, *Propaganda State in Crisis*, 104.

106. Brandenberger, *National Bolshevism*, 35–36, and chap. 2 more generally.

107. Yekelchyk, *Stalin's Empire of Memory*, 19. For more on the creation and support of national cultures in the 1930s, see Yuri Slezkine, "The USSR as a Communal Apartment, or How a Socialist State Promoted Ethnic Particularism," *Slavic Review* 53, no. 2 (Summer 1994): 445–447.

108. Brandenberger, *National Bolshevism*, 37–42; and Brandenberger, *Propaganda State in Crisis*, 142–161.

109. David L. Hoffmann, "Was There a 'Great Retreat' from Soviet Socialism? Stalinist Culture Reconsidered," *Kritika: Explorations in Russian and Eurasian History* 5, no. 4 (Fall 2004): 653.

110. "Postanovlenie Vserossiiskogo tsentral'nogo ispolnitel'nogo Komiteta ot 20 avgusta 1932, 'Ob utverzhdenie polozheniia o mezhduvedomstvennom Komitete po okhrane pamiatnikov revoliutsii, iskusstva i kul'tury pri Prezidiume VTsIK," in Anisimov, *Okhrana pamiatnikov istorii i kul'tury*, 58–59.

111. "Ob okhrane istoricheskikh pamiatnikov: Postanovlenie VTsIK i SNK RSFSR ot 10 avgusta 1933," KGIOP (Arkhiv Komiteta po gosudarstvennomu kontroliu, ispol'zovaniiu i okhrane pamiatnikov istorii i kul'tury), f. 950.III, d. N-3353, l.2.

112. TsGALI SPb (Tsentral'nyi gosudarstvennyi arkhiv literatury i iskusstva Sankt-Peterburga), f. 32, op. 1, d. 71, l. 10.

113. TsGALI SPb, f. 32, op. 1, d. 71, l. 13.

114. TsGALI SPb, f. 32, op. 1, d. 71, l. 19.

115. TsGALI SPb, f. 32, op. 1, d. 71, l. 22.

116. Iu. N. Zhukov, *Kogda gremeli pushki: Spasenie pamiatnikov zodchestva v gody Velikoi Otechestvennoi voiny; V pomoshch' lektoru* (Moscow: Obshchestvo 'Znanie' RSFSR, 1990), 8. On the Pushkin centennial, see Stephanie Sandler, "The 1937 Pushkin Jubilee as Epic Trauma," in *Epic Revisionism: Russian History and Literature as Stalinist Propaganda*, ed. Kevin M. F. Platt and David Brandenberger (Madison: University of Wisconsin Press, 2006), 193–213.

117. Zhukov, *Kogda gremeli pushki*, 11; Leningrad's Department for the Protection of Monuments was created in November 1938. KGIOP, f. 950.III, d. N-3353, l. 6.

118. Zhukov, *Kogda gremeli pushki*, 13.

119. Serhy Yekelchyk notes how postwar authorities in Ukraine distanced themselves from their predecessors, who destroyed churches to create new urban spaces and were later accused of being "monsters of the Bukharin-Trotskyite gang" and "lackeys of the foreign bourgeois intelligence services." See Yekelchyk, *Stalin's Empire of Memory*, 123.

120. Zhukov notes that the regional organ for monument protection in Leningrad had remained intact under different names and guises since 1917. Zhukov, *Kogda gremeli pushki*, 6–11.

2. THESE MONUMENTS MUST BE PROTECTED!

1. On Hitler's plans for the creation of a German Empire in the East, see Wendy Lower, *Nazi Empire-Building and the Holocaust in Ukraine* (Chapel Hill: University of North Carolina Press, 2005); Mark Mazower, *Hitler's Empire: How the Nazis Ruled Europe* (New York: Penguin, 2008); Karel C. Berkhoff, *Harvest of Despair: Life and Death in Ukraine under Nazi Rule* (Cambridge, MA: Belknap Press of Harvard University Press, 2004); Kay, *Exploitation, Resettlement, and Mass Murder*.

2. See V. K. Vinogradov, V. P. Gusachenko, O. I. Nazhestkin, and V. L. Peshcherskii, eds., *Sekrety Gitlera na stole u Stalina: Razvedka i kontrrazvedka o podgotovke germanskoi agressii protiv SSSR, mart-iiun' 1941; Dokumenty iz tsentral'nogo arkhiva FSB Rossii* (Moscow: Izdatel'stvo ob"edineniia Mosgorarkhiv, 1995).

3. Geoffrey P. Megargee, *War of Annihilation: Combat and Genocide on the Eastern Front, 1941* (New York: Rowman and Littlefield, 2006), 19–24.

4. Diary entry for 8 July 1941, in Franz Halder, *The Halder War Diary, 1939–1942*, ed. Charles Burdick and Hans-Adolf Jacobsen (Novato, CA: Presidio, 1988), 458.

5. "Vypiska iz protokola zasedaniia Chrezvychainoi gosudarstvennoi komissii po ustanovleniiu i rassledovaniiu zlodeianii nemetsko-fashistskikh zakhvatchikov i ikh soobshchnikov o prichinennom imi ushcherbe grazhdanam, obshchestvennym organizatsiiam, predpriiatiiam i uchezhdeniiam Leningrada i ego prigorodov: 15 iiunia 1945 g.," in Kh. Kh. Kamalov, R. B. Serdnak, and Iu. S. Tokarev, eds., *Deviat'sot geroicheskikh dnei: Sbornik dokumentov i materialov o geroicheskoi bor'be trudiashchikhsia Leningrada v 1941–1944gg* (Leningrad: Nauka, 1966), 399; V. A. Ezhov, "Vosstanovlenie Leningrada," in *Vozrozhdenie: Vospominaniia, ocherki i dokumenty o vosstanovlenii Leningrada*, ed. V. A. Kutuzov and E. G. Levina (Leningrad: Lenizdat, 1977), 5.

6. The exact number of people who died during the siege is still unknown, but historians now believe that the number is close to 1 million. Richard Bidlack and Nikita Lomagin note that between 1.6 and 2 million people died within the city and in battles surrounding Leningrad over the course of the siege. They estimate the number of people who died from starvation, cold, and enemy bombardment to be in the range of 900,000. See Bidlack and Lomagin, eds., *The Leningrad Blockade, 1941–1944: A New Documentary History from the Soviet Archives,* trans. Marion Schwarz (New Haven, CT: Yale University Press, 2012), 1, 270–275.

7. "Iz doklada professora L.A. Il'ina na sobranii sovetskoi intelligentsia Leningrada, 14 ianvaria 1942," in T. Malinina, ed., *Iz istorii sovetskoi arkhitektury 1941–1945 gg.* (Moscow: Izdatel'stvo Nauka, 1978), 23. Il'in was killed by shrapnel from a German shell on 11 December 1942.

8. P. D. Baranovskii, "Avtobiografiia," in *Petr Baranovskii: Trudy, vospominaniia sovremennikov,* ed. Iu. A. Bychkov et al. (Moscow: Otchii Dom, 1996), 12; S. F. Vitushkin, ed., *". . . I nichto ne zabyto": Dokumenty i materialy o zlodeianiiakh nemetsko-fashistskikh okkupantov na Novgorodskoi zemle (1941–1944)* (Novgorod: Kirillitsa, 1996), 22.

9. See Vasily Grossman's account in *A Writer at War: A Soviet Journalist with the Red Army, 1941–1945,* ed. Anthony Beevor, trans. Luba Vinogradova (Toronto: Knopf, 2005), 54–55.

10. L. V. Maksakova, *Spasenie kul'turnykh tsennostei v gody Velikoi Otechestvennoi voiny* (Moscow: Nauka, 1990), 67.

11. Qualls, *From Ruins to Reconstruction,* 1, 15–23.

12. For more on the connection of writers to St. Petersburg's landscape, especially during the late nineteenth and twentieth centuries, see Anna Lisa Crone and Jennifer Day, *My Petersburg/Myself: Mental Architecture and Imaginative Space in Modern Russian Letters* (Bloomington, IN: Slavica, 2004). Not all depictions of the city's beautiful vistas, however, were positive. Nikolai Gogol, for example, described St. Petersburg as deceitful and not at all the beautiful city it seemed to be at first glance. See his "Nevsky Prospekt" in *Plays and Petersburg Tales,* ed. and trans. Christopher English (New York: Oxford University Press, 1995).

13. RNB OR (Rossiiskaia natsional'naia biblioteka, otdel rukopisei), f. 1015, d. 57, l. 150. Diary entry from 30 November 1941.

14. Blinov, "Obshchestvo 'Staryi Peterburg – Novyi Leningrad,'" 69.

15. Richard Bidlack, "The Political Mood in Leningrad during the First Year of the Soviet-German War," *Russian Review* 59, no. 1 (January 2000): 99.

16. John Barber, "Popular Reactions in Moscow to the German Invasion of June 22, 1941," *Soviet Union/Union Soviétique* 18, nos. 1–3 (1991): 7. Bidlack, too, argues that the that there was a significant amount of pressure on people to enlist, especially as time progressed. Bidlack, "The Political Mood," 99.

17. In Estonia, J. Maide, the deputy chief of the Estonian rural security network (*Omakaitse*) expressed his willingness to work with the Germans to throw off Soviet rule and regain independence for the Estonian people. He wrote the following after the German invasion: "Having learned on 22 June about the declaration of war and Greater Germany's military actions against Russia, a weight was lifted from the heart of every

Estonian. Finally the war, which we awaited like a messiah, had begun. No doubt it was clear that the troubles were far from over and that war would bring unforeseen difficulties. But that didn't scare us anymore. We awaited the moment when the German army would come and liberate Estonia from Communism." "Spravka zamestitelia nachal'nika Glavnogo upravleniia 'Omakaitse' Ia.Iu. Maide o deiatel'nosti organizatsii v 1941 g.," in N. I. Vladimirtsev et. al, eds., *Pribaltiiskii natsionalism v dokumentakh NKVD, MVD i MGB SSSR* (Moscow: Ob'edinennaia redaktsiia MVD Rossii, 2011), 53.

18. On the enthusiastic reception of German troops by Ukrainian villagers, see Berkhoff, *Harvest of Despair,* 20–21.

19. See Karel C. Berkhoff, *Motherland in Danger: Soviet Propaganda during World War II* (Cambridge, MA: Harvard University Press, 2012).

20. For a text of Molotov's speech, see http://www.fordham.edu/halsall/mod/1941molotov.html (accessed 29 October 2013).

21. Bidlack and Lomagin state that from 28 June, *Leningradskaia pravda* commissioned noted historians to publish articles on the past and present wars. On 9 July the historian V. Mavrodin published an article chronicling victories against the German foe. Several other articles followed in this vein. Bidlack and Lomagin, *The Leningrad Blockade,* 54–55.

22. Brandenberger, *National Bolshevism,* 118–119. Petr Aliakrinskii produced a propaganda poster in July 1942 which depicts these Russian heroes in military regalia surrounding Stalin's quote. See Brandenberger, *National Bolshevism,* 119; and Peter Kort Zegers and Douglas Druick, eds., *Windows on the War: Soviet TASS Posters at Home and Abroad, 1941–1945* (Chicago: Art Institute of Chicago, 2011), 84.

23. Argyrios K. Pisiotis, "Images of Hate in the Art of War," in *Culture and Entertainment in Wartime Russia*, ed. Richard Stites (Bloomington: Indiana University Press, 1995), 142,

24. Ehrenburg's *Pravda* article, "The Justification of Hate," is reproduced in James von Geldern and Richard Stites, eds., *Mass Culture in Soviet Russia: Tales, Poems, Songs, Movies, Plays, and Folklore, 1917–1953* (Bloomington: Indiana University Press, 1995), 401–405.

25. Ehrenburg, "The Justification of Hate," 403–404.

26. The destruction of the Spanish Civil War especially signaled a need for preservation in European states as well. See, for example, Nicholas, *The Rape of Europa,* 46–49.

27. See A. M. Kuchumov, *Stat'i, vospominaniia, pis'ma,* ed. N. S. Tret'iakov (St. Petersburg: Art-Palac, 2004), 62.

28. Lambourne, *War Damage in Western Europe,* 41–45. For a study of monument protection in France immediately before the war and during the Vichy period, see Karlsgodt, *Defending National Treasures.*

29. See V. K. Makarov, "Okhrana pamiatnikov iskusstva i stariny v usloviiakh voennogo vremeni v Zapadnoi Evrope," KGIOP, f. 950-VI-2, d. N-127, l. 10; and KGIOP, f. 950-VI-2, d. N-128, l. 2 (ob).

30. After the city was besieged and frantic efforts began to protect monuments, Lev Il'in stressed the importance of learning from the experiences of countries in the West. KGIOP, f. 950-VI-2, d. N-131, l. 1.

31. N. V. Baranov, *Siluety blokady: Zapiski glavnogo arkhitektora goroda* (Leningrad: Lenizdat, 1982), 23.

32. Sergei Nikolaevich Davydov, "Podvig arkhitektora Belekhova," in *Podvig veka: Khudozhniki, skul'ptury, arkhitektory, iskusstvovedy v gody Velikoi Otechestvennoi voiny i blokady Leningrada; Vospominaniia, dnevniki, pis'ma, ocherki, literaturnye zapisi,* ed. Nina Papernaia (Leningrad: Lenizdat, 1969), 285.

33. GMGS (Gosudarstvennyi muzei gorodskoi skul'putry), f. Otdel pamiatnikov i memorial'nykh dosok, d. 48, ch. 1, l. 36.

34. TsGALI SPb, f. 341, op. 1, d. 76, ll. 65–66.

35. N. N. Baranov and V. G. Isachenko, *Glavnyi arkhitektor Leningrada Nikolai Baranov: Tvorcheskii put' i sud'ba* (St. Petersburg: Stroiizdat, 2001), 18.

36. This was a relatively new method of monument protection widely practiced in the West. See Lambourne, *War Damage in Western Europe,* 42.

37. Mikhail Bobrov, *Khraniteli angela: Zapiski blokadnogo al'pinista* (St. Petersburg: Izdatel'stvo Sankt-Peterburgskogo gumanitarnyi universitet profsoiuzov, 1998), 25. Camouflage work was carried out in other cities as well. In Novgorod, for example, some church cupolas with gold leaf were covered with canvas in the early days of the war. See Vitushkin, *". . . I nichto ne zabyto,"* 22.

38. GMGS, f. Otdel pamiatnikov i memorial'nykh dosok, d. 48, ch. 1, ll. 37–38.

39. Ibid.

40. P. K. Baltun, *Russkii muzei – evakuatsiia, blokada, vosstanovlenie (iz vospominanii muzeinogo rabotnika)* (Moscow: Izobratitel'noe iskusstvo, 1981), 25.

41. I. V. Krestovskii, "Ukrytiia i okhrana pamiatnikov Leningrada v gody blokady," KGIOP, f. 950-VI-2, d. N-1233, ll. 6–7. Reproduced as Krestovskii, "Ukrytiia i okhrana pamiatnikov Leningrada v gody blokady (1941–44)," *Zabveniiu ne podlezhit: Stat'i, vospominaniia, dokumenty* 7 (2006): 5–14. Video of this can be seen in the recent documentary film *Blokada.* See Sergei Loznitsa, dir., *Blokada* (St. Petersburg: St. Petersburg Documentary Film Studio, 2006), DVD.

42. Several other statues and moveable historic monuments in London were either encased in sand and brick or evacuated. See Philip Ziegler, *London at War, 1939–1945* (New York: Knopf, 1995), 54.

43. KGIOP, f. 950-VI-2, d. N-1233, l. 2.

44. The report is from 8 July. GMGS, f. Otdel pamiatnikov i memorial'nykh dosok, d. 35, ch. 2, ll. 3–5.

45. For a map of statues buried in the Summer Garden, see Iu. Iu. Bakhareva, T. V. Kovaleva, and T. G. Shishkina, eds., *Arkhitektory blokadnogo Leningrada* (St. Petersburg: NP-Print, 2005), 51.

46. V. M. Koval'chuk and A. N. Chistikov, eds., *Leningrad v gody Velikoi Otechestvennoi Voiny: Ocherki. Dokumenty. Fotografii* (St. Petersburg: Izdatel'stvo-poligraficheskii servisnyi tsentr, 2005), 37.

47. KGIOP, f. 950-VI-2, d. N-1233, l. 2.

48. GMGS, f. Otdel pamiatnikov i memorial'nykh dosok, d. 35, ch. 2, l. 4.

49. L. Rudnev, "Arkhitektory na zashchite goroda Lenina," *Literatura i iskusstva,* 14 March 1942.

50. Richard Bidlack, "Foreword: Historical Background to the Siege of Leningrad," in *Writing the Siege of Leningrad: Women's Diaries, Memoirs, and Documentary Prose,* ed. Cynthia Simmons and Nina Perlina (Pittsburgh: University of Pittsburgh Press, 2002), xiii.

51. D. S. Likhachev, *Reflections on the Russian Soul: A Memoir,* trans. Bernard Adams (New York: Central European University Press, 2000), 220.

52. Bidlack, "The Political Mood in Leningrad," 100.

53. Lambourne, *War Damage in Western Europe,* 2. In his discussion of Sevastopol during the Second World War, Karl Qualls notes that the Germans deliberately targeted monuments for destruction, as Nazi Germany's campaign in the USSR was "a total war not just on the physical present but also on the mythical past." Qualls, *From Ruins to Reconstruction,* 23.

54. "Das Verhalten der Truppe im Ostraum." Issued on 12 October 1941. http://www.ns-archiv.de/krieg/untermenschen/reichenau-befehl.php (accessed 11 July 2013). See also the trial transcript of the International Military Tribunal at Nuremberg from 21 February 1946, where evidence is presented to show the intentional destruction of cultural and historic monuments. S. Paul A. Joosten, ed., *The Trial of the Major War Criminals before the International Military Tribunal,* vol. 8 (Nuremberg: International Military Tribunal, 1947).

55. Alexander Dallin, *German Rule in Russia, 1941–1945: A Study in Occupation Policies* (New York: St. Martin's, 1957), 71.

56. Baranov, *Siluety blokady,* 20.

57. The commission, created in July 1942, was subordinate to the All-Union Committee for Artistic Affairs. See *Pamiatniki zodchestva razrushennye ili povrezhdennye nemetskimi zakhvatchikami: Dokumenty i materialy; Vypusk I* (Moscow: Gosudarstvennoe arkhitekturnoe izdatel'stvo Akademii arkhitektury SSSR, 1942), 36.

58. *Pamiatniki zodchestva razrushennye ili povrezhdennye,* 3.

59. Harrison Salisbury, *The 900 Days: The Siege of Leningrad* (Cambridge, MA: Da Capo, 2003), 298.

60. Likhachev, *Reflections on the Russian Soul,* 222.

61. Vera Inber, *Leningrad Diary,* trans. Serge M. Wolff (London: Hutchinson of London, 1971), 26.

62. Parts of Knyazev's diary have been reproduced in Ales Adamovich and Danil Granin, eds., *A Book of the Blockade,* trans. Hilda Perham (Moscow: Raduga, 1983), 255.

63. B. I. Zagurskii, "*Iskusstvo,*" in *Ocherki istorii Leningrada,* vol. 5, *Period Velikoi Otechestvennoi voiny Sovetskogo Soiuza, 1941–1945gg,* ed. V. M. Koval'chuk et. al. (Moscow: Izdatel'stvo Akademii Nauk, 1967), 604.

64. Baranov, *Siluety blokady,* 43; Bobrov, *Khraniteli angela,* 23.

65. TsGA SPb (Tsentral'nyi gosudarstvennyi arkhiv Sankt-Peterburga), f. 7384, op. 17, d. 598, l. 24; A. R. Dzeniskevich, ed., *Leningrad v osade: Sborniki dokumentov o geroicheskoi oborone Leningrada v gody Velikoi Otechestvennoi voine; 1941–1945* (St. Petersburg: Liki Rossii, 1995), 522–527.

66. TsGALI SPb, f. 333, op. 3, d. 3, l. 44.

67. Bobrov, *Khraniteli angela,* 67.

68. RNB OR, f. 1117, op. 1, ch. 1, d. 157, l. 1 (ob).

69. N. V. Baranov, *Glavnyi arkhitektor goroda: Tvorcheskaia i organizatsionnaia deiatel'nost* (Moscow: Stroizdat, 1979), 16.

70. TsGALI SPb, f. 341, op. 1, d. 81, l. 13. Preservationists in Moscow carried out documentation work on many of the city's monuments as well. Malinina, *Iz istorii sovetskoi arkhitektury,* 5.

71. TsGALI SPb, f. 341, op. 1, d. 81, ll. 18–22.

72. "Iz doklada arkhitektora B. Rubanenko na X plenume Pravleniia SSA SSSR o deiatel'nosti leningradskikh arkhitektorov v pervye mesiatsy osady goroda," in Malinina, *Iz istorii sovetskoi arkhitektury,* 28.

73. Krestovskii, "Ukrytiia i okhrana pamiatnikov Leningrada v gody blokady," 11.

74. TsGALI SPb, f. 341, op. 1, d. 81, l. 13; TsGALI SPb, f. 341, op. 1, d. 91, l. 5.

75. "Postanovlenie Voennogo soveta Leningradskogo fronta o snizhenii norm khleba," in Dzeniskevich, *Leningrad v osade*, 194–195.

76. E. Levina, "Pis'ma k drugu," 200.

77. TsGALI SPb, f. 341, op. 1, d. 81, l. 13; TsGALI SPb, f. 341, op. 1, d. 91, l. 5.

78. KGIOP, f. 50, d. P-70, l. 208. Belekhov would later accuse the Architectural-Planning Administration and the Union of Architects of allowing "many needed architects" to be evacuated. See TsGA SPb, f. 7384, op. 17, d. 598, l. 41.

79. TsGA SPb, f. 7384, op. 17, d. 598, l. 29.

80. According to the Hunger Plan, "Many tens of millions of people in this territory will become superfluous and will die or must emigrate to Siberia. Attempts to rescue the population there from death through starvation by obtaining surpluses from the black earth zone can only come at the expense of provisioning Europe. They prevent the possibility of Germany holding out until the end of the war, they prevent Germany and Europe from resisting the blockade. With regard to this, absolute clarity must reign." Quoted in Timothy Snyder, *Bloodlands: Europe between Hitler and Stalin* (New York: Basic Books, 2010), 162–163; and Kay, *Exploitation, Resettlement, Mass Murder*, 134.

81. N. A. Lomagin, ed., *V tiskakh goloda: Blokada Leningrada v dokumentakh germanskikh spetssluzhb i NKVD* (St. Petersburg: Evropeiskii Dom, 2000), 178.

82. Dzeniskevich, *Leningrad v osade*, 298.

83. RNB OR, f. 1015, d. 57, l. 169. Diary entry from 4 January 1942.

84. Vsevolod Vishnevskii, *Leningrad: Dnevniki voennykh let; V 2-kh knigakh; Kniga pervaia; 2 noiabria 1941 goda–31 dekabria 1942 goda* (Moscow: Voenizdat, 2002), 72.

85. KGIOP, f. Belekhova, op. 1, d. 43 (unpaginated).

86. Alexander Werth, *Leningrad* (London: Hamish Hamilton, 1944), 32.

87. KGIOP, f. Belekhova, d. 48 (unpaginated); Bobrov, *Khraniteli angela*, 22; Werth, *Leningrad*, 30.

88. D. Arkin, "Monumenty russkim geroiam," *Literatura i iskusstva*, 15 August 1942, 2.

89. TsGALI SPb, f. 333, op. 3, d. 3, l. 63.

90. For a report on the condition of the Mikhailovskii Palace, see RNB OR, f. 1117, d. 158, l. 2.

91. "Sokhranenie khudozhestvennykh pamiatnikov Leningrada," *Literatura i iskusstvo*, 25 December 1943.

92. Salisbury, *The 900 Days*, 504. Bidlack and Lomagin, *The Leningrad Blockade*, 285.

93. In certain places where damage was extensive, city officials and architects covered the destruction with plywood, which had the design of the predestruction facade painted on it. See references to this in Polina Barskova, "The Spectacle of the Besieged City: Repurposing Cultural Memory in Leningrad, 1941–1944," *Slavic Review* 69, no. 2 (Summer 2010): 353–354.

94. Boris Rest and Sergei Varshavsky, *Saved for Humanity: The Hermitage during the Siege of Leningrad, 1941–1944*, trans. Arthur Shakarovsky-Raffe (Leningrad: Aurora Art, 1985), 188. These problems persisted throughout the period of the blockade and into the postwar years. See TsGALI SPb, f. 341, op. 1, d. 101, ll. 1–2.

95. TsGA SPb, f. 7384, op. 17, d. 598, ll. 38–39. See also TsGALI SPb, f. 341, op. 1, d. 101, ll. 1–2.

96. KGIOP, f. Belekhova, op. 1, d. 41 (unpaginated).

97. TsGA SPb, f. 7384, op. 17, d. 598, ll. 14–15, 44.

98. RNB OR, f. 1117 (B. I. Zagurskii), op. 1, d. 157, l. 1 (ob).

99. KGIOP, f. 50, d. P-70, ll. 168–169.

100. Baranov, *Siluety blokady*, 85.

101. TsGALI SPb, f. 341, op. 1, d. 87, l. 9. See also Iu. Iu. Bakhareva, "Okhrana pamiatnikov Leningrada v gody Velikoi otechestvennoi voiny," in *Okhrana pamiatnikov Sankt-Peterburga*, ed. Bakhareva et.al. (St. Petersburg: Propilei, 2008), 64–65.

102. Vera Ketlinskaia, "Eto i est' Leningrad!," *Literaturnaia gazeta*, 3 February 1945.

103. Salisbury, *The 900 Days*, 551.

104. "Ob ispolzovanii arkhitektorov goroda Leningrada po svoei spetsial'nosti (reshenie ispol'nitelnogo komiteta Leningradskogo gorodskogo soveta ot 21 Jan 1943 N.38, p.45)," *Biulleten' Leningradskogo gorodskogo soveta deputatov trudiashchikhsia*, 1943, nos. 3–4: 9–10; TsGALI SPb, f. 341, op. 1, d. 90, l. 41.

105. TsGALI SPb, f. 341, op. 1, d. 96, l. 42.

106. TsGALI SPb, f. 341, op. 1, d. 100, l. 30.

107. Baranov, *Siluety blokady*, 116.

108. TsGALI SPb, f. 341, op. 1, d. 96, l. 39; TsGALI SPb, f. 266, op. 1, d. 22, ll. 2, 4.

109. I. A. Vaks and N. M. Ol', "Budushchie restavratory," in Kutuzov and Levina, *Vozrozhdenie*, 228.

110. Baranov, *Siluety blokady*, 117.

111. TsGALI SPb, f. 266, op. 1, d. 22, l. 2; I. A. Vaks, "Podgotovka masterov khudozhestvennoi otdelki zdanii," *Arkhitektura Leningrada*, nos. 1–2 (1944): 24–25.

112. Vaks and Ol', "Budushchie restavratory," 231.

113. The page from Baranov's diary is reprinted in his memoirs. See Baranov, *Siluety blokady*, 118–119.

3. PROJECTING SOVIET POWER

1. Donald Filtzer, *Soviet Workers and Late Stalinism: Labour and the Restoration of the Stalinist System after World War II* (New York: Cambridge University Press, 2002), 13.

2. See Martin Blackwell, "Regime City of the First Category: The Experience of the Return of Soviet Power to Kyiv, Ukraine, 1943–1946" (PhD diss., Indiana University, 2005); Andrew Day, "Building Socialism: The Politics of the Soviet Cityscape in the Stalin Era" (PhD diss., Columbia University, 1998; Jeffrey W. Jones, *Everyday Life and the "Reconstruction" of Soviet Russia during and after the Great Patriotic War, 1943–1948* (Bloomington: Slavica, 2008); and Qualls, *From Ruins to Reconstruction*. The situation was only gradually improved throughout the first postwar years, and by 1949, even though much was restored, many residential buildings in urban centers remained in ruins. See E. Iu. Zubkova et al., eds., *Sovetskaia zhizn' 1945–1953* (Moscow: Rosspen, 2003), 168–169.

3. A. V. Karasev, "Vozrozhdenie goroda-geroia," *Istoriia SSSR* 5, no. 3 (1961): 116. Many wooden structures were also disassembled and used for fuel during the blockade as a means of saving the trees in the historic parks of Leningrad. See Baranov, *Siluety blokady*, 54.

4. A. Z. Vakser, *Leningrad poslevoennyi, 1945–1982 gody* (St. Petersburg: Izdatel'stvo Ostrov, 2005), 21. For details, see *AKT Leningradskoi gorodskoi komissii o prednamerennom istreblenii nemetsko-fashistskimi varvarami mirnykh zhitelei Leningrada i ushcherbe, nanesennom khoziaistvu i kul'turno-istoricheskim*

pamiatnikam goroda za period voiny i blokady (Leningrad: Ogiz-Gospolitizdat, 1945), 32–34.

5. *AKT Leningradskoi gorodskoi komissii*, 33.

6. *AKT Leningradskoi gorodskoi komissii*, 28.

7. Blair A. Ruble, *Leningrad: Shaping a Soviet City* (Los Angeles: University of California Press, 1989), 51.

8. See the State Defense Committee's decree from 29 March 1944, "O pervoocherednykh meropriiatiiakh po vosstanovleniiu promyshlennosti i gorodskogo khoziaistva Leningrada v 1944." *Resheniia partii i pravitel'stva po khoziaistvennym voprosam: Tom 3, 1941–1952* (Moscow: Izdatel'stvo politicheskoi literatury, 1968), 195–200.

9. RGASPI (Rossiiskii gosudarstvennyi arkhiv sotsial'no-politicheskoi istorii), f. 77, op. 1, d. 793, l. 41.

10. Ia. O. Rubanchik, "My otstoiali tebia, Leningrad, my tebia vosstanovim," *Arkhitektura Leningrada*, no. 1 (1945): 16–22.

11. See, for example, V. Lavrov's article which discusses the "urgent need" to restore monuments contributing to the architectural ensembles of cities and towns. "Neotlozhnye voprosy vosstanovleniia pamiatnikov Russkogo zodchestva," *Arkhitektura SSSR*, 1944, no. 8: 24–30.

12. M. P. Pavlova, "Sostoianie okhrany pamiatnikov arkhitektury i organizatsii restavratsionnykh rabot v 1940-e–1960-e gg," in *Pamiatniki arkhitektury v Sovetskom Soiuze: Ocherki istorii arkhitekturnoi restavratsii*, ed. A. S. Shchenkov (Moscow: Pamiatniki istoricheskoi mysli, 2004), 232.

13. KGIOP, f. 950-II-2, d. N-3349/1, l. 3 (ob).

14. See Qualls's discussion of local planners' placing historic monuments at the center of Sevastopol's restoration plans. Qualls, *From Ruins to Reconstruction*, chap. 4.

15. Ruble, *Leningrad*, 50.

16. Vakser, *Leningrad poslevoennyi*, 71.

17. For more on eclectic architectural styles linking monuments, see Buckler, *Mapping St. Petersburg*, 55–60.

18. See Lambourne, *War Damage in Western Europe*, 187–188; Jeffry M. Diefendorf, "Introduction: New Perspectives on a Rebuilt Europe," in *Rebuilding Europe's Bombed Cities*, ed. Jeffry M. Diefendorf (London: Macmillan, 1990), 5.

19. Diefendorf, "Introduction," 5.

20. See Andrew Day, "The Rise and Fall of Stalinist Architecture," in Cracraft and Rowland, *Architectures of Russian Identity*, 174.

21. See Qualls, *From Ruins to Reconstruction*. See also his "Accommodation and Agitation in Sevastopol: Redefining Socialist Space in the Postwar 'City of Glory,'" in *Socialist Spaces: Sites of Everyday Life in the Eastern Bloc*, ed. David Crowley and Susan E. Reid (New York: Berg, 2002).

22. Ultimately, Qualls notes, local architects and party and government leaders in Sevastopol were able to advance their plans for the reconstruction of the city by seizing on "Stalin's recent promotion of building according to local conditions to remove Moscow-based architects and to develop a reconstruction plan . . . that championed an image of the city that was more in harmony with its traditions and history." As in Leningrad, local planners in Sevastopol made Russian military and imperial history the centerpiece of the reconstruction. Qualls, *From Ruins to Reconstruction*, 47.

23. V. A. Kamenskii, "Pervoocherednye zadachi arkhitektorov Leningrada," *Arkhitektura Leningrada*, no. 1 (1945): 1.

See also Lisa Kirschenbaum's discussion of these issues in Kirschenbaum, *The Legacy of the Siege of Leningrad,* 128–129.

24. N. V. Baranov, "O plane vosstanovleniia Leningrada: Iz doklada glavnogo arkhitektora Leningrada N.V. Baranova na rashirennom zasedanii pravleniia SSA s aktivom moskovskikh arkhitektorov 10-X-1944 g.," *Arkhitektura Leningrada,* no. 1 (1945): 3. See also "Leningrad stanet eshche nariadnee: Beseda s glavnym inzhenerom stroitel'nogo upravleniia Lengorispolkoma, D.M. Trofimkimym," in *Vechernii Leningrad,* 5 April 1946. In this article the author discusses facade work and notes that the Birzha, the Ethnographic Museum of the Academy of Science, the Russian Museum, the Engineers' Castle, the Mikhailovskii Manezh, the Arctic Museum, the House of Art, and others were worked on first.

25. See the diary entry for 17 August 1945 in Boldyrev, *Osadnaia Zapis',* 349.

26. TsGA SPb, f. 7384, op. 17, d. 1108, l. 12 (ob).

27. N. V. Baranov, "O plane vosstanovleniia Leningrada," 8.

28. In Leningrad, as in other places, the role of historic architectural ensembles in the formation of the city was crucial. See Lavrov, "Neotlozhnye voprosy vosstanovleniia pamiatnikov," 26.

29. N. Baranov, "Arkhitekturnyi oblik Leningrada," *Vechernii Leningrad,* 20 April 1946. See also TsGANTD SPb (Tsentral'nyi gosudarstvennyi arkhiv nauchno-teknicheskoi dokumentatsii Sankt-Peterburga), f. 17, op. 2–1, d. 2, l. 76.

30. KGIOP, f. 950.VI-I, d. N-393, l. 3. V. K. Makarov expressed similar feelings in an appeal to Leningrad's artistic community to restore the suburban palaces. He wrote, "When they place a wounded soldier on the operating table, the surgeon does not throw up his hands in despair, but quickly and capably begins the rewarding work of returning life and meaning to this maimed, but once beautiful organism. This is how we must act!" See RNB OR, f. 1135, op. 1, d. 24, l. 5.

31. See, for example, V. A. Kamenskii, "Zhiloi dom v ansemble goroda," *Arkhitektura i stroitel'stvo Leningrada,* November 1946, 16.

32. Ia. O. Rubanchik discussed this in an article on the restoration of Nevskii Prospekt. "A number of labor-intensive reconstruction and restoration works, which at first glance are not given great significance, play a significant role in the formation of the prospect's ensemble. Such work includes the reconstruction of the first floors flanking the former Catherine kostel and the Armenian church." See Rubanchik, "Vosstanovlenie Nevskogo Prospekta," *Arkhitektura i stroitel'stvo Leningrada* 3, no. 9 (1948): 16; Buckler, *Mapping St. Petersburg,* 1–3.

33. KGIOP, f. 950-II-2, d. N-3349/1, l. 14 (ob).

34. TsGA SPb, f. 7384, op. 17, d. 1108, l. 1. This letter was from 1944. In 1948 Baranov again called for work to be done on the Admiralty and placed a great deal of importance on the ensemble principle: "Considering the significance of the stated building in the ensemble of our city . . ." See KGIOP, f. 50, d. P-71, l. 253.

35. TsGA SPb, f. 7384, op. 26, d. 57, l. 2.

36. Baranov, "O plane vosstanovleniia Leningrada," 4–5.

37. Such imagery had been used throughout the war, as Soviet artists juxtaposed Red Army soldiers with heroic knights and warriors from Russian history, including Dmitrii Donskoi, Alexander Nevskii, and Alexander Suvorov. Even in the postwar period, similar images were used to link the Soviet present with the Russian past. A 1946 propaganda poster

by Victor Ivanov captioned "Glory to the Russian People – A People of Epic Heroes, A People of Creative Talents!," for example, used similar imagery. The poster presented an architect reviewing plans for Moscow set against the city's historic core. Looming above the architect is the founder of Moscow, Yuri Dolgorukii, implying a link between the heroic battles of Russian history and the new battles on the restoration front. Reproduced in Brandenberger, *National Bolshevism,* 195.

38. Brumfield, *A History of Russian Architecture,* 228.

39. "Kakie doma stroim: Beseda s glavnym arkhitektorom Leningrada, chlenom-korrespondentom Akademii arkhitektury SSSR, N.V. Baranovym," *Vechernii Leningrad,* 25 January 1946.

40. TsGALI SPb, f. 277, op. 1, d. 18, l. 6 (ob).

41. TsGALI SPb, f. 277, op. 1, d. 18, ll. 6 (ob)–7. TsGA SPb, f. 2076, op. 5, d. 43, l. 112 (ob).

42. Iu. L. Kosenkova, *Sovetskii gorod 1940-kh–pervoi poloviny 1950-kh godov: Ot tvorcheskikh poiskov k praktike stroitel'stva* (Moscow: URSS, 2000), 247–249.

43. On the decision to leave the village of Oradour-sur-Glane in ruins as a commemoration of Nazi brutality, see Farmer, *Martyred Village.*

44. For a discussion of the motives for leaving historic monuments in ruins, see Lambourne, *War Damage in Western Europe,* 179–180.

45. GMGS, f. Otdel pamiatnikov i memorial'nykh dosok, d. 36–37, ch. 2, l. 12b.

46. The damage is now commemorated by plaques that attribute the destruction to German shells and bombs. See, for example, Kirschenbaum, *The Legacy of the Siege of Leningrad,* 190.

47. A. S. Shchenkov and M. P. Pavlova, "Stanovlenie metodiki arkhitekturnoi restavratsii v pervoe poslevoennoe desiatiletie," in Shchenkov, *Pamiatniki arkhitektury,* 299.

48. See, for example, Igor' Grabar', ed., *Pamiatniki iskusstva razrushennye nemetskimi zakhvatchikami v SSSR: Sbornik statei* (Moscow: Izdatel'stvo Akademii Nauk SSSR, 1948).

49. S. Tsimbal, "Iasnoe nebo," *Vechernii Leningrad,* 26 June 1946.

50. Tsimbal, "Iasnoe nebo," 2.

51. Another article in *Vechernii Leningrad* stated the following: "Our glorious city is taking on its beautiful appearance anew. On the place of ruins beautiful buildings were raised in the shortest time. Leningraders are restoring the maimed residential buildings, destroyed by the enemy." *Vechernii Leningrad,* 17 December 1945.

52. Lambourne, *War Damage in Western Europe,* 96.

53. For a discussion of the use of Peter the Great in creating Soviet identity under Stalin, see Kevin M. F. Platt, *Terror and Greatness: Ivan and Peter as Russian Myths* (Ithaca, NY: Cornell University Press, 2011).

54. KGIOP, f. 50, d. P-70, l. 144.

55. A. A. Kedrinskii et al., eds, *Vosstanovlenie pamiatnikov arkhitektury Leningrada,* 2nd ed. (Leningrad: Stroiizdat, 1987), 282.

56. RGAE (Rossiiskii gosudarstvennyi arkhiv ekonomii), f. 9588, op. 1, d. 39, ll. 229–237.

57. Vsevolod Rozhdestvenskii, "U pamiatnika (Rasskaz iz tsikla 'Legendy Leningrada')," *Leningradskaia pravda,* 23 December 1945.

58. According to Baranov, the historic lessons embodied in the city's monuments inspired people to defend the city and

save it from the Germans. "It needs to be remembered," he wrote, "that during the difficult days of the ordeal, in the period of the heroic defense of Leningrad, the architectural appearance of the city promoted the steadfastness and determination of its defenders, who were determined to die rather than allow the iron [*kovanyi*] boot of the German fascist onto the beautiful squares, streets and avenues of the city." N. V. Baranov, "Zadachi leningradskikh arkhitektorov v realizatsii piatiletnego plana vosstanovleniia i razvitiia g. Leningrada i oblasti," *Arkhitektura i stroitel'stvo Leningrada,* November 1946, 4. In the plan for the development and restoration of Leningrad, delivered by Baranov on 25 December 1945, he wrote, "The external appearance of Leningrad unwittingly educates. . . . To this you may add the patriotic feelings of the population. It is no secret that Leningraders loved their city very much in the days of the Defense of Leningrad, which many of us lived through. In that great epic . . . Leningrad's external appearance played a well-known role." TsGA SPb, f. 7384, op. 26, d. 57, l. 4.

59. For a history of the medal "For the Defense of Leningrad," see V. S. Grigor'ev, *"Za oboronu Leningrada": Istoriia medali* (St. Petersburg, 1993).

60. "Godovshchina velikoi pobedy Krasnoi Armii pod Leningradom. (Material dlia dokladchikov i besedchikov)," *Bloknot agitatora,* no. 2 (1945): 32.

61. F. Samoilov, "Trekhletie so dnia pobedy sovetskikh voisk pod Leningradom," *Bloknot agitatora,* no. 2 (1947): 18.

62. TsGAIPD SPb (Tsentral'nyi gosudarstvennyi arkhiv istoriko-politicheskikh dokumentov Sankt Peterburga), f. 25, op. 10, d. 431, l. 1.

63. Samoilov, "Trekhletie so dnia pobedy sovetskikh voisk pod Leningradom," 18.

64. Vakser, *Leningrad poslevoennyi,* 75. See also Harrison Salisbury, "Art in Leningrad Flourishes Again: Cultural Centers and Historic Palaces Are Largely Free of Scars of Battle," *New York Times,* 12 November 1949.

65. RGAE, f. 9588, op. 1, d. 67, ll. 192–193.

66. Trade colleges Number 9 (in operation since January 1944 and discussed in the previous chapter) and Number 11 (in operation since October 1945). See, for example, "Iunye restavratory: Arkhitekturno-khudozhestvennoe remeslennoe uchilishche," *Vechernii Leningrad,* 19 April 1946; "Shkola masterov-khudozhnikov: Uchilishche v Solianom pereulke," *Vechernii Leningrad,* 23 August 1946; "Budushchie mastera: Remeslennoe uchilishche N.11," *Vechernii Leningrad,* 31 August 1946; "Budushchie restavratory: V arkhitekturo-khudozhestvennom remeslennom uchilishche," *Vechernii Leningrad,* 1 November 1946; "Lepshchiki i zhivopistsy: Arkhitekturno-khudozhestvennoe remeslennoe uchilishche," *Vechernii Leningrad,* 4 January 1947.

67. Kedrinskii et al., eds, *Vosstanovlenie pamiatnikov,* 30.

68. TsGANTD SPb, f. 386, op. 1–4, d. 19, l. 6 (ob). LARM was created on the basis of a decision of the executive committee of the city soviet on 19 March 1945, and confirmed by a decree of the Soviet government on 9 May 1945. It began work in July of that year.

69. TsGANTD SPb, f. 386, op. 1–4, d. 24, l. 3.

70. TsGANTD SPb, f. 386, op. 1–4, d. 24, l. 20; TsGANTD SPb, f. 386, op. 1–4, d. 66, ll. 20–22.

71. Although the authorities sought to accomplish these tasks as quickly as possible, statues and spires remained

concealed until the spring and summer of 1945. Strategic imperatives led preservationists to delay certain restorative actions, and even pushed Leningrad's authorities to demand that the camouflage on the city's spires and cupolas be repaired between May and August 1944. KGIOP, f. 50, d. P-70, ll. 153, 160.

72. TsGANTD SPb, f. 386, op. 1–4, d. 18, l. 18; Mikhail Bobrov, *Khraniteli angela: Zapiski blokadnogo al'pinista* (St. Petersburg: Izdatel'stvo SPb Gumanitarnogo universiteta profsoiuzov, 1998), 101.

73. GMGS, f. Otdel pamiatnikov i memorial'nykh dosok, d. 48, ch. 1 (unpaginated).

74. Ibid.

75. For the plan to remove the sculptures from the ground, see TsGALI SPb, f. 277, op. 1, d. 85, l. 11.

76. TsGALI SPb, f. 277, op. 1, d. 85, l. 1.

77. RNB OR, f. 1015, d. 61, ll. 11–13. Diary entry from 15 August 1945.

78. TsGA SPb, f. 7384, op. 17, d. 1447, l. 21. A Leningrad city soviet executive committee decision from 1944, for example, ordered that materials from destroyed buildings be gathered and used for construction where needed. The decision also included instructions for how to properly disassemble and gather the construction materials. See *Biulleten' Leningradskogo gorodskogo soveta deputatov trudiashchikh sia*, nos. 3–4 (1994): 8–12.

79. See Levina, "Pis'ma k drugu," 210.

80. "Anichkov most 2 iiunia," *Leningradskaia pravda*, 3 June 1945.

81. The statues were returned to their pedestals on the bridge by the same organization that removed them in 1941, thirteen days ahead of schedule. See TsGA SPb, f. 7384, op. 17, d. 1447, l. 39.

82. Rubanchik, "Vosstanovlenie Nevskogo Prospekta," 18.

83. RNB OR, f. 1015, d. 61, l. 13.

84. The organization "Monumentskulptura" refused work on the Manchurian Lions at Peter I's Cottage, for example, because it did not possess the necessary hoisting machinery. This task was passed on to "Stal'konstruktsiia," the very same organization which carried out the restoration of the monument to Peter I at the Engineers' Castle. See TsGA SPb, f. 7384, op. 17, d. 1447, l. 84.

85. Konstantin Fedin, "Svidanie s Leningradom, zapiski 1944 goda," *Novyi mir* 4–5 (1944): 45.

86. TsGA SPb, f. 7384, op. 17, d. 1108, l. 12 (ob).

87. TsGALI SPb, f. 277, op. 1, d. 167, l. 4.

88. The city soviet decreed that the heavily damaged Tauride Palace, for example, was to be completely restored by 1 September 1945, and allocated one million rubles for this work. KGIOP, f. 157, d. P-781, l. 103, l. 95. The plan, however, turned out to be much too ambitious. Indeed, with the amount of work needed to be done in the city, very few monuments were actually restored that quickly. Taking into account the deficiencies in material and labor supplies, the authorities revised their plans and aimed to have the interiors and facades not only at the Tauride Palace but at the other monuments housing the party committee and soviet restored by the end of 1947, at a cost of nearly seven million rubles. TsGA SPb, f. 7384, op. 29, d. 174, l. 97.

89. KGIOP, f. 163, d. P-187, l. 73. The commission was composed of Baranov, Belekhov, A. A. Khodyrev (the chief of the Administration of Construction), and A. M. Shabrov (the chief of the State Architectural-Construction Control).

90. See the account of the director of the museum, P. K. Baltun, of the

restoration in the early postwar years. Baltun, *Russkii musei,* 86.

91. KGIOP, f. 163, d. P-818, ll. 224–224 (ob).

92. KGIOP, f. 163, d. P-818, l. 220. This Soviet government order from 27 May 1947 was signed by Stalin.

93. Kedrinskii et al., eds., *Vosstanovlenie pamiatnikov,* 190.

94. See, for example, "O meropriiatiiakh po uluchsheniiu vneshnego blagoustroistva goroda Leningrada. (Reshenie ispolnitel'nogo komiteta Leningradskogo gorodskogo soveta deputatov trudiashchikhsia ot 19 aprelia 1945, N.144, p.3)," *Biulleten' Leningradskogo gorodskogo soveta deputatov trudiashchikhsia,* no. 9 (1945): 5–6. TsGALI SPb, f. 277, op. 1, d. 18, l. 8.

95. I. Z. Maseev, "Pervye tipovye," in *Vozrozhdenie: Vospominaniia, ocherki i dokumenty o vosstanovlenii Leningrada,* ed. V. A. Kutuzov and E. G. Levina (Leningrad: Lenizdat, 1977), 236. It was suggested that in the interests of architectural harmony all windows without glass on the main streets be covered with plywood and painted the same color as the facade of the building. See "O meropriiatiiakh po uluchsheniiu vneshnego blagoustroistva goroda Leningrada. (Reshenie ispolnitel'nogo komiteta Leningradskogo gorodskogo soveta deputatov trudiashchikhsia ot 15 avgusta 1944, N.119, p.3-z)," *Biulleten' Leningradskogo gorodskogo soveta deputatov trudiashchikhsia,* no. 16 (1944): 2.

96. "Blagoustroistvo goroda – zabota kazhdogo leningradtsa," *Leningradskaia pravda,* 8 May 1945.

97. GARF (Gosudarstvennyi arkhiv Rossiiskoi Federatsii), f. A-150, op. 2, d. 961, ll. 15–19. See also "O podgotove k fasadnym rabotam v 1946 godu. (Reshenie Ispolnitel'nogo Komiteta Leningradskogo gorodskogo soveta deputatov trudiashchikhsia ot 28 fevralia 1946, N.169, p.2-b)," *Biulleten' Leningradskogo gorodskogo soveta deputatov trudiashchikhsia,* no. 6 (1946): 3.

98. TsGANTD SPb, f. 386, op. 1–4, d. 67, l. 18.

99. "Na fasadakh leningradskikh zdanii," *Vechernii Leningrad,* 10 August 1946.

100. "Fasad dvortsa," *Vechernii Leningrad,* 20 October 1946.

101. "O podgotove k fasadnym rabotam v 1946 godu. (Reshenie ispolnitel'nogo komiteta Leningradskogo gorodskogo soveta deputatov trudiashchikhsia ot 28 fevralia 1946, N.169, p.2-b)," *Biulleten' Leningradskogo gorodskogo soveta deputatov trudiashchikhsia,* no. 6 (1946): 3.

102. "O khode rabot po remontu i okraske fasadov vedomstvennykh zdanii. (Reshenie ispolnitel'nogo komiteta Leningradskogo gorodskogo soveta deputatov trudiashchikhsia ot 7 iiulia 1947, N.242, p.1-b)," *Biulleten' Leningradskogo gorodskogo soveta deputatov trudiashchikhsia,* no. 15 (1947): 5. Work had begun at these monuments of architecture before, however. In July 1946, it was believed that the Pushkin Theater was one of the objectives that was on track to be completed on time. See also TsGA SPb, f.7 384, op. 25, d. 30, l. 178.

103. This decision listed several locations, including the spit of Vasilievskii Island, Art Square, Ostrovskii Square, the square at Smolnyi, Nevskii Prospekt, Sennaia Square, the square at the Chemical-Technological Institute, and others. See "O khode rabot po remontu i okraske fasadov vedomstvennykh zdanii," 5.

104. See the stenographic report of this meeting. TsGA SPb, f. 7384, op. 25, d. 30, ll. 175–187.

105. TsGA SPb, f. 7384, op. 25, d. 30, l. 177.

106. TsGA SPb, f. 7384, op. 25, d. 30, l. 186.

107. TsGA SPb, f. 7384, op. 25, d. 30, l. 187.

108. See the stenographic report of the meeting. TsGA SPb, f. 7384, op. 25, d. 245, ll. 69–81.

109. TsGA SPb, f. 7384, op. 25, d. 245, l. 78.

110. Ibid.

111. The poor work on facades of departmental buildings was discussed in *Leningradskaia pravda.* One article noted that work was very unsatisfactory, and that restoration of the city's prewar appearance was in danger of not becoming a reality, and the author went on to single out several who were supposedly at fault. See "V Ispolkome Lengorsoveta," *Leningradskaia pravda,* 9 June 1945.

112. Anne Gorsuch, "'There's No Place like Home': Soviet Tourism in Late Stalinism," *Slavic Review* 62, no. 4 (Winter 2003): 771.

113. This particular quotation comes from the "Otchet o rabote ehkskursionnogo biuro za 1946." TsGALI, f. 277, op. 1, d. 253, l. 1.

114. The bureau's yearly reports note that the majority of tourist-related tours and other activities generally focused on these four areas.

115. TsGAIPD SPb, f. 3401, op. 1, d. 5, l. 22.

116. GARF, f. A-150, op. 2, d. 980, ll. 168–169.

117. The documents from the Main Administration for the Protection of Monuments in Moscow and the State Inspectorate for the Protection of Monuments in Leningrad often reference occupants and the difficulties they present. See, for example, RGAE, f. 9588, op. 1, d.40, ll. 27–30, 188–190.

118. TsGALI SPb, f. 341, op. 1, d. 245, ll. 8–10.

119. TsGALI SPb, f. 341, op. 1, d. 245, l. 8; RGAE, f. 9588, op. 1, d. 69, ll. 77–78.

120. TsGALI SPb, f. 341, op. 1, d. 245, l. 8 (ob).

121. K. Dmitrev, "Restavratsiia Inzhernernogo Zamka," *Leningradskaia pravda,* 7 April 1945.

122. See the documents in KGIOP, f. 167, d. Inzhenernyi zamok (no delo number and unpaginated). The documents in this file mainly discuss the catastrophic problems at the castle between 1944 and 1949.

123. KGIOP, f.167, d. Inzhenernyi zamok (no delo number and unpaginated). The report is dated 12 February 1948.

124. RGAE, f. 9588, op. 1, d. 67, l. 161.

125. KGIOP, f. 167, d. Inzhenernyi zamok (no delo number and unpaginated). The letter was sent to *Izvestiia* in 1949.

126. TsGALI SPb, f. 341, op. 1, d. 245, ll. 9–10. In 1950 it was proposed that the building be used as the Leningrad Museum of the Revolution (which was housed in part of the Winter Palace until 1944). The Leningrad party leadership petitioned the central government for fifteen million rubles in order to restore the premises, but the request was turned down. See RGASPI, f. 17, op. 132, d. 440, l. 6.

127. Kedrinskii et al., *Vosstanovlenie pamiatnikov,* 233.

128. "Ne beregut pamiatnikov proshlogo," *Vechernii Leningrad,* 22 February 1946. Another letter sent to the press evoked the ensemble principle in complaining about the lack of work carried out on the Rostral Columns on the spit of Vasilievskii Island. See "U Rostral'nykh kolonn," *Vechernii Leningrad,* 3 June 1946.

129. TsGALI SPb, f. 333, op. 1, d. 342, ll. 8–9.

130. KGIOP, f. 163, d. P-818, l. 207.

131. RGASPI, f. 17, op. 132, d. 98, l. 29–29 (ob).

132. In a lecture delivered to the city's architectural community in 1949,

Belekhov, the head of Leningrad's State Inspectorate for the Preservation of Monuments (GIOP), extolled the successes achieved in restoring the city's monuments. Since 1945, 263 million rubles had been allocated and spent on the preservation and restoration of historic monuments and landmarks. According to Belekhov, in 1938 only 9 million was spent on monuments. In 1945, following the victory over the Germans, that figure climbed to 39 million. In 1946 the amount rose to 60 million, in 1947 to almost 80 million, and in 1948 to 84 million. KGIOP, f. 950. VI-1, d. N-393, l. 6.

133. L.L. Rakov, "Pamiatnik geroiam nashego goroda: K godovshchine so dnia otkrytiia vystavki 'Geroicheskaia oborona Leningrada,'" *Leningradskaia pravda,* 30 May 1945.

4. "WHEN IVAN COMES, THERE WILL BE NOTHING LEFT"

1. S. N. Balaeva, *Zapiski khranitelia Gatchinskogo dvortsa, 1924–1956: Dnevniki; Stat'i,* ed. N. S. Batenin (St. Petersburg, Iskusstvo Rossii, 2005), 159.

2. Anne Gorsuch argues that postwar Soviet tourism was used to reinforce patriotic Soviet identity in reaction to the developing Cold War. See Gorsuch, "'There's No Place like Home.'" This type of tourism was used by other regimes at around the same time.

3. Peterhof – later known as Petrodvorets – was founded by the first Russian emperor on the shores of the Gulf of Finland to the southwest of the city. Designed by the French architect Jean Le Blond on the model of Versailles, the park immediately became famous for its opulent fountain system adorned with gilded allegorical statues. In the decades after Peter's death, Rastrelli transformed the modest palace into an impressive baroque complex. The Italian-born architect also built the baroque Catherine Palace in Tsarskoe Selo – later named Pushkin – during Elizabeth's reign (1741–1762). The park surrounding the palace in Pushkin was designed during Catherine the Great's rule as an English garden, replete with manmade ponds and ruins. Both Pavlovsk and Gatchina were closely associated with Catherine's son, Paul. In the late 1700s, the Scottish architect Charles Cameron designed and built the neoclassical palace in Pavlovsk for the heir to the throne. Although the castle-like palace at Gatchina was used by Paul as a large-scale military camp to drill his soldiers, it was originally built and owned by Catherine's lover, Count Grigorii Orlov, in the 1770s and 1780s.

4. Fyodor Dostoevsky's novel *The Idiot,* for example, is in large part a story of St. Petersburg's well-to-do enjoying the summer at their dachas in Pavlovsk. See Dostoevsky, *The Idiot,* trans. David Magarshack (New York: Penguin, 1955).

5. For a history of the development of suburbia in England, see Robert Fishman, *Bourgeois Utopias: The Rise and Fall of Suburbia* (New York: Basic Books, 1987).

6. Stephen Lovell discusses the surroundings of Leningrad and their importance as places of retreat for people in the imperial period. See Lovell, *Summer Folk: A History of the Dacha, 1710–2000* (Ithaca, NY: Cornell University Press, 2003), 28–57.

7. N. S. Tret'iakov, ed., "'My . . . dolzhny schitat' sebia mobilizovannymi dlia bor'by i pobedy . . .': Iz dnevnikov khranitelei prigorodnykh dvortsov-muzeev Leningrada; 1941–1945 gg.," *Otechestvennye arkhivy,* no. 1 (2007): 83.

8. See the diary of Lyubov Vasilievna Shaporina, in Veronique Garros, Natalia Korenevskaya, and Thomas Lahusen, eds.,

Intimacy and Terror: Soviet Diaries of the 1930s, trans. Carol Flath (New York: New Press, 1995), 347.

9. A. I. Zelenova, *Dvorets v Pavlovske* (Leningrad: Lenizdat, 1986), 5.

10. "Soobshchenie Chrezvychainoi Gosudarstvennoi Komissii po ustanovleniiu i rassledovaniiu zlodeianii nemetsko-fashistskikh zakhvatchikov i ikh soobshchnikov: O razrusheniiakh pamiatnikov iskusstva i arkhitektury v gorodakh Petrodvorets, Pushkin i Pavlovsk," *Arkhitektura Leningrada,* nos. 1–2 (1944): 16.

11. Baranov, *Siluety blokady,* 8.

12. These plans were developed in the mid-1930s, after the damage to artistic and historic monuments in the Spanish Civil War had become known. N. S. Tret'iakov, "Spasenie istoriko-kul'turnykh pamiatnikov prigorodnykh muzeinykh kompleksov Leningrada v gody Velikoi Otechestvennoi voiny i pervyi poslevoennyi period (1941–1948)" (Candidate of Science diss., Leningrad State University, 1991), 44–48.

13. Tret'iakov, "Spasenie istoriko-kul'turnykh pamiatnikov," 59.

14. A. I. Zelenova, "Snariady rvutsia v Pavlovske: Iz vospominanii direktora dvortsa-muzeia Anny Ivanovny Zelenovoi," in Papernaia, *Podvig veka,* 20.

15. V. I. Piliavskii, "Razrusheniia prigorodov Leningrada," *Arkhitektura Leningrada,* nos. 1–2 (1944): 21.

16. For a more detailed discussion of the evacuation of art and cultural valuables, see Maksakova, *Spasenie kul'turnykh tsennostei,* 49–81. See also G. V. Vilinbakhov, ed., *Ermitazh: Khronika voennykh let, 1941–1945; Dokumenty arkhiva Gosudarstvennogo Ermitazha* (St. Petersburg: Izdatel'stvo Gosudarstvennogo Ermitazha, 2005). Museum workers packed many of the moveable valuables from the suburbs into storage boxes and shipped them by train to Novosibirsk and Sarapul. Zelenova, *Dvorets v Pavlovske,* 5.

17. Ia. I. Shurygin, *Petergof: Letopis' vostanovleniia* (St. Petersburg: Arbis, 2000), 66.

18. Shurygin, *Petergof,* 76.

19. Zelenova, "Snariady rvutsia v Pavlovske," 20.

20. Tret'iakov, *"Spasenie istoriko-kul'turnykh pamiatnikov prigorodov,"* 42–48.

21. See Barber, "Popular Reactions in Moscow," 5–18.

22. Zelenova, *Dvorets v Pavlovske,* 6.

23. E. L. Turova describes how shells damaged the Catherine Palace and some of the pavilions in Pushkin from 14 September onward. See Turova, "Snariady rvutsia v Pushkine: Iz dnevnika khranitelia Ekaterininskogo parka, Evgenii Leonidovny Turovoi," in Papernaia, *Podvig veka,* 18.

24. RNB OR, f. 1015, d. 57, l. 86.

25. Piliavskii, "Razrusheniia prigorodov Leningrada," 21.

26. RNB OR, f. 1015, d. 57, l. 89 (ob).

27. For the letter, see Papernaia, ed., *Podvig Veka,* 19.

28. Daniil Granin, "Vstupitel'noe slovo," in *Vozrozhdennye iz pepla: Petrodvorets, Pushkin, Pavlovsk; Al'bom,* ed. I. M. Gurevich, G. D. Khodasevich, and V. A. Belanina (Leningrad: Avrora, 1989), 14. In September 2007, I spoke with Granin at a conference in St. Petersburg on the blockade. He told me that on New Year's Eve 1941, the Germans occupying Pushkin gathered in the Catherine Palace to celebrate. The Soviet forces could have fired on the palace and taken the lives of several Germans, including high commanders, but Granin said that they simply could not bring themselves to do it.

29. Werth, *Leningrad*, 42.

30. Piliavskii, "Razrusheniia prigorodov Leningrada," 21.

31. See, for example, *Soobshchenie Komissii po okhrane i vosstanovleniiu arkhitekturnykh pamiatnikov: Pamiatniki zodchestva, razrushennye ili povrezhdennye nemetskimi zakhvatchikami; Dokumenty i materialy.* Vypusk 1 (Moscow: Izdatel'stvo Akademii Arkhitektury, 1942).

32. See, for example, "Gitlerovskim vandalam-gromilam ne udastsia skryt' svoikh prestuplenii v Iasnoi Poliane," *Literatura i iskusstvo,* 13 January 1942.

33. Baranov, *Siluety blokady,* 149.

34. Shurygin, *Petergof,* 60.

35. Zelenova, *Dvorets v Pavlovske,* 7.

36. For a detailed account of German theft of cultural valuables from the Soviet Union, see Boitsov and Vasil'eva, eds., *Kartoteka 'Z'*; and M. S. Zinich, *Pokhishchennye sokrovishcha: Vyvoz natsistami rossiiskikh kul'turnykh tsennostei* (Moscow: Institut rossiiskoi istorii, RAN, 2003). Several reports and articles published about the destruction in the suburbs emphasize that there was a special commission set up in Germany to process and catalogue valuables taken from occupied regions.

37. For a popular history of the search for the Amber Room, see Catherine Scott-Clark and Andrew Levy, *The Amber Room: The Fate of the World's Greatest Lost Treasure* (New York: Berkley Books, 2005).

38. In 2000, Russia's deputy minister of culture, Pavel V. Khoroshilov, stated that "the Amber Room has always represented the most painful, the most poignant of our losses." Quoted in Celestine Bohlen, "Arts Abroad: A Homecoming for Treasures Looted in War," *New York Times,* 27 April 2000.

39. For a detailed review of the condition of the Catherine Palace at the beginning of February 1944, see E. P. Turova's report to the head of the Administration for Artistic Affairs, B. I. Zagurskii. RNB OR, f. 1117, d. 223, ll. 1–5.

40. RNB OR, f. 1117, d. 223, l. 2.

41. Konstantin Fedin, "Svidanie s Leningradom, zapiski 1944 goda," *Novyi mir* 4–5 (1944): 48.

42. Baranov, *Siluety blokady,* 147; Fedin, "Svidanie s Leningradom," 48.

43. Baranov, *Siluety blokady,* 147. Baranov also noted that the palace had been turned into a "vile cave" by the German "degenerates." Baranov, *Siluety blokady,* 148.

44. See "Soobshchenie Chrezvychanoi Gosudarstvennoi Komissii," 19.

45. For a detailed review of the condition of the Pavlovsk Palace at the beginning of February 1944, see A. I. Zelenova's report to the head of the Administration for Artistic Affairs, B. I. Zagurskii. RNB OR, f. 1117, d. 222, ll. 1–3.

46. D. Rudnev and M. Sivolobov, "V Gatchine," *Pravda,* 28 January 1944. See also Vera Inber's account in Inber, *Leningrad Diary,* trans. Serge M. Wolff and Rachel Grieve (London: Hutchinson of London, 1971), 184–185.

47. A. I. Zelenova, "Vozrozhdenie: Iz vospominanii direktora Pavlovskogo dvortsa-muzeia Anny Ivanovny Zelenovoi," in Papernaia, *Podvig veka,* 332.

48. Fedin, "Svidanie s Leningradom," 49.

49. This account is from one of the future restorers, A. P. Udalenkov, and is found in Shurygin, *Petergof,* 28. See Shurygin for a much more detailed account of the damage. M. Tikhomirova also includes a great deal of information in her recollections of the period. See Tikhomirova, *Pamiatniki, liudi, sobytiia: Iz zapisok muzeinogo rabotnika* (Leningrad:

Izdatel'stvo "Khudozhnik RSFSR," 1970), 51–60.

50. V. Piliavskii, "Vandalizm nemetsko-fashistskikh zakhvatchikov v prigorodakh Leningrada," *Arkhitektura SSSR,* no. 7 (1944): 36; Shurygin, *Petergof,* 28; Tikhomirova, *Pamiatniki, liudi, sobytiia,* 53.

51. "My otomstim za tebia, Petergof!," *Pravda,* 28 January 1944.

52. Preservation movements in other countries during this period also recognized the importance of historical monuments in telling the story of the nation. See Koshar, *Germany's Transient Pasts,* 224; See also Johnson, *How St. Petersburg Learned to Study Itself.*

53. N. Denisov, "Tri goroda (ot spetsial'nogo korrespondenta 'Krasnoi zvezdy')," *Krasnaia zvezda,* 27 January 1944.

54. "Soobshchenie Chrezvychanoi Gosudarstvennoi Kommissii," 16.

55. Fedin, "Svidanie s Leningradom," 49.

56. Werth, *Leningrad,* 42.

57. Nikolai Tikhonov, "Kamni Petergofa vzyvaiut o mshchenii," *Krasnaia zvezda,* 25 January 1944, 3.

58. See Bevan's discussion of the destruction of architecture during war as a deliberate policy to annihilate opposing cultures. Bevan, *The Destruction of Memory,* 28. During the war there were discussions of the Germans' treatment of historic monuments in Western Europe and elsewhere in the Soviet press. See, for example, I. Matsa, "Gitlerovskie vandaly," *Literatura i iskusstva,* 29 May 1943.

59. On the use of hate for mobilizational purposes during the war, see Serhy Yekelchyk, "The Civic Duty to Hate: Stalinist Citizenship as Political Practice and Civic Emotion (Kiev, 1943–53)," *Kritika: Explorations in Russian and Eurasian History* 7, no. 3 (Summer 2006): 532. See also Pisiotis, "Images of Hate in the Art of War."

60. Lambourne, *War Damage in Western Europe,* 101.

61. It should be noted that the Leningrad authorities also discussed the destruction of monuments in the city itself as acts deliberately meant to destroy historic monuments and erase Russian culture. See "Chrezvychainaia Gosudarstvennaia Komissiia po ustanovleniiu i rassledovaniiu zlodeianii nemetsko-fashistskikh zakhvatchikov i ikh soobshchnikov," *AKT Leningradskoi gorodskoi komissii.*

62. Lambourne, *War Damage in Western Europe,* 121.

63. Bantjes, "Making Sense of Iconoclasm," 171.

64. Yekelchyk notes that the destruction of a historic area in Kiev was blamed on the Germans and used to incite hatred and feelings of vengeance. See Yekelchyk, "The Civic Duty to Hate," 534. An article in the press noted the following in regard to hatred and vengeance: "The ashes of Peterhof burn the hearts of our warriors, calling for them to advance more quickly, and beat the enemy with more force." See A. Mikhailov and V. Vasilevskii, "Pepel Petergofa," *Krasnaia zvezda,* 21 January 1944.

65. "My otomstim za tebia, Petergof!," *Pravda,* 28 January 1944; Tikhonov, "Kamni Petergofa vzyvaiut o mshchenii."

66. Tret'iakov argues that the hate summoned up by the destruction of the palaces made people want to restore them. The restoration therefore took on a political character. See Tret'iakov, "Spasenie istoriko-kul'turnykh pamiatnikov," 177.

67. Tikhonov, "Kamni Petergofa vzyvaiut o mshchenii," 3. Tikhonov wrote elsewhere that "the ruins of Peterhof, Pavlovsk, Pushkino and Gatchina

appeared before the victorious Leningrad forces, calling for vengeance with all the heartrending tragedy of their ruins, shell holes and charred and crumbling walls. Even those of the men who had never before seen their splendor in peacetime could not help being moved at the sight of what the barbarians had done to this heritage of our past." See Tikhonov, "Victory: Leningrad in January 1944," in *Heroic Leningrad: Documents, Sketches and Stories of Its Siege and Relief,* trans. J. Fineberg (Moscow: Foreign Languages Publishing House, 1945), 149.

68. Piliavskii, "Razrusheniia prigorodov Leningrada," 23. Having visited Pushkin on the day after liberation, Ol'ga Berggol'ts likewise expressed the opinion that the palaces should be restored. See Ol'ga Berggol'ts, "My prishli v Pushkin," in *Ol'ga Berggol'ts: Izbrannye proizvedeniia v dvukh tomakh; Tom 2,* ed. A. Ruleva (Leningrad: "Khudozhestvennaia literature, 1967), 258.

69. Il'ia Ehrenburg, "Vechnyi gorod," in *Deviat'sot dnei: Literaturno-khudozhestvennyi sbornik,* ed. A. M. Amsterdam and M. M. Smirnov (Leningrad: Lenizdat, 1948), 506. The article was written in July 1945.

70. See Salisbury, review of *The Palaces of Leningrad,* by Victor and Audrey Kennett, *Journal of the Society of Architectural Historians* 33, no. 3 (1974): 255–256.

71. Susan Massie, for example, states that when P. S. Popkov, chairman of the city soviet, first saw the ruins, he said they should be razed to the ground. See Massie, *Pavlovsk: The Life of a Russian Palace* (Toronto: Little, Brown, 1990), 277.

72. Rudy Koshar discusses the debates surrounding ruined monuments in Germany after World War II. He notes that although there was some sentiment for having ruins preserved, in general there was an "allergy to ruins," making people want to see them removed or restored to their former appearance. See Koshar, *From Monuments to Traces: Artifacts of German Memory, 1870–1990* (Los Angeles: University of California Press, 2000), 153–154.

73. E. I. Katonin stated that this was how he felt when he returned to the city from evacuation shortly after the blockade was lifted. He made this statement at a 29 March 1946 meeting to discuss the work of Leningrad's Preservation Inspectorate. The stenographic report notes applause from the audience. See KGIOP, f. 950-II-2, d. N-3349/1, l. 16.

74. RNB OR, f.1135, op. 1, d. 24, ll. 4 (ob)–5.

75. KGIOP, f. 226-G, d. P-1024, ll. 92, 93, 94, 96.

76. Malinina, ed., *Iz istorii sovetskoi arkhitektury,* 128–129.

77. This quote comes from Zelenova's account of the meeting. See Zelenova, "Vozrozhdenie," 334. Shortly after the meeting Oleinik was released from the Red Army and began work as the head restorer in Pavlovsk.

78. Tikhomirova, *Pamiatniki, liudi, sobytiia,* 58. Zelenova also discusses this meeting. See Zelenova, "Vozrozhdenie," 336–337.

79. GMZ Pavlovsk (Gosudarstvennyi muzei-zapovednik Pavlovsk), f. Nauchno-vospomogatel'ny fond, Inv. 11708/3, ch. 1, l. 60.

80. KGIOP, f. 226-G, d. P-1024, l. 71 (ob).

81. The discussion of creating historic and artistic museums in the palaces came up at a number of points during the conference. See KGIOP, f. 226-G, d. P-1024, ll. 54–54, 61 (ob), 67 (ob)–68, 72–74, 77,

79. See also Balaeva, *Zapiski khranitelia Gatchinskogo dvortsa,* 146.

82. GMZ Pavlovsk, f. Nauchno-vospomogatel'ny fond, Inv. 11708/3, ch. 1, l. 61.

83. Elena Zubkova discusses the aspirations of Soviet citizens in the immediate postwar period. She notes that many romanticized the years of the 1930s and yearned for a better, easier life. See Zubkova, *Russia after the War,* 25–26, 34–35.

84. For a discussion of the need to create a healthy and patriotic citizenship to suit the needs of the modern state, see Hoffmann, *Stalinist Values.*

85. For more on this, see Andrei Dzeniskevich and John Barber, eds., *Life and Death in Besieged Leningrad, 1941–44* (New York: Palgrave Macmillan, 2005).

86. See, for example, the articles "O letnem otdykhe trudiashchikhsia" and "Vosstanovim zdorov'e leningradtsev," *Leningradskaia pravda,* 1 June 1945.

87. Due to the level of damage in Peterhof, most of the interior was to be used for more contemporary purposes. In 1948 Nikolai Baranov wrote that alongside exhibition halls there would be a concert hall, a restaurant, and a library. See Baranov, *Arkhitektura i storitel'stvo Leningrada* (Leningrad: Leningradskoe gazetno-zhurnal'noe i knizhnoe izdatel'stvo, 1948), 70.

88. KGIOP, f. 226-G, d. P-1024, ll. 61–62.

89. GMZ Pavlovsk, f. Nauchno-vospomogatel'ny fond, Inv. 11708/3, ch. 1, l. 63.

90. Preservationists and architects stressed that that palaces should be restored as close to the original as possible and that falsifications should be avoided at all costs. See the project for the restoration of the Pavlovsk Palace, TsGANTD SPb, f. 386, op. 1–4, d. 21, l. 54. Likewise, the Leningrad Architectural-Restoration Workshops refused to use imitations in their work. For example, see TsGALI SPb, f. 277, op. 1, d. 566, l. 9.

91. TsGALI SPb, f.277, op. 1, d. 82, l. 5 (ob).

92. Piliavskii, "Razrusheniia prigorodov Leningrada," 23. Oleinik, in his address to the participants of the meeting in which restoration was discussed, also noted that there was indeed enough documentary material in Leningrad to allow for restoration.

93. KGIOP, f. Fond Belekhova, op. 1, d. 49 (unpaginated). See Tikhomirova's discussion of the activities of suburban palace-museum workers throughout the blockade. Tikhomirova, *Pamiatniki, liudi, sobyttiia,* 7–50.

94. KGIOP, f. Fond Belekhova, op. 1, d. 58 (unpaginated).

95. "Vosstanovlenie leningradskikh dvortsov," *Literatura i iskusstvo,* 27 May 1944. See also Malinina, *Iz istorii sovetskoi arkhitektury,* 129–130. Suzanne Massie writes that the committee from Moscow arrived in March before the conference discussed above. The documents and press coverage, however, discuss only the May visit. See Massie, *Pavlovsk,* 280.

96. KGIOP, f. 226-G, d. P-1024, l. 50 (ob); f. Fond Belekhova, op. 1, d. 61 (unpaginated).

97. RGASPI, f. 77, op. 1, d. 793, l. 45.

98. Massie, *Pavlovsk,* 280.

99. KGIOP, f. 226-G, d. P-1024, l. 50 (ob).

100. KGIOP, f. 226-G, d. P-1024, l. 50 (ob).

101. KGIOP, f. Fond Belekhova, op. 1, d. 61 (unpaginated). Others made the connection between the restoration of historic monuments in the West and in Russia. E. I. Katonin discussed this at a meeting in 1946: "The restoration of the Cathedral in Reims after the barbarous bombardment

of German artillery comes to mind, and we have to believe that we will restore our suburbs, since the task that confronted the French was a much more difficult task than the one before us." See KGIOP, f. 950-II-2, d. N-3349/1, l. 16.

102. See Belekhov's letter to the chairman of the Committee for Artistic Affairs, M. B. Khrapchenko, KGIOP, f. Fond Belekhova, op. 1, d. 61 (unpaginated). Preservationists in the USSR in the postwar period depended on support from the public, and especially the intelligentsia, in the work to save historic monuments that were either damaged by the Germans or had fallen into disrepair. See the speech by M. I. Rzianin (head of GUOP) at the all-Union gathering of leading workers from the republican administrations for architectural affairs in December 1944. Kosenkova, *Sovetskii gorod 1940-kh–pervoi poloviny 1950-kh godov*, 257–258.

103. See N. N. Belekhov's letter to A. I. Shchusev, KGIOP, f. Fond Belekhova, op. 1, d. 61 (unpaginated). See also KGIOP, f. 226-G, d. P-1024, l. 50 (ob).

104. In November 1944, for example, Khrapchenko and Mordvinov wrote to Molotov asking for help in preserving the suburban palaces. See RGAE, f. 9342, op. 1, d. 2, l. 90.

105. Letter from 17 June 1944. See Kuchumov, *Stat'i, vospominaniia, pis'ma*, 123.

106. Massie, *Pavlovsk*, 280–281.

107. See Makarov's diary entry from 27 May in Tret'iakov, "'My . . . dolzhny schitat' sebia mobilizovannymi," 96.

108. See "Ob organizatsii otdelov kulturno-prosvetitel'noi raboty pri ispolnitel'nom komitete Leningradskogo gorodskogo soveta i ispolkomakh raisovetov deputatov trudiashchikhsia. (Reshenie ispolnitel'nogo komiteta Leningradskogo gorodskogo soveta deputatov trudiashchikhsia ot 22 fevralia 1945, N.138, p.10-b)," *Biulleten' Leningradskogo gorodskogo soveta deputatov trudiashchikhsia*, no. 4 (1945): 8–9.

109. TsGA SPb, f. 2076, op. 5, d. 43, l. 64.

110. TsGA SPb, f. 7384, op. 29, d. 48, l. 2; TsGA, f. 2076, op. 5, d. 43, l. 65; "O piatiletnem plane vosstanovleniia i razvitiia gorodskogo khoziaistva Leningrada na 1946–1950 gg. Reshenie XIII sessii Leningradskogo gorodskogo soveta deputatov trudiashchikhsia ot 17 ianvaria 1947 g." *Vechernii Leningrad*, 1 February 1947.

111. P. Lonopel'ko, "Prigorody Leningrada: Novyi tsikl lektsii v lektorii Gorkoma VKP(b)," *Vechernii Leningrad*, 12 June 1947.

112. M. P. Pavlova and A. S. Shchenkov, "Restavratsionnaia praktika," in Shchenkov, *Pamiatniki arkhitektury v Sovetskom Soiuze*, 344.

113. Shurygin, *Petergof*, 10.

114. KGIOP, f. Fond Belekhova, op. 1, d. 58 (unpaginated).

115. TsGA SPb, f. 2076, op. 5, d. 43, ll. 126–126 (ob). The parks in Pushkin and Pavlovsk, it was believed, would be restored completely by 1947.

116. TsGA SPb, f. 7384, op. 17, d. 1180, l. 51; TsGALI SPb, f. 411, op. 2, d. 4, l. 3.

117. N. V. Kukushkin, "Vesnoi 1944 goda . . . ," in Kutuzov and Levina, *Vozrozhdenie*, 29.

118. TsGAIPD SPb, f. 25, op. 10, d. 431, ll. 8–9. See A. A. Kedrinskii et. al., *Letopis' vozrozhdeniia: Vostanovlenie pamiatnikov arkhitektury Leningrada i prigorodov, razrushennykh v gody Velikoi Otechestvennoi voiny nemetsko-fashistskimi zakhvatshchikami* (Leningrad: Izdatel'stvo literature po stroitel'stvu, 1971), 53.

119. KGIOP, f. 226-G, d. P-1037, ll. 123–124.

120. Zelenova, "Vozrozhdenie: Iz vospominanii direktora Pavlovskogo

dvortsa-muzeia Anny Ivanovny Zelenovoi," in Papernaia, *Podvig veka,* 340.

121. TsGALI SPb, f. 277, op. 1, d. 82, l. 5. Because Pavlovsk was officially part of Leningrad province, the people who were available there for *voskresniki* were, for the most part, allocated to agricultural work.

122. Shurygin, *Petergof,* 93–94.

123. Shurygin, *Petergof,* 100–102.

124. See, for example, a discussion held by the Department of Cultural-Enlightenment Work about the restoration of the Catherine Park by 1948. It was estimated that the park would soon be completely restored to its former appearance. TsGALI SPb, f. 277, op. 1, d. 566, l. 31.

125. During the first year of restoration, the lack of skilled workers was acutely felt by all industries and establishments in the city. The city soviet and party committee were actively engaged in recruiting workers from all over the Soviet Union, especially Leningraders who had been evacuated. This recruitment process concerned the suburban palaces as well. See TsGA SPb, f. 7384, op. 17, d. 1207, ll. 2, 3, 43, 69.

126. TsGA SPb, f. 7384, op. 17, d. 1180, l. 32.

127. Baranov, *Siluety blokady,* 158.

128. KGIOP, f. 226-G, d. P-1024, l. 49.

129. See KGIOP, f. 226-G, d. P-1024, l. 43–46 for the letter to Beria, as well as letters to Grabar', Mordvinov, and Khrapchenko asking them to support the request. See also KGIOP, f. Fond Belekhova, op. 1, d. 61 (unpaginated).

130. See the reply to Belekhov from the deputy people's commissar of the NKVD, Chernyshov, dated 25 October 1944. KGIOP, f. Fond Belekhova, op. 1, d. 59 (unpaginated).

131. KGIOP, f. Fond Belekhova, op. 1, d. 61 (unpaginated); TsGA SPb, f. 7384, op. 17, d. 1447, ll. 7, 14. Requests were made in November 1944 and January 1945.

132. KGIOP, f. 246–1, d. P-1079, l. 33.

133. TsGA SPb, f. 7384, op. 17, d. 1447, ll. 40, 44. Work on the palaces in Peterhof and Pushkin was assigned to Construction Trust 6 in March 1945.

134. TsGA SPb, f. 7384, op. 17, d. 1447, l. 44; TsGA SPb, f. 7384, op. 17, d. 1446, l. 30.

135. TsGALI SPb, f. 277, op. 1, d. 82, ll. 7–9. In March 1946 Pavlovsk remained very poorly supplied with lumber. To overcome this obstacle, Zelenova wrote N. V. Baranov and asked that a woodcutting area be allotted to the administration of the Pavlovsk Palace-Museum. TsGALI SPb, f. 277, op. 1, d. 78, l. 47.

136. TsGALI SPb, f. 277, op. 1, d. 82, ll. 24–25 (ob).

137. Karasev, "Vozrozhdenie gorodageroia," 122. G. T. Kedrov, a participant in the restoration efforts in the city, noted that "in the first years of restoration, there was a sharp deficiency in the workforce, production equipment, engineers . . . without which normal work was impossible." See Kedrov, "Istoki rosta," in Kutuzov and Levina, *Vozrozhdennie,* 35.

138. Normalcy and stability, according to Sheila Fitzpatrick, remained elusive at least until Stalin's death in 1953. I use the term "normalcy" here to denote a general improvement in the economic system during the postwar years. See Fitzpatrick, "Postwar Soviet Society: The 'Return to Normalcy,' 1945–1953," in *The Impact of World War II on the Soviet Union,* ed. Susan J. Linz (Totowa, NJ: Rowman and Allanheld, 1985), 129.

139. As would become clear, twenty-seven million rubles was obviously not enough money for the task at hand. See TsGALI SPb, f. 277, op. 1, d. 167, ll. 19–20.

140. TsGALI SPb, f. 277, op. 1, d. 256, l. 3.

141. TsGA SPb, f. 2076, op. 5, d. 43, l. 127 (ob). When Popkov appealed to the central government in 1948 to have the Great Palace in Peterhof restored as a base of cultural-enlightenment work, he made the argument that the facade of the palace was a "component part of the Great Cascade fountains." TsGALI SPb, f. 277, op. 1, d. 562, l. 9.

142. TsGALI SPb, op. 1, d. 554, l. 80; RGASPI, f. 17, op. 132, d. 440, l. 15.

143. TsGALI SPb, f. 277, op. 1, d. 566, l. 8.

144. "Pavlovskii dvorets vosstanavlivaetsia," *Leningradskaia pravda,* 9 October 1946.

145. Of the 1947 allotment of 3.4 million rubles, 400,000 was assigned for Pushkin and 1.8 million for Petrodvorets, and the remaining 1.2 million was to be shared by Pavlovsk, Gatchina, and Oranienbaum. The decision to raise the funding was approved by the Soviet government. See TsGALI SPb, f. 277, op. 1, d. 328, l. 73. For the extra funds in 1948, see TsGALI SPb, f. 277, op. 1, d. 552, l. 113. Again, as in 1947, the money came partially from residential projects on Moscow Highway.

146. TsGALI SPb, f. 341, op. 1, d. 245, l. 12.

147. TsGALI SPb, f. 277, op. 1, d. 658, l. 21.

148. TsGALI SPb, f. 341, op. 1, d. 245, ll. 12–13.

149. TsGALI SPb, f. 277, op. 1, d. 562, ll. 6–7, 9, 18–19.

150. TsGALI SPb, f. 277, op. 1, d. 552, ll. 150–151.

151. TsGALI SPb, f. 277, op. 1, d. 811, ll. 9–10.

152. TsGALI SPb, f. 277, op. 1, d. 813, l. 2; TsGALI SPb, f. 277, op. 1, d. 1079, ll. 46, 48.

153. An exhibit devoted to Pushkin was opened in 1945 in the Lyceum. TsGA SPb, f. 7384, op. 29, d. 174, l. 34.

154. "V prigorodakh Leningrada," *Vechernii Leningrad,* 8 April 1946.

155. TsGALI SPb, f. 277, op. 1, d. 673, l. 1.

156. TsGALI SPb, f. 277, op. 1, d. 673, l. 3.

157. Shurygin, *Petergof,* 103.

158. See, for example, "Vystavka v Aleksandrovskom dvortse," *Bolshevistskoe slovo,* 6 June 1946; E. Gladkova, "Pushkinskaia vystavka v Litsee," *Bolshevistskoe slovo,* 9 June 1946.

159. A. Kuchumov, "V Ekaterininskom dvortse," *Bolshevistskoe slovo,* 23 November 1946.

160. TsGALI SPb, f. 277, op. 1, d. 673, l. 2.

161. "Dokladnaia zapiska professora P.V. Preis 'O vosstanovlenii arkhitekturnykh pamiatnikov razrushennykh fashistami.'" KGIOP, f. Fond Belekhova, op. 1, d. 61 (unpaginated).

162. TsGALI SPb, f. 277, op. 1, d. 71, l. 2 (ob).

163. TsGALI SPb, f. 277, op. 1, d. 554, l. 67.

164. TsGALI SPb, f. 277, op. 1, d. 813, l. 33. Efforts to restore the suburban palaces and parks were also the subject of an exhibit in the House of Architects in 1946. Images of the destroyed palaces, restoration work, and plans to further restore the palaces were put on display. See "V soiuze arkhitektorov (khronika 1946 g.)," *Arkhitektura i stroitel'stva Leningrada: Sbornik* (November 1946): 70.

5. BECOMING "LENINGRADERS"

1. See, for example, Qualls's discussion of Moscow's vision for the city of Sevastopol in the early postwar years. Qualls, *From Ruins to Reconstruction,* 55–61. On plans for the construction of memorials, see Nina Tumarkin, *The Living and the Dead: The Rise and Fall of the Cult of World War II in Russia* (New York: Basic Books, 1994), 82–84.

2. Amir Weiner argues that the war became a prism through which the world was viewed and that the emerging myth of war became a central part of the Soviet people's identity. See Weiner, *Making Sense*

of War: The Second World War and the Fate of the Bolshevik Revolution* (Princeton, NJ: Princeton University Press, 2001), 17–20.

3. This point is made by Lisa Kirschenbaum. She writes, "Understood as a 'historic event' even as it occurred, the siege rapidly became the subject of commemorations." See Kirschenbaum, "Commemorations of the Siege of Leningrad: A Catastrophe in Memory and Myth," in *The Memory of Catastrophe,* ed. Peter Gray and Kendrick Oliver (New York: Manchester University Press, 2004), 106.

4. Kirschenbaum, "Commemorations of the Siege of Leningrad," 106. See also Lisa A. Kirschenbaum, "Gender, Memory, and National Myths: Ol'ga Berggol'ts and the Siege of Leningrad," *Nationalities Papers* 28, no. 3 (2000): 551.

5. Elena S. Seniavskaia, "Heroic Symbols: The Reality and Mythology of War," *Russian Studies in History* 37, no. 1 (Summer 1998): 62.

6. Tumarkin, likewise, notes how the Victory Day celebrations were used by the central leadership to promote restoration after the war. See Tumarkin, *The Living and the Dead,* 103–105.

7. Karl Qualls has shown how the authorities in Sevastopol attempted to inculcate a sense of civic identity in residents, noting that "if someone gained pride of place, and emotional attachment to the city, it was thought that he or she would work harder (and sacrifice more) to see it rebuilt." See Qualls, "Local-Outsider Negotiations in Postwar Sevastopol's Reconstruction, 1944–53," in *Provincial Landscapes: Local Dimensions of Soviet Power, 1917–1953,* ed. Donald Raleigh (Pittsburgh: Pittsburgh University Press, 2001), 278.

8. E. Iu. Zubkova et al., eds., *Sovetskaia zhizn', 1945–1953* (Moscow: Rosspen, 2003), 276–278. See also Elizabeth White, "After the War Was Over: The Civilian Return to Leningrad," *Europe-Asia Studies* 59, no. 7 (November 2007): 1145–1161.

9. Ruble, *Leningrad,* 51; Vakser, *Leningrad poslevoennyi,* 7.

10. Ruble, *Leningrad,* 51.

11. See Ruble, "The Leningrad Affair and the Provincialization of Leningrad," *Russian Review* 42, no. 3 (1983): 308.

12. RGASPI, f. 77, op. 1, d. 793, ll. 74–75.

13. RGASPI, f. 77, op. 1, d. 793, l. 71.

14. Kuznetsov's statements about Leningrad patriotism were met with "thunderous applause." "Rech' tov: A.A. Kuznetsova na predvybornom sovesh-chanii predstavitelei trudiashchikhsia Vyborgskogo raiona g. Leningrada 16 ianvar'ia 1946 goda," *Leningradskaia pravda,* 20 January 1946, 2.

15. Similar issues were witnessed in other areas of the Soviet Union that had been devastated by the war. Martin Blackwell, for example, notes that Kiev's party leadership was confronted with problems surrounding reconstruction and labor mobilization. He writes that in 1946, "a privileged and politically volatile population of demobilized servicemen and their families, as well as a formerly occu-pied population uninterested in involving itself with reconstruction, now dominated the city." See Blackwell, "Regime City of the First Category," 154.

16. RGASPI, f. 77, op. 1, d. 793, l. 72.

17. Boldyrev, *Osadnaia Zapis',* 344. For a discussion of official attempts to instill Soviet values in the peasant migrants coming to Moscow in the First Five-Year Plan, see David L. Hoffmann, *Peasant Metropolis: Social Identities in Moscow, 1929–1941* (Ithaca, NY: Cornell University Press, 1994), 2–5 and chap. 6.

18. One needs to be wary of mood reports produced by the secret police,

party activists, and informants. The individuals compiling the reports sought out troublesome information, and as a result these documents have a tendency to skew the reality of the situation. For a discussion of state surveillance and the compilation of *svodki,* see Peter Holquist, "'Information Is the Alpha and Omega of Our Work': Bolshevik Surveillance in Its Pan-European Context," *Journal of Modern History* 69, no. 3 (September 1997): 415–450; See also Sarah Davies' study of public opinion in Stalin's Russia based on *svodki.* Davies, *Popular Opinion in Stalin's Russia: Terror, Propaganda, and Dissent, 1934–1941* (New York: Cambridge University Press, 1997).

19. TsGAIPD SPb, f. 25, op. 10, d. 434, ll. 44–45.

20. TsGAIPD SPb, f. 25, op. 10, d. 454, l. 70.

21. Ibid.

22. See, for example, TsGAIPD SPb, f.25, op.10, d. 431, l. 24.

23. TsGAIPD SPb, f. 25, op. 10, d. 453, l. 47.

24. TsGAIPD SPb, f. 25, op. 10, d. 454, ll. 9–10.

25. The architect E. Levina, for example, was enraged about the fact that several architects were evacuated in the spring of 1942. She felt they were turning their backs on the city when it needed their help most of all. See Levina, "Pis'ma k drugu," 202–203.

26. TsGAIPD SPb, f. 25, op. 10, d. 442, l. 59.

27. TsGAIPD SPb, f. 25, op. 10, d. 453, l. 207.

28. TsGAIPD SPb, f. 25, op. 10, d. 453, l. 13 (ob). Rebecca Manley notes that being in evacuation could become a mark of shame, as was the case with Tatiana Borisovna Lozinskaia, who wrote to a fellow Leningrader soon after her return to the city that "those who had lived through the blockade had a 'stern and severe expression in their eyes. And I always feel somewhat ashamed in front of them.'" See Manley, "The Evacuation and Survival of Soviet Civilians, 1941–1946" (PhD diss., University of California, Berkeley, 2004), 268.

29. TsGAIPD SPb, f. 25, op. 10, d. 442, l. 60.

30. Nikolai Punin, *Mir svetel liubov'iu: Dnevniki i pis'ma,* ed. L. A. Zykov (Moscow: Artist. Rezhisser. Teatr, 2000), 385.

31. Boldyrev, *Osadnaia zapis',* 333.

32. TsGAIPD SPb, f. 25, op. 10, d. 442, l. 76.

33. TsGAIPD SPb, f. 25, op. 10, d. 453, l. 208.

34. TsGAIPD SPb, f. 25, op. 10, d. 453, l. 151.

35. Elizabeth White notes that newcomers to the city were "encouraged to become 'Leningraders.'" White, "After the War Was Over," 1159.

36. John R. Gillis, "Memory and Identity: The History of a Relationship," in *Commemorations: The Politics of National Identity,* ed. John R. Gillis (Princeton, NJ: Princeton University Press, 1004), 5. See also Pierre Nora, "Between Memory and History: *Les Lieux de Mémoire,*" trans. Marc Roudebush, *Representations* 26 (Spring 1989).

37. For an excellent review of the interpretations of war remembrance, see T. G. Ashplant, Graham Dawson, and Michael Roper, "The Politics of War Memory and Commemoration: Contexts, Structures and Dynamics," in *The Politics of War Memory and Commemoration,* ed. T. G. Ashplant, Graham Dawson, and Michael Roper (New York: Routledge, 2000).

38. Jay Winter and Emmanuel Sivan, "Setting the Framework," in *War and*

Remembrance in the Twentieth Century, ed. Jay Winter and Emmanuel Sivan (New York: Cambridge University Press, 1999), 38.

39. Catherine Merridale, "War, Death, and Remembrance in Soviet Russia," in Winter and Sivan, *War and Remembrance in the Twentieth Century,* 82. For a much more cynical discussion of Soviet commemorations, see Tumarkin, *The Living and the Dead,* 101.

40. TsGAIPD SPb, f. 25, op. 10, d. 434, l. 65.

41. Some establishments in dire need of workers for restoration petitioned the authorities for the right to reevacuate people, stipulating that the reevacuees would be Leningraders. See TsGA SPb, f. 7384, op. 17, d. 1207, l. 43.

42. TsGAIPD SPb, f. 25, op. 10, d. 434, l. 10. In teaching the "main qualities of Leningraders," propagandists in the Kirov District gave a number of talks, including but not limited to the following: "Women of the Factory in the Days of the Great Patriotic War," "Patriotism of Leningraders – Kirovtsy," "Leningrad – The Most Outstanding Cultural Center," and "The Revolutionary Tradition of the Kirov Factory." TsGAIPD SPb, f. 25, op. 10, d. 434, l. 27 (ob).

43. TsGAIPD SPb, f. 25, op. 10, d. 453, l. 47.

44. "Pamiatniki bor'by i pobedy: Muzei oborony goroda za god posetilo 800 tysiach chelovek," *Vechernii Leningrad,* 18 January 1947.

45. On the function of museums, see Carol Duncan, "Art Museums and the Ritual of Citizenship," in *Exhibiting Cultures: The Poetics and Politics of Museum Display,* ed. Ivan Karp and Steven D. Lavine (Washington, DC: Smithsonian Institution Press, 1991).

46. For a range of strategies employed by Leningraders to survive the blockade, including cannibalism and other criminal acts, see Bidlack and Lomagin, eds., *The Leningrad Blockade,* 262–328.

47. For more on this topic, see Berkhoff, *Motherland in Danger.*

48. See the short description of the exhibit written by one of its guides, Raisa Solomonovna Bogorad. GMMOBL (Gosudarstvennyi memorial'nyi muzei oborony i blokady Leningrada), f. RDF, op. 1r, d. 75, AKT 468–90 (1), ll. 1–4.

49. M. A. Sergeevna and A. A. Shishkin, "Izdaniia, stavshie rarietami," *Zabveniiu ne podlezhit: Stati, vospominaniia, dokumenty* 5 (2005): 170. R. S. Bogorad, one of the guides, noted that she led five hundred excursions between November 1941 and December 1943. GMMOBL, f. RDF, op. 1r, d. 75, AKT 468–90 (1), ll. 1–4.

50. GMMOBL, f. RDF, op. 1r, d. 75, AKT 226–90 (2); TsGALI SPb, f. 277, op. 1, d. 691, l. 1.

51. M. B. Rabinovitch, *Vospominaniia dolgoi zhizni* (St. Petersburg: Evropeiskii Dom, 1996), 234.

52. GMMOBL, f. RDF, op. 1r, d. 75, AKT 226–90 (2). The exhibition was run by the Administration for Artistic Affairs. In 1945, when the Department of Cultural-Enlightenment Work was established under the Executive Committee of the city soviet, the exhibition was transferred to its authority. See "Ob organizatsii otdelov kul'turno-prosvetitel'noi raboty pri ispolnitel'nom komitete Leningradskogo gorodskogo soveta i ispolkomakh raisovetov deputatov trudiashchikhsia. (Reshenie ispolnitel'nogo komiteta Leningradskogo gorodskogo soveta deputatov trudiashchikhsia ot 22 fevralia 1945, N.138, p.10-b)," *Biulleten' Leningradskogo gorodskogo soveta deputatov trudiashchikhsia,* no. 4 (1945): 8–9.

53. N. D. Khudiakova, "K 60-letiiu osnovaniia Muzeia oborony Leningrada: Sud'ba muzeia," *Zabveniiu ne podlezhit: Stati, vospominaniia, dokumenty* 4 (2004): 9.

54. "Pamiatnik bor'by i pobedy."

55. Khudiakova, "K 60-letiiu osnovaniia Muzeia oborony Leningrada," 10. See also TsGAIPD SPb, f. 25, op. 18, d. 195, l. 2.

56. Khudiakova, "K 60-letiiu osnovaniia Muzeia oborony Leningrada," 10; L. L. Rakov, "Vystavka 'Oborona Leningrada,'" in *Khudozhniki goroda-fronta: Vospominaniia i dnevniki leningradskikh khudozhnikov*, ed. I. A. Brodskii (Leningrad: Khudozhnik RSFSR, 1973), 399.

57. N. D. Khudiakova, "'I vse zhe verili v pobedu' (Iz blokadnogo dnevnika 1941–1943 gg.)," *Zabveniiu ne podlezhit: Stati, vospominaniia, dnevniki* 2 (2001): 67.

58. TsGALI SPb, f. 333, op. 2, d. 21, ll. 15–17. For examples of artwork created during the blockade, see Brodskii, ed., *Khudozhniki goroda-fronta;* V. E. Loviagina, I. A. Silant'eva, and Iu. V. Usatova, eds., *Blokadnyi dnevnik: Zhivopis' i grafika blokadnogo vremeni; Al'bom-katalog* (St. Petersburg: Gosudarstvennyi muzei istorii Sankt-Peterburga, 2005); Papernaia, ed., *Podvig veka*.

59. RNB OR, f. 1117, op. (unnumbered), ch. 1, d. 157, l. 49. For the plan presented to the Party Committee for approval in February, as well as notes on its shortcomings, see TsGAIPD SPb, f. 25, op. 10, d. 467a, ll. 1–11.

60. TsGAIPD SPb, f. 25, op. 18, d. 195, l. 2.

61. TsGAIPD SPb, f. 25, op. 10, d. 468, l. 2.

62. Ibid.

63. See party secretary A. I. Makhanov's letter to Zhdanov, Kuznetsov, and Ia. F. Kapustin about the need to turn the exhibition into a museum. He argued that it would only be natural to transform it into a museum, given that such a large amount of materials had been collected. TsGAIPD, f. 25, op. 10, d. 468, l. 38. Reports about the work of the exhibition throughout 1945 emphasized that one of the main goals was to have it turned into a permanent museum. TsGALI SPb, f. 277, op. 1, d. 110, l. 53

64. TsGA SPb, f. 7384, op. 17, d. 1446, l. 65 (ob).

65. For the decree see TsGALI SPb, f. 277, op. 1, d. 1, l. 10 and l. 18. For the corresponding Leningrad city soviet decision, see TsGA SPb, f. 7384, op. 18, d. 1688, l. 147. Even after the exhibition had been turned into a republic-level museum of second-category stature, Leningrad authorities continued to petition to have it given first-category stature. See the party committee's project decree from 1947. TsGA SPb, f. 7384, op. 29, d. 296, ll. 51–52.

66. When the Museum of the Defense of Leningrad opened, the size of its layout had increased to almost two times that of the exhibition, and the number of exhibits on display increased by over a thousand. See TsGAIPD SPb, f. 25, op. 18, d. 195, l. 2.

67. See Weiner, *Making Sense of War*.

68. "Muzei oborony Leningrada," *Vechernii Leningrad*, 25 January 1946.

69. "Oblik velikogo goroda: Izbirateli v Muzee oborony Leningrada," *Vechernii Leningrad*, 8 December 1946.

70. See *Muzei oborony Leningrada: Putevoditel'* (Leningrad: Gosudarstvennyi izdatel'stvo "Iskusstvo," 1948), 5–10. See also *Vystavka "Geroicheskaia oborona Leningrada": Ocherk-putevoditel'* (Leningrad: Gosudarstvennyi izdatel'stvo "Iskusstvo," 1945), 5–11.

71. See *Vystavka "Geroicheskaia oborona Leningrada,"* 10.

72. TsGALI SPb, f. 277, op. 1, d. 692, l. 23.

73. *Muzei oborony Leningrada*, 7, 196.

74. See *Muzei oborony Leningrada* for more information on the holdings of each hall.

75. Kirschenbaum, "Commemorations of the Siege of Leningrad," 107.

76. TsGALI SPb, f. 277, op. 1, d. 135, l. 5.

77. "Pamiat' o velikoi bitve: Slava goroda-geroiia," *Vechernii Leningrad,* 26 January 1946.

78. "Relikvii velikoi pobedy: Novye zaly v Muzee Oborony Leningrada," *Leningradskaia pravda,* 20 January 1949.

79. "Pamiatnik bor'by i pobedy."

80. Inber, *Leningrad Diary,* 204.

81. L. L. Rakov, "Pamiatnik geroiam nashego goroda," *Leningradskaia pravda,* 30 April 1945.

82. TsGAIPD SPb, f. 25, op. 10, d. 468, l. 59.

83. TsGA SPb, f. 7384, op. 17, d. 1446, l. 111; GMMOBL, f. RDF, op. 1r, d. 75, AKT 120–91 (3).

84. TsGAIPD SPb, f. 25, op. 10, d. 468, l. 59.

85. "O piatiletnem plane vosstanovleniia i razvitiia gorodskogo khoziaistva Leningrada na 1946–1950 gg.: Reshenie XIII sessii Leningradskogo gorodskogo soveta deputatov trudiashchikhsia ot 17 ianvaria 1947," *Vechernii Leningrad,* 1 February 1947.

86. See TsGALI SPb, f. 277, op. 1, d. 135, l. 12; TsGALI SPb, f. 277, op. 1, d. 328, l. 2 and l. 8.

87. For the creation of the exhibit devoted to postwar restoration, see TsGAIPD SPb, f. 4440, op. 1, d. 16, l. 2. For plans to create the others, see TsGALI SPb, f. 277, op. 1, d. 110, l. 28.

88. TsGALI SPb, f. 277, op. 1, d. 100, l. 28; TsGAIPD SPb, f. 25, op. 10, d. 613a, l. 6. The territory given to the museum to display military technology was formerly the private plot of the Museum of Socialist Agriculture. In 1945 the plot was transferred to the Museum of Defense, paved, and used as a display ground. See TsGAIPD SPb, f. 25, op. 2, d. 5371, l. 15.

89. TsGALI SPb, f. 277, op. 1, d. 86, l. 5.

90. TsGALI SPb, f. 277, op. 1, d. 689, l. 5; GMMOBL, f. RDF, op. 1r, d. 75, AKT 63–93.

91. Trips were made to places where especially fierce battles took place, including Nevskaia Dubrovka, Siniavinskie Vysoty, Pulkovo, Krasnoe Selo, Pushkin, Petrokrepost', and the Karelian Peninsula, among others. See TsGALI SPb, f. 277, op. 1, d. 457, l. 3; TsGALI SPb, op. 1, d. 245, l. 1.

92. V. Andrianova, "Dar trudiashchikhsia muzeiu: Novye eksponaty v Muzee oborony Leningrada," *Vechernii Leningrad,* 18 May 1946.

93. Andrianova, "Dar trudiashchikhsia muzeiu."

94. "1,000 novykh dokumentov," *Leningradskaia pravda,* 26 March 1949.

95. TsGALI SPb, f. 277, op. 1, d. 457, l. 3.

96. D. Smirnova, "Pamiatnye eksponaty: Popolnenie Muzeia oborony Leningrada," *Vechernii Leningrad,* 17 June 1947.

97. TsGALI SPb, f. 277, op. 1, d. 689, l. 5; GMMOBL, f. RDF, op. 1r, d. 75, AKT 63–93.

98. TsGALI SPb, f. 277, op. 1, d. 692, l. 5. Kovalev replaced Rakov as director of the museum in May 1947.

99. TsGAIPD SPb, f. 25, op. 18, d. 195, ll. 3–5.

100. TsGALI SPb, f. 277, op. 1, d. 245, l. 4; TsGAIPD SPb, f. 25, op. 10, d. 613a, l. 5.

101. TsGAIPD SPb, f. 25, op. 18, d. 92, l. 7.

102. "Materialy po istorii Gosudarstvennogo memorial'nogo muzeia oborony i blokady Leningrada," *Zabveniiu ne podlezhit: Sbornik statei* 1 (1999): 70–74.

103. TsGAIPD SPb, f. 25, op. 18, d. 92, l. 7.

104. TsGAIPD SPb, f. 25, op. 18, d. 195, l. 3.

105. "Tovarishchi-agitatory! Organizuiete ekursii na vystavku 'Geroicheskaia oborona Leningrada,'" *Bloknot agitatora,* 1945, nos. 8–9: 63.

106. TsGAIPD SPb, f. 25, op. 18, d. 195, l. 1.

107. See TsGAIPD SPb, f. 25, op. 10, d. 434, l. 16; and TsGAIPD SPb, f. 25, op. 10, d. 453, l. 50.

108. TsGAIPD SPb, f. 25, op. 18, d. 195, l. 3.

109. Karen Petrone, *Life Has Become More Joyous, Comrades: Celebrations in the Time of Stalin* (Bloomington: Indiana University Press, 2000), 204–205.

110. For a brief discussion of Victory Day celebrations, see Tumarkin, *The Living and the Dead,* 103–104.

111. TsGALI SPb, f. 411, op. 2, d. 4, l. 152

112. Ibid.

113. See, for example, "Godovshchina velikoi pobedy Krasnoi Armii pod Leningradom. (Material dlia dokladchikov i besedchikov)," *Bloknot agitatora,* 1945, no. 2: 1–36; "Vtoraia godovshchina velikoi pobedy Krasnoi Armii pod Leningradom. (Material dlia dokladchikov i besedchikov)," *Bloknot agitatora,* 1946, no. 2: 1–26.

114. TsGALI SPb, f. 277, op. 1, d. 492, l. 3 (ob).

115. TsGALI SPb, f. 411, op. 2, d. 4, l. 152; TsGALI SPb, f. 277, op. 1, d. 492, l. 5 (ob). As 27 January drew closer, activists' work intensified. A report from the Primorskii district notes that activists carried out discussions and lectures at all establishments, factories, and educational institutes from 26 January onward. See TsGAIPD SPb, f. 25, op. 10, d. 539, l. 26 (ob).

116. TsGALI SPb, f. 277, op. 1, d. 492, ll. 3–5 (ob).

117. In 1945, for example, the Department of Agitation and Propaganda of the city party committee sent 184 lecturers to organizations and establishments to give talks on the significance of the blockade and defense of the city. See TsGAIPD SPb, f. 25, op. 10, d. 539, l. 4. The political administration of the Leningrad Military District also appointed people to give lectures and talks to gatherings of workers. In 1946, for instance, it assigned 150 people who participated in the battles outside Leningrad to deliver talks to workers. See "Rasskazy o Velikoi Pobedy," *Vechernii Leningrad,* 26 January 1946. Lecturers from the Musuem of the Defense of Leningrad were also sent to establishments in the city to give talks on the victory outside Leningrad during this period. See "Vstrechi s geroiami, lektsii, ekskursii," *Leningradskaia pravda,* 26 January 1949.

118. TsGAIPD SPb, f. 25, op. 10, d. 539, l. 29.

119. The celebrations surrounding the October Revolution were not listed in this report. See TsGAIPD SPb, f. 25, op. 10, d. 530, l. 25.

120. The museum officially opened on 27 January 1946; on that day, four thousand people visited it in the first hour. "Otkrytie Muzeia oborony Leningrada," *Vechernii Leningrad,* 27 January 1946. On 26 and 27 January 1947, about ten thousand people visited the museum. See "V chest' slavnoi godovshchiny," *Leningradskaia pravda,* 28 January 1947. The central press also noted the great rise in attendance at the museum on the days surrounding the anniversary. See "Leningrad otmechaet godovshchinu velikoi pobedy," *Pravda,* 26 January 1947.

121. TsGAIPD SPb, f. 25, op. 10, d. 539, l. 26 (ob); "U bratskikh mogil zashchitnikov Leningrada," *Leningradskaia pravda,* 28 January 1947; "Vozlozhenie venkov na mogily zashchitnikov Leningrada," *Leningradskaia pravda,* 28 January 1949; "Torzhestvo v Leningrade," *Pravda,* 28 January 1949.

122. "Na bratskikh mogilakh: Mitingi v Volodarskom raione," *Vechernyi Leningrad*, 27 January 1947.

123. Commenting on Armistice Day celebrations in London, historian Mark Connely has noted that "it was not just an occasion of grief and consolation; it was also a day of pride and of re-dedication to a set of ideals." Mark Connely, *The Great War, Memory and Ritual: Commemoration in the City and East London, 1916–1939* (Suffolk: Boydell Press, 2002), 149.

124. "Nakanune tret'eu godovshchiny osvobozhdeniia Leningrada ot blokady: Na raionnykh torzhestvennykh zasedaniakh," *Leningradskaia pravda*, 26 January 1947.

125. Petrone, *Life Has Become More Joyous, Comrades*, 15.

126. TsGAIPD SPb, f. 25, op. 10, d. 539, l. 3.

127. For examples of concert programs for 1945 and 1949, see RNB OR, f. 1117, d. 388, ll. 11–16. For more detailed plans for the evening at the Kirov Theater in 1949, see TsGAIPD SPb, f. 25, op. 18, d. 178, ll. 8–14.

128. TsGAIPD SPb, f. 25, op. 10, d. 539, l. 1; "Ukaz Preziduma Verkhovnogo Soveta SSSR: O nagrazhdenii goroda Leningrada ordenom Lenina," *Bloknot agitatora*, no. 3 (1945): 1.

129. RGASPI, f. 78, op. 1, d. 1040, ll. 1–3.

130. "Rech' tov. Popkova P.S.," *Bloknot agitatora*, no. 3 (1945): 6–12.

131. Each of the speeches given in subsequent years at the Kirov Theater told the story of the blockade, stressed the importance of the city's traditions, and then emphasized the need for restoration. See, for example, the speeches from 1947 to 1949 in TsGA SPb, f. 7384, op. 25, d. 238, ll. 1–38; TsGA SPb, f. 7384, op. 25, d. 475, ll. 1–26; TsGA SPb, f. 7384, op. 25, d. 745, ll. 1–35.

132. TsGAIPD SPb, f. 25, op. 18, d. 178, ll. 6–7.

133. For example, see the plan for 1946. TsGA SPb, f. 7384, op. 25, d. 63, l. 42.

134. TsGAIPD SPb, f. 25, op. 10, d. 539, l. 6.

135. "Leningrad prazdnichnyi," *Leningradskaia pravda*, 28 January 1949.

136. GMMOBL, f. RDF, op. 1k, d. 10 (p. 25), l. 1. The poem was written by Tat'iana Bulakh on 20 January 1943.

6. Cold War Complications

1. David Priestland notes that the Cold War was of "supreme importance to all aspects of Soviet politics" and that literature on the period needs to "pay greater attention to the interaction between domestic and international forces." See Priestland, "Cold War Mobilization and Domestic Politics: The Soviet Union," in *The Cambridge History of the Cold War*, Vol. 1, *Origins*, ed. Melvyn P. Leffler and Odd Arne Westad (New York: Cambridge University Press, 2012), 443.

2. For documents relating to ideology and ideological demands in the postwar period, see D. G. Nadzhafov, ed., *Stalin i kosmopolitizm: 1945–1953; Dokumenty* (Moscow: Izdatel'stvo Materik, 2005).

3. Shelia Fitzpatrick, "Conclusion: Late Stalinism in Historical Perspective," in Fürst, *Late Stalinist Russia*, 272; Nikolai Krementsov, *The Cure: The Story of Cancer and Politics from the Annals of the Cold War* (Chicago: University of Chicago Press, 2002), 109; Kees Boterbloem, *The Life and Times of Andrei Zhdanov, 1896–1948* (Montreal: McGill-Queens University Press, 2004), 256. See also Ethan Pollock, *Stalin and the Soviet Science Wars* (Princeton, NJ: Princeton University Press, 2006), 7.

4. Vladislav Zubok and Constantine Pleshakov, *Inside the Kremlin's Cold War:*

From Stalin to Khrushchev (Cambridge, MA: Harvard University Press, 1996), 31–32.

5. Timothy Johnston argues that the Soviet Union's official diplomatic identity remained firmly rooted in the increasingly fractious collaboration between the great powers until the fall of 1947. Johnston, *Being Soviet: Identity, Rumour, and Everyday Life under Stalin, 1939–1953* (Oxford: Oxford University Press, 2011), 127–132.

6. Andrei Zhdanov, "The Two-Camp Policy (September 1947)," in *From Stalinism to Pluralism: A Documentary History of Eastern Europe since 1945*, ed. Gale Stokes, 2nd ed. (New York: Oxford University Press, 1996), 38–42.

7. Gorlizki and Khlevniuk, *Cold Peace*, 31–32.

8. Boterbloem, *The Life and Times of Andrei Zhdanov*, 256, 270.

9. Leningrad's intelligentsia, for example, had focused more on local patriotism and the history of the city than on Soviet patriotism in fiction and propaganda during the siege. Aileen G. Rambow, "The Siege of Leningrad: Wartime Literature and Ideological Change," in *The People's War: Responses to World War II in the Soviet Union*, ed. Robert W. Thurston and Bernd Bonwetsch (Chicago: University of Illinois Press, 2000), 167.

10. Elena Zubkova's work on the postwar period has been particularly enlightening on the popular desire for change in the postwar years. See Zubkova, *Russia after the War*.

11. Amir Weiner, for example, notes that the authorities in the Vinnytsia region of Ukraine could only claim to have rid the area of "the nationalist menace" in 1949. Weiner, *Making Sense of War*, 133. See also Statiev, *The Soviet Counterinsurgency*, 97–138.

12. There is large body of literature on the return of slave laborers and POWs to the Soviet Union after the war. For a brief but incisive discussion of the treatment of returning Soviet citizens, see Nick Baron, "Remaking Soviet Society: The Filtration of Returnees from Nazi Germany, 1944–49," in *Warlands: Population Resettlement and State Reconstruction in the Soviet-East European Borderlands, 1945–50*, ed. Peter Gatrell and Nick Baron (New York: Palgrave Macmillan, 2009), 89–116. For a much more detailed study of the fate of Soviet citizens returning from German captivity, see Pavel Polian, *Zhertvy dvukh diktatur: Zhizn', trud, unizhenie i smert' sovetskikh voennoplennykh i ostarbeiterov na chuzhbine i na rodine* (Moscow: Rosspen, 2002).

13. Tanja Penter, "Local Collaborators on Trial: Soviet War Crimes Trials under Stalin (1945–1953)," *Cahiers du monde russe* 49, no. 2 (2008): 342.

14. Nikita Lomagin has recently noted that "in connection with the worsening situation at the front, until the middle of August 1941 Leningrad was in many ways left to its own devices. The traditional hierarchy of relations, in which Leningrad relied on the directives of Moscow, was broken for a certain period of time, which in the end led to serious frictions between Stalin and the Leningrad leadership." Lomagin, *Neizvestnaia blokada: V 2-kh knigakh; Kniga 1-aia*, 2nd ed. (St. Petersburg: Neva, 2004), 547.

15. See, for example, Donald Filtzer's study of labor in the postwar period. He discusses the government's repressive control over society and the need to restore the economy as quickly as possible. Filtzer, *Soviet Workers and Late Stalinism*; Sheila Fitzpatrick also notes the regime's desire to reassert control over society after the

war. Fitzpatrick, "Postwar Soviet Society," 130; see also Zubkova, *Russia after the War.*

16. Gorlizki and Khlevniuk, *Cold Peace,* 31–32.

17. "Iz stenogrammy vystupleniia sekretaria TsK VKP(b) A.A. Zhdanova na soveshchanii v Agitprope TsK po voprosam propagandy," in Nadzhafov, *Stalin i kosmopolitizm,* 46–50.

18. Boterbloem, *The Life and Times of Andrei Zhdanov,* 277; Gorlizki and Khlevniuk, *Cold Peace,* 34.

19. See "Proekt postanovleniia Orgbiuro TsK VKP(b) 'O zhurnalakh 'Zvezda' i 'Leningrad' s pravkoi I.V. Stalina: 14 avgusta 1946," in Nadzhafov, *Stalin i kosmopolitizm,* 66–69; Serhy Yekelchyk, "Celebrating the Soviet Present: The *Zhdanovshchina* Campaign in Ukrainian Literature and Arts," in *Provincial Landscapes: Local Dimensions of Soviet Power, 1917–1953,* ed. Donald Raleigh (Pittsburgh: Pittsburgh University Press, 2001), 256. The archival record shows that Stalin was indeed the author and driving force behind this campaign and others. For a discussion of Stalin's role, see Gorlizki and Khlevniuk, *Cold Peace,* 31–38.

20. Quoted in Krementsov, *The Cure,* 111; see "Zakrytoe pis'mo TsK VKP(b) o dele professorov Kliuevoi i Roskina: 16 iiulia 1947," in Nadzhafov, *Stalin i kosmopolitizm,* 123–127; see also Pollock, *Stalin and the Soviet Science Wars.*

21. "Plan meropriiatii po propaganda sredi naseleniia idei sovetskogo patriotizma: Dokument Agitpropa TsK, 18 aprelia 1947," in Nadzhafov, *Stalin i kosmopolitizm,* 110–116.

22. Ibid., 110–111, 114.

23. Amir Weiner, "The Making of a Dominant Myth: The Second World War and the Construction of Political Identities within the Soviet Polity," *Russian Review* 55, no. 3 (1996): 660.

24. Priestland, "Cold War Mobilization and Domestic Politics," 445.

25. "Plan meropriiatii," in Nadzhafov, *Stalin i kosmopolitizm,*112.

26. Ibid., 112–113. In light of the international situation, the party organization of the Leningrad Department of Cultural-Enlightenment Work instructed that talks should be held among the laborers of Leningrad to discuss international developments. It also insisted that in further educational work the "glorious history of our motherland," the heroism of the Soviet people during the war, and the history of the party (as well as Lenin and Stalin) should be emphasized. See TsGAIPD SPb, f. 2853, op. 2, d. 10, ll. 57–58. The glorification of the country's past was to be emphasized in all manner of official activities. Leningrad's Excursion Bureau, for example, stated in 1945 that its main task was "the education of laborers in the spirit of Soviet patriotism," which included "the popularization of the glorious past and the heroic present of the Hero-City Leningrad." TsGALI SPb, f. 277, op. 1, d. 3, l. 87.

27. For a fascinating discussion of how the past was presented in Ukraine during the postwar period, see Yekelchyk, *Stalin's Empire of Memory,* 11.

28. Matiushkin, *Sovetskii patriotizm,* 237.

29. Brandenberger, *National Bolshevism,* 198.

30. David Hoffmann discusses the use of Russia's past in the prewar period as a means to provide a common heritage for the entire Soviet population. See Hoffmann, *Stalinist Values,* 159–162. For further discussion of the rehabilitation of Russia's past, see Brandenberger, *National Bolshevism;* Platt and Brandenberger, eds., *Epic Revisionism.* For the classic argument that sees the rehabilitation as a betrayal

of socialism, see Timasheff, *The Great Retreat.*

31. Yekelchyk, *Stalin's Empire of Memory,* 123.

32. See "Iz vystupleniia N.N. Voronina na soveshchanii po okhrane pamiatnikov arkhitektury," in Malinina, *Iz istorii sovetskoi arkhitektury,* 46.

33. RGAE, f. 9432, op. 1, d. 12, l. 53.

34. RGAE, f. 9432, op. 1, d. 14, l. 89.

35. RGAE, f. 9432, op. 1, d. 14, l. 87.

36. Several documents present Leningrad as the front runner in the restoration of monuments, noting that in 1948 all the monuments under state protection were either restored or in the process of restoration. See RGAE, f. 9588, op. 1, d. 40, l. 48; RGAE, f. 9588, op. 1, d. 67, ll. 192–195.

37. RGAE, f. 9588, op. 1, d. 21, l. 1 (ob); RGAE, f. 9588, op. 1, d. 40, ll. 27–30.

38. Even though the Main Administration for the Protection of Monuments of Architecture had been created under the authority of the Committee for Architectural Affairs, it was still a relatively young organization, having begun its duties only in 1944. Throughout the 1930s there had been a series of administrations which began work, but shortly after were shut down or transferred to other institutions. RGAE, f. 9588, op. 1, d. 38, ll. 100–102.

39. RGAE, f. 9588, op. 1, d. 38, l. 102.

40. See "Postanovlenie Soveta Ministrov RSFSR ot 22 maia 1947 g., N.389 'Ob okhrane pamiatnikov arkhitektury,'" in Anisimov, *Okhrana pamiatnikov istorii i kul'tury,* 53–55.

41. Ibid.

42. One of the points in the law suggested that the procurator of the Russian republic order local procuracies to "intensify the battle with those who break the laws on the protection of architectural monuments." Ibid., 55.

43. RGAE, f. 9588, op. 1, d. 67, l. 43.

44. RGAE, f. 9432, op. 1, d. 34, l. 17.

45. This law was signed by the chairman of the Council of Ministers (USSR), I. Stalin. "Postanovlenie Soveta Ministrov SSSR ot 14 October 1948 g., N.3898, 'O merakh uluchsheniia okhrany pamiatnikov kul'tury,'" in Anisimov, *Okhrana pamiatnikov istorii i kul'tury,* 57–59.

46. See the appendix to the above law, "Polozhenie ob okhrane pamiatnikov kul'tury," in Anisimov, *Okhrana pamiatnikov istorii i kul'tury,* 59–67.

47. John Farrell discusses these new laws briefly in the context of the post-Stalin period when preservation activists were calling for an all-Union voluntary society to oversee preservation in the Soviet Union. See Farrell, "If These Stones Could Only Speak: Historical and Cultural Preservation in a Soviet Context, 1955–1966" (PhD diss., University of California, Davis, 2004), 27–28, 99–102.

48. The fact that preservation was now considered an all-Union matter was a point that Belekhov emphasized at a meeting of architects in Leningrad in 1949. TsGALI SPb, f. 341, op. 1, d. 245, l. 4.

49. RGAE, f. 9588, op. 1, d. 40, l. 22.

50. RGASPI, f. 17, op. 132, d. 248, ll. 22, 24.

51. RGAE, f. 9588, op. 1, d. 68, l. 17. In late 1948 and early 1949, the Committee for Architectural Affairs sent a flurry of such letters to various organizations demanding that work be carried out on the basis of the October 1948 decree. For further examples from Leningrad, see RGAE, f. 9588, op. 1, d. 68, ll. 8, 9, 10, 12.

52. TsGALI SPb, f. 277, op. 1, d. 813, l. 40.

53. See, for example, RGASPI, f. 17, op. 132, d. 440, l. 22.

54. Yekelchyk, *Stalin's Empire of Memory,* 120.

55. Kirschenbaum, *The Legacy of the Siege of Leningrad,* 14.

56. For a good example of this type of literature from a number of different authors, see A. V. Amsterdam and M. M. Smirnov, eds., *Deviat'sot dnei: Literaturno-khudozhestvennyi sbornik* (Leningrad: Lenizdat, 1948). This is a compilation of articles and stories published in com memoration of the fifth anniversary of the lifting of the blockade.

57. During the war, for example, the party leadership raised the idea of compiling a chronicle of Leningrad and the surrounding region. This work was carried out under the Department of Agitation and Propaganda of the Leningrad party city committee. Work continued after the war ended. See TsGAIPD SPb, f. 25, op. 2, d. 5287, ll. 1a–2.

58. Andrei Dzeniskevich, *Blokada i politika: Oborona Leningrada v politicheskoi kon"iunkture* (St. Petersburg: Nestor, 1998), 10.

59. This point has been overlooked by historians. Lisa Kirschenbaum, for example, states that "building victory monuments did not become part of the immediate postwar effort to repair and revitalize the city. Until the mid-1950s, planners largely followed the prescription for the city articulated by the architect Valentin Kamenskii in 1945: 'Quickly heal the wounds inflicted by the German-fascist barbarians.'" Kirschenbaum, *The Legacy of the Siege of Leningrad,* 115. She does note, however, that there were architectural plans and competitions during the war, and that architects continued to discuss plans after the war. According to Kirschenbaum, the lack of monuments built in the postwar period was the "result of a need to allocate scarce reconstruction funds to restoring essential services." Kirschenbaum, *The Legacy of the Siege of Leningrad,* 133. Likewise, Ol'ga Rusinova argues that the idea of creating a large-scale architectural-sculptural memorial came only at the end of the 1950s. See Rusinova, "Dolgovechnee kamnia i bronzy: Obrazy blokady v monumental'nykh ansambliakh Leningrada," in *Pamiat' o blockade: Svidetel'stva ochividtsev i istoricheskoe soznanie obshchestva,* ed. M. V. Loskutova (St. Petersburg: Novoe Izdatel'stvo, 2006), 336. Finally, P. M. Bulushev and V. I. Ganshin mention that there were architectural competitions for a monument during the war, but they gloss over the postwar year to pick up in 1963 when the Council of Ministers made the decision to create the monument that now exists on Victory Square. See P. M. Bulushev and V. I. Ganshin, *Podvigu tvoemu, Leningrad: Monument geroicheskim zashchitnikam goroda* (Leningrad: Lenizdat, 1980), 8–13.

60. TsGAIPD SPb, f. 25, op. 2, d. 5066, l. 2.

61. TsGA SPb, f. 7384, op. 17, d. 1447, l. 3.

62. TsGA SPb, f. 7384, op. 17, d. 1447, l. 6.

63. TsGA SPb, f. 7384, op. 17, d. 1447, l. 7.

64. For the party decision to have the monument erected, see TsGAIPD SPb, f. 25, op. 2, d. 5371, l. 34.

65. See Baranov's paper delivered on 25 December 1945 to the executive committee of the Leningrad city soviet. TsGA SPb, f. 7384, op. 26, d. 57, ll. 31–32. See also Baranov's discussion of the monument. TsGA SPb, f. 7384, op. 17, d. 1447, ll. 3–13.

66. For correspondence between the Leningrad authorities and the Central Committee in Moscow, see RGASPI, f. 17, op. 125, d. 368, ll. 108–109; RGASPI f. 17, op. 125, d. 471, l. 29; TsGA SPb, f. 7384, op. 29, d. 174, l. 32. In the draft decree about Leningrad's "General Plan" in the postwar period, a series of monuments reflecting the defense of Leningrad and the war were

envisioned. See RGAE, f. 9432, op. 1, d. 216, l. 14. The outline of the five-year plan for Leningrad's restoration can be found in *Vechernii Leningrad*. See "O piatiletnom plane vosstanovleniia i razvitiia gorodskogo khoziaistva Leningrada na 1946–1950 gg.: Reshenie XIII sessii Leningradskogo gorodskogo soveta deputatov trudiashchikhsia ot 17 Jan 1947 g.," *Vechernii Leningrad*, 1 February 1947.

67. See the memoirs of Aleksei Andreevich Gonchukov. TsGAIPD SPb, f. 4000, op. 18, d. 333, l. 57.

68. GMMOBL, f. RDF, op. 1K, d. 10 (p. 25), l. 39. Written by Tat'iana Bulakh in her diary on 20 January 1943. Francesco Bartolomeo Rastrelli was one of the most famous St. Petersburg architects of the eighteenth century.

69. The connection between the city's historic architecture and commemorations of the blockade can also be seen in certain projects for constructing monuments to the heroic defense. B. R. Rubanenko's and I. I. Fomin's plan for the reconstruction of Gostiny Dvor, for example, envisioned a monument to the heroic defense of Leningrad in the building's central courtyard. See Iu. Iu. Bakhareva, "Arkhitekturnye konkursy v blokadnom Leningrade: Gostinyi dvor," *Relikviia* 1, no. 8 (2005): 30–35.

70. Other authors have noted the destruction of the blockade memory with the onset of the Leningrad Affair. Harrison Salisbury was perhaps the first to discuss it, in Salisbury, *The 900 Days*, 581. Most recently, Lisa Kirschenbaum has argued, quite correctly, that the Leningrad Affair was in part an attempt to extinguish local loyalties that had developed out of the blockade. See Kirschenbaum, *The Legacy of the Siege of Leningrad*, 143–147.

71. Viktoria Kalendarova, "Formiruia pamiat': Blokada v leningradskix gazet i dokumental'nom kino v poslevoennye desiatiletiia," in Loskutova, *Pamiat' o blokade*, 284.

72. TsGALI SPb, f. 277, op. 1, d. 694, l. 1.

73. For a discussion of press coverage of the war and Stalin's role in it, see Jeffrey Brooks, *Thank You, Comrade Stalin!: Soviet Public Culture from Revolution to Cold War* (Princeton, NJ: Princeton University Press, 2000), chaps. 7 and 8.

74. See "Postanovlenie Politbiuro o sniatii s dolzhnostei A.A. Kuznetsova, M.I. Rodionova, P.S. Popkova," from 15 February 1949, in O. V. Khlevniuk et. al, eds., *Politbiuro TsK VKP(b) i Sovet Ministrov SSSR, 1945–1953* (Moscow: Rosspen, 2002), 66–68.

75. Memorial (Arkhiv Memoriala Sankt-Peterburga), f. 5 (Neopublikovannaia memuaristika), ed. khr., Grigorii Iosifovich Mishkevich, l. 64.

76. "Postanovlenie ob"edinennogo plenuma Leningradskogo obkoma i gorkoma VKP(b) po itogam obsuzhdeniia postanovleniia Politbiuro 'ob antipartiinykh deistviiakh' A.A. Kuznetsova, M.I. Rodionova i P.S. Popkova," from 22 February 1949, in V. V. Denisov et. al., eds., *TsK VKP(b) i regional'nye partiinye komitety, 1945–1953* (Moscow: Rosspen, 2004), 185–189. See also V. V. Sadovin's recollections of the meeting. TsGAIPD SPb, f. 4000, op. 18, d. 585, ll. 2–5.

77. Nadezhda Mandelstam first used the term "the plague" to discuss how enemies of the people "infected" all those they came in contact with during the terror of 1937–1938. See Mandelstam, *Hope against Hope: A Memoir*, trans. Max Hayward (New York: Modern Library, 1999), 197. Sheila Fitzpatrick also uses the term to show how family, friends, and acquaintances of an accused person were affected by the terror. See Fitzpatrick, *Everyday Stalinism: Extraordinary Life in*

Extraordinary Times; Soviet Russia in the 1930s (New York: Oxford University Press, 1999), 199.

78. A. N. Iakovlev, ed., *Reabilitatsiia: Politicheskie protsessy 30–50-kh godov* (Moscow: Izdatel'stvo politicheskoi literatury, 1990), 312.

79. V. I. Demidov and V. A. Kutuzov note that the those people affected by the purge had lived and worked (or their bosses had) in Leningrad during the 1940s, including the period of the blockade. See Demidov and Kutuzov, *"Leningradskoe delo"* (Leningrad: Lenizdat, 1990), 7; Iakovlev, *Reabilitatsiia,* 318–319. A letter to N. S. Khrushchev in 1954 about the Leningrad Affair notes that even elderly and extended family members of the accused were subject to imprisonment and exile. See "Spravka ob osuzhdennykh po 'leningradskomu delu,'" in Khlevniuk, *Politbiuro TsK VKP(b) i Sovet Ministrov,* 306–307.

80. TsGAIPD SPb, f. 4000, op. 18, d. 585, ll. 7–8. The author of these recollections of the Leningrad Affair was one of the fifty arrested on 15 August 1952. It should further be noted that a significant number of party officials in Leningrad during the postwar period had lived through the blockade. In 1948, four out of every five people in the Leningrad party organization were "members of the heroic defense of Leningrad." See Z. S. Mironenko and V. A. Ezhov, eds., *Ocherki istorii Leningradskoi organizatsii KPSS: Tom III – 1945–1985* (Leningrad: Lenizdat, 1985), 18.

81. Kees Boterbloem, "The Death of Andrei Zhdanov," *Slavonic and East European Review* 80, no. 2 (April 2002): 287; Timothy Dunmore, *Soviet Politics, 1945–1953* (London: Macmillan, 1984), 124–125; Werner G. Hahn, *Postwar Soviet Politics: The Fall of Zhdanov and the Defeat of Moderation, 1946–53* (Ithaca, NY: Cornell University Press, 1982), chaps. 3 and 4.

82. Gorlizki and Khlevniuk, *Cold Peace,* chap. 3.

83. Benjamin Tromly, "The Leningrad Affair and Soviet Patronage Politics, 1949–1950," *Europe-Asia Studies* 56, no. 5 (July 2004): 707.

84. Richard Bidlack, "Ideological or Political Origins of the Leningrad Affair? A Response to David Brandenberger," *Russian Review* 64, no. 1 (2005): 90–95. See also Lomagin, *Neizvestnaia blokada.*

85. David Brandenberger stresses the ideological factors that brought on the purge of Leningraders. He argues that Leningraders had overstepped the limits of permissibility in their calls for the creation of a Communist Party for the Russian Republic to be centered in Leningrad. See Brandenberger, "Stalin, the Leningrad Affair and the Limits of Postwar Russocentrism," *Russian Review* 63, no. 2 (2004): 241–255.

86. Kirschenbaum takes this position as well. She argues, quite correctly, that the purge "operated against local identities, putting an end to the wartime tolerance of local loyalties in general and of Leningraders' insistence on the uniqueness of their experiences in particular." See Kirschenbaum, *The Legacy of the Siege of Leningrad,* 143–144.

87. Weiner, *Making Sense of War,* 8.

88. Joshua Rubenstein, "Introduction: Night of the Murdered Poets," in *Stalin's Secret Pogrom: The Postwar Inquisition of the Jewish Anti-Fascist Committee,* ed. Joshua Rubenstein and Oleg Naumov (New Haven, CT: Yale University Press, 2001), 25. This case of course is much more complicated. It must be seen in light of the anticosmopolitanism campaign of the postwar period, and the increase in

anti-Semitism, especially after the creation of the state of Israel in 1948. Nevertheless, the fact that Jews were persecuted for expressing the Jewish experience in the war is similar to the persecution of Leningraders for their particularistic myth.

89. See "Dokladnaia zapiska G.F. Aleksandrova i zaveduiushchego Otdelom vneshnei politiki TsK VKP(b) M.A. Suslova V.M. Molotovu i sekretariu TsK VKP(b) A.A. Kuznetsovu s predlozheniem prekratit' deiatel'nost' Antifashistskogo Komiteta sovetskikh uchenykh i Evreiskogo Antifashistskogo Komiteta v SSSR," in Nadzhafov, *Stalin i kosmopolitizm*, 98–101. See also "Dokladnaia zapiska Agitpropa TsK A.A. Zhdanovu po voprosu izdaniia 'Chernoi knigi,'" ibid., 103–105. *The Black Book* had been published in English in the United States by the time that this report was sent to Zhdanov in early February 1946.

90. V. A. Kutuzov discusses how the purged Leningraders were replaced by people sent from Moscow, and how these new leaders of the Leningrad party and soviet organizations continued to decimate the former leadership. The new party boss, V. A. Andrianov (a close associate of Malenkov), for example, began to purge people under the principle "the more, the better." See Kutuzov, "'Leningradskoe delo': Sud'by ispolnitelei," in *Rossiiskaia gosudarstvennost': Istoriia i sovremennost'*, ed. M. V. Khodiakov (St. Petersburg: Znamenitye Universanty, 2003), 614. The Orgbiuro confirmed Andrianov's position as first secretary of the Leningrad party on 7 March 1949. RGASPI, f. 17, op. 116, d. 420, l. 7.

91. RGAPSI, f. 17, op. 132, d. 103, l. 75.

92. See the report entitled "O nekotorykh nedostatkakh i merakh uluchsheniia agitatsionno-massovoi i kul'turno-prosvetitel'noi raboty v leningradskoi partiinoi organizatsii." RGASPI, f. 17, op. 132, d. 114, ll. 159–163.

93. Arlen Blium notes that some of these books were put back into circulation once the Leningrad Affair was deemed to be a falsified crime during the early Khrushchev period. Others, however, remained in special repositories until Perestroika. See Blium, "Blokadnaia tema v tsenzurnoi blokade: Po arkhivnym dokumentam glavlita SSSR," *Neva*, no. 1 (2004): 239. Many of the books were blacklisted because they presented Kuznetsov and the other Leningrad leaders in a positive light, or because they were mentioned at all. One book, for example, was taken out of circulation because Kuznetsov was mentioned along with other leaders of the party. RGASPI, f. 17, op. 132, d. 319, l. 209. A commission sent to Leningrad to carry out a verification of the party membership also noted that in the first half of 1949, five thousand books and journals were taken from the libraries of Leningrad University because they included materials written by enemies of the people. RGASPI, f. 17, op. 132, d. 103, l. 76.

94. See, for example, I. Bykov and I. Khrenov, "Velikaia pobeda pod Leningradom (k shestiletiiu razgroma nemetsko-fashistskikh zakhvatchikov pod Leningradom)," *Leningradskaia pravda*, 27 January 1950. See also Kalendarova, "Formiruia pamiat'," 285.

95. Each year around 27 January there were a number of articles outlining the celebrations taking place throughout Leningrad. From 1950 onward there are no reports of this at all. The archives also reveal no trace of preparations, speeches, or events as they do for the years between 1944 and 1949.

96. Memorial, f. 5 (Neopublikovannaia memuaristika), ed. khr., Grigorii

Iosifovich Mishkevich, l. 65. This information comes from G. I. Mishkevich (one of the subdirectors of the museum), who heard it from the former director, L. L. Rakov. V. A. Kutuzov, who interviewed Mishkevich, notes these accusations as well.

97. V.A. Kutuzov, "Muzei oborony Leningrad," *Dialog* 24 (August 1988): 24.

98. In September, for example, the Orgburo of the Central Committee decided to send two instructors from Agitprop to Leningrad for twenty days to review the work of the museum. RGASPI, f. 17, op. 116, d. 460, l. 9. A gathering of the museum's party organization on 19 October 1949 noted that a commission from the Central Committee provided a plan to help with the reconstruction of the museum's layout and narrative. It also noted that the commission from Moscow planned to return to Leningrad and review the changes being made. TsGAIPD SPb, f. 4440, op. 2, d. 11, ll. 5, 9.

99. See the "Postanovlenie Obshchego zakrytogo partiinogo sobraniia chlenov i kandidatov partiinoi partorganizatsii Muzeia oborony Leningrada ot 19 oktiabria 1949," TsGAIPD SPb, f. 4440, op. 2, d. 11, l. 13.

100. See the discussion of the "Zakrytoe partiinoe sobranie partiinoi organizatsii Muzeia oborony Leningrada ot 18 noiabria 1949 goda," TsGAIPD, f. 4440, op. 2, d. 11, ll. 16–25.

101. TsGAIPD SPb, f. 4440, op. 2, d. 11, l. 22.

102. Soon after the Leningrad Affair began, the museum's second director, Lev L'vovich Rakov, who had become synonymous with the museum, was arrested and sentenced under article 58 to twenty-five years' imprisonment. Not long after that, another museum worker, Grigorii Iosifovich Mishkevich, was arrested for being part of the "anti-Soviet center" that was the museum. See his account of his arrest and interrogation in Memorial, f. 5 (Neopublikovannaia memuaristika), ed. khr., Grigorii Iosifovich Mishkevich, ll. 36–74.

103. TsGALI SPb, f. 277, op. 1, d. 1198, ll. 13–14; TsGALI SPb, f. 277, op. 1, d. 1384, ll. 2–5.

104. TsGALI SPb, f. 277, op. 1, d. 1198, l. 11. Following the purge of Leningrad's leaders and the arrest of several museum workers, including the director, V. P. Kovalev, L. A. Dubinin was appointed the new director. He was one of the propagandists sent from Moscow to Leningrad in August 1949 to provide guidance for the Leningrad party organization in propaganda work. RGASPI, f. 17, op. 116, d. 452, l. 7.

105. Kutuzov, "Muzei oborony Leningrada," 26.

106. By the end of 1951 the museum's party members and workers began to doubt whether the museum would ever open again. Many questions were asked at meetings about the fate of the museum. See TsGAIPD SPb, f. 4440, op. 2, d. 20, ll. 35–40; TsGAIPD SPb, f. 4440, op. 2, d. 24, ll. 1–4.

107. TsGALI SPb, f. 277, op. 1, d. 1561, l. 1.

108. Brandenberger, *National Bolshevism*, 194.

CONCLUSION

1. On the use of *Alexander Nevskii* for patriotic ends, see Richard Taylor, *Film Propaganda: Soviet Russia and Nazi Germany* (New York: I. B. Tauris, 1998), 85–98.

2. For a discussion of the film's reception, see David Brandenberger, "The Popular Reception of S.M. Eisenstein's *Aleksandr Nevskii*," in Platt and Brandenberger, *Epic Revisionism*, 233–252.

3. The consequences of betraying the fatherland were emphasized in a 9 June 1934 article in *Pravda*. The article stated that "the defense of the fatherland is the supreme law of life. And he who raises his hand against his country, he who betrays his country should be destroyed." It went on to list penalties for betraying the fatherland, including death by shooting, imprisonment, and confiscation of property. Family members were also to bear responsibility for the "acts of traitors." "Za rodinu," 1.

4. Both Andrew Day and Karl Qualls, for example, note that while planners in Moscow sought to use postwar restoration to redesign Stalingrad and Sevastopol as memorials to the war, local planners fought to have their cities' urban planning traditions and heritage feature prominently in postwar designs. See Day, "Building Socialism," 184–187, 198; and Qualls, *From Ruins to Reconstruction,* chap. 2.

5. Iakovlev, ed., *Reabilitatsiia,* 320. During this period of hesitant de-Stalinization, the new leadership deemed many of the criminal allegations made against the Soviet people to be fabrications and attributed them to Stalin's "cult of personality" or his henchmen. Soviet newspapers announced that the Doctor's Plot – a supposed conspiracy of Jewish doctors who allegedly conspired to murder members of the top party leadership – was a falsification. The post-Stalin leadership quickly announced a mass amnesty of Gulag prisoners sentenced for nonpolitical crimes and later dismantled the system. Gorlizki and Khlevniuk, *Cold Peace,* 167.

6. Kirschenbaum, *The Legacy of the Siege of Leningrad,* 152; Tumarkin, *The Living and the Dead,* 110–111.

7. Dzeniskevich, *Blokada i politika,* 14–16.

8. For a complete list of plaques established in the city since the Khrushchev period, along with illustrations, see V. N. Timofeev, E. N. Poretskina, and N. N. Efremov, *Memorial'nye doski Sankt-Peterburga: Spravochnik* (St. Petersburg: Art-Biuro, 1999), 522–563.

9. Leningraders themselves funded the construction of this monument through donations. P. M. Bulushev and V. I. Ganshin, *Podvigu tvoemu, Leningrad: Monument geroicheskim zashchitnikam goroda* (Leningrad: Lenizdat, 1980), 13.

10. T. M. Shmakova, "Rodom iz leningradskoi blokady," *Trudy Gosudarstvennogo muzeia istorii Sankt-Peterburga* 9 (2004): 62.

11. A. A. Shishkin, "Slovo o muzee," *Zabveniiu ne podlezhit* 1 (1999): 9.

12. Baltun, *Russkii muzei;* Baranov, *Siluety blokady;* Brodskii, ed., *Khudozhniki goroda-fronta;* S. N. Razgonov, *Khraniteli vechnogo* (Moscow: Molodaia gvardiia, 1975); Kedrinskii et al., eds., *Letopis' vozrozhdeniia;* Kedrinskii et al., eds., *Vosstanovlenie pamiatnikov arkhitektury Leningrada;* Papernaia, ed., *Podvig veka;* Tikhomirova, *Pamiatniki, liudi, sobytiia.*

13. Bakhareva, Kovaleva, and Shishkina, eds., *Arkhitektory blokadnogo Leningrada;* Kuchumov, *Stat'i, vospominaniia, pis'ma;* Loviagina, Silant'eva, and Usatova, eds., *Blokadnyi dnevnik;* Shurygin, *Petergof;* Vilinbakhov, ed., *Ermitazh;* V. N. Vologdina, ed., *Iz istorii Kunstkamery, 1941–1945* (St. Petersburg: RAN Kunstkamera, 2003); Zelenova, *Stat'i, vospominaniia, pis'ma;* Balaeva, *Zapiski khranitelia Gatchinskogo dvortsa.*

14. Joseph Brodsky, "A Guide to a Renamed City," in *Less than One: Selected Essays* (New York: Farrar, Straus and Giroux, 1986), 91.

BIBLIOGRAPHY

PRIMARY SOURCES

Archives

Citations of most archival materials are by *fond* (collection), *opis'* (finding aid), *delo* (file), *list* (page), and are abbreviated f., op., d., l. Some citations include *chast'* (part), abbreviated as "ch.," in either the finding aid or the file.

GARF (Gosudarstvennyi arkhiv Rossiiskoi Federatsii) [State Archive of the Russian Federation]

f. A-150. Gosudarstvennyi komitet Soveta Ministrov RSFSR po delam stroitel'stvo i arkhitektury.

GMGS (Gosudarstvennyi muzei gorodskoi skul'ptury) [State Museum of City Sculpture]

f. Otdel pamiatnikov i memorial'nykh dosok.

GMMOBL (Gosudarstvennyi memorial'nyi muzei oborony i blokady Leningrada) [State Memorial Museum of the Defense and Blockade of Leningrad]

f. Rukopisno-dokumental'nyi fond.

GMZ Gatchina (Arkhiv Gosudarstvennogo muzeia-zapovednika "Gatchina") [Archive of the State Museum and National Park "Gatchina"]

GMZ Pavlovsk (Arkhiv Gosudarstvennogo muzeia-zapovednika "Pavlovsk") [Archive of the State Museum and National Park "Pavlovsk"]

f. Nauchno-vospomogatel'ny fond.

KGIOP (Arkhiv Komiteta po gosudarstvennomu kontroliu, ispol'zovaniiu i okhrane pamiatnikov istorii i kul'tury Sankt-Peterburga) [Archive of the Committee for State Control, Use, and Preservation of Monuments of History and Culture of St. Petersburg]

f. Belekhova.

f. 3. Kuntskamera.

f. 50. Admiralteistvo.

f. 157. Tavricheskii dvorets.

f. 163. Zimnii dvorets.

f. 166. Muzei etnografii.

f. 166–1. Mikhailovskii dvorets.

f. 167. Inzhenernyi zamok.

f. 226. Ekaterininskii park (Pushkin).

f. 226-G. Prigorodnye dvortsy i parki.

f. 226–1. Ekaterininskii dvorets (Pushkin).

f. 246–1. Pavlovskii dvorets (Pavlovsk).

f. 950. Nauchno-metodicheskii otdel.

Memorial (Arkhiv Memoriala Sankt-Peterburga) [Archive of the St. Petersburg Branch of Memorial]

f. 5. Neopublikovannaia memuaristika.

RGAE (Rossiiskii gosudarstvennyi arkhiv

ekonomiki) [Russian State Archive of the Economy]
f. 9432. Komitet po delam arkhitektury pri Sovmin SSSR.
f. 9588. Upravlenie okhrany pamiatnikov arkhitektury.
RGASPI (Rossiiskii gosudarstvennyi arkhiv sotsial'no-politicheskoi istorii) [Russian State Archive of Socio-Political History].
f. 17. Tsentral'nyi komitet VKP (b).
f. 77. Andrei Aleksandrovich Zhdanov.
f. 78. Mikhail Ivanovich Kalinin.
RNB OR (Rossiiskaia natsional'naia biblioteka otdel rukopisei) [Manuscript Division of the Russian National Library]
f. 1117. Boris Ivanovich Zagurskii.
f. 1015. Anna Petrovna Ostroumova-Lebedeva.
f. 1035. Vladimir Kuz'mich Makarov.
TsGA SPb (Tsentral'nyi gosudarstvennyi arkhiv Sankt-Peterburga) [Central State Archive of St. Petersburg]
f. 568. Kuibyshevskii raionnyi sovet narodnykh deputatov Sankt-Peterburga.
f. 2076. Planovaia komissiia ispolkoma Leningradskogo gorodskogo soveta.
f. 7384. Sankt-Peterburgskii gorodskoi sovet narodnykh deputatov.
TsGAIPD SPb (Tsentral'nyi gosudarstvennyi arkhiv istoriko-politicheskikh dokumentov Sankt-Peterburga) [Central State Archive of Historico-Political Documents of St. Petersburg].
f. 25. Leningradskii gorodskoi komitet KPSS.
f. 2853. Gorodskoi otdel kul'turno-prosvetitel'noi raboty.
f. 3401. Organ upravlenie proektno-stroitel'nogo ob"edineniia "Restavrator."
f. 3462. Dvortsovo-parkovyi muzei-zapovednik, Pushkin.
f. 4000. Institut istorii partii leningradskogo Obkoma KPSS.
f. 4440. Muzei Oborony Leningrada.
TsGALI SPb (Tsentral'nyi gosudarstvennyi arkhiv literatury i iskusstva Sankt-Peterburga) [Central State Archive of Literature and Art of St. Petersburg]
f. 32. Obshchestvo Staryi-Peterburg – Novyi Leningrad.
f. 266. Vysshee khudozhestvenno-promyshlennoe uchilishche im. V. I. Mukhinoi.
f. 277. Otdel kul'turno-prosvetitel'noi raboty Lengorispolkoma.
f. 333. Upravlenie po delam iskusstv Lengorispolkoma.
f. 341. Leningradskoe otdelenie Soiuza arkhitektorov SSSR.
f. 411. Direktsiia Pushkinskogo prigorodnogo dvortsa-muzeia i parka.
TsGANTD SPb (Tsentral'nyi gosudarstvennyi arkhiv nauchno-teknicheskoi dokumentatsii Sankt-Peterburga) [Central State Archive of Scientific and Technical Documentation of St. Petersburg]
f. 17. Upravlenie tipovogo eksperimental'nogo proektirovaniia zhilykh i obshestvennykh zdanii.
f. 386. Arkhitekturno-planirovochnoe upravlenie lengorispolkoma.
USHMM (United States Holocaust Memorial Museum Archive)
RG-06.025. Postwar Trials in the Soviet Union.

Russian and Soviet Periodicals

Arkhitektura i stroitelstvo Leningrada
Arkhitektura Leningrada
Arkhitektura SSSR
Biulleten' Leningradskogo gorodskogo soveta deputatov trudiashchikhsia
Bloknot agitatora
Bolshevistskoe slovo
Krasnaia zvezda

Leningradskaia pravda
Literatura i iskusstvo
Literaturnaia gazeta
Mir iskusstva
Novyi mir
Pravda
Starye gody
Vecherniaia Moskva
Vechernii Leningrad
Zvezda

Published Archival Documents, Memoirs, and Other Primary Materials

Adamovich, Ales, and Danil Granin, eds. *A Book of the Blockade.* Translated by Hilda Perham. Moscow: Raduga, 1983.

AKT Leningradskoi gorodskoi komissii o prednamerennom istreblenii nemetsko-fashistskimi varvarami mirnykh zhitelei Leningrada i ushcherbe, nanesennom khoziaistvu i kul'turno-istoricheskim pamiatnikam goroda za period voiny i blokady. Leningrad: Ogiz-Gospolitizdat, 1945.

Amsterdam, A. V., and M. M. Smirnov, eds. *Deviat'sot dnei: Literaturno-khudozhestvennyi sbornik.* Leningrad: Lenizdat, 1948.

Anisimov, G. G., ed. *Okhrana pamiatnikov istorii i kul'tury.* Moscow: Sovetskaia Rossiia, 1973.

———, ed. *Okhrana pamiatnikov istorii i kul'tury: Dekrety, postanovleniia, rasporiazheniia Pravitel'stva SSSR i Pravitel'stva RSFSR, 1917–1968.* Moscow: Institut istorii Akademii Nauk SSSR, 1968.

Avvakumov, S. I., ed. *Geroicheskii Leningrad, 1917–1942.* Leningrad: Gospolitizdat, 1943.

———, ed. *Leningrad v Velikoi otechestvennoi voine: Tom I; 22 iiunia 1941–22 iiunia 1943.* Leningrad: Gospolitizdat, 1944.

Bakhareva, Iu. Iu, T. V. Kovaleva, and T. G. Shishkina, eds. *Arkhitektory blokadnogo Leningrada.* St. Petersburg: NP-Print, 2005.

Balaeva, S. N. *Zapiski khranitelia Gatchinskogo dvortsa, 1924–1956: Dnevniki; Stat'i.* Edited by N. S. Batenin. St. Petersburg: Iskusstvo Rossii, 2005.

Baltun, P. K. *Russkii muzei – evakuatsiia, blokada, vosstanovlenie (iz vospominanii muzeinogo rabotnika).* Moscow: Izobratitel'noe iskusstvo, 1981.

Baranov, N. V. *Arkhitektura i stroitel'stvo Leningrada.* Leningrad: Leningradskoe gazetno-zhurnal'noe i knizhnoe izdatel'stvo, 1948.

———. *Glavnyi arkhitektor goroda: Tvorcheskaia i organizatsionnaia deiatel'nost.* Moscow: Stroizdat, 1979.

———. "O plane vosstanovleniia Leningrada: Iz doklada glavnogo arkhitektora Leningrada N.V. Baranova na rashirennom zasedanii pravleniia SSA s aktivom moskovskikh arkhitektorov 10-X-1944 g." *Arkhitektura Leningrada,* no. 1 (1945): 3–9.

———. *Siluety blokady: Zapiski glavnogo arkhitektora goroda.* Leningrad: Lenizdat, 1982.

———. "Zadachi leningradskikh arkhitektorov v realizatsii piatiletnego plana vosstanovleniia i razvitiia g. Leningrada i oblasti." *Arkhitektura i stroitel'stvo Leningrada,* November 1946, 1–7.

Baranovskii, P. D. "Avtobiografiia." In *Petr Baranovskii: Trudy, vospominaniia sovremennikov,* edited by Iu. A. Bychkov, O. P. Baranovskaia, V. A. Desiatnikov, and A. M. Ponomarev, 7–14. Moscow: Otchii Dom, 1996.

Bely, Andrei. *Petersburg.* Edited and translated by Robert A. Maguire and John E. Malmstad. Bloomington: Indiana University Press, 1978.

Benois, Alexander. "Chudesa i blagorazumie." In *Aleksandr Benua razmyshliaet,* edited by I. S. Zil'bershtein and

A. N. Savinov, 55–61. Moscow: Sovetskii Khudozhnik, 1968.

———. *Moi dnevnik: 1916–1917–1918.* Edited by N. I. Aleksandrova and T. V. Esina. Moscow: Russkii Put', 2003.

———. "Zhivopisnyi Peterburg." *Mir iskusstva* 1 (1902): 1–5.

Berggol'ts, Ol'ga. "My prishli v Pushkin." In *Ol'ga Berggol'ts: Izbrannye proizvedeniia v dvukh tomakh; Tom 2*, edited by A. Ruleva, 248–259. Leningrad: "Khudozhestvennaia literatura, 1967.

Bergholz, Olga. "In Leningrad during Those Days." In *Heroic Leningrad: Documents, Sketches and Stories of Its Siege and Relief*, translated by J. Fineberg, 141–145. Moscow: Foreign Languages Publishing House, 1945.

Bidlack, Richard, and Nikita Lomagin, eds. *The Leningrad Blockade, 1941–1944: A New Documentary History from the Soviet Archives.* Translated by Marian Schwartz. New Haven, CT: Yale University Press, 2012.

Bobrov, Mikhail. *Khraniteli angela: Zapiski blokadnogo al'pinista.* St. Petersburg: Izdatel'stvo Sankt-Peterburgskogo gumanitarnyi universitet profsoiuzov, 1998.

Boitsov, M. A., and T. A. Vasil'eva, eds. *Kartoteka "Z" operativnogo shtaba "Reikhsliaiter Rozenberg": Tsennosti kul'tury na okkupirovannykh territoriiakh Rossii, Ukrainy i Belorussii, 1941–1942.* Moscow: Izdatel'stvo Moskovskogo Universiteta, 1998.

Boldyrev, A. N. *Osadnaia Zapis' (Blokadnyi dnevnik).* Edited by V. S. Garbuzova and I. M. Streblin-Kamenskii. St. Petersburg: Evropeiskii Dom, 1998.

Brodskii, I. A., ed. *Khudozhniki goroda-fronta: Vospominaniia i dnevniki leningradskikh khudozhnikov.* Leningrad: Izdatel'stvo "Khudozhnik RSFSR," 1973.

Brodsky, Joseph. "A Guide to a Renamed City." In *Less than One: Selected Essays*, 69–94. New York: Farrar, Straus and Giroux, 1986.

Bychkov, Iu. A., O. P. Baranovskaia, V. A. Desiatnikov, and A. M. Ponomarev, eds. *Petr Baranovskii: Trudy, vospominaniia sovremennikov.* Moscow: Otchii Dom, 1996.

Clark, Katerina, and Evgeny Dobrenko, with Andrei Artizov and Oleg Naumov, eds. *Soviet Culture and Power: A History in Documents, 1917–1953.* Translated by Marian Schwartz. New Haven, CT: Yale University Press, 2007.

Davydov, Sergei Nikolaevich. "Podvig arkhitektora Belekhova." In *Podvig veka: Khudozhniki, skul'ptury, arkhitektory, iskusstvovedy v gody Velikoi Otechestvennoi voiny i blokady Leningrada; Vospominaniia, dnevniki, pis'ma, ocherki, literaturnye zapisi*, edited by Nina Papernaia, 285–288. Leningrad: Lenizdat, 1969.

Denisov, V. V., A. V. Kvashonkin, L. N. Malashenko, A. I. Miniuk, M. Iu. Prozumenshchikov, and O. V. Khlevniuk, eds. *TsK VKP(b) i regional'nye partiinye komitety, 1945–1953.* Moscow: Rosspen, 2004.

Dostoevsky, Fyodor. *The Idiot.* Translated by David Magarshack. New York: Penguin, 1955.

Dzeniskevich, A. R., ed. *Leningrad v osade: Sbornik dokumentov o geroicheskoi oborone Leningrada v gody Velikoi Otechestvennoi voine; 1941–1945.* St. Petersburg: Liki Rossii, 1995.

Ehrenburg, Il'ia. "Vechnyi gorod." In *Deviat'sot dnei: Literaturno-khudozhestvennyi sbornik*, edited by A. M. Amsterdam and M. M. Smirnov, 501–507. Leningrad: Lenizdat, 1948.

Ezhov, V. A. "Vosstanovlenie Leningrada." In *Vozrozhdenie: Vospominaniia, ocherki i dokumenty o vosstanovlenii Leningrada,* edited by V. A. Kutuzov and E. G. Levina, 5–18. Leningrad: Lenizdat, 1977.

Fedin, Konstantin. "Svidanie s Leningradom, zapiski 1944 goda." *Novyi mir* 4–5 (1944): 41–53.

Garros, Veronique, Natalia Korenevskaya, and Thomas Lahusen, eds. *Intimacy and Terror: Soviet Diaries of the 1930s.* Translated by Carol Flath. New York: New Press, 1995.

"Godovshchina velikoi pobedy Krasnoi Armii pod Leningradom. (Material dlia dokladchikov i besedchikov)." *Bloknot agitatora,* no. 2 (1945): 1–36.

Gogol, Nikolai. "Nevsky Prospekt." In *Nikolai Gogol: Plays and Petersburg Tales,* edited and translated by Christopher English, 3–36. New York: Oxford University Press, 1995.

Grabar', Igor', ed., *Pamiatniki iskusstva razrushennye nemetskimi zakhvatchikami v SSSR: Sbornik statei.* Moscow: Izdatel'stvo Akademii Nauk SSSR, 1948.

Grossman, Vasily. *A Writer at War: A Soviet Journalist with the Red Army, 1941–1945.* Edited by Antony Beevor. Translated by Luba Vinogradova. Toronto: Knopf, 2005.

Halder, Franz. *The Halder War Diary, 1939–1942.* Edited by Charles Burdick and Hans-Adolf Jacobsen. Novato, CA: Presidio, 1988.

Iakovlev, A. N., ed. *Reabilitatsiia: Politicheskie protsessy 30–50-kh godov.* Moscow: Izdatel'stvo politicheskoi literatury, 1990.

Inber, Vera. *Leningrad Diary.* Translated by Serge M. Wolff. London: Hutchinson of London, 1971.

Joosten, S. Paul A., ed. *The Trial of the Major War Criminals before the International Military Tribunal.* Vol. 8. Nuremberg: International Military Tribunal, 1947.

Kamalov, Kh. Kh., R. B. Serdnak, and Iu. S. Tokarev, eds. *Deviat'sot geroicheskikh dnei: Sbornik dokumentov i materialov o geroicheskoi bor'be trudiashchikhsia Leningrada v 1941–1944 gg.* Leningrad: Nauka, 1966.

Kamenskii, V. A. "Pervoocherednye zadachi arkhitektorov Leningrada." *Arkhitektura Leningrada,* no. 1 (1945): 1–2.

———. "Zhiloi dom v ansemble goroda." *Arkhitektura i stroitel'stvo Leningrada,* November 1946, 15–18.

Kedrov, G. T. "Istoki rosta." In *Vozrozhdenie: Vospominaniia, ocherki i dokumenty o vosstanovlenii Leningrada,* edited by V. A. Kutuzov and E. G. Levina, 35–41. Leningrad: Lenizdat, 1977.

Khlevniuk, O. V., Y. Gorlizki, L. P. Kosheleva, A. I. Miniuk, M. Iu. Prozumenshchikov, L. A. Rogovaia, and S. V. Somonova, eds. *Politbiuro TsK VKP(b) i Sovet Ministrov SSSR, 1945–1953.* Moscow: Rosspen, 2002.

Khudiakova, N. D. "'I vse zhe verili v pobedu' (Iz blokadnogo dnevnika 1941–1943 gg.)." *Zabveniiu ne podlezhit: Stati, vospominaniia, dnevniki* 2 (2001): 57–68.

———. "K 60-letiiu osnovaniia Muzeia oborony Leningrada: Sud'ba muzeia." *Zabveniiu ne podlezhit: Stati, vospominaniia, dokumenty* 4 (2004): 9–19.

Kochina, Elena. *Blockade Diary.* Translated by Samuel C. Ramer. Ann Arbor, MI: Ardis, 1990.

Kosenkova, Iu. L. *Sovetskii gorod 1940-kh–pervoi poloviny 1950-kh godov: Ot tvorcheskikh poiskov k praktike stroitel'stva.* Moscow: URSS, 2000.

Koval'chuk, V. M., and A. N. Chistikov, eds. *Leningrad v gody Velikoi Otechestvennoi voiny: Ocherki. Dokumenty. Fotografii.* St. Petersburg: Izdatel'stvo-poligraficheskii servisnyi tsentr, 2005.

Krestovskii, I. V. "Ukrytiia i okhrana pamiatnikov Leningrada v gody blokady (1941–44)." *Zabveniiu ne podlezhit: Stat'i, vospominaniia, dokumenty* 7 (2006): 5–14.

Kuchumov, A. M. *Stat'i, vospominaniia, pis'ma.* Edited by N. S. Tret'iakov. St. Petersburg: Art-Palas, 2004.

Kukushkin, N. V. "Vsenoi 1944 goda . . ." In *Vozrozhdenie: Vospominaniia, ocherki i dokumenty o vosstanovlenii Leningrada,* edited by V. A. Kutuzov and E. G. Levina, 28–29. Leningrad: Lenizdat, 1977.

Lavrov, V. "Neotlozhnye voprosy vosstanovleniia pamiatnikov Russkogo zodchestva." *Arkhitektura SSSR,* no. 8 (1944): 24–30.

"Leningrad zimoi 1941–42 gg. Risunki arkhitektorov." *Arkhitektura SSSR,* no. 2 (1943): 16–18.

Levina, E. "Pis'ma k drugu." In *Leningradtsy v dni blokady: Sbornik,* edited by E. Korol'chuk and A. Volkova, 195–220. Leningrad: Leningradskoe gazetno-zhurnal'noe i knizhnoe izdatel'stvo, 1947.

Likhachev, D. S. *Reflections on the Russian Soul: A Memoir.* Translated by Bernard Adams. New York: Central European University Press, 2000.

Lomagin, N. A., ed. *V tiskakh goloda: Blokada Leningrada v dokumentakh germanskikh spetssluzhb i NKVD.* St. Petersburg: Evropeiskii Dom, 2000.

Loviagina, V. E., I. A. Silant'eva, and Iu. V. Usatova, eds. *Blokadnyi dnevnik: Zhivopis' i grafika blokadnogo vremeni; Al'bom-katalog.* St. Petersburg: Gosudarstvennyi muzei istorii Sankt-Peterburga, 2005.

Loznitsa, Sergei, dir. *Blokada.* St. Petersburg: St. Petersburg Documentary Film Studio, 2006. DVD.

Lukomsky, G. K. *Staryi Peterburg: Progulki po starinnym kvartalam stolitsy.* St. Petersburg: Kolo, 2002.

Malinina, T., ed. *Iz istorii sovetskoi arkhitektury 1941–1945 gg.* Moscow: Izdatel'stvo Nauka, 1978.

Mandelstam, Nadezhda. *Hope against Hope: A Memoir.* Translated by Max Hayward. New York: Modern Library, 1999.

Maseev, I. Z. "Pervye tipovye." In *Vozrozhdenie: Vospominaniia, ocherki i dokumenty o vosstanovlenii Leningrada,* edited by V. A. Kutuzov and E. G. Levina, 236–240. Leningrad: Lenizdat, 1977.

Matiushkin, N. I. *Sovetskii patriotizm – moguchaia dvizhushchaia sila sotsialisticheskogo obshchestva.* Moscow: Gosudarstvennoe izdatel'stvo politicheskoi literatury, 1952.

Molotov, V. M. *The International Situation and the Soviet Union.* New York: International Publishers, 1935.

Muzei oborony Leningrada: Putevoditel'. Leningrad: Gosudarstvennoe izdatel'stvo "Iskusstvo," 1948.

Nadzhafov, D. G., ed. *Stalin i kosmopolitizm: 1945–1953; Dokumenty.* Moscow: Izdatel'stvo Materik, 2005.

Nenarokov, A. P., ed. *Kul'turnoe stroitel'stvo v SSSR, 1917–1927: Razborka edinoi gosudarstvennoi politiki v oblasti kul'tury; Dokumenty i materialy.* Moscow: Nauka, 1989.

Obshchestvo Staryi Peterburg, 1921–1923. Petrograd, 1923.

Osipova, Lidiia. *"Dnevnik kollaborantki."* In *"Svershilos' Prishli nemtsy!" Ideinyi kollaboratsionizm v SSSR v period Velikoi Otechestvennoi voiny,* edited by O. V. Budnitskii and G. S. Zelenina, 63–188. Moscow: Rosspen, 2012.

Pamiatniki zodchestva razrushennye ili povrezhdennye nemetskimi zakhvatchikami: Dokumenty i materialy; Vypusk I. Moscow: Gosudarstvennoe arkhitekturnoe izdatel'stvo Akademii arkhitektury SSSR, 1942.

Papernaia, Nina, ed. *Podvig veka: Khu-*

dozhniki, skul'ptory, arkhitektory, iskusstvovedy v gody Velikoi otechestvennoi voiny i blokady Leningrada; Vospominaniia, dnevniki, pis'ma, ocherki, literaturnye zapisi. Leningrad: Lenizdat, 1969.

Piliavskii, V. I. "Razrusheniia prigorodov Leningrada." *Arkhitektura Leningrada,* nos. 1–2 (1944): 21–23.

———. "Vandalizm nemetsko-fashistskikh zakhvatchikov v prigorodakh Leningrada." *Arkhitektura SSSR,* no. 7 (1944): 35–39.

Piotrovskii, B. B. *Stranitsy moei zhizni.* St. Petersburg: Nauka, 1995.

Piotrovskii, M. B., ed. *Gosudarstvennyi Ermitazh: Muzeinye rasprodazhi 1928–1929 godov; Arkhivnye dokumenty.* St. Petersburg: State Hermitage, 2006.

Punin, Nikolai. *Mir svetel liubov'iu: Dnevniki i pis'ma.* Edited by L. A. Zykov. Moscow: Artist. Rezhisser. Teatr, 2000.

Pushkin, A. S. "The Bronze Horseman." In *The Portable Nineteenth-Century Russian Reader,* edited by George Gibian, translated by Walter Arndt, 8–21. New York: Penguin, 1993

P. V., "Ocherednye vandalizmy vedomstv." *Starye gody,* January 1913, 49–50.

Pylaev, Mikhail. *Staryi Peterburg.* St. Petersburg: Izdatel'stvo A. S. Suvorina, 1887.

Rabinovitch, M. B. *Vospominaniia dolgoi zhizni.* St. Petersburg: Evropeiskii Dom, 1996.

Rakov, L. L. "Vystavka 'Oborona Leningrada.'" In *Khudozhniki goroda-fronta: Vospominaniia i dnevniki leningradskikh khudozhnikov,* edited by I. A. Brodskii, 399–404. Leningrad: Khudozhnik RSFSR, 1973.

"Rech' tov. Popkova P.S." *Bloknot agitatora,* no. 3 (1945): 6–12.

Resheniia partii i pravitel'stva po khoziaistvennym voprosam: Tom 3, 1941–1952. Moscow: Izdatel'stvo politicheskoi literatury, 1968.

Riegl, Alois. "The Modern Cult of Monuments: Its Essence and Its Development." Translated by Karen Bruckner and Karen Williams. In *Historical and Philosophical Issues in the Conservation of Cultural Heritage,* edited by Nicholas Stanley Price, M. Kirby Talley Jr., and Alessandra Melucco Vaccaro, 69–83. Los Angeles: Getty Conservation Institute, 1996.

Rostislavov, A. "Zhertva 'sobytii.'" *Starye gody,* January 1907, 21–23.

Rubanchik, Ia. O. "My otstoiali tebia, Leningrad, my tebia vosstanovim." *Arkhitektura Leningrada,* no. 1 (1945): 16–22.

———. "Vosstanovlenie Nevskogo Prospekta." *Arkhitektura i stroitel'stvo Leningrada* 3, no. 9 (1948): 11–22.

Samoilov, F. "Trekhletie so dnia pobedy sovetskikh voisk pod Leningradom." *Bloknot agitatora,* no. 2 (1947): 18–37.

Serapina, N. M., ed. *Ermitazh, kotoryi my poteriali: Dokumenty 1920–1930 godov.* St. Petersburg: Izdatel'stvo Zhurnal Neva, 2002.

Sharikov, K. G., ed. *Leningrad v Velikoi otechestvennoi voine: Tom II; 23 iiunia–24 marta 1944.* Leningrad: Lenizdat, 1947.

Shmakova, T. M. "Rodom iz leningradskoi blokady." *Trudy Gosudarstvennogo muzeia istorii Sankt-Peterburga* 9 (2004): 61–63.

Shurygin, Ia. I. *Petergof: Letopis' vostanovleniia.* St. Petersburg: Arbis, 2000.

Simmons, Cynthia, and Nina Perlina, eds. *Writing the Siege of Leningrad: Women's Diaries, Memoirs, and Documentary Prose.* Pittsburgh: University of Pittsburgh Press, 2002.

"Soobshchenie Chrezvychainoi Gosudarstvennoi Komissii po ustanovleniiu i rassledovaniiu zlodeianii nemetsko-fashistskikh zakhvatchikov i ikh soobshchnikov: O razrusheniiakh pamiatnikov iskusstva i arkhitektury v gorodakh Petrodvorets, Pushkin i Pavlovsk." *Arkhitektura Leningrada,* nos. 1–2 (1944): 16–20.

Soobshchenie Komissii po okhrane i vosstanovleniiu arkhitekturnykh pamiatnikov: Pamiatniki zodchestva, razrushennye ili povrezhdennye nemetskimi zakhvatchikami; Dokumenty i materialy. Vypusk 1. Moscow: Izdatel'stvo Akademii arkhitektury SSSR, 1942.

Stalin, Joseph. *Works.* Vol. 13 (July 1930–January 1934). Moscow: Foreign Languages Publishing House, 1954.

Stokes, Gale, ed. *From Stalinism to Pluralism: A Documentary History of Eastern Europe since 1945.* 2nd ed. New York: Oxford University Press, 1996.

Tikhomirova, M. *Pamiatniki, liudi, sobytiia: Iz zapisok muzeinogo rabotnika.* Leningrad: Izdatel'stvo Khudozhnik RSFSR, 1970.

Tikhonov, N. S. "Victory: Leningrad in January 1944." In *Heroic Leningrad: Documents, Sketches and Stories of Its Siege and Relief,* translated by J. Fineberg, 146–152. Moscow: Foreign Languages Publishing House, 1945.

Timofeev, V. N., E. N. Poretskina, and N. N. Efremov. *Memorial'nye doski Sankt-Peterburga: Spravochnik.* St. Petersburg: Art-Biuro, 1999.

Tret'iakov, N. S., ed. "'My . . . dolzhny schitat' sebia mobilizovannymi dlia bor'by i pobedy . . .': Iz dnevnikov khraniteli prigorodnykh dvortsov-muzeev Leningrada; 1941–1945 gg." *Otechestvennye arkhivy,* no. 1 (2007): 82–97.

Turova, E. L. "Snariady rvutsia v Pushkine: Iz dnevnika khranitelia Ekaterininskogo parka, Evgenii Leonidovny Turovoi." In *Podvig veka: Khudozhniki, skul'ptory, arkhitektory, iskusstvovedy v gody Velikoi Otechestvennoi voiny i blokady Leningrada; Vospominaniia, dnevniki, pis'ma, ocherki, literaturnye zapisi,* edited by Nina Papernaia, 17–18. Leningrad: Lenizdat, 1989.

"Ukaz Preziduma Verkhovnogo Soveta SSSR: O nagrazhdenii goroda Leningrada ordenom Lenina." *Bloknot agitatora,* no. 3 (1945): 1.

"V soiuze arkhitektorov (khronika 1942–1945 gg.)." *Arkhitektura Leningrada,* no. 1 (1945): 28–31.

"V soiuze arkhitektorov (khronika 1946 g.)." *Arkhitektura i stroitel'stva Leningrada: Sbornik,* November (1946): 70.

Vaks, I. A. "Podgotovka masterov khudozhestvennoi otdelki zdanii." *Arkhitektura Leningrada,* nos. 1–2 (1944): 24–25.

Vaks, I. A., and N. M. Ol'. "Budushchie restavratory." In *Vozrozhdenie: Vospominaniia, ocherki i dokumenty o vosstanovlenii Leningrada,* edited by V. A. Kutuzov and E. G. Levina, 228–233. Leningrad: Lenizdat, 1977.

Vereshchagin, V. "Starye gody." *Starye gody,* January 1907, 1.

Vilinbakhov, G. V., ed. *Ermitazh: Khronika voennykh let, 1941–1945; Dokumenty arkhiva Gosudarstvennogo Ermitazha.* St. Petersburg: Izdatel'stvo Gosudarstvennogo Ermitazha, 2005.

Vinogradov, V. K., V. P. Gusachenko, O. I. Nazhestkin, and V. L. Peshcherskii, eds. *Sekrety Gitlera na stole u Stalina: Razvedka i kontrrazvedka o podgotovke germanskoi agressii protiv SSSR, mart–iiun' 1941; Dokumenty iz tsentral'nogo arkhiva FSB Rossii.* Moscow: Izdatel'stvo ob"edineniia Mosgorakhiv, 1995.

Vishnevskii, Vsevolod. *Leningrad: Dnevniki voennykh let; V 2-kh knigakh; Kniga pervaia; 2 noiabria 1941 goda–31 dekabria 1942 goda.* Moscow: Voenizdat, 2002.

———. *Leningrad: Dnevniki voennykh let; V 2-kh knigakh; Kniga vtoraia; 1 ianvaria*

1943 goda–28 sentiabria 1944 goda; 1–9 maia 1945 goda. Moscow: Voenizdat, 2002.

Vitushkin, S. F., ed. *"... I nichto ne zabyto": Dokumenty i materialy o zlodeianiiakh nemetsko-fashistskikh okkupantov na Novgorodskoi zemle (1941–1944)*. Novgorod: Kirillitsa, 1996.

Vladimirtsev, N. I., V. M. Komissarov, V. D. Krivets, V. F. Nekrasov, B. S. Neshkin, and S. M. Shtutman, eds. *Pribaltiiskii natsionalism v dokumentakh NKVD, MVD i MGB SSSR*. Moscow: Ob"edinennaia redaktsiia MVD Rossii, 2011.

Vologdina, V. N., ed. *Iz istorii Kunstkamery, 1941–1945*. St. Petersburg: RAN Kunstkamera, 2003.

von Geldern, James, and Richard Stites, eds. *Mass Culture in Soviet Russia: Tales, Poems, Songs, Movies, Plays, and Folklore, 1917–1953*. Bloomington: Indiana University Press, 1995.

"Vtoraia godovshchina velikoi pobedy Krasnoi Armii pod Leningradom. (Material dlia dokladchikov i besedchikov)." *Bloknot agitatora*, no. 2 (1946): 1–26.

Vystavka "Geroicheskaia oborona Leningrada": Ocherk-putevoditel'. Leningrad: Gosudarstvennyi izdatel'stvo "Iskusstvo," 1945.

Werth, Alexander. *Leningrad*. London: Hamish Hamilton, 1944.

Zagurskii, B. I. "*Iskusstvo*." In *Ocherki istorii Leningrada*. Tom 5, *Period Velikoi Otechestvennoi voiny Sovetskogo Soiuza, 1941–1945gg*, edited by V. M. Koval'chuk, G. P. Aleksandrov, E. A. Boltin, Iu. I. Zavarukhin, S. P. Kniazev, Sh. M. Levin, N. E. Nosov, G. L. Sobolev, and A. L. Fraiman, 602–648. Moscow: Izdatel'stvo Akademii Nauk, 1967.

Zegers, Peter Kort, and Douglas Druick, eds. *Windows on the War: Soviet TASS Posters at Home and Abroad, 1941–1945*. Chicago: Art Institute of Chicago, 2011.

Zelenova, A. I. *Dvorets v Pavlovske*. Leningrad: Lenizdat, 1986.

———. "Snariady rvutsia v Pavlovske: Iz vospominanii direktora dvortsa-muzeia Anny Ivanovany Zelenovoi." In *Podvig veka: Khudozhniki, skul'ptory, arkhitektory, iskusstvovedy v gody Velikoi Otechestvennoi voiny i blokady Leningrada; Vospominaniia, dnevniki, pis'ma, ocherki, literaturnye zapisi*, edited by Nina Papernaia, 20–29. Leningrad: Lenizdat, 1989.

———. *Stat'i, vospominaniia, pis'ma*. Edited by N. S. Tret'iakov. St. Petersburg: Art-Palas, 2006.

———. "Vozrozhdenie: Iz vospominanii direktora Pavlovskogo dvortsa-muzeia Anny Ivanovny Zelenovoi." In *Podvig veka: Khudozhniki, skul'ptory, arkhitektory, iskusstvovedy v gody Velikoi Otechestvennoi voiny i blokady Leningrada; Vospominaniia, dnevniki, pis'ma, ocherki, literaturnye zapisi*, edited by Nina Papernaia, 332–341. Leningrad: Lenizdat, 1989.

Zhdanov, Andrei. "The Two-Camp Policy (September 1947)." In *From Stalinism to Pluralism: A Documentary History of Eastern Europe since 1945*, edited by Gale Stokes, 38–42. 2nd ed. New York: Oxford University Press, 1996.

Zhilinskii, I. I. "Blokadnyi dnevnik." Pts. 1 and 2. *Voprosy Istorii*, nos. 5–6 (1996): 5–27; no. 7 (1996): 3–13.

Zubkova, E. Iu., L. P. Kosheleva, G. A. Kuznetsova, A. I. Miniuk, and L. A. Rogovaia, eds. *Sovetskaia zhizn' 1945–1953*. Moscow: Rosspen, 2003.

SECONDARY SOURCES

Antonov, V. V., and A. V. Kobak, eds. *Utrachennye pamiatniki arkhitektury*

Peterburga-Leningrada: Katalog vystavki. Leningrad: Khudozhnik RSFSR, 1988.

Ashplant, T. G., Graham Dawson, and Michael Roper. "The Politics of War Memory and Commemoration: Contexts, Structures and Dynamics." In *The Politics of War Memory and Commemoration,* edited by T. G. Ashplant, Graham Dawson, and Michael Roper, 3–86. New York: Routledge, 2000.

Bailes, Kendall. *Technology and Society under Lenin and Stalin: Origins of the Soviet Technological Intelligentsia, 1917–1941.* Princeton, NJ: Princeton University Press, 1978.

Bakhareva, Iu. Iu. "Arkhitekturnaia zhizn' Leningrada v gody Velikoi Otechestvennoi voiny." In *Arkhitektory blokadnogo Leningrada,* edited by Iu. Iu. Bakhareva, T. V. Kovaleva, and T. G. Shishkina, 6–19. St. Petersburg: Gosudarstvennyi Muzei Istorii Sankt-Peterburga, 2005.

———. "Arkhitekturnye konkursy v blokadnom Leningrade: Gostinyi dvor." *Relikviia* 1, no. 8 (2005): 30–35.

———. "Arkhitekturnyi konkurs 1942 g." In *Prostranstvo Sankt-Peterburga: Pamiatniki kul'turnogo naslediia i sovremennaia gorodskaia sreda; Materialy nauchno-prakticheskoi konferentsii, Sankt-Peterburg, 18–19 noiabria 2002,* edited by B. M. Matveev, 237–248. St. Petersburg: Filologicheskii fakultet SpbGU, 2003.

———. "Okhrana pamiatnikov Leningrada v gody Velikoi otechestvennoi voiny." In *Okhrana pamiatnikov Sankt-Peterburga,* edited by Iu. Iu. Bakhareva, S. A. Vesnin, I. P. Dubrovskaia, and N. V. Marushina, 51–69. St. Petersburg: Propilei, 2008.

Bantjes, Adrian A. "Making Sense of Iconoclasm: Popular Responses to the Destruction of Religious Images in Revolutionary Mexico." In *Iconoclasm: Contested Objects, Contested Terms,* edited by Stacy Boldrick and Richard Clay, 169–188. Burlington, VT: Ashgate, 2007.

Baranov, N. N., and V.G. Isachenko. *Glavnyi arkhitektor Leningrada Nikolai Baranov: Tvorcheskii put' i sud'ba.* St. Petersburg: Stroiizdat, 2001.

Barber, John. "Popular Reactions in Moscow to the German Invasion of June 22, 1941." *Soviet Union/UnionSoviétique* 18, nos. 1–3 (1991): 5–18.

Barber, John, and Mark Harrison. *The Soviet Home Front, 1941–1945: A Social and Economic History of the USSR in World War II.* New York: Longman, 1991.

Baron, Nick. "Remaking Soviet Society: The Filtration of Returnees from Nazi Germany, 1944–49." In *Warlands: Population Resettlement and State Reconstruction in the Soviet-East European Borderlands, 1945–50,* edited by Peter Gatrell and Nick Baron, 89–116. New York: Palgrave Macmillan, 2009.

Barskova, Polina. "The Spectacle of the Besieged City: Repurposing Cultural Memory in Leningrad, 1941–1944." *Slavic Review* 69, no. 2 (Summer 2010): 327–355.

Bartov, Omer. *The Eastern Front: German Troops and the Barbarisation of Warfare.* 2nd ed. New York: St. Martin's, 2001.

Bater, James H. *St. Petersburg: Industrialization and Change.* London: Edward Arnold, 1976.

Bennett, Tony. *The Birth of the Museum: History, Theory, Politics.* New York: Routledge, 1995.

Berkhoff, Karel C. *Harvest of Despair: Life and Death in Ukraine under Nazi Rule.* Cambridge, MA: Belknap Press of Harvard University Press, 2004.

———. *Motherland in Danger: Soviet Propaganda during World War II* (Cambridge, MA: Harvard University Press, 2012.

Bevan, Robert. *The Destruction of Memory: Architecture at War.* London: Reaktion Books, 2006.

Bidlack, Richard. "Foreword: Historical Background to the Siege of Leningrad." In *Writing the Siege of Leningrad: Women's Diaries, Memoirs, and Documentary Prose,* edited by Cynthia Simmons and Nina Perlina, ix–xxvi. Pittsburgh: University of Pittsburgh Press, 2002.

———. "Ideological or Political Origins of the Leningrad Affair? A Response to David Brandenberger." *Russian Review* 64, no. 1 (2005): 90–95.

———. "The Political Mood in Leningrad during the First Year of the Soviet-German War." *Russian Review* 59, no. 1 (2000): 96–113.

———. "Survival Strategies in Leningrad during the First Year of the Soviet-German War." In *The People's War: Responses to World War II in the Soviet Union,* edited by Robert Thurston and Bernd Bonwetsch, 84–107. Chicago: University of Illinios Press, 2000.

Bittner, Stephen V. *The Many Lives of Khrushchev's Thaw: Experience and Memory in Moscow's Arbat.* Ithaca, NY: Cornell University Press, 2008.

Blackwell, Martin. "Regime City of the First Category: The Experience of the Return of Soviet Power to Kyiv, Ukraine, 1943–1946." Ph.D. diss., Indiana University, 2005.

Blinov, P. M. "Obshchestvo 'Staryi Peterburg – Novyi Leningrad.'" *Pamiatniki otechestva: Al'minakh Vserossiiskogo obshchestva okhrany pamiatnikov istorii kul'tury,* no. 2 (1987): 45–51.

Blium, Arlen. "Blokadnaia tema v tsenzurnoi blokade: Po arkhivnym dokumentam glavlita SSSR." *Neva,* no. 1 (2004): 238–245.

Boguslavskii, G. A. "Kul'turnoe nasledie i khudozhestvennyi mir Petrograda v 1918–1920 godakh." In *Peterburgskoe chteniia, 97: Materialy entsiklopedicheskoi biblioteki "Sankt-Peterburg-2003,"* edited by T. A. Slavina, 199–203. St. Petersburg: Russko-Baltiiskii informatsionnyi tsentr BLITs, 1997.

Boldrick, Stacy, and Richard Clay, eds. *Iconoclasm: Contested Objects, Contested Terms.* Burlington, VT: Ashgate, 2007.

Bonwetsch, Bernd. "The War as a 'Breathing Space': Soviet Intellectuals and the 'Great Patriotic War.'" In *The People's War: Responses to World War II in the Soviet Union,* edited by Robert W. Thurston and Bernd Bonwetsch, 137–153. Chicago: University of Illinois Press, 2000.

Boterbloem, Kees. "The Death of Andrei Zhdanov." *Slavonic and East European Review* 80, no. 2 (April 2002): 267–287.

———. *The Life and Times of Andrei Zhdanov, 1896–1948.* Montreal: McGill-Queens University Press, 2004.

Boym, Svetlana. *The Future of Nostalgia.* New York: Basic Books, 2001.

Brandenberger, David. *National Bolshevism: Stalinist Mass Culture and the Formation of Modern Russian National Identity, 1931–1956.* Cambridge, MA: Harvard University Press, 2002.

———. "The Popular Reception of S.M. Eisenstein's *Aleksandr Nevskii.*" In *Epic Revisionism: Russian History and Literature as Stalinist Propaganda,* edited by Kevin M. F. Platt and David Brandenberger, 233–252. Madison: University of Wisconsin Press, 2006.

———. *Propaganda State in Crisis: Soviet Ideology, Indoctrination, and Terror under Stalin, 1927–1941.* New Haven, CT: Yale University Press, 2011.

———. "Stalin, the Leningrad Affair and the Limits of Postwar Russocentrism." *Russian Review* 63, no. 2 (2004): 241–255.

Brooks, Jeffrey. *Thank You, Comrade Stalin!: Soviet Public Culture from Revolution to Cold War.* Princeton, NJ: Princeton University Press, 2000.

Brumfield, William Craft. *A History of Russian Architecture.* New York: Cambridge University Press, 1993.

Buckler, Julie. *Mapping St. Petersburg: Imperial Text and Cityshape.* Princeton, NJ: Princeton University Press, 2005.

Bucur, Maria, and Nancy M. Wingfield. "Introduction." In *Staging the Past: The Politics of Commemoration in Nabsburg Central Europe, 1848 to the Present,* edited by Maria Bucur and Nancy M. Wingfield, 5–12. West Lafayette, IN: Purdue University Press, 2001.

Budnitskii, O. V., and G. S. Zelenina. "Ideinyi kollaboratsionizm v gody Velikoi Otechestvennoi voiny." In *"Svershilos' Prishli nemtsy!" Ideinyi kollaboratsionizm v SSSR v period Velikoi Otechestvennoi voiny,* edited by O. V. Budnitskii and G. S. Zelenina, 4–62. Moscow: Rosspen, 2012.

Bulushev, P. M., and V. I. Ganshin. *Podvigu tvoemu, Leningrad: Monument geroicheskim zashchitnikam goroda.* Leningrad: Lenizdat, 1980.

Chistikov, A. N., and N. B. Lebina. *Obyvatel' i reformy: Kartiny povsednevnoi zhizni gorozhan.* St. Petersburg: Dmitrii Bulanin, 2003.

Choay, Francoise. *The Invention of the Historic Monument.* Translated by Lauren M. O'Connell. New York: Cambridge University Press, 2001.

Clark, Katerina. *Petersburg: Crucible of Cultural Revolution.* Cambridge, MA: Harvard University Press, 1995.

Clay, Richard. "Bouchardon's Statue of Louis XV: Iconoclasm and the Transformation of Signs." In *Iconoclasm: Contested Objects, Contested Terms,* edited by Stacy Boldrick and Richard Clay, 93–122. Burlington, VT: Ashgate, 2007.

Colton, Timothy. *Moscow: Governing the Socialist Metropolis.* Cambridge, MA: Belknap Press of Harvard University Press, 1998.

Connely, Mark. *The Great War, Memory and Ritual: Commemoration in the City and East London, 1916–1939.* Suffolk: Boydell Press, 2002.

Conquest, Robert. *Power and Policy in the USSR: The Study of Soviet Dynastics.* New York: St. Martin's, 1961.

Corney, Frederick. *Telling October: Memory and the Making of the Bolshevik Revolution.* Ithaca, NY: Cornell University Press, 2004.

Cracraft, James. *The Petrine Revolution in Russian Architecture.* Chicago: University of Chicago Press, 1988.

———. *The Revolution of Peter the Great.* Cambridge, MA: Harvard University Press, 2003.

Cracraft, James, and Daniel Rowland, eds. *Architectures of Russian Identity: 1500 to the Present.* Ithaca, NY: Cornell University Press, 2003.

———. "Introduction." In *Architectures of Russian Identity: 1500 to the Present,* edited by James Cracraft and Daniel Rowland, 1–6. Ithaca, NY: Cornell University Press, 2003.

Crone, Anna Lisa, and Jennifer Day. *My Petersburg/Myself: Mental Architecture and Imaginative Space in Modern Russian Letters.* Bloomington, IN: Slavica, 2004.

Crowley, David, and Susan E. Reid, eds., *Socialist Spaces: Sites of Everyday Life in the Eastern Bloc.* New York: Berg, 2002.

Dallin, Alexander. *German Rule in Russia, 1941–1945: A Study in Occupation Policies.* New York: St. Martin's, 1957.

Davies, Sarah. *Popular Opinion in Stalin's*

Russia: Terror, Propaganda, and Dissent, 1934–1941. New York: Cambridge University Press, 1997.

Day, Andrew. "Building Socialism: The Politics of the Soviet Cityscape in the Stalin Era." PhD diss., Columbia University, 1998.

———. "The Rise and Fall of Stalinist Architecture." In *Architectures of Russian Identity: 1500 to the Present*, edited by James Cracraft and Daniel Rowland, 172–190. Ithaca, NY: Cornell University Press, 2003.

Dean, Martin. *Collaboration in the Holocaust: Crimes of the Local Police in Belorussia and Ukraine, 1941–44*. New York: St. Martin's, 2000.

Demidov, V. I., and V. A. Kutuzov. *"Leningradskoe delo."* Leningrad: Lenizdat, 1990.

Diefendorf, Jeffry M. *In the Wake of War: The Reconstruction of German Cities after World War II*. New York: Oxford University Press, 1993.

———. "Introduction: New Perspectives on a Rebuilt Europe." In *Rebuilding Europe's Bombed Cities*, edited by Jeffry M. Diefendorf, 1–15. London: Macmillan, 1990.

———, ed. *Rebuilding Europe's Bombed Cities*. London: Macmillan, 1990.

Duncan, Carol. "Art Museums and the Ritual of Citizenship." In *Exhibiting Cultures: The Poetics and Politics of Museum Display*, edited by Ivan Karp and Stephen D. Lavine, 88–103. Washington, DC: Smithsonian Institution Press, 1991.

Dunham, Vera. *In Stalin's Time: Middleclass Values in Soviet Fiction*. New York: Cambridge University Press, 1976.

Dunmore, Timothy. *Soviet Politics, 1945–1953*. London: Macmillan, 1984.

Dzeniskevich, Andrei, and John Barber, eds. *Life and Death in Besieged Leningrad, 1941–44*. New York: Palgrave Macmillan, 2005.

Dzeniskevich, A. R. *Blokada i politika: Oborona Leningrada v politicheskoi kon"iunkture*. St. Petersburg: Nestor, 1998.

———. *Front u zavodskikh sten: Maloizuchennye problemy oborony Leningrada, 1941–1944*. St. Petersburg: Nestor, 1998.

Edele, Mark. "More than Just Stalinists: The Political Sentiments of Victors, 1945–1953." In *Late Stalinist Russia: Society between Reconstruction and Reinvention*, edited by Juliane Fürst, 167–191. London: Routledge, 2006.

———. *Soviet Veterans of the Second World War: A Popular Movement in an Authoritarian Society, 1941–1991*. Oxford: Oxford University Press, 2008.

Egorov, Iu. A. *The Architectural Planning of St. Petersburg*. Translated by Eric Dluhosch. Athens: Ohio University Press, 1969.

Erikson, John. *The Road to Stalingrad: Stalin's War with Germany*. Boulder, CO: Westview, 1984.

Ermolov, Igor'. *Tri goda bez Stalina: Okkupatsiia; Sovetskie grazhdane mezhdu natsistami i bol'shivakami*. Moscow: Tsentrpoligraff, 2010.

Evdokimov, P. B., ed. *Liudskie poteri SSSR v Velikoi Otechestvennoi voine: Sbornik statei*. St. Petersburg: Izdatel'stvo Russko-Baltiiskii informatsionnyi tsentr BLITS, 1995.

Farmer, Sarah. *Martyred Village: Commemorating the 1944 Massacre at Oradour-sur-Glane*. Los Angeles: University of California Press, 1999.

Farrell, John. "If These Stones Could Only Speak: Historical and Cultural Preservation in a Soviet Context, 1955–1966." PhD diss., University of California, Davis, 2004.

Figes, Orlando, and Boris Kolonitskii.

Interpreting the Russian Revolution: The Language and Symbols of 1917. New Haven, CT: Yale University Press, 1999.

Filtzer, Donald. *Soviet Workers and Late Stalinism: Labour and the Restoration of the Stalinist System after World War II*. New York: Cambridge University Press, 2002.

———. "The Standard of Living of Soviet Industrial Workers in the Immediate Postwar Period, 1945–1948." *Europe-Asia Studies* 51, no. 6 (September 1999): 1013–1014.

Fishman, Robert. *Bourgeois Utopias: The Rise and Fall of Suburbia*. New York: Basic Books, 1987.

Fitzpatrick, Sheila. "Conclusion: Late Stalinism in Historical Perspective." In *Late Stalinist Russia: Society between Reconstruction and Reinvention,* edited by Juliane Fürst, 269–282. New York: Routledge, 2006.

———. *The Cultural Front: Power and Culture in Revolutionary Russia*. Ithaca, NY: Cornell University Press, 1992.

———. *Everyday Stalinism: Extraordinary Life in Extraordinary Times; Soviet Russia in the 1930s*. New York: Oxford University Press, 1999.

———. "Postwar Soviet Society: The 'Return to Normalcy,' 1945–1953." In *The Impact of World War II on the Soviet Union,* edited by Susan J. Linz, 129–156. Totowa, NJ: Rowman and Allanheld, 1985.

———. *Stalin's Peasants: Resistance and Survival in the Russian Village after Collectivization*. New York: Oxford University Press, 1996.

Freeman, Kirilly. *Bronzes to Bullets: Vichy and the Destruction of French Public Statuary, 1941–1944*. Stanford, CA: Stanford University Press, 2009.

Fritz, Stephen G. *Ostkrieg: Hitler's War of Extermination in the East*. Lexington: University Press of Kentucky, 2011.

Fürst, Juliane, ed. *Late Stalinist Russia: Society between Reconstruction and Reinvention*. New York: Routledge, 2006.

———. *Stalin's Last Generation: Soviet Post-War Youth and the Emergence of Mature Socialism*. New York: Oxford University Press, 2010.

Gamboni, Dario. *The Destruction of Art: Iconoclasm and Vandalism since the French Revolution*. London: Reaktion Books, 1997.

Gartenschläger, Uwe. "Living and Surviving in Occupied Minsk." In *The People's War: Responses to World War II in the Soviet Union,* edited by Robert W. Thurston and Bernd Bonwetsch, 13–28. Chicago: University of Illinois Press, 2000.

Geppert, Dominik, ed. *The Postwar Challenge: Cultural, Social, and Political Change in Western Europe, 1945–58*. New York: Oxford University Press, 2003.

Gillis, John R. *Commemorations: The Politics of National Identity*. Princeton, NJ: Princeton University Press, 1994.

———. "Memory and Identity: The History of a Relationship." In *Commemorations: The Politics of National Identity,* edited by John. R. Gillis, 3–24. Princeton, NJ: Princeton University Press, 1994.

Gorlizki, Yoram, and Oleg Khlevniuk. *Cold Peace: Stalin and the Soviet Ruling Circle, 1945–1953*. New York: Oxford University Press, 2004.

Gorodetsky, Gabriel. *Grand Delusion: Stalin and the German Invasion of Russia*. New Haven, CT: Yale University Press, 1999.

Gorsuch, Anne. "'There's No Place like Home': Soviet Tourism in Late Stalinism." *Slavic Review* 62, no. 4 (Winter 2003): 760–785.

Goscilo, Helena, and Stephen M. Norris, eds. *Preserving Petersburg: History, Memory, Nostalgia*. Bloomington: Indiana University Press, 2008.

Granin, Daniil. "Vstupitel'noe slovo." In *Vozrozhdennye iz pepla: Petrodvorets, Pushkin, Pavlovsk; Al'bom,* edited by I. M. Gurevich, G. D. Khodasevich, and V. A. Belanina, 13–15. Leningrad: Avrora, 1989.

Gray, Peter, and Kendrick Oliver, eds. *The Memory of Catastrophe*. New York: Manchester University Press, 2004.

Grigor'ev, V. S. *"Za oboronu Leningrada": Istoriia medali*. St. Petersburg, 1993.

Hagenloh, Paul. *Stalin's Police: Public Order and Mass Repression in the USSR, 1926–1941*. Baltimore: Johns Hopkins University Press, 2009.

Hahn, Werner G. *Postwar Soviet Politics: The Fall of Zhdanov and the Defeat of Moderation, 1946–53*. Ithaca, NY: Cornell University Press, 1982.

Hassell, James. "The Planning of St. Petersburg." *The Historian* 36, no. 2 (February 1974): 248–263.

Heer, Hannes, and Klaus Naumann, eds. *War of Extermination: The German Military in World War II, 1941–1944*. New York: Berghahn Books, 2000.

Hellberg-Hirn, Elena. *Imperial Imprints: Post-Soviet St. Petersburg*. Helsinki: SKS Finnish Literature Society, 2003.

Hobsbawm, Eric, and Terrence Ranger, eds. *The Invention of Tradition*. New York: Cambridge University Press, 1983.

Hoffmann, David L. *Peasant Metropolis: Social Identities in Moscow, 1929–1941*. Ithaca, NY: Cornell University Press, 1994.

———. *Stalinist Values: The Cultural Norms of Soviet Modernity, 1917–1941*. Ithaca, NY: Cornell University Press, 2003.

———. "Was There a 'Great Retreat' from Soviet Socialism? Stalinist Culture Reconsidered." *Kritika: Explorations in Russian and Eurasian History* 5, no. 4 (Fall 2004): 651–674.

Holguin, Sandie. "'National Spain Invites You': Battlefield Tourism during the Spanish Civil War." *American Historical Review* 110, no. 5 (December 2005): 1399–1426.

Holquist, Peter. "'Information Is the Alpha and Omega of Our Work': Bolshevik Surveillance in Its Pan-European Context." *Journal of Modern History* 69, no. 3 (September 1997): 415–450.

———. *Making War, Forging Revolution: Russia's Continuum of Crisis, 1914–1921*. Cambridge, MA: Harvard University Press, 2002.

Idzerda, Stanley J. "Iconoclasm during the French Revolution." *American Historical Review* 60, no. 1 (October 1954): 13–26.

Johnson, Emily D. *How St. Petersburg Learned to Study Itself: The Russian Idea of Kraevedenie*. University Park, PA: Penn State University Press, 2006.

Johnston, Timothy. *Being Soviet: Identity, Rumour, and Everyday Life under Stalin, 1939–1953*. Oxford: Oxford University Press, 2011.

Jones, Jeffrey W. *Everyday Life and the "Reconstruction" of Soviet Russia during and after the Great Patriotic War, 1943–1948*. Bloomington: Slavica, 2008.

Jones, Jeffrey Wade. "'In My Opinion This Is All a Fraud!': Concrete, Culture, and Class in the 'Reconstruction' of Rostov-on-Don, 1943–1948." PhD diss., University of North Carolina at Chapel Hill, 2000.

Kalendarova, Viktoria. "Formiruia pamiat': Blokada v leningradskikh gazet i dokumental'nom kino v poslevoennye desiatiletiia." In *Pamiat' o blokade: Svidetel'stva ochevidtsev i istoricheskoe soznanie obshchestva,* edited by Marina

Loskutova, 275–295. St. Petersburg: Novoe Izdatel'stvo, 2005.

Karasev, A. V. "Vozrozhdenie goroda-geroia." *Istoriia SSSR* 5, no. 3 (1961): 116–128.

Karlsgodt, Elizabeth Campbell. *Defending National Treasures: French Art and Heritage under Vichy.* Stanford, CA: Stanford University Press, 2011.

Karp, Ivan, and Stephen Lavine, eds. In *Exhibiting Cultures: The Poetics and Politics of Museum Display.* Washington, DC: Smithsonian Institution Press, 1991.

Kay, Alex J. *Exploitation, Resettlement, Mass Murder: Political and Economic Planning for German Occupation Policy in the Soviet Union, 1940–1941.* New York: Berghahn Books, 2006.

Kedrinskii, A. A., M. G. Kolotov, B. N. Ometov, and A. G. Raskin, eds. *Vosstanovlenie pamiatnikov arkhitektury Leningrada.* 2nd ed. Leningrad: Stroiizdat, 1987.

Kedrinskii, A. A., M. G. Kolotov, L. A. Mederskii, and A. G. Raskin, eds. *Letopis' vozrozhdeniia: Vostanovlenie pamiatnikov arkhitektury Leningrada i prigorodov, razrushennykh v gody Velikoi Otechestvennoi voiny nemetsko-fashistskimi zakhvatshchikami.* Leningrad: Izdatel'stvo literatura po stroitel'stvu, 1971.

Kelly, Catriona. "Introduction: Iconoclasm and Commemorating the Past." In *Constructing Russian Culture in the Age of Revolution: 1881–1940,* edited by Catriona Kelly and David Shepherd, 227–237. New York: Oxford University Press, 1998.

———. "Socialist Churches: Heritage Preservation and 'Cultic Buildings' in Leningrad, 1924–1940." *Slavic Review* 71, no. 4 (Winter 2012): 792–823.

Kenez, Peter, and Richard Stites, eds. *Bolshevik Culture: Experiment and Order in the Russian Revolution.* Bloomington: Indiana University Press, 1985.

Khlevniuk, Oleg. "The Objectives of the Great Terror." In *Soviet History, 1937–1938: Essays in Honour of R.W. Davies,* edited by Julian Cooper, Maureen Perrie, and E. A. Rees, 158–176. London: Palgrave Macmillan, 1995.

Kirschenbaum, Lisa A. "Commemorations of the Siege of Leningrad: A Catastrophe in Memory and Myth." In *The Memory of Catastrophe,* edited by Peter Gray and Kendrick Oliver, 106–117. New York: Manchester University Press, 2004.

———. "Gender, Memory, and National Myths: Ol'ga Berggol'ts and the Siege of Leningrad." *Nationalities Papers* 28, no. 3 (2000): 551–564.

———. *The Legacy of the Siege of Leningrad, 1941–1945: Myths, Memories, and Monuments.* New York: Cambridge University Press, 2006.

Koshar, Rudy. "Building Pasts: Historic Preservation and Identity in Twentieth-Century Germany." In *Commemorations: The Politics of National Identity,* edited by John R. Gillis, 215–238. Princeton, NJ: Princeton University Press, 1994.

———. *From Monuments to Traces: Artifacts of German Memory, 1870–1990.* Los Angeles: University of California Press, 2000.

———. *Germany's Transient Pasts: Preservation and National Memory in the Twentieth Century.* Chapel Hill: University of North Carolina Press, 1998.

Kotkin, Stephen. *Magnetic Mountain: Stalinism as a Civilization.* Los Angeles: University of California Press, 1995.

Koval'chuk, V. M. *900 dnei blokady: Leningrad 1941–1944.* St. Petersburg: Dmitrii Bulanin, 2005.

Koval'chuk, V. M., G. P. Aleksandrov, E. A. Boltin, Iu. I. Zavarukhin, S. P. Kniazev, Sh. M. Levin, N. E. Nosov, G. L. Sobolev, and A. L. Fraiman, eds. *Ocherki istorii Leningrada*. Tom 5, *Period Velikoi Otechestvennoi voiny Sovetskogo Soiuza, 1941–1945gg*. Moscow: Izdatel'stvo Akademii Nauk, 1967.

Kovalev, Boris. *Natsistskaia okkupatsiia i kollaboratsionizm v Rossii, 1941–1944*. Moscow: Tranzitkniga, 2004.

Kramer, Alan. *Dynamic of Destruction: Culture and Mass Killing in the First World War*. New York: Oxford University Press, 2007.

Krementsov, Nikolai. *The Cure: The Story of Cancer and Politics from the Annals of the Cold War*. Chicago: University of Chicago Press, 2002.

Krylova, Anna. "'Healers of Wounded Souls': The Crisis of Private Life in Soviet Literature, 1944–1946." *Journal of Modern History* 73, no. 2 (June 2001): 307–331.

Kul'chinskaia, E. D. "Ot museefikatsii k unichtozheniiu naslediia. 1920-e gody." In *Pamiatniki arkhitektury v Sovetskom Soiuze: Ocherki istorii arkhitekturnoi restavratsii*, edited by A. S. Shchenkov, 21–33. Moscow: Pamiatniki istoricheskoi mysli, 2004.

———. "Teatralizatsiia i mifologizatsiia kul'tury: Unichtozhenie i pereomyslenie naslediia; Konets 1920 kh–1930-e gody." In *Pamiatniki arkhitektury v Sovetskom Soiuze: Ocherki istorii arkhitekturnoi restavratsii*, edited by A. S. Shchenkov, 33–44. Moscow: Pamiatniki istoricheskoi mysli, 2004.

Kutuzov, V. A. '"Leningradskoe delo': Sud'by ispolnitelei." In *Rossiiskaia gosudarstvennost': Istoriia i sovremennost'*, edited by M. V. Khodiakov, 613–623. St. Petersburg: Znamenitye Universanty, 2003.

———. "Muzei oborony Leningrad." *Dialog* 24 (August 1988): 21–27.

Lambourne, Nicola. *War Damage in Western Europe: The Destruction of Historic Monuments during the Second World War*. Edinburgh: Edinburgh University Press, 2001.

Lenoe, Matthew E. *Closer to the Masses: Stalinist Culture, Social Revolution, and Soviet Newspapers*. Cambridge, MA: Harvard University Press, 2004.

———. "In Defense of Timasheff's Great Retreat." *Kritika: Explorations in Russian and Eurasian History* 5, no. 4 (Fall 2004): 721–730.

Levesque, Jean. "'Part-Time Peasants': Labour Discipline, Collective-Farm Life, and the Fate of Soviet Socialized Agriculture after the Second World War, 1945–1953." PhD diss., University of Toronto, 2003.

Lincoln, W. Bruce. *Sunlight at Midnight: St. Petersburg and the Rise of Modern Russia*. New York: Basic Books, 2002.

Linz, Susan J., ed. *The Impact of World War II on the Soviet Union*. Totowa, NJ: Rowman and Allanheld, 1985.

Lomagin, Nikita. *Neizvestnaia blokada: V 2-kh knigakh*. 2nd ed. St. Petersburg: Neva, 2004.

Loskutova, Marina, ed. *Pamiat' o blokade: Svidetel'stva ochevidtsev i istoricheskoe soznanie obshchestva*. St. Petersburg: Novoe Izdatel'stvo, 2005.

Lovell, Stephen. *Summer Folk: A History of the Dacha, 1710–2000*. Ithaca, NY: Cornell University Press, 2003.

Lower, Wendy. *Nazi Empire-Building and the Holocaust in Ukraine*. Chapel Hill: University of North Carolina Press, 2005.

Luppov, S. P. *Istoriia stroitel'stva Peterburga v pervoi chetverti XVIII veka*. Leningrad: Izdatel'stvo Akademii Nauk SSSR, 1957.

Maddox, Steven. "The Memory of the Blockade and Its Function in the Immediate Postwar Restoration of Leningrad." In *Bitva za Leningrad: Diskussionnye problemy*, edited by Nikita Lomagin, 272–302. St. Petersburg: Evropeiskii Dom, 2009.

———. "Prestupleniia i nakazanie: Karatel'nye otriady v leningradskoi oblasti, 1941–1945." Translated by L. G. Novikova. In *SSSR vo Vtoroi mirovoi voine: Okkupatsiia. Kholokost. Stalinizm*, edited by O. V. Budnitskii, 26–48. Moscow: Rosspen, 2014.

———. "'These Monuments Must Be Protected!' Stalin's Turn to the Past and Historic Preservation during the Blockade of Leningrad." *Russian Review* 70 (October 2011): 608–626.

Maksakova, L. V. *Spasenie kul'turnykh tsennostei v gody Velikoi Otechestvennoi voiny*. Moscow: Nauka, 1990.

Mally, Lynn. *Culture of the Future: The Proletkult Movement in Revolutionary Russia*. Los Angeles: University of California Press, 1990.

Manley, Rebecca. "The Evacuation and Survival of Soviet Civilians, 1941–1946." PhD diss., University of California, Berkeley, 2004.

———. *To Tashkent Station: Evacuation and Survival in the Soviet Union at War*. Ithaca, NY: Cornell University Press, 2009.

Massie, Susan. *Pavlovsk: The Life of a Russian Palace*. Toronto: Little, Brown, 1990.

Mazower, Mark. *Hitler's Empire: How the Nazis Ruled Europe*. New York: Penguin, 2008.

McMeekin, Sean. *History's Greatest Heist: The Looting of Russia by the Bolsheviks*. New Haven, CT: Yale University Press, 2008.

Megargee, Geoffrey P. *War of Annihilation: Combat and Genocide on the Eastern Front, 1941*. New York: Rowman and Littlefield, 2006.

Meng, Michael. *Shattered Spaces: Encountering Jewish Ruins in Postwar Germany and Poland*. Cambridge, MA: Harvard University Press, 2011.

Merridale, Catherine. *Ivan's War: The Red Army, 1939–1945*. London: Faber and Faber, 2005.

———. "War, Death, and Remembrance in Soviet Russia." In *War and Remembrance in the Twentieth Century*, edited by Jay Winter and Emmanuel Sivan, 61–83. New York: Cambridge University Press, 1999.

Milward, Alan S. *The Reconstruction of Western Europe, 1945–1951*. Los Angeles: University of California Press, 1984.

Mironenko, Z. S., and V. A. Ezhov, eds., *Ocherki istorii Leningradskoi organizatsii KPSS: Tom III – 1945–1985*. Leningrad: Lenizdat, 1985.

Mueller, Rolf-Dieter. *The Unknown Eastern Front: The Wehrmacht and Hitler's Foreign Soldiers*. Translated by David Burnett. New York: I. B. Tauris, 2012.

Nelson, Robert S., and Margaret Olin. "Introduction." In *Monuments of Memory, Made and Unmade*, edited by Robert S. Nelson and Margaret Olin, 1–10. Chicago: University of Chicago Press, 2003.

Nicholas, Lynn H. *The Rape of Europa: The Fate of Europe's Treasures in the Third Reich and the Second World War*. New York: Knopf, 1994.

Nora, Pierre. "Between Memory and History: *Les Lieux de Memoire*." Translated by Marc Roudebush. *Representations* 26 (Spring 1989): 7–25.

Nove, Alec. *An Economic History of the USSR*. 3rd ed. New York: Penguin Books, 1992.

Odom, Anne, and Wendy Salmond, eds. *Treasures into Tractors: The Selling of*

Russia's Cultural Heritage, 1918–1938. Seattle: University of Washington Press, 2009.

Overy, Richard. *Russia's War: A History of the Soviet War Effort: 1941–1945.* New York: Penguin, 1997.

Pavlova, M. P. "Sostoianie okhrany pamiatnikov arkhitektury i organizatsii restavratsionnykh rabot v 1940-e–1960-e gg." In *Pamiatniki arkhitektury v Sovetskom Soiuze. Ocherki istorii arkhitekturnoi restavratsii,* edited by A. S. Shchenkov, 228–296. Moscow: Pamiatniki istoricheskoi mysli, 2004.

Pavlova, M. P., and A. S. Shchenkov, "Restavratsionnaia praktika." In *Pamiatniki arkhitektury v Sovetskom Soiuze: Ocherki istorii arkhitekturnoi restavratsii,* edited by A. S. Shchenkov, 344–358. Moscow: Pamiatniki istoricheskoi mysli, 2004.

Penter, Tanja. "Local Collaborators on Trial: Soviet War Crimes Trials under Stalin (1945–1953)." *Cahiers du monde russe* 49, no. 2 (2008): 341–364.

Peterson, Zoe Bakeeff. "The Architectural Heritage of Leningrad." *American Slavic and East European Review* 4, nos. 3/4 (December 1945): 18–34.

Petrone, Karen. *Life Has Become More Joyous, Comrades: Celebrations in the Time of Stalin.* Bloomington: Indiana University Press, 2000.

Pisiotis, Argyrios K. "Images of Hate in the Art of War." In *Culture and Entertainment in Wartime Russia,* edited by Richard Stites, 141–156. Bloomington: Indiana University Press, 1995.

Platt, Kevin M. F. *Terror and Greatness: Ivan and Peter as Russian Myths.* Ithaca, NY: Cornell University Press, 2011.

Platt, Kevin M. F., and David Brandenberger, eds. *Epic Revisionism: Russian History and Literature as Stalinist Propaganda.* Madison: University of Wisconsin Press, 2006.

Polian, Pavel. *Zhertvy dvukh diktatur: Zhizn', trud, unizhenie i smert' sovetskikh voennoplennykh i ostarbeiterov na chuzhbine i na rodine.* Moscow: Rosspen, 2002.

Pollock, Ethan. *Stalin and the Soviet Science Wars.* Princeton, NJ: Princeton University Press, 2006.

Priestland, David. "Cold War Mobilization and Domestic Politics: The Soviet Union." In *The Cambridge History of the Cold War,* vol. 1, *Origins,* edited by Melvyn P. Leffler and Odd Arne Westad, 442–463. New York: Cambridge University Press, 2012.

Qualls, Karl. "Accommodation and Agitation in Sevastopol: Redefining Socialist Space in the Postwar 'City of Glory.'" In *Socialist Spaces: Sites of Everyday Life in the Eastern Bloc,* edited by David Crowley and Susan E. Reid, 23–45. New York: Berg, 2002.

———. *From Ruins to Reconstruction: Urban Identity in Sevastopol after World War II.* Ithaca, NY: Cornell University Press, 2009.

———. "Local-Outsider Negotiations in Postwar Sevastopol's Reconstruction, 1944–53." In *Provincial Landscapes: Local Dimensions of Soviet Power, 1917–1953,* edited by Donald Raleigh, 276–298. Pittsburgh: Pittsburgh University Press, 2001.

———. "Raised from Ruins: Restoring Popular Allegiance through City Planning in Sevastopol, 1943–1954." PhD diss., Georgetown University, 1998.

Raleigh, Donald, ed. *Provincial Landscapes: Local Dimensions of Soviet Power, 1917–1953.* Pittsburgh: Pittsburgh University Press, 2001.

Rambow, Aileen G. "The Siege of Leningrad: Wartime Literature and Ideological Change." In *The People's War: Responses to World War II in the Soviet Union,* edited by Robert W. Thurston and Bernd Bonwetsch, 154–170. Chicago: University of Illinois Press, 2000.

Raskin, A. G. "Sokhranenie arkhitekturno-khudozhestvennykh pamiatnikov Leningrada v nachale voiny i period blokady (iiun' 1941–ianvar' 1944)." *Pamiatniki istorii kul'tury Sankt-Peterburga. Kraevedcheskie zapiski: Issledovaniia i materialy,* no. 9 (2004): 5–18.

Razgonov, S. N. *Khraniteli vechnogo.* Moscow: Molodaia gvardiia, 1975.

Rest, Boris, and Sergei Varshavsky, *Saved for Humanity: The Hermitage during the Siege of Leningrad, 1941–1944.* Translated by Arthur Shakarovsky-Raffe. Leningrad: Aurora Art, 1985.

Riasanovsky, Nicholas. *Nicholas I and Official Nationality in Russia, 1825–1855.* Berkeley: University of California Press, 1961.

Rubenstein, Joshua. "Introduction: Night of the Murdered Poets." In *Stalin's Secret Pogrom: The Postwar Inquisition of the Jewish Anti-Fascist Committee,* edited by Joshua Rubenstein and Oleg Naumov, 1–64. New Haven, CT: Yale University Press, 2001.

Ruble, Blair A. "The Leningrad Affair and the Provincialization of Leningrad." *Russian Review* 42, no. 3 (1983): 301–320.

———. *Leningrad: Shaping a Soviet City.* Los Angeles: University of California Press, 1990.

Rudling, Per. "The Khatyn Massacre in Belorussia: A Historical Controversy Revisited." *Holocaust and Genocide Studies* 26, no. 1 (Spring 2012): 29–58.

Rusinova, Ol'ga. "Dolgovechnee kamnia i bronzy: Obrazy blokady v monumental'nykh ansambliakh Leningrada." In *Pamiat' o blockade: Svidetel'stva ochividtsev i istoricheskoe soznanie obshchestva,* edited by M. V. Loskutova, 335–364. St. Petersburg: Novoe Izdatel'stvo, 2006.

Salisbury, Harrison. *The 900 Days: The Siege of Leningrad.* Cambridge, MA: Da Capo, 2003.

———. Review of *The Palaces of Leningrad,* by Victor and Audrey Kennett. *Journal of the Society of Architectural Historians* 33, no. 3 (1974): 255–256.

Sandler, Stephanie. "The 1937 Pushkin Jubilee as Epic Trauma." In *Epic Revisionism: Russian History and Literature as Stalinist Propaganda,* edited by Kevin M. F. Platt and David Brandenberger, 193–213. Madison: University of Wisconsin Press, 2006.

Scherer, David. *Policing Stalin's Socialism: Repression and Social Order in the Soviet Union, 1924–1953.* New Haven, CT: Yale University Press, 2009.

Scott-Clark, Catherine, and Andrew Levy. *The Amber Room: The Fate of the World's Greatest Lost Treasure.* New York: Berkley Books, 2005.

Semiriaga, M. I. *Kollaboratsionizm: Priroda, tipologiia i proiavleniia v gody Vtoroi mirovoi voiny.* Moscow: Rosspen, 2000.

Seniavskaia, Elena S. "Heroic Symbols: The Reality and Mythology of War." *Russian Studies in History* 37, no. 1 (Summer 1998): 61–87.

Sergeevna, M. A., and A. A. Shishkin. "Izdaniia, stavshie raritetami." *Zabveniiu ne podlezhit: Stati, vospominaniia, dokumenty* 5 (2005): 170–177.

Shchenkov, A. S. "Kratkaia kharteristika obshche kul'turnoi situatsii." In *Pamiatniki arkhitektury v Sovetskom Soiuze: Ocherki istorii arkhitekturnoi restavratsii,* edited by A. S. Shchenkov, 7–14. Moscow: Pamiatniki istoricheskoi mysli, 2004.

———, ed. *Pamiatniki arkhitektury v Sovetskom Soiuze: Ocherki istorii arkhi-*

tekturnoi restavratsii. Moscow: Pamiatniki istoricheskoi mysli, 2004.

Shchenkov, A. S., and M. P. Pavlova. "Stanovlenie metodiki arkhitekturnoi restavratsii v pervoe poslevoennoe desiatiletie." In *Pamiatniki arkhitektury v Sovetskom Soiuze: Ocherki istorii arkhitekturnoi restavratsii,* edited by A. S. Shchenkov, 297–307. Moscow: Pamiatniki istoricheskoi mysli, 2004.

Shishkin, A. A. "Slovo o muzee." *Zabveniiu ne podlezhit* 1 (1999): 3–11.

Sichynsky, Volodymyr. *Destruction of Ukrainian Monuments of Art and Culture under the Soviet Russian Administration between 1917–1957.* New York: Ukrainian Congress Committee of America, 1958.

Slezkine, Yuri. "The USSR as a Communal Apartment, or How a Socialist State Promoted Ethnic Particularism." *Slavic Review* 53, no. 2 (Summer 1994): 414–452.

Snyder, Timothy. *Bloodlands: Europe between Hitler and Stalin.* New York: Basic Books, 2010.

Sontag, John P. "The Soviet War Scare of 1926–1927." *Russian Review* 34, no. 1 (January 1975): 66–77.

Statiev, Alexander. *The Soviet Counterinsurgency in the Western Borderlands.* New York: Cambridge University Press, 2010.

Stites, Richard, ed. *Culture and Entertainment in Wartime Russia.* Bloomington: Indiana University Press, 1995.

———. "Iconoclastic Currents in the Russian Revolution: Destroying and Preserving the Past." In *Bolshevik Culture: Experiment and Order in the Russian Revolution,* edited by Peter Kenez and Richard Stites, 1–24. Bloomington: Indiana University Press, 1985.

———. *Revolutionary Dreams: Utopian Vision and Experimental Life in the Russian Revolution.* New York: Oxford University Press, 1989.

———. "Soviet Russian Wartime Culture: Freedom and Control, Spontaneity and Consciousness." In *The People's War: Responses to World War II in the Soviet Union,* edited by Robert W. Thurston and Bernd Bonwetsch, 171–184. Chicago: University of Illinois Press, 2000.

Stroud, Gregory. "The Past in Common: Modern Ruins as a Shared Urban Experience of Revolution-Era Moscow and St. Petersburg." *Slavic Review* 65, no. 4 (Winter 2006): 712–735.

Taylor, Richard. *Film Propaganda: Soviet Russia and Nazi Germany.* New York: I. B. Tauris, 1998.

Thurston, Robert W., and Bernd Bonwetsch. *The People's War: Responses to World War II in the Soviet Union.* Chicago: University of Illinois Press, 2000.

Timasheff, Nicholas. *The Great Retreat: The Growth and Decline of Communism in Russia.* New York: E. P. Dutton, 1946.

Tret'iakov, N. S. "Spasenie istoriko-kul'turnykh pamiatnikov prigorodov muzeinykh kompleksov Leningrada v gody Velikoi Otechestvennoi voiny i pervyi poslevoennyi period (1941–1948)." Candidate of Science diss., Leningrad State University, 1991.

Tromly, Benjamin. "The Leningrad Affair and Soviet Patronage Politics, 1949–1950." *Europe-Asia Studies* 56, no. 5 (July 2004): 707–729.

Tumarkin, Nina. *The Living and the Dead: The Rise and Fall of the Cult of World War II in Russia.* New York: Basic Books, 1994.

Tur'inskaia, Khristina. *Muzeinoe delo v Rossii v 1907–1936 gody.* Moscow: Institut etnografii i antropologii im. N. N. Miklukho-Maklaia Rossiiskaia Akademiia Nauk, 2001.

Vakser, A. Z. *Leningrad poslevoennyi, 1945–*

1982 gody. St. Petersburg: Izdatel'stvo Ostrov, 2005.

———. "Nastroenii Leningradtsev poslevoennogo vremeni, 1945–1953 gody." *Nestor*, no. 1 (2001): 303–328.

———. "Posle pobedy. Poslevoennye budni russkogo Troia." *Rodina*, no. 1 (2003): 155–158.

Velikanova, Olga. "The Myth of the 'Besieged Fortress': Soviet Mass Perception in the 1920s–1930s." Working paper no. 7, Stalin-Era Research and Archives Project, Centre for Russian and East European Studies, University of Toronto, 2002.

———. *Popular Perceptions of Soviet Politics in the 1920s: Disenchantment of the Dreamers*. New York: Palgrave Macmillan, 2013.

Viola, Lynne. *Peasant Rebels under Stalin: Collectivization and the Culture of Peasant Resistance*. New York: Oxford University Press, 1999.

———. *The Unknown Gulag: The Lost World of Stalin's Special Settlements*. New York: Oxford University Press, 2009.

Viola, Lynne, V. P. Danilov, N. A. Ivnitskii, and Denis Kozlov, eds. *The Tragedy of the Soviet Countryside*. Vol. 1, *The War against the Peasantry, 1927–1930*. Translated by Steven Shabad. New Haven, CT: Yale University Press, 2005.

Weiner, Amir. "The Making of a Dominant Myth: The Second World War and the Construction of Political Identities within the Soviet Polity." *Russian Review* 55, no. 3 (1996): 638–660.

———. *Making Sense of War: The Second World War and the Fate of the Bolshevik Revolution*. Princeton, NJ: Princeton University Press, 2001.

———. "Saving Private Ivan: From What, Why, and How?" *Kritika: Explorations in Russian and Eurasian History* 1, no. 2 (Spring 2000): 305–336.

Werth, Alexander. *Russia at War: 1941–1945*. London: Barrie and Rockliff, 1964.

White, Elizabeth. "After the War Was Over: The Civilian Return to Leningrad." *Europe-Asia Studies* 59, no. 7 (November 2007): 1145–1161.

Winter, Jay, and Emmanuel Sivan. "Setting the Framework." In *War and Remembrance in the Twentieth Century*, edited by Jay Winter and Emmanuel Sivan, 6–39. New York: Cambridge University Press, 1999.

Winter, J. M., and Blain Baggett. *1914–1918: The Great War and the Shaping of the Twentieth Century*. London: BBC Books, 1996.

Wortman, Richard. *Scenarios of Power: Myth and Ceremony in Russian Monarchy*. Vol. 1, *From Peter the Great to the Death of Nicholas I*. Princeton, NJ: Princeton University Press, 1995.

Yekelchyk, Serhy. "Celebrating the Soviet Present: The *Zhdanovshchina* Campaign in Ukrainian Literature and Arts." In *Provincial Landscapes: Local Dimensions of Soviet Power, 1917–1953*, edited by Donald Raleigh, 255–275. Pittsburgh: Pittsburgh University Press, 2001.

———. "The Civic Duty to Hate: Stalinist Citizenship as Political Practice and Civic Emotion (Kiev, 1943–53)." *Kritika: Explorations in Russian and Eurasian History* 7, no. 3 (Summer 2006): 529–556.

———. *Stalin's Empire of Memory: Russian-Ukrainian Relations in the Soviet Historical Imagination*. Toronto: University of Toronto Press, 2004.

Zhukov, Iu. N. *Kogda gremeli pushki: Spasenie pamiatnikov zodchestva v gody Velikoi Otechestvennoi voiny; V pomoshch' lektoru*. Moscow: Obshchestvo 'Znanie' RSFSR, 1990.

———. *Stanovlenie i deiatel'nost sovetskikh organov okhrany pamiatnikov istorii i kul'tury, 1917–1920*. Moscow: Nauka, 1989.

Ziegler, Philip. *London at War, 1939–1945*. New York: Knopf, 1995.

Zima, V. F. *Golod v SSSR 1946–1947 godov: Proizkhzhdenie i posledstviia*. Moscow: Rossiiskaia academia nauk, Institut istorii Rossii, 1996.

Zinich, M. S. *Pokhishchennye sokrovishcha: Vyvoz natsistami rossiiskikh kul'turnykh tsennostei*. Moscow: Rossiiskaia academia nauk, Institut istorii Rossii, 2003.

Zubkova, Elena. *Russia after the War: Hopes, Illusions, and Disappointments, 1945–1957*. Translated by Hugh Ragsdale. Armonk, NY: M. E. Sharpe, 1998.

Zubok, Vladislav. *A Failed Empire: The Soviet Union in the Cold War from Stalin to Gorbachev*. Chapel Hill: University of North Carolina Press, 2007.

Zubok, Vladislav, and Constantine Pleshakov. *Inside the Kremlin's Cold War: From Stalin to Khrushchev*. Cambridge, MA: Harvard University Press, 1996.

INDEX

Page numbers in italics refer to illustrations.

STEVEN MADDOX is Assistant Professor of History at Canisius College.

Printed and bound by CPI Group (UK) Ltd, Croydon, CR0 4YY

09/06/2025

14685931-0001